Global Public Goods and Sustainable Development in the Practice of International Organizations

Global Public Goods and Sustainable Development in the Practice of International Organizations

Responding to Challenges of Today's World

Edited by

Ewa Latoszek and Agnieszka Kłos

BRILL

LEIDEN | BOSTON

Library of Congress Cataloging-in-Publication Data

Names: Latoszek, Ewa, editor. |
Kłos, Agnieszka, editor.
Title: Global public goods and sustainable development in the practice of international organizations : responding to challenges of today's world / edited by Ewa Latoszek and Agnieszka Kłos.
Description: Boston : Brill, [2023] | Includes bibliographical references and index.
Identifiers: LCCN 2023045792 (print) | LCCN 2023045793 (ebook) | ISBN 9789004536319 (hardback) | ISBN 9789004687264 (ebook)
Subjects: LCSH: Public goods. | Sustainable development. | International cooperation.
Classification: LCC HB846.5 .G5526 2023 (print) | LCC HB846.5 (ebook) | DDC 338.9–dc23/eng/20231005
LC record available at https://lccn.loc.gov/2023045792
LC ebook record available at https://lccn.loc.gov/2023045793

Typeface for the Latin, Greek, and Cyrillic scripts: "Brill". See and download: brill.com/brill-typeface.

ISBN 978-90-04-53631-9 (hardback)
ISBN 978-90-04-68726-4 (e-book)
DOI 10.1163/9789004687264

This book is printed on acid-free paper and produced in a sustainable manner.

Figures and Tables

Figures

Tables

Abbreviations

AI	Artificial intelligence
AoA	Agreement on Agriculture
BCE	Butterfly Conservation Europe
CARINFONET	Central Asian Republics Information Network
CBAM	Carbon Border Adjustment Mechanism
CCAP	Climate Change Action Plan
CCRT	Catastrophe Containment and Relief Trust
CDC	Centers for Disease Control and Prevention
CDIP	Committee on Development and Intellectual Property
CEAS	Common European Asylum System
CEPF	Critical Ecosystem Partnership Fund
CEPI	Coalition for Epidemic Preparedness Innovations
CETA	EU – Canada Comprehensive Economic and Trade Agreement
CFI	Cities of the Future Index (EasyPark)
CFR	Charter of Fundamental Rights of the European Union
CIMI	Cities in Motion Index (IESE)
CIT	Corporate income tax
CJEU	Court of Justice of the European Union
CMEMS	Copernicus Marine Environment Monitoring Service
CoE	Council of Europe
COVAX	COVID-19 Vaccines Global Access
COVID-19	Coronavirus disease 2019
CSO	Civil society organization
CSR/RBC	Corporate social responsibility/responsible business conduct
DESA	Department of Economic and Social Affairs of the United Nations
DFCTA	Deep and Comprehensive Free Trade Area
DFI	Development finance instrument
DG CLIMA	Directorate-General for Climate Action
DG CNECT	Directorate-General for Communications Networks, Content and Technology
DG COMM	Directorate-General for Communication
DG ENV	Directorate-General for the Environment
DG MOVE	Directorate-General for Mobility and Transport
DG SANTE	Directorate-General for Health and Food Safety
EAM	European Agenda on Migration
EaP	Eastern Partnership
EBC	European Central Bank
EBCC	European Bird Census Council

EBRD	European Bank for Reconstruction and Development
ECA	Export Credit Agency
ECDC	European Centre for Disease Prevention and Control
ECF	Extended Credit Facility
EC	European Commission
ECHR	European Court of Human Rights
ECOFiN	Financial Affairs Council
EEA	European Environment Agency
EEC	European Economic Community
EFF	Extended Fund Facility
EFSA	European Food Safety Authority
EHII	European Health Information Initiative
EIB	European Investment Bank
EIGE	European Institute for Gender Equality
EIONET	European Environment Information and Observation Network
EMA	European Medicines Agency
EMDE	Emerging market and developing economy
EMU	Economic and Monetary Union
EP	European Parliament
EPO	European Patent Office
ERCC	Emergency Response Coordination Centre
ERDF	European Regional Development Fund
ESIF	European Structural and Investment Fund
EU	European Union
EU ETS	EU Emissions Trading System
EUIPO	European Union Intellectual Property Office
Euratom	European Atomic Energy Community
EWRS	Early Warning and Response System
FCL	Flexible Credit Line
FCTC	Framework Convention on Tobacco Control
FDA	Food and Drug Administration
FDI	Foreign direct investment
FSB	Financial Stability Board
FTA	Free trade agreement
GAPH	Global Alliance on Health and Pollution
GATT	General Agreement on Tariffs and Trade
GCM	Global Compact for Migration
GCR	Global Compact on Refugees
GDP	Gross domestic product
GEF	Global Environment Facility
GHG	Global health governance

GMP	Good manufacturing practice
GNI	Gross national income
GPG	Global public good
GSP	Generalized System of Preferences
GVC	Global value chain
HERA	Health Emergency Preparedness and Response Authority
HIPC	Heavily indebted poor countries
IBRD	International Bank for Reconstruction and Development
ICD	International Classification of Diseases
ICSID	International Centre for Settlement of Investment Disputes
ICT	Information and communication technology
IDA	International Development Association
IFC	International Finance Corporation
IFRC	International Federation of Red Cross and Red Crescent Societies
IGO	Intergovernmental organization
IHME	Institute for Health Metrics and Evaluation
ILO	International Labour Organization
IMF	International Monetary Fund
IO	International organization
IOM	International Organization for Migration
IP	Intellectual property
IPRS	Intellectual property rights
JRC	Joint Research Centre
LDC	Least developed country
MDG	Millennium Development Goal
MDRI	Multilateral Debt Relief Initiative
MEA	Multilateral environmental agreement
MENA	Middle East and North Africa
MFN	Most favored nation
MIA	Measure of international authority
MIGA	Multilateral Investment Guarantee Agency
NATO	North Atlantic Treaty Organization
NGO	Non-governmental organization
NICE	National Institute for Clinical Excellence (UK)
NPMA	New Pact on Migration and Asylum
OCA	Optimum currency area
OSCE	Organization for Security and Co-operation in Europe
ODA	Official development assistance
OECD	Organisation for Economic Co-operation and Development
OIHP	Office International d'Hygiène Publique
OP	Technical Assistance Operational Program

PCT	Patent Cooperation Treaty
PLL	Precautionary and Liquidity Line
PRGF	Poverty Reduction and Growth Facility
PRGT	Poverty Reduction Growth Trust
PSI	Policy Support Instrument
RCF	Rapid Credit Facility
R&D	Research and development
RES	Renewable energy sources
RFI	Rapid Financing Instrument
RRF	Resilience and Recovery Framework
RSD	Refugee status determination
RTA	Regional trade agreement
SBA	Stand-by Arrangement
SCF	Stand-by Credit Facility
SCI	Smart City Index (IMD – SUTD)
SCM	Agreement the Agreement on Subsidies and Countervailing Measures
SD	Sustainable development
SDG	Sustainable Development Goal
SDR	Special drawing rights
SGP	Stability and Growth Pact
SME	Small and medium-sized enterprises
SMM	Special Monitoring Mission
SPI	Social Progress Index
STECF	Scientific, Technical and Economic Committee for Fisheries
TBL	Triple bottom line
TCA	EU – UK Trade and Cooperation Agreement
TEU	Treaty on European Union
TFEU	Treaty on the Functioning of the European Union
TREE	Training for Rural Economic Empowerment
TRIPS	Trade-Related Aspects of Intellectual Property Rights
TSD	Trade and sustainable development
TVET	Technical and vocational education and training
UNDP	United Nations Development Programme
UNESCO	United Nations Educational, Scientific and Cultural Organization
UNFCCC	United Nations Framework Convention on Climate Change
UNHCR	United Nations High Commissioner for Refugees
UNSC	United Nations Statistical Commission
UN	United Nations
WALoc	Weighted average length of credit
WB	World Bank

WBG	World Bank Group
WHO	World Health Organization
WIPO	World Intellectual Property Organization
WTO	World Trade Organization
VSS	Voluntary Sustainability Standards

Notes on Contributors

Ewa Latoszek, Prof

is Full Professor (economics) and Head of the Jean Monnet Chair of the European Union, Warsaw School of Economics (SGH); Director of Jean Monnet Centre of Excellence (CEWSE). In her career, she was awarded several international and national awards, including the EUI (Florence, Italy) fellowship, two awards from the Minister of Science and Higher Education for scientific and organizational achievements, the Bronze and Silver Cross of Merit awarded by the president of Poland, and over 20 Rector of Warsaw School of Economics Awards. In her research, she specializes in global and regional studies, development economics, European integration, and EU policies. She also coordinated several international and national grants, including the FP7. She has been a visiting professor in many universities, including EUI (Florence), LSE, Canterbury University (New Zealand), and NUS (Singapore). She has also served as the expert in two EC Advisory Groups under Horizon 2020. As an expert, she participated in the process of Polish accession to EU. She also contributed significantly to establishing the cooperation of SGH with Ernst & Young in the field of education in Poland as the Director of Joint Post-diploma Studies. Main functions: President of the Polish European Community Studies Association (PECSA); member of a Steering Committee of the Research Alliance for Development, the World Bank (RAD); member of the Polish Academy of Sciences; Deputy Dean at Warsaw School of Economics; Coordinator of European Studies, Warsaw School of Economics; member of board of ECSA. She is an author of more than 200 publications, including articles, chapters, and monographs related to European integration and international organizations. Email: elatos@sgh.waw.pl, ORCID ID: 0000-0002-2354-9536.

Agnieszka Kłos, PhD

is Assistant Professor at the Jean Monnet Chair of the European Union, Warsaw School of Economics (SGH). Her research interests include international finance, public finance, international relations, and European studies. Author of numerous articles and book chapters in the field of public finance, the EU budget, and the management of instruments financed from EU funds. She has been awarded many times by the Rector of the Warsaw School of Economics for scientific and organizational achievements. She is a member of the editorial board of the *Review of European Affairs* and a reviewer for *Review of European Affairs* and *Studia Europejskie – European Studies*. She has almost 20 years of experience in the management of public funds (national and foreign). She worked at the Ministry of Agriculture and Rural Development, the Ministry of

Finance, the National Economy Bank (BGK), and the Marshal's Office of the Mazowieckie Voivodeship in Warsaw. She participated in study visits to the Ministry of Finance in Germany and the Ministry of the Economy in France. She has also received and coordinated many international grants co-funded by the National Bank of Poland, Ministry of Foreign Affairs, Erasmus+ (Lifelong Learning Programme) and others. She was the Treasurer and the Vice President of the Polish European Community Studies Association (PECSA). She was a member of the Association of Brokers and Advisers and a member of the Polish Economic Society. She is an expert/teacher in EU finance issues at the Academy of European Careers Foundation. Email: aklos1@sgh.waw.pl, ORCID ID: 0000-0003-1947-046X.

Aleksandra Borowicz, PhD

is Assistant Professor in the Department of International Economics and Economic Development at the Faculty of Economics at the University of Gdansk. She specializes in international economics, with a focus on international trade, foreign direct investment, and the economics of European integration. She has experience in applying for and implementing projects co-financed by the European Union. She is a member of the Team Europe Network at the European Commission in Poland. She is a member of the board of PECSA (Polish European Community Studies Association). She also holds a seat on the editorial boards of two journals: *Review of European Affairs*, published by PECSA, and *European Integration Studies*, published by Kaunas University of Technology. Email: aleksandra.borowicz@ug.edu.pl, ORCID ID: 0000-0001-6183-7902.

Leiza Brumat, PhD

is Senior Research Fellow at Eurac Research (Bolzano/Bozen, Italy) where she works on her research project "Policy Implementation in Global South Regionalism: Multilevel Migration Governance in South America" (POLIM), funded by the Autonomous Province of Bolzano/Bozen. She is also an Associate Research Fellow at the Institute for Comparative Regional Integration Studies of the United Nations University (UNU-CRIS). She is an international relations analyst and was awarded a PhD by FLACSO Argentina and an MA in international relations and negotiation by FLACSO and the Universidad de San Andrés. Her previous positions include Research Fellow at the Migration Policy Centre (MPC) of the European University Institute (EUI), Lecturer in international relations, regional integration, and international organizations at UADE and at the Universidad de San Andrés, in her native city Buenos Aires, as well as a Research Fellow for the National Council of Scientific and Technical Research (CONICET) of Argentina. She has done research and teaching activities at the Università di Bologna and the Universidad Complutense de Madrid. She has provided policy advice for the European Union, the Mercosur, and the IOM. She has extensively published on regionalism, regional and global migration governance, and the free movement of persons. Her latest publications include *The Dynamics of Regional Migration Governance* (edited with Andrew Geddes, Marcia Vera-Espinoza, and Leila Hadj-Abdou, Edward Elgar, 2019), *Migration and Mobility in the European Union* (with Andrew Geddes and Leila Hadj-Abdou, Palgrave Macmillan, 2020), and *Freedom of Movement in South America: Rethinking Regional Migration Policy* (Routledge, forthcoming). Email: leiza.brumat@eurac.edu, ORCID ID: 0000-0001-5764-0170.

Giuseppe T. Cirella, PhD, Dr. Hab
is Professor of Human Geography, and works at the Faculty of Economics, University of Gdansk, Sopot, Poland, where he received his equivalency Doctor of Habilitation (Dr. Hab.) in economics and finance. He specializes in economic development, environmental social science, and sustainability. His interdisciplinary background also includes sociopolitical research throughout Eastern Europe, Africa, and China. After completing a PhD at Griffith University, Australia, within the Centre for Infrastructure Engineering and Management, on developing a sustainability-based index, he founded the Polo Centre of Sustainability in Italy. Notably, he has held professorships and scientific positions at Saint Petersburg State University, Russia; Inner Mongolia University of Science and Technology, China; Life University, Cambodia; and the Free University of Bozen, Italy. In his early career, he worked with the Canadian International Development Agency in Indonesia as well as with Radarsat International in Brazil. He is also on the editorial board of a number of internationally renowned academic peer-reviewed journals and has edited a number of books. Email: gt.cirella@ug.edu.pl, ORCID ID: 0000-0002-0810-0589.

Rasa Daugėlienė, PhD
is Associate Professor at the Scientific Group of Public Governance Research in the Department of Social Science, Arts, and Humanities at Kaunas University of Technology, Lithuania. She specializes in the economics of EU integration, the macroeconomic stability of state economies, the workings of the EU internal market, as well as innovative public governance methods. She has experience in evaluating research projects as well as in their implementation (e.g., the H2020 project "FEDORA: Future-Oriented Science Education to Enhance Responsibility and Engagement"). She is an expert of the Lithuanian Science Council as well as an expert at the Quality Agency for Higher Education in Latvia (AIKA). She is a member of the editorial board of two international

scientific journals: *Acta Informatica Pragensia* (published by Prague University of Economics and Business, Czechia) and *Current Issues in Management of Business and Society Development* (conference proceedings published by the University of Latvia). She is Editor in Chief of *European Integration Studies*, an international scientific journal (published by Kaunas University of Technology). Email: rasa.daugeliene@ktu.lt, ORCID ID: 0000-0002-5232-7270.

Agnieszka Domańska, PhD, Dr. Hab
is Associate Professor at the Warsaw School of Economics (SGH), the International Political Economy Department (ZMPE) at the Institute of International Studies (ISM), College of Socio-Economics (KES). An economist with a record of research and publications, she is also an experienced lecturer who has taught across Europe and beyond. Her research interests include international economic relations, international business cycle synchronization, transmission of macroeconomic shocks, the effects of international economic policy, the EU transport system, and cooperation between science and business in high-tech industries. She is a permanent member of the following academic societies: INFER; the Polish European Community Studies Association (PECSA); IISES; and the Polish Economic Society. For a number of years, she served as the President of the Staszic Institute. Since 2020 she has been the President of the Polish branch of Principles for Responsible Management Education (PRIME). She serves as the topic editor at the *Review of European Affairs*, published by PECSA. Email: adomansk@sgh.waw.pl, ORCID ID: 0000-0002-4303-9680.

Małgorzata Dziembała, PhD, Dr. Hab
Doctor habilitatus of economic science, PhD in economics, is Associate Professor, Head of the Department of International Economic Relations, University of Economics, in Katowice, Poland. Her research focuses on European economic integration, European Union regional policy, and competitiveness of the regions, international cooperation of the regions, including cross-border cooperation, and innovation policy. She publishes extensively and is the author or co-author of articles and chapters in monographs comprising more than a hundred publications. Her academic teaching refers to issues of international economics, management of EU funds, and international business. She has delivered lectures in France, Finland, Switzerland, the US, and other countries. She gained practical experience in the field of EU cohesion policy, including European territorial cooperation. She was the expert of the Polish Ministry of Regional Development during preparation of the Operational Programme of Cross-border Cooperation, Czech Republic – Republic of Poland, 2007–2013, within the European Territorial Cooperation objective. Email: malgorzata.dziembala@ue.katowice.pl, ORCID ID: 0000-0002-8992-8627.

Lenka Fojtíková, Prof.
is Professor of International Economic Relations, PhD in Economics, Vice-Rector for External Relations at PRIGO University, Havířov, Czech Republic. Her research focuses on international trade, WTO, EU trade policy, and European economic integration. She is the author or co-author of six monographs, more than 40 articles and conference papers that have been indexed in the Web of Science database and Scopus, and many others. Regarding research and publication, she has been successful in cooperating with partners at other universities in the Czech Republic and abroad. Her academic teaching focuses on international economics, the European Union, and the economic policies of selected countries. She supervised PhD students. She has delivered lectures in Japan, China, Belgium, Cyprus, Italy, Portugal, Spain, and Romania. She is a member of the editorial board of the *Review of Economic Perspectives – Národohospodářský obzor*, published by Masaryk University in Brno, *European Studies: The Review of European Law, Economics and Politics*, published by the Czech Association for European Studies (ČAES) in Olomouc, *Creative and Knowledge Society* published by the Pan-European University in Bratislava, Slovakia, and the *Almanach. Aktuální otázky světové ekonomiky a politiky*, published by the Economic University in Bratislava, Slovakia. She has extensive experience of organizing international scientific conferences. She has been a professional guarantor of the International Conference on European Integration (ICEI) since 2012. She has also been a member of the Scientific Council of the Faculty of International Relations at the Economic University in Prague, the Faculty of Economics at VSB-Technical University of Ostrava, and PRIGO University in Havířov. Email: lenka.fojtikova@vsb.cz, ORCID ID: 0000-0002-1544-2421.

Katja Zajc Kejžar, Prof.
is Full Professor in the School of Economics and Business at the University of Ljubljana. Her research interests include various aspects of international economics, European economic integration, global governance, global value chains, and industrial restructuring and evolution. She has been a visiting researcher at the Department of Economics, University of Bologna, and a guest lecturer at Shanghai University of International Business and Economics, the University of Antwerp, and the University of Rijeka. Her bibliography includes over 60 papers/book chapters, including publications in high-ranking international journals, such as *Review of World Economics, The World Economy, Open Economies Review, Small Business Economics, Journal of International Trade & Economic Development*, and *Applied Economics*. She has contributed to several European, national, and international projects with a research focus on global and regional economic integration processes. She was a founding member of

the European Communities Studies Association of Slovenia (ECSA Slovenia) and served as its Vice President. Email: katja.zajc@ef.uni-lj.si, ORCID ID: 0000-0003-1360-6899.

Ewa Kosycarz, PhD
holds a PhD in the field of Public Finance. Her research areas cover state budgets, public expenditures, and public health-care systems. Her scientific interests include: efficiency, effectiveness, and the resilience of health-care systems at the macro-, mezzo- and microeconomic levels. She was an Advisor to the Secretary of State in the Performance Budget Department of the Prime Minister's Chancellery. She cooperated with the Ministry of Finance in several projects concerning performance measurement, including training for government officials from several ministries and public agencies. She was commissioned by the Ministry of Finance to prepare a list of indicators used in the state performance budget. She cooperated with the Agency for Health Technology Assessment and Pricing. Email: ekosyc@sgh.waw.pl, ORCID ID: 0000-0003-4272-6195.

Anatoliy Kruglashov, Prof.
is a political scientist and historian, and works as Head of the Department of Political Science and Public Administration, and Director of the Research Institute of European Integration and Regional Studies, Chernivtsi Jury Fedkovych National University, Ukraine. He is the titular member in the Group of Independent Experts on the European Chapter of Self-Government, Congress of Local and Regional Authorities, Council of Europe, since 2014. His research interests mainly cover European integration with special attention to EU policy towards Eastern Partnership countries, security studies, CEE and post-Soviet space political processes, political regionalism and ethno-politics, history of political ideas and political science, public administration and self-government. He has been Invited Scholar and Professor at the University of Alberta (Edmonton, Canada), Professor at Jagellonian University (Krakow, Poland), and Professor at the European Humanities University (Belarus and Lithuania). He has been invited to lecture in Germany, Poland, Slovakia, Russia, and Romania. He has also run several European and national research and didactic projects. He is the author of recent publications (articles and chapters in some books): *Chernivtsi Region Cross-border Cooperation: Global Challenges versus Local Opportunities* (Lviv, 2022), *Eastern Partnership vis-à-vis Challenges and Doubts* (Lublin, 2020), *Turbulent Neighborhood: Ukraine and the EU Relations under Ongoing Pressure* (Warsaw, 2017), *Securing Insecure: Ukraine on the Margins of the European Integration Process* (Chișinău, 2018), *Ukraine Approaching the EU: How to Avoid the "Fata Morgana" Case* (Chișinău –

Tbilisi – Chernivtsi, 2017), *Hardships of Dialogue: Civil Society Communication with Authorities in Ukraine* (Wien, 2016), *Ukraine – Romania Dialogue: Moving ahead from Distrust and Suspicions* (Oradea – Debrecen, 2016), and others. Email: akruglas@gmail.com, ORCID ID: 0000-0003-0611-2698.

Andrzej Latoszek, MA
gained his MA degree in finance and banking at the Warsaw School of Economics (SGH). He has also earned a diploma in real estate brokerage at the Warsaw University of Life Sciences (SGGW) and a diploma in property management from the Institute of Spatial Management and Housing in Warsaw. He is a licensed real estate broker and property manager. In his professional work, he focuses on banking relating to international cooperation and the role of international organizations in supporting the Polish economy and the transformation process. He has a wide range of professional experiences working in the banking sector (for, among others, Alior Bank, Bank Gospodarstwa Krajowego (BIK), which is the Polish national development bank, and PEKAO S.A.), dealing with international investment projects (structured export finance), trade finance, and restructuring corporate debt. Email: andrzej.latoszek@gmail.com.

Mirela Mărcuț, PhD
is Lecturer at the University of Oradea, in Romania. Her research interests include digital policies and governance, as well as smart cities, with a particular focus on the European Union. In 2017, she was awarded the Henri Rieben Scholarship at the Jean Monnet Foundation for Europe to study the beginnings of the information society in Europe. In 2020, she held a postdoctoral research scholarship in Darmstadt, Germany, studying the governance of smart cities. Her main publications include *The Socioeconomic Evolution of the European Union: Exploring the Electronic Frontier* (2016), *Crystallizing the EU Digital Policy: Exploring the Digital Single Market* (2017), and *The Governance of Digital Policies* (2020), all published by Springer. Email: mirelamarcut@uoradea.ro, ORCID ID: 0000-0003-2832-9249.

Willem Molle, Prof.
is Emeritus Professor in the School of Economics, Erasmus University Rotterdam, Netherlands. He is a leading academic in his field. His research and publications mostly concern European and worldwide economic and social policy processes and institutional developments. He has published some widely acclaimed handbooks on these subjects. On the global level he has published *Governing the World Economy* (Routledge, 2014). These works and his numerous other books and articles show his capacity to apply theoretical insights with assessments of a wide ranging number of subjects in order to get

to consistent strategic solutions. He has also broad experience in policy advice. He has been associated with ECORYS Research and Consulting in several senior roles. He has contributed to many multinational projects for international organizations. Email: wtmmolle-c@telfort.nl, ORCID ID: 0000-0001-7690-0951.

Marta Pachocka, PhD
is an economist and political scientist. Assistant Professor in the Department of Political Studies, the Institute of International Studies of the Collegium of Socio-Economics of the Warsaw School of Economics (SGH); researcher and co-coordinator of the Laboratory of Urban and Regional Migration Policies at the Centre of Migration Research (CMR) of the University of Warsaw (UW); and former Head of the Migration Policies Research Unit at CMR (2018–2022). She has considerable experience as both a team leader and member in implementing cross-sector and multi-stakeholder projects co-funded by the National Science Centre (Poland), National Bank of Poland, Capital City of Warsaw, various ministries, EU Programmes (Horizon 2020, Horizon Europe, Lifelong Learning Programme, Erasmus+, Creative Europe), and others. She is on the board of the Polish European Community Studies Association (PECSA) and the Research Committee RC46 "Migration and Citizenship" of the International Political Science Association (IPSA). She supports the European Commission Representation in Poland as an EU expert member of the Team Europe Direct Poland network. She is also a member of the International Steering Committee of the Metropolis Project, focused on international migration and migration policies. She is a member of several national and international associations, including UACES, IMISCOE, IPSA, IASF, IPPA, and the Consultative Forum of the EU Agency for Asylum (since 2022) on behalf of the CMR UW. She was a Visiting Research Fellow at the Centre for European Studies of Sciences Po Paris (2015) and a Visiting Scholar at the Carleton University (2022). She was a Visiting Professor in Bratislava (2015) and Tartu (2016). She has authored or co-authored book chapters, journal articles, working papers, research reports, and other texts in Polish, English, French, or German covering international relations and economics, migration studies, and EU studies, which has given her considerable experience and expertise to co-edit books and special issues of journals highly recognized by international publishers (including Wiley, Routledge, and Emerald). Her main research interests include EU studies and migration studies. Email: marta.pachocka@gmail.com, ORCID ID: 0000-0002-6930-5078.

Nina Ponikvar, PhD
is an Associate Professor of Economics at the School of Economics and Business, University of Ljubljana, in the Academic Unit for Economics. Her

research interests include various aspects of firm performance, such as growth, profit margins, survival, and market exit, and the role of firm and industry characteristics, as well as economic valuation methods, and heterodox macroeconomic models of small open economies. She has published several papers in high-ranking scientific journals and monographs. She teaches microeconomics, macroeconomics, and managerial economics university courses. Email: nina.ponikvar@ef.uni-lj.si, ORCID ID: 0000-0003-3976-211X.

Magdalena Proczek, PhD, Dr. Hab
is Associate Professor at the Warsaw School of Economics (SGH). She graduated from SGH and engaged in postgraduate studies in pedagogy (SGH) and intellectual property protection (Maria Curie-Skłodowska University, Lublin). Her research interests include the activities of international organizations, international relations, and European studies. She is a frequent author, co-author, and editor of academic articles, monographs, reviews, etc. She has also received and coordinated many grants (including Jean Monnet Permanent Course (1995–1998), Jean Monnet – Lifelong Learning Programme (2013–2015), Jean Monnet Centre of Excellence at WSE – CEWSE (2016–2019), Jean Monnet "Policy Debate with the Academic World," (2016–2018), Jean Monnet "Support to Associations" (2016–2019), Strategic Partnerships Erasmus+ (2016–2019), Jean Monnet Module (2019–2022). She has worked at many Polish universities and supervised more than 240 MA and BA theses. She has received the Warsaw School of Economics Rector's Team Award for Teaching 11 times, as well as numerous other awards, such as the Minister of National Education and Sport Team Award, as well as for her doctoral and habilitation dissertations. She is a member of many professional bodies and organizations, including the Polish European Community Studies Association and the Polish Economic Society. She has organized many conferences and national and international seminars related to European Union studies. She has collaborated with international organizations such as the World Bank, UNDP, UNHCR, Amnesty International, the Robert Schuman Foundation, the US Embassy in Poland, the National School for Public Administration, the National Bank of Poland, etc. Email: mprocz@sgh.waw.pl, ORCID ID: 0000-0001-7888-7850.

Ewa Osuch-Rak, PhD
is Assistant Professor at the Jean Monnet Chair of the European Union, Warsaw School of Economics (SGH). PhD in the field of social sciences in the discipline of economics and finance (PhD thesis was awarded a distinction). Research and development project manager with over 12 years of experience in project initiation, organization, and administration. She worked for public institutions, such as Polish Agency for Enterprise Development (PARP) and the Polish

Academy of Sciences (PAN), and for private organizations, such as high-tech companies in the space and energy sector. She graduated from SGH (MA in International Relations, 2009; postgraduate managerial program "Innovation Manager," 2013). Author of articles covering innovation, technology transfer, space industry, as well as sustainable development, and co-editor of a monograph: *Facing the Challenges in the European Union: Re-thinking EU Education and Research for Smart and Inclusive Growth* (Polish European Community Studies Association, 2015). Recipient a Young Scientist's Research Grant funded by the Polish Ministry of Science and Higher Education (2015). Visiting Scholar at Haas School of Business, University of California, Berkeley (2013). Laureate of 2nd Degree Team Prizes of the Rector of the SGH for scientific achievement. Laureate of the prestigious Polish Ministry of Science and Higher Education's program Top 500 Innovators Science-Management-Commercialization (MBA level). Email: eosuch@sgh.waw.pl, ORCID ID: 0000-0002-6919-9391.

Angela Maria Romito, Prof., LLM
is Associate Professor of European Union Law, Faculty of Political Science, University of Bari Aldo Moro, Italy. Fully qualified as Full Professor of EU Law since December 18, 2021, following nationally held competition procedure (Abilitazione Scientifica Nazionale). She holds a Law degree cum laude from the University of Bari and an LLM from the School of Law/Center of International Legal Education at the University of Pittsburgh (2001). Lawyer in Bari since July 1997. Teaching experience since 2005. Member of the editorial boards of *Studi sull'integrazione europea* (since 2006, and referee since 2022), *SudinEuropa* (since 1996), *Papers di Diritto europeo* (since 2021), and the Polish legal review *Public Administration and Security Studies* (since 2018). Member of Società Italiana di diritto internazionale (SIDI) and Associazione italiana studiosi di diritto dell'Unione europea (AISDUE). Member of MIUR – PRIN project 2007 "European Citizenship and Political Rights: Problems and Perspectives," scientific coordinator: Professor Ennio Triggiani. Member of MIUR-PRIN 2017; Prot. 20174EH2MR "International Migrations, State, Sovereignty and Human Rights: Open Legal Issues." Referee for the Italian National Agency for the Evaluation of Universities and Research Institutes (ANVUR). She is a winner of several national and international fellowships. Author of two books: *La tutela giurisdizionale nell'Unione europea tra effettività del sistema e garanzie individuali* (Bari, 2015) and *Ruolo e funzioni dell'European Competition Network." Dal Regolamento* (CE) *1/2003 alla direttiva* ECN+ (Bari, 2020). Her research interests include judicial protection in the EU, European citizenship, European competition law, European Union law, international private law, and international commercial law. Email: angelamaria.romito@uniba.it, ORCID ID: 0000-0002-0486-5859.

Aleksandra Szczerba, PhD, Dr. Hab
is Professor of Law at the Jacob of Paradies University in Gorzów Wielkopolski, Poland. An external expert of the European Institute for Gender Equality and expert of Team Europe. Visiting Professor at the University of Bari Aldo Moro, Italy. Anti-discrimination lawyer at the Office of the Commissioner for Human Rights. She specializes in EU law and anti-discrimination law. Her research interests include the principle of gender equality, the area of freedom, security, and justice (AFSJ), and the EU internal market. She is an author and co-editor of several books and articles published both in Polish and English. Email: szczerba.aleksandra@gmail.com, ORCID ID: 0000-0001-7857-0554.

Piotr Stolarczyk, PhD
holds a PhD from the Warsaw School of Economics (SGH) in Poland, presently Assistant Professor of Economics and Finance at Lazarski University in Warsaw. His academic teaching covers Economics, International Trade and Finance. He graduated from SGH with an MA in finance and banking. He also holds an MSc in European Union business and law from Aarhus University in Denmark and an EMBA degree from Warsaw University. He gained professional experience working for many years in the public and private sectors in Poland and abroad. Currently, he works in the banking sector dealing with international investment projects (export finance) and trade finance. Previously, he worked in the European Parliament where he was involved in the work of the EP Committee on Economic and Monetary Affairs. He frequently comments on the economy and finance. His opinion articles have been published in leading Polish and international newspapers. Email: piotrstolarczyk@o2.pl, ORCID ID:0000-0001-8225-1417.

Diego Caballero Vélez, PhD
is postdoctoral Researcher at the Centre of Migration Research (CMR) at the University of Warsaw. He holds a PhD in political science, EU politics and international relations from the Sant'Anna School of Advanced Studies in Pisa, Italy. He has spent visiting periods at the Migration Policy Centre (European University Institute),Refugee Studies Centre (University of Oxford) and the Warsaw School of Economics (SGH). In addition, he has presented research papers at seminars in several universities, such as the University of Oxford, the University of Catania, and SGH, as well as published with internationally recognized scientific journals. He was a teaching assistant at the Catholic University of Applied Sciences of Mainz and at the University of Pisa. Research interests: European migration, asylum and security policies, political economy, EU external action, and multilevel governance. Apart from his research experience, he has worked at the Research Executive Agency (European Commission) as a Blue

Book trainee. Recent publications: "When Exit Policies Determine the Entry Policies: The Case of *Karta Polaka*," *International Migration* (2022, with J. Misiuna), and "Producing Public Goods in the EU: European Integration Processes in the Fields of Refugee Protection and Climate Stability," *European Politics and Society* (2021, with M. Pachocka). Email: d.caballerovelez@gmail.com, ORCID ID: 0000-0003-3646-9823.

Anna Wójtowicz, PhD

works at the Warsaw School of Economics, Collegium of Socio-Economics. Her research interests include energy for sustainable development, renewable energy sources, international economics, and development economics. She has participated in many national and international conferences. She is the author and co-author of numerous publications in the field of sustainable development, renewable energy sources, energy policy of member countries of the EU, and development economics. She has participated in the work of the organizing committee of the international congress of the project "Centre of Excellence at Warsaw School of Economics on the European Union's Security and Stability in a New Economic, Social & Geopolitical Settlement." Her academic teaching covers development economics, European integration, sustainable development, business cycle analysis, foreign market research, as well as macroeconomics and microeconomics. Member of the Polish European Community Studies Association (PECSA). Email: awojtow@sgh.waw.pl, ORCID ID: 0000-0002-2337-7455.

Introduction

Ewa Latoszek and Agnieszka Kłos

1 Key Arguments Presented in This Volume

Given the importance of international organizations in today's world, the purpose of this publication is to present the scale of activities carried out by international organizations (IOs), their role in solving selected problems related to the current challenges of the world, and the effectiveness of actions taken to balance global development. This publication is an original research work aimed at acquiring new knowledge about basic phenomena and observable facts on the role of international organizations in creating, managing, and providing global public goods (GPGs) for better implementation of sustainable development (SD). The publication is of key importance for the theory and practice of international and development economics, the more so because their role has increased significantly in the current global situation, marked by the pandemic, the war in Ukraine, and the deepening economic crisis. The fact that international organizations have come to serve as a forum where attempts are made to reconcile the conflicting interests of its members is of particular importance nowadays, given that member states seem to be losing the ability to deal with the flagrant incongruities existing within their own societies. They begin to rely – to an increasing extent – on international organizations as coordinators of activities within the gradually expanding areas of international cooperation.

According to scholars researching the process of globalization, the role of international organizations in responding to new global and regional challenges related to economic, financial, and social changes has become noticeably more prominent over the past decade (Gygli et al., 2019; McCormick, 2022; Diehl & Frederking, 2010; Carbaugh, 2016). The changes which have taken place in the world have increased the pressure to build a new global architecture for the 21st century based on deepening the interdependence of the main actors in international relations (that is, international governmental organizations and institutions, states, and NGOs) to face the current economic, political, financial, and social challenges. But today, as the global community confronts a comprehensive and interconnected array of compelling economic, development, and security challenges which require effective coexistence of these actors, the importance of IOs in solving this problems is much greater than ever. Nowadays at the center of world sustainability stand the new policy towards the ways of providing and regulating global public goods by IOs as the global uncertainty is on the rise fueled by political, geo-economic, and social tensions. The COVID-19 pandemic and the war in Ukraine have accelerated and focused attention on these shifts, while creating challenges of its own. It has exposed the risk of a breakdown of global cooperation and trust. But no matter what the emerging threats are, it has also highlighted the interconnected nature of economies, which rely on stable and predictable international rules and resilient channels of multilateral cooperation.

Today, global public goods – their management and provision – are one of the most important issues in international relations and their study has not only an academic but also a distinctly utilitarian value (Kaul et al., 2003). Questions about how to maintain peace and democracy, impede global warming, fight the pandemic or avoid the global economic and financial crisis are becoming increasingly relevant to a globalized world. Despite the threats and the obvious benefits of collective actions of the international community for the common good and the wider security of the world for future generations, the practice of all subjects involved in this area leaves much to be done and is in principle still a road to nowhere, no matter if it has absorbed huge amounts of private and public money and still is unable to provide what civilians need the most – security, stability, sustainability.

It is currently necessary to provide a multidimensional analysis of the impact of international organizations on mitigating the threats emerging in the global economy and reconciling the conflicting interests of its members through a more effective provision, management, and use of global goods in the process of implementing sustainable development. The aim of the study is twofold. Firstly, it is believed to be the first study of this kind to carry out a multidimensional analysis of the impact of international organizations on mitigating global economic, social, and political challenges in the world, increasing in complexity and number, and to reconcile the conflicting interests of the organizations' members through much more effective use of global goods to foster sustainable development. Secondly, it provides further evidence for the policy debate on the scope and importance of international organizations in the process of optimal (efficient) management and use of a wide range of public goods in the implementation of the concept of sustainable development. Moreover, the sustainable development of the world has raised concerns within scholars for decades (Alves & Biancarelli, 2020; Sachs et al., 2019; Independent Group, 2019; Gupta & Vegelin, 2016; Stiglitz, 2019). From a different angle, the validity of the debate notwithstanding, very little attention in it has been paid to the question of the independence of sustainable development with global public goods provision by IOs, which has become an extremely urgent and important problem in the times of COVID-19 and the war in Ukraine. This publication seeks to answer the following questions: (1) What are the stages of the evolution of GPGs in the globalizing world? (2) What are the main elements of the sustainable development paradigm, considering the ongoing changes in the world? (3) What are the main elements of GPGs? (4) What actors of international relations have enough power to rule and provide GPGs? (5) What are the most important instruments and dimensions of the contemporary GPG in regards to their impact on the world's SD?

The IO policy towards the regulation/provision/management of global public goods has to adopt and reflect the challenges of our times by building fairer and more sustainable globalization based on modernized rules and stronger enforcement action. It is only by doing so that we can generate in a responsible and sustainable manner the opportunities that citizens and the planet need. The provision of global public goods by IOs has the potential to influence not only the economy or politics, but also our daily lives through the constant spread of democratic openness and empowered citizenship on a global scale to make all of them more sustainable. Especially as global public goods are provided largely without a relevant, up-to-date theory, often failing to keep up with the rapidly evolving world. Furthermore, the perception of global public goods varies across population groups in today's multifactor world.

2 Statement of Purpose

Many member states and other participants of international relations regard the activities of IOs as inadequate and doubt their ability to cope with increasingly complex and numerous challenges, such as financial instability, the environment and climate change, health and the fight against major pandemics, multilateral trade, everyday security, etc., which are no longer only national goals but global public goods. On the other hand, in today's economy the production of private goods has taken precedence over the provision of public goods. Therefore, if SD is to become reality, the debate on global public goods needs to be pursued. This book critically examines how effectively global institutions comply with their commitments to provide global public goods. It analyzes how their effectiveness can be improved through accountability measures designed to increase the global institutions' compliance with the assumptions of sustainable development, and to deliver better results not only through influencing the policy of member states to be more effective towards implementation of global public goods, but also through securing adequate resources (private and public) for these goods.

This publication is an original research work aimed at acquiring new knowledge about basic phenomena and observable facts, as the role of international organizations in the implementation of the concept of sustainable development is of key importance for the theory and practice of international economics and development economics. It is all the more important, given the current global situation, marked by the pandemic and a deepening economic crisis. In fact, international organizations have come to serve as a forum for attempts to reconcile the conflicting interests of their members. It is of particular importance nowadays, given that member states seem to be losing the ability to deal with the flagrant incongruities existing within their own general public. They begin to rely – to an increasing extent – on international organizations as coordinators of activities within the gradually expanding areas of international cooperation. Given the importance of international organizations in today's world, the publication would present the scale of activities carried out by international organizations and their role in solving selected problems related to the current challenges of the world economy, as well as the scope and effectiveness of actions taken to balance global development.

3 Methodology

The starting point of the research publication presents, by the method of synthesis and deduction, the impact of international organizations on mitigating the threats emerging in the global economy and reconciling the conflicting interests of its members through a more effective management of global goods in the process of implementing sustainable development. Due to the interdisciplinary and complex nature of this analysis, mixed research methods were employed (Creswell et al., 2003) to integrate quantitative and qualitative analyzes and results.

In order to achieve the purpose of this publication, the following methods were employed:

– The methods of literature analysis, including critical analysis of literature of discipline (Popay et al., 2006) as well as for the purpose of the review of scientific literature, and content analysis (Krippendorff, 2004) were used. To make this process comprehensive, published literature related to the global goods, sustainable development, and international organizations was analyzed using standardized techniques). Peer-reviewed scientific papers and books were accessed in online databases (Science Direct, Research, Academy, Google Scholar) using different combinations of search terms. The Boolean operators AND and OR were used to make this search more effective. Publications, books, scientific magazines, articles, acts, reports of the European Commission, European Central Bank, United Nations, Organisation for Economic Co-operation and Development, World Bank, and international scientific institutes and others were analyzed to gather the theoretical base for empirical research. Such a wide range of literature allowed the researchers to find and analyze the most appropriate and the most recent literature and document as well as to state clearly what has been researched so far in this area to avoid duplications and if so, what types of actions are deemed necessary.

- Quantitative methods – of time series of economic indicators, descriptive analysis of statistical data and reports of expert groups, visual presentation of results, tabular description of materials and data obtained from reports of the European Commission, European Central Bank, United Nations, UNIDO, United Nations Conference on Trade and Development, Organisation for Economic Co-operation and Development, World Bank and other institutions and also statistical materials published by these organizations, as well as international scientific institutes.
- The case study method to show the prospects in the implementation of actions taken by the international organizations on mitigating the threats emerging in the global economy and reconciling the conflicting interests of its members through a more effective management of global goods in the process of implementing sustainable development.

The analysis was carried out accordingly to the type of data collected. Due to discrepancies in data from these sources, the empirical analysis was preceded by a thorough verification of the data. Qualitative data was analyzed in line with the principles of thematic analysis (Braun & Clarke, 2006;).

4 Setup

Members of society of today should be aware that regardless of the pros and cons, it has to be admitted that the concept of SD is one of the most important strategies of economic development and has the potential to influence not only the economy but also our daily lives to make them more sustainable. Especially in the context of the effective creation, management, and use of global public goods by international organizations. Yet, we do not have a sufficiently developed research approach that allows us to look at the different aspects of their importance in the context of SD. This book examines the issue of interdependence between three elements: international organizations, global public goods, and sustainable development, which has not been comprehensively analyzed yet and discussed in the literature. The publication comprises six parts consisting of 16 chapters, including this introductory chapter and a concluding one. The chapters address a variety of topics consistent with the book objectives.

The discussion in the book starts with Part 1, which highlights the key features of global public goods and global governance. It consist of two chapters. In Chapter 1 Katja Zajc Kejžar and Nina Ponikvar focus on analyzing the interconnectivity of sustainable development and global public goods in today's practice of international organizations facing new challenges such as COVID-19, the war in Ukraine, climate change, rapid developments in new technologies, economic and social foundations of our lives, etc. This part presents the evolution and the main features of global public goods (GPGs) as well as their role in the world economy of today. This chapter contributes to the understanding of the changing nature of GPGs and frames the discussion on the adjustments needed in the definition and provision of GPGs by the main stakeholders, including international organizations, in the context of the new sustainable development paradigm. The analysis provided here makes two important contributions. First, it specifies what global public goods are and answers the question of how international organizations streamline the use of global public goods. Secondly, the analysis highlights the correlation between the increase of utility and effectiveness of global public goods and the implementation of the sustainable development concept in contemporary circumstances.

In Chapter 2, Willem Molle characterizes the modern system of global governance, the process of its evolution up to the present, its theoretical backgrounds, as well as its strengths and weaknesses. To address the considerable challenges that the system faces nowadays, the author analyzes how adequate this system is to solve these challenges in such an unstable world and what the consequences of these changes could be for various aspects of social life and for the relationships between the major actors of the world economy. Molle concentrates in this chapter on three important sets of concrete questions: the first one concerns the scope of globalization and the growth of global institutions capable of delivering new global public goods; the second one touches on the issue of theoretical explanations of these developments and the main characteristics of the system of global governance as it has evolved to the present with special attention to the ensuing shift in authority to IOs; and the third one raises the problem of the main weaknesses of the current system of global governance, how the lack of legitimacy of existing institutions can be addressed, and what should be done to improve the performance of institutions.

Part 2 focuses on international security and SDGs. Chapter 3 by Anatoliy Kruglashov argues that the global order is in a dramatic transition phase, from the so-called unipolar to a multipolar system of international relations. This makes international relations less predictable so that global and regional actors tend towards chaotic moves and actions. The first victim of this trend is international security. Rapid growth of local and regional conflicts and fears unleashed by COVID-19 are only a few of the risks the global community is facing. The new stage of the Russo – Ukrainian War thoroughly proves the aggravated state of global insecurity. International organizations have been founded in order to promote global development and pave a way towards peaceful and rational solutions in the area of security. Still, the UN is hardly a successful case as a provider of global security. NATO seems much stronger but its power is limited as well. The EU seeks to play an active role in resolving most crucial regional and global problems, but it is burdened with too many internal problems by itself. Numerous issues also impaired the activity of OSCE and Council of Europe. This chapter deals with the UN, the OSCE, NATO, the Council of Europe, and, finally, EU policies regarding the most crucial security challenges. How do they try to cope with the key issues of the lack of security? What are the advantages and disadvantages of those international organizations vis-à-vis key threats and the risks of global disorder? What kind of solutions do they look for in order to increase their capacity to introduce more peaceful and secure politics to the world? All of these activities by international organizations in the realm of security are analyzed by applying the concepts of hard, soft and smart powers.

In Chapter 4 Leiza Brumat, Diego Caballero Vélez, and Marta Pachocka argue that IOs actively link SD to migration as a political strategy for mitigating the effects of the overlapping and fragmented character of global migration governance. The literature acknowledges this governance character in the legislation and regimes that regulate different types of migrants and migration, and that migration is an area in which states' interests are very divergent, so collective action is more unlikely). This has powerful effects on individuals' access to rights and mobility In this chapter, the authors argue that IOs are aware that states' interests are more likely to converge in a SD agenda rather than the migration agenda because the SD agenda is perceived as more legitimate. They analyze refugee protection as a global public good to show how IOs actively include migration into their SD agendas to broaden the opportunities for cooperation in this highly contested area. They show how and why IOs strategically "use" SD to enhance global migration governance by looking at the cases of the UNHCR and the EU.

In Chapter 5 Angela Maria Romito and Aleksandra Szczerba describe the European legal system for protecting human rights, highlighting the relevant tools of the European Union through the prism of the rule of law as an "umbrella principle." The principle at stake – the rule of law – is the backbone of any modern constitutional democracy. Within the EU legal system, it is enshrined in Article 2 of the Treaty on European Union (TEU) and it is a prerequisite for the protection of all the other fundamental values, including fundamental rights and democracy. The concept of the rule of law includes, inter alia, principles such as legality, according to which the legislative process must be transparent, accountable, democratic, and pluralistic; offer legal certainty; prohibit the arbitrary exercise of executive power; provide effective judicial protection by independent and impartial courts and effective judicial review, including respect for fundamental rights; ensure separation of powers; and guarantee equality before the law. These principles have been recognized by the Court of Justice of the European Union. They shall ensure that all public authorities always act within the limits set by the law, in accordance with the values of democracy and fundamental rights, and under the supervision of an independent and impartial judge. The recent behavior of governments, such as that of Poland and Hungary, has contributed to intensifying the debate on strengthening the rule of law and the necessary involvement of an active civil society.

Economic globalization has brought progress in many areas of social life and influenced the living standards of many people around the world. International trade significantly contributed to this development, following the liberalization processes that occurred in the world after World War II. However, growing production and trade deplete resources, pollute the air, oceans, and soil, and have a negative impact on the environment and health of people. The chapters in Part 3 concentrate on the empirical verification of the theory of global public goods and sustainable development through the prism of multilateral trade in the activities of the OECD, the WTO, and the EU. The focus is on the importance of multilateral trade to foster sustainable development.

In Chapter 6 Lenka Fojtíková introduces some facts and shows critical areas in trade liberalization, which is carried out under the WTO multilateral framework and supported by the OECD in order to achieve sustainable development in the world. Firstly, the author presents an interaction between economic development and environmental sustainability in practical examples. The chapter proves that the cooperation on the creation of a suitable institutional framework, which would protect the environment and not create new barriers to trade, is necessary on local, regional, national, and international levels. Secondly, the role of the World Trade Organization (WTO) and the

Organisation for Economic Co-operation and Development (OECD) in achieving the Sustainable Development Goals (SDGs) is discussed. The chapter presents the institutional and legal frameworks of both organizations that deal with environment-related issues. Besides this, special attention is given to the multilateral trade principles, such as non-discrimination, transparency, and predictability, to implement measures in order to achieve environmental goals and not create barriers to trade. Thirdly, the author analyzes the trade liberalization process in three areas that play the most important role in ensuring market access for environmental goods and services. Thus, the liberalization of agricultural trade, trade in services, and intellectual property represent the most sensitive topics in the area of multilateral trade liberalization in which the author develops a critical debate on the real achievements of the WTO and the OECD on the way to achieving sustainable development.

In addition to these analyzes, in Chapter 7 Piotr Stolarczyk reviews the rules governing the provision of financing for international trade with particular focus on the functioning of so-called export credits. The starting point for the author's analysis is the observation of the growing importance of trade as such in generating national income. An open and non-discriminatory system of international trade has become crucial to ensure the sustainable development of the world. The liberalization of trade that has been going on for many years created highly competitive environment for international trade. In such a reality, maintaining the appropriate shape of regulations that will ensure the non-discriminatory nature of world trade and, at the same time, free access to the global market of goods and services, has become of high importance. The WTO and the OECD are the organizations that ensure the compliance with the regulations. According to the author, they are also the regulators of an open and non-discriminatory trading system as a public good. The author analyzes the provisions of the Agreement on Subsidies and Countervailing Measures, the WTO Agreement on Agriculture, and the OECD Consensus, with special focus on regulations concerning export credits. The author pays attention to the special rules concerning least developed countries, which are shaped to support their development in a competitive system of international trade.

In Chapter 8 Aleksandra Borowicz and Rasa Daugėlienė provide an overview and space for critical debate on the role of the EU as an international organization in the creation of a multilateral trade regime in the context of the SDGs through the trade channel. As a key player on the global economic and political scene, the European Union is the creator of the world trade regime, next to World Trade Organization (WTO). Through the trade policy, it impacts the fulfillment of the SDGs. Firstly, the authors discuss international trade as a global public good by indicating the features of global public goods.

The chapter proves that the characteristic non-rivalry and non-excludability of international trade portrays trade as a global public good. Therefore, it is expected that trade policy shall play an essential role in the delivery of SDGs. The authors reveal which targets set in Agenda 2030 are directly correlated with trade. Secondly, the chapter presents EU trade policy as a holistic area of policymaking, the complex character and direct linkages of EU priorities with SDGs, and the progress of EU member states on the road to the achievement of the SDGs. Thirdly, the authors analyze EU trade policy towards third countries in terms of covering the agreements by the SDGs. The analysis presented in the chapter is based on 11 agreements with various third countries. The chapter gives an overview and space for critical debate on the role of the EU as an international organization in the creation of a multilateral trade regime in the context of the SDGs through the trade channel.

Part 4 focuses on financial stability and GDP in the activities of the World Bank, the IMF, and the EU. The issue of financial system stability has gained importance in recent years. The global financial crisis of 2007+ has forced a revision of thinking about the economy. Globalization stimulates close multilevel connections between various economic entities and international organizations, as well as between the international organizations themselves. These connections also contribute to the stability of the financial system. However, financial system stability is a difficult, multifaceted, and often controversial topic. The spread of communicable diseases (especially the COVID-19 pandemic), changes in today's multilateral trade and financial system structures, the impact of climate change, international and internal security crises (such as the war in Ukraine) all clearly illustrate the urgency of concerted global actions of all actors in international relations, with the World Bank/World Bank Group, IMF, and EU at the forefront.

Chapter 9 by Ewa Latoszek and Andrzej Latoszek examines the role of the World Bank in fostering sustainable growth in the world via increasing its involvement in the management and production of global public goods parallel to its statutory activities focused on planned financial support for member states. The main aim is to analyze and suggest ways in which the World Bank can strengthen its abilities in GPGs production to assist member states to meet their development objectives together with sustainable growth goals. This chapter explores the backgrounds of changes that took place in World Bank priorities over the decades and the ways in which this organization is able to combine its main statutory aims with delivering GPGs to foster sustainable growth. By doing so, it also highlights the contingencies besetting the process and offers some cues into World Bank's current stance towards the most important challenges in this area.

In Chapter 10 Magdalena Proczek presents the International Monetary Fund (IMF), which ensures the stability of the international financial and economic system by controlling, regulating, and assisting its members. This organization conducts ongoing bilateral and multilateral surveillance of member countries' financial and economic policies, which is an important part of the IMF's work to balance development and manage global public goods. In the process of surveillance and regulation, the Fund identifies potential risks to macroeconomic and financial stability. The analysis highlights that the IMF recommends necessary adjustments and, if required, supports member states in preparing and implementing adjustment and recovery programs, which are often combined with providing financing and technical assistance during the implementation of the programs.

Chapter 11, written by Agnieszka Kłos, presents the issues related to the coordination of the fiscal policy at European Union level. The creation of the economic and monetary union is one of the stages of tightening and deepening the integration of the European Union member states. It manifests itself in the creation of rules for the coordination of fiscal and monetary policy. As the common euro currency was launched, the monetary policy was delegated to a supranational level. But it did not concern fiscal policy, which remained with the eurozone countries' domestic governments. The fiscal framework of the EU is an institutional safeguard against the externalities of the domestic fiscal policies in the economic and monetary union. Commonly agreed principles and institutions aim to ensure the long-lasting stability of public finances so as to protect the autonomy and effectiveness of the centralized monetary policy. However, not all member states respect these rules. The author presents the changes in the coordination of fiscal rules prepared by the European Commission and makes an attempt to assess how the coordination of fiscal policy at the EU level affects ensuring the conditions for sustainable development.

Part 5 focuses on green energy, health care, and digitalization as international global public goods. The authors of the chapters in this part argue that IOs should pay more attention the most important challenges of today's world, which include green energy, health care, the digitalization process, knowledge and intellectual property management, and making cities smarter from the viewpoint of global public goods and sustainable growth. Neglecting these issues can impede regional and international efforts to enhance the equitable distribution of GPGs for making the world more sustainable.

In Chapter 12, Anna Wójtowicz underlines that the progressive process of globalization has resulted in numerous threats that take up a much broader dimension in the modern economy: the degradation of natural resources, climate change, and strong dependence of many developed economies on imports of energy resources, with individual states often unable to deal with the effects of global challenges on their own. This chapter aims to show the importance of global public goods such as environmental protection and energy conservation and to verify whether the actions taken by IOs in favor of the green transition fit into the model of sustainable development. The analysis includes IOs such as the United Nations, the World Bank, and the European Bank for Reconstruction and Development, but special attention is paid to the European Union and the European Investment Bank, as these organizations have taken on the extremely ambitious challenge of achieving EU climate neutrality by 2050.

The purpose of Chapter 13, by Ewa Kosycarz, is to show the role of international institutions in the process of delivering global health-related public goods that meet the 2030 SDGs. The author presents examples of global public goods in global health and indicates that the Sustainable Development Goals (which can be implemented through the provision of global goods) allows the raising of the level of global health. Attention is also paid to public goods in global health at the regional level, giving the example of the European Union. In this context, experiences from the COVID-19 pandemic are discussed in particular. The EU's role in providing global public goods in health care, as perceived by EU institutions, also seems to be important. Reference is made to the reasons for starting work on the EU Global Health Strategy. The author also draws attention to the causes of difficulties and, consequently, failures in the provision of public goods in global health.

Chapter 14, written by Ewa Osuch-Rak, presents the international intellectual property (IP) system, which is complex and dichotomous in nature. It involves, on the one hand, the need to stimulate technological progress by maintaining an adequate level of IP protection and, on the other hand, the need to create appropriate conditions for the diffusion of innovation and technology transfer. Both technological development and technology transfer are essential to the achievement of SDGs. The aim of the chapter is to discuss the role of selected international organizations in realizing the concept of sustainable development, based on the study of their programs and activities related to IP. Firstly, the author gives an overview of the relation between IP and economic growth, highlighting the complex and ambiguous nature of this relationship, which makes the management of the international IP regime require special competencies. Secondly, the author presents both IP and knowledge as global public goods, emphasizing the differences between them. Thirdly, the author analyzes the approach of selected international organizations to sustainable development. These organizations form the architecture of the international IP system: the World Trade Organization (WTO), the World Intellectual Property Organization (WIPO), the European Union (EU), and the Organisation for Economic Co-operation and Development (OECD). This chapter reveals many contemporary challenges of the international IP system and proves that international organizations may alleviate tensions and ambiguities within it in order to achieve the SDGs.

Part 6 is devoted to the issues of digital transformation and the concepts of smart cities, which are increasingly important for strategic sustainable development. An important challenge of today's world is digitalization, which is essential for all aspects of our lives. This phenomenon is analyzed in Chapter 15 by Malgorzata Dziembała and Mirela Mărcuţ, who underline that digitalization is a process of transformation of society and the economy fueled by technological development and deployment. Not only does it include the growing use of digital technologies in all facets of life, but digitalization also brings about new ways of doing things. New business models (such as e-government) are just some examples of these transformations. Nevertheless, transformation does not automatically entail positive processes and results, but can also trigger negative effects. The digital divide is one of the prime illustrations of the various challenges that people must face in the digital age. Taking into account the fact that, similar to other processes of digitalization, the digital divide does not stop at state borders, international organizations must assume a role in channeling them for the better. Multilateralism is the solution, considering that states share similar socioeconomic challenges and interests. By promoting cooperation between three groups of actors (employers, workers, and member states), the International Labour Organization (ILO) ensures that its approach is incorporated in implemented policies or adopted standards. Additionally, the EU also promotes the development of digital economy by supporting digital education in Europe, digitalizing European industry, and other initiatives. These two organizations operate on different scales and with different competences, but they tackle the same challenge. Hence, the aim of the chapter is to discuss the roles of the ILO and the EU in offering guidance and a governance "umbrella." The challenges and threats resulting from digitalization of the education system, labor market, and institutions are discussed. Additionally, the role of the ILO and the EU in promoting mechanisms, policies, and activities that help their members address digital challenges, which require an upgrade of skills, reskilling and adaptation, is presented.

Chapter 16 is based on case research of smart settlements with a specific focus on Poland. It is written by Agnieszka Domańska and Giuseppe T. Cirella, who focus on the issue of the smart city as a key platform between sustainability and public good. Sustainability is inherently linked to the advancement of the standard of living, mental and physical health care, and protection of the natural environment. These aspects are strongly intertwined with the responsibility and general understanding that public resources should be utilized for the good of communities. This conceptually "obvious" relationship is directly interconnected with urbanization and the idea of smart cities. This can be broken down in two ways: on the one hand, smart cities are meant to serve most of the sustainability goals on a territorial scale, while on the other, in a technical and organizational sense they depend on the public goods and municipally managed resources that enable them to function. Spotlighting key international strategies (e.g., the SDGs), the fostering of inclusive, safe, and resilient cities that better facilitate urban spaces are highlighted in SDG 11. From this perspective, the EU develops delivery initiatives and policy for various smart city projects central to its member states. The focus of this chapter is to show how the two title concepts, "sustainability" (seen from the overall perspective of Agenda 2030) and "smart cities," are interrelated by definition and through the goals they serve. Linkages between them manifest human needs and present commonalities through various overlapping indicators. Namely, measuring and reporting progress in achieving goals by both and showing how actual practical engagement of given international organizations affects their outcome. Secondarily, the role of international and supranational bodies supporting city smartness is discussed with attention to how the EU supports and funds smart city concepts in Poland. Highlighted projects linking the two title concepts are illustrated.

The volume concludes with a brief evaluation by the book's editors, Ewa Latoszek and Agnieszka Kłos. They summarize the answers to the research questions provided by the authors of the chapters and reflect on the importance of these contributions.

5 The Book's Added Value

This publication is an original research work presenting new knowledge about a number of fundamental phenomena and observable facts relating to the role of international organizations in the distribution of global public goods and their contribution to the attainment of the Sustainable Development Goals.

The added value of the book results from the informed choice of the subject matter; it presents the current situation as well as global and regional challenges from an interdisciplinary perspective. Its value also lies in the skillful selection of global public goods that are discussed, considered by the authors as the most important, in the accuracy of the concepts used and their expert explanation, as well as a remarkable line-up of contributors.

In subsequent chapters, the authors present a multidimensional analysis of the role of selected IOs in mitigating threats that emerge within the global economy and in reconciling the conflicting interests of its members through a more effective management of global goods in the process of implementing the principles of sustainable development. A multifactor analysis of various areas (e.g., external security, trade, financial stability, health, democracy and human rights, migration, green energy, intellectual property law) expounds the essence of IOs and their role in the process of distribution of GPGs and their optimal (effective) management with a perspective of attaining the SDGs.

The publication was prepared by a skillfully selected international and interdisciplinary team of researchers, including distinguished professors and doctors of economics and finance, political science, law, and sociology. Each author is an expert in his/her discipline and subject, conversant with both theory and practice. They are accomplished academics with important scientific achievements, participants in international research projects, members of scientific associations, editors of academic journals, and recognized visiting lecturers at foreign universities. The research team consists of academics from leading research centers, including the University of Gdansk, the Kaunas University of Technology, the Warsaw School of Economics, the Migration Policy Centre of the European University Institute, the University of Economics in Katowice, PRIGO University, Erasmus University Rotterdam, the University of Ljubljana, Université Libre de Bruxelles, Warsaw University, and Chernivtsi Jury Fedkovych National Universit. Many combine research work with practice.

6 Target Audience

The book's impact is threefold: it contributes to the development of theory, practice, and teaching. This book brings a significant added value to both theory and practice (business, public administration and non-governmental organizations), not only as an original and creative piece of work, but also because the analysis of these research areas is an ambitious endeavor aimed at delivering valuable results. Its target audience consists of members of institutions shaping or influencing economic and social policy, such as political parties, trade unions, non-governmental organizations, as well as students and academics. It may also serve as further reading for students of international finance, international economic relations, sustainable development, international organizations, economic development, European studies, global management, and economics. The book is a compendium of knowledge: it introduces and defines the concept of the public good, discusses the essence of IOs and sustainable development, and provides an analysis of selected organizations and the methods they use for the distribution of specific public goods. It has been written with a broad target audience in mind, and with a view to help readers grasp a number of complex issues. Understanding the subject of IO in the context of the distribution of public goods and sustainable development does not require any prior (specialist) knowledge. Conclusions presented by the contributors may serve as a starting point for further research and political debate on the scope of operations and the importance of IOs in the process of optimal (effective) management and the use of a wide range of public goods in implementing the concept of sustainable development.

References

Alves, E. E. C., & Biancarelli, A. M. (2020). Financial cooperation initiatives in Latin America: Conditions of origins, subsistence and eventual vanishing. *Economics and Business Review*, 20(4), 51–71. doi:10.18559/ebr.2020.4.4

Braun, V., & Clarke, V. (2006). Using thematic analysis in psychology. *Qualitative Research in Psychology, 3*(2), 77–101.

Carbaugh, R. J. (2016). International Economics. Cengage Learning.

Creswell, J. W., Plano Clark, V. L., Gutmann, M. L., & Hanson, W. E. (2003). Advance mixed methods research designs. In A. Tashakkori & C. Teddlie (Eds.), *Handbook of mixed methods in social and behavioral research* (pp. 209–240). Sage.

Diehl, P. F., & Frederking B. (Eds.). (2010). *The politics of global governance: International organizations in an interdependent world.* Lynne Rienner Publishers.

Gupta, J., & Vegelin, C. (2016). Sustainable development goals and inclusive development. *International Environmental Agreements: Politics, Law and Economics, 16*(3), 433–448.

Gygli, S., Haelg, F., Potrafke, N., & Sturm, J.-E. (2019). The KOF Globalisation Index revisited. *Review of International Organizations, 14*, 543–574.

Independent Group of Scientists appointed by the Secretary General. (2019). *Global sustainable development report: The future is now: Science for achieving sustainable development.* United Nations. Retrieved September 10, 2020, from https://sustainabledevelopment.un.org/content/documents/24797GSDR_report_2019.pdf

Kaul, I., Conceição, P., Le Goulven, K., Mendoza, R. U. (Eds.). (2003). *Providing global public goods: Managing globalization.* Oxford University Press.

Krippendorff, K. (2004). Reliability in content analysis: Some common misconceptions and recommendations. *Human Communication Research, 30*(3), 411–433.

McCormick, J. (2022). *Introduction to global studies*. Bloomsbury.

Popay, J., Roberts, H., Sowden, A., Petticrew, M., Arai, L., Rodgers, M., & Duffy, S. (2006). *Guidance on the conduct of narrative synthesis in systematic reviews: A product from the ESRC Methods Programme*. Lancaster University.

Sachs, J., Schmidt-Traub, G., Kroll, C., Lafortune, G., & Fuller, G. (2019). *Sustainable development report 2019*. Bertelsmann Stiftung and Sustainable Development Solutions Network (SDSN).

Stiglitz, J. (2019). *People, power, and profits: Progressive capitalism for an age of discontent*. Penguin UK.

PART 1

Global Public Goods, Sustainable Development and International Organizations: An Outline of the Theory

CHAPTER 1

Global Public Goods in Light of the New Paradigm of Sustainable Development under the Challenges Facing Today's World

Katja Zajc Kejžar and Nina Ponikvar

1 Introduction

The COVID-19 pandemic has proven that the survival of humanity in the event of a crisis depends on its collective response and action. After decades of taking world peace for granted, the Russo – Ukrainian War undermines our feeling of safety from war. Even without the latest challenges facing the world, the rapid process of globalization, the deepening of economic integration, and the increase in cross-border flows worldwide have placed global public goods (hereafter GPGs) and the possibilities for intervention at the center of discussions initiated by international organizations in the past decades. Climate change, security, and health issues are just some of the challenges facing the global community. In addition, outstanding scientific and technological advances, particularly high-speed communication networks and advances in transportation, have increased the extent to which the world's population is affected by the above influences and perceives them in their daily lives.

Consequently, the awareness created by these challenges, cross-border externalities, and spillover effects increases the pressure on national governments and international organizations to address this issue. Addressing exigent global challenges via GPGs provision is crucial to improve global welfare. However, many obstacles prevent proper allocation of resources to providing GPGs. Apart from movement towards global governance in terms of regulating transport and communication, resulting in high payoffs and little loss of national autonomy (Buchholz & Sandler, 2021), there's no strong commitment to govern the provision of GPGs at the global level. One of the initiatives to address this challenge is the United Nations 2030 Agenda for Sustainable Development (United Nations, 2015). Some of the Sustainable Development Goals (hereafter SDGs) are directly related to the provision of global public goods and have the ambitious goal of being a major global development framework.

The purpose of this chapter is to discuss the evolution of the concept of GPGs and to address the main features and challenges related to GPGs, their provision and financing. We aim to identify the causes of inefficiencies in the provision of GPGs and assess the impact of globalization processes, economic growth, and technological progress on the scope and diversity of GPGs. The chapter contributes to an understanding of the changing nature of GPGs and provides a framework for discussing the adjustments needed in the definition and provision of GPGs in the context of the new sustainable development paradigm.

The content of the chapter is structured along four sections and a conclusion. In Section 1, we first outline the characteristics and discuss the concept of public goods. In Section 2, we continue by introducing and discussing global public goods. Section 3 focuses on the provision and financing of GPGs, while Section 4 places GPGs in the context of sustainable development and the SDGs.

2 Characteristics of Public Goods

The concept of public goods, also known as collective consumption goods, comes from microeconomics and welfare economics. It was developed by Paul Samuelson (1954), although the concept as such goes back at least to the 18th century, where the "common good" was mentioned by David Hume (1739). Public goods can be distinguished from its private counterpart based on two principles, namely the rivalry in consumption and excludability from consumption. To understand what a public good is, it is useful first to examine the characteristics of a private good. In a market transaction a buyer gains access to a good (or service) in exchange for money or, sometimes, in exchange for another good. Buyers and sellers meet through the price mechanism, and if everything works in a textbook perfect way, the economy can reach a state of maximum efficiency in which resources are put to their most productive uses. A key condition for a market transaction, however, is that the ownership or use of a good can be transferred or denied conditional on the offsetting exchange – the payment of its price. Thus private goods tend to be excludable and rival in consumption. A piece of cake, once consumed, cannot be enjoyed by others (Kaul et al., 1999). With public goods, matters are different. Pure public goods are characterized by the properties of non-rivalry and non-excludability in consumption (Cornes & Sandler, 1994).

Non-rivalry (non-congestion) generally means that consumption of such a good by one consumer does not prevent consumption by other consumers. More specifically, an additional consumer of the public good does not reduce the utility of existing consumers and marginal costs are zero when an additional individual consumer engages in the consumption of the public good. Thus, non-rivalry allows a public good to be used by multiple consumers.

This means that the total utility from consuming a public good is the sum of the utilities of all individuals consuming that public good. Since markets are not able to detect the total utility, but only observe individual utility from the consumption of a public good via individual demand, the market is not able to ensure allocatively efficient quantities of public goods to be produced (Stiglitz, 1988). Regulation of the volume of production is therefore necessary to ensure sufficient production of public goods.

Non-excludability is another characteristic usually associated with public goods. In the case of non-excludability, no consumer can be excluded from consuming a good. This means that free riders, consumers who do not contribute to the payment of a public good, can participate in its consumption. When a public good is characterized by both non-rivalry and non-excludability, both regulation of the volume of production and collective financing of a public good (direct taxation or subsidization of private spending) are essential to ensure the allocative efficiency of the production and consumption of public goods (Silvestre, 2012).

Table 1.1 presents the taxonomy of goods according to their characteristics of rivalry and excludability, distinguishing between pure and impure public goods (Buchholz & Sandler, 2021). Pure public goods are consistent with the above definition as completely non-rivalrous and non-excludable. In the case of pure public goods, the marginal cost of providing the good to another consumer is zero, and no one can be excluded from the benefit of the good. In modern democracies, few cases of pure public goods come to mind. Samuelson's (1954) examples of the lighthouse, traffic lights, national defense, and world peace (Kaul et al., 1999) are a few cases of pure public goods. But several impure public goods that are excludable and/or congestible, thus carrying one of the private goods' characteristics, can be found. Such goods are, for example, tertiary education, motorways, public libraries, museums, and sporting facilities, as well as certain aspects of urban infrastructure (Economides & Philippopoulos, 2020). Impure public goods are not entirely non-rivalrous nor non-excludable. Club goods are a subtype of impure public goods. They are characterized by

TABLE 1.1 Taxonomy of good types by excludability and rivalrousness

	Rivalrous	**Non-rivalrous**
Excludable	Private goods	Club goods
Non-excludable	The tragedy of the commons	Pure public goods

SOURCE: GRAVES (2020)

excludability in consumption, being available only to club members (members of a particular organization or institution), although they are characterized by non-rivalry up to a certain congestion threshold. Accordingly, they are often classified as a subtype of public goods that begin to behave like private goods above a certain level of consumption or number of consumers. That is, above a certain level, additional members of the club, i.e., additional consumers, lead to a congestion effect that may be viewed as introducing rival consumption (Coase, 1974; Baumol & Blinder, 2015). Regardless of the type of public good, the provision of public goods is a central function of governments.

In sum, public goods represent an example of market failure, which prevents markets from achieving an allocatively efficient level of output. Unlike private goods, public goods justify either the governmental direct provision, regulation of the volume of production or merely financing of the public good (Thöne & Kreuter, 2020).

3 Global Public Goods

GPGs have captured the attention of economists and social scientists since they were discovered based on the standardization of measurement system, the defining of property rights, and the opening of trading systems, showing the need for international public goods provision in the absence of a supranational government (Buchholz & Sandler, 2021). Since the end of the 20th century, the key international institutions such as the World Bank and the United Nations have recognized the growing importance of goods with benefits that spill over national borders. Such goods have benefits that extend beyond the country of origin. Some authors (e.g., Sandler, 2002) differentiate between regional public goods, providing benefits within regions, international public goods, providing benefits to more than one country, and GPGs, where benefits evolve worldwide.

As explained, global public goods, unlike country-specific or regional public goods, are not bound by geographic boundaries. Moreover, global public goods are multidimensional and include sociological and temporal dimensions in addition to geographic ones to reflect the complexity of the real world (Kaul et al., 1999). Therefore, we can define global public goods as goods whose benefits span multiple countries, inhabitants, and generations, which are global and inherently public at the same time (Kaul & Mendoza, 2003). "Global public goods are institutions, mechanisms, and outcomes that provide quasi-universal benefits to more than one group of countries, extending to both current and future generations" (Birdsall & Diofasi, 2015). Consequently, GPGs provide benefits to people regardless of their country's level of development.

GPGs play a key role in securing social, economic, and political progress and are fundamental to addressing global risks such as security, climate change, infectious diseases, and financial crises.

There are four particular characteristics of GPGs that we need to observe in order to distinguish between different types of GPGs (Buchholz & Sandler, 2021), i.e., non-rivalry, non-excludability, the existence of spillover effects and the technology of aggregation. The first and the second characteristic relate to GPGs as public goods and involve the degree of non-rivalry and non-excludability from consumption. These two characteristics of the GPGs imply that Pareto optimum level of the provision of GPGs cannot be achieved by provision decisions of individual countries. When non-rivalry is complete, an additional country using the GPG does not reduce the benefits from other countries and marginal cost of including additional country in the consumption is zero. An example of such a GPG is a thickened stratospheric ozone layer, where the benefits of one country are not smaller when other countries benefit from less ultraviolet exposure as well (Buchholz & Sandler, 2021). Non-excludability means that once provided, GPGs benefits are unconditionally available to all countries, i.e., regardless of their payment. For example, the stratospheric ozone shield, preserving biodiversity, controlling infectious diseases, are GPGs which are non-excludable (Buchholz & Sandler, 2021). The third characteristics of GPGs involves the range of benefit spillovers. GPGs are related to global benefit spillovers while smaller ranges of benefit spillovers result in transregional, regional, transnational, and national public goods (Sandler & Arce, 2002). The fourth characteristic of GPGs is related to technology of aggregation (also called aggregator technology). Buchholz and Sandler (2021, p. 496) differentiate between seven types of aggregator technologies:

- Summation, where the overall level of GPG equals the sum of the countries' contributions (e.g., limiting greenhouse emissions or preserving biodiversity, curbing organized crime in a globalized world, developing smart city platforms and strategies)
- Weighted sum, where the overall level of GPG equals a weighted sum of the countries' contribution (e.g., controlling the spread of an infectious disease, reducing acid rain, system of canals and waterways)
- Weakest link, where the smallest contribution of the world's countries determines the GPG's aggregate level (e.g., maintaining the functionality of a global network, surveillance of a disease outbreak)
- Weaker link, where the smallest contribution of the world's countries has the greatest influence on the GPG's aggregate level, followed by the second smallest contribution, and so on (e.g., inhibiting the spread of financial instability, inhibiting crop disease diffusion)

- Threshold, where benefits from the GPG only arise once its cumulative contributed quantity surpasses a threshold amount (e.g., establishing an early-warning system for disasters, suppressing large-scale forest fires, or curbing flooding)
- Best shot, where largest contribution by a country determines the GPG's aggregate level (e.g., diverting a comet, developing financial or agricultural best practices, providing satellite launch facility)
- Better shot, where largest contribution by a country has the greatest influence on the GPG's aggregate level, followed by the second largest contribution, and so on (uncovering best treatment regimes for diseases, limiting the diffusion of transnational terrorist campaigns, biohazard facility)

Table 1.2 maps the above-described aggregator technology categories to three general types of GPGs, i.e., pure GPGs, impure GPGs, and club goods.

The overview of the literature covering the GPGs topics (Buchholz & Sandler, 2021) by the area of interest show that global public health, environment preservation, climate change mitigation, global public health, and security are considered as fundamental GPG-related areas:

- *Natural environment*, where GPGs are related to protecting essential ecosystems and preserving biodiversity, reversing ozone layer depletion and curbing climate change, adopting universal regulatory practices related to these topics (for more on green energy, see Chapter 12)
- *Health*-related GPGs, such as identifying virulent pathogens, eradicating infectious diseases, developing disease treatment regimes (for more, see Chapter 13)
- *Security and food safety issues* related to fostering cybersecurity, reducing transnational terrorism, and maintaining world peace (for more, see Part 2)
- *Economic, social, and other conditions*, such as discovering scientific breakthroughs, preserving cultural heritage, adopting universal regulatory practices and international trade rules, ameliorating global financial and/or economic crises, addressing refuge flows, and promoting smart city platforms (for more on these issues, see Parts 3 and 4 and Chapters 14–16)

Bostrom (2013) argues that mitigating existential risk is another issue that should be treated as a GPG, if not the most important one. Another example of a GPG is knowledge (Stiglitz, 1999). It fulfills both theoretical criteria, since an additional consumer of knowledge does not diminish the amount of knowledge available (non-rivalry) and, moreover, additional consumers can hardly be prevented from accessing existing knowledge (non-excludability), all the more so in the era of digitalization.

The scope and the variety of GPGs have been steadily increasing due to technological advances, processes of globalization, economic growth, and

TABLE 1.2 Examples of GPGs according to aggregator technology categories and three general types of GPGs

	Pure public goods	Impure public goods	Club goods
Summation	Greenhouse gas emissions limitation Biodiversity conservation	Organized crime curbing Peacekeeping assets deployment	INTELSAT communication network
Weighted sum	Infectious outbreak spread control	Acid rain and pollution reduction	System of canals and waterways
Weakest link	Global network maintenance	Financial crises surveillance Disease outbreak surveillance	Air traffic control system
Weaker link	Financial instability contagion prevention Maintaining sterilization	Inhibiting pests Crop disease diffusion	Global internet network
Threshold	Early-warning system for natural disasters	Suppressing forest fires Curbing flooding	Crisis management counterterrorism force
Best shot	Eliminating a rogue country Diverting a comet	Developing financial or agricultural best practices	Satellite launch facility
Better shot	Treatment regimes for diseases	Limiting terrorist campaigns Drug trafficking prevention	Biohazard facility

SOURCE: BUCHHOLZ AND SANDLER (2021)

population expansion. As discussed in Buchholz and Sandler (2021), advances in technologies lead to the rise of novel GPGs, such as nuclear waste sequestration, the internet, satellite-based communication networks, supersonic air travel, and ozone-depleting chlorofluorocarbons. Economic growth and population expansion in some parts of the world relates to climate change and its mitigation as one of the most crucial GPGs nowadays. By using the newest monitoring technologies, the global public bads (hereafter GPBs) can be marked, such as the accumulation of atmospheric greenhouse gases, the melting of the icecaps, deforestation of the rainforest, the spread of the deserts.

Further, some national public goods are becoming global as their consequences extend to neighboring countries and beyond, such as transnational terrorism and civil wars. The integration of markets requires the development of a common response to market crisis while the high-speed communication enables sharing of ideas, threats, knowledge, misinformation, panics, and best practices within the global community.

4 Provision and Financing of GPGs

In case of non-excludability, compulsory collective financing (e.g., financing by general taxes) of public good provision is the best option to overcome the free-rider issue. But other possibilities of financing exist in the case of goods characterized with excludability in consumption. One possibility is mandatory collective financing of a public good, which leads to uniform and free access to public goods for all members of society. The oppositeto mandatory collective financing is the case where individuals are free to choose the amount they want by paying a price (usually called a use price), with that price determined by a market-based mechanism. Of course, anything in between is possible, e.g., combining policy-based and market-based mechanisms, as well as outcomes for other pricing systems, such as average cost or marginal cost pricing (Economides & Philippopoulos, 2020).

Even though GPGs are related to the same issues as the public goods provision and collective action, additional features are of particular importance in the case of GPGs. The provision and financing are more complex in the case of GPGs, contrary to country-specific public goods that are provided by national governments and financed via national tax systems. The required geographical scale of the collective action is greater in the case of GPGs compared to national counterparts. Consequently, the provision capabilities of the GPGs are more heterogeneous (Chen & Zeckhauser, 2018). GPGs involve countries or institutions to act as the agents, while public goods involve individuals as agents. With countries as agents, their sovereignty needs to be considered with respect to provision and agreement. Various institutions, such as coalition formation (e.g., voluntary cooperation by a subgroup of countries), public private partnerships, non-governmental organizations (hereafter NGOs) and multilateral organizations are important actors in the provision of GPGs (Buchholz & Sandler, 2021).

Barret and Dannenberg (2022) use an experiment to investigate the decision to link trade cooperation to the provision of a GPG. They study a unilateral approach, in which players decide independently and without commitment, and a multilateral approach, in which players decide by, and are committed through, an agreement. Results confirm the superiority of the multilateral approach, where the agreement by a majority coupled with commitment by this majority are required for successful provision of the public good. This supports the crucial role of international organizations (hereafter IOs) for the optimal provision and adequate financing arrangements of the GPGs.

In recent years, especially after the global financial and economic crisis (2008/2009), we have witnessed a weakening of the multilateral foundations of the world economic order created after World War II under the umbrella of the Bretton Woods institutions and the system of UN agencies. Growing skepticism and disrespect for global/international agreements and even threats to withdraw from IOs on behalf of narrow national interests further undermine the already weak foundations of the multilateral format. The question arises: Are international institutions (e.g., the World Bank, IMF, WTO, WHO) capable of playing a decisive role in the governance of GPGs? Given the growing scope and number of GPGs, on the one hand, and the erosion of the institutional strength of IOs, on the other, IOs do not seem well equipped to handle the complex task of managing GPGs. According to economist Ravi Kanbur (2001), IOs need to change their approach and governance systems and, in particular, rethink their country-by-country approach to allocating funding.

The multilateral design needs to address the provision as well as the financing of GPGs, following the fairness principle. Namely, on the one hand, some countries have an incentive to contribute less, creating the so-called free-rider problem at the international level, which results in the provision of GPGs being less than globally desired (Kornek & Edenhofer, 2020). Thus, in the case of GPGs, economic efficiency is maximized when economic activities – and the policies to regulate them – extend across national borders. Indeed, similar to all public goods, the provision of GPGs will be structurally undersupplied if left to markets or individual countries that have suboptimal incentives to spend (Kopiński & Wróblewski 2021). Since the provision of GPGs cannot be done single-handedly by national governments, collaboration between multiple countries is required. Chen and Zeckhauser (2018) show that GPGs are particularly challenging due to the substantial asymmetries among nations. Namely, in the case of GPGs, there is an absence of a central authority possessing tax and expenditure responsibilities to provide an efficient level of public good. Consequently, voluntary arrangements must replace coercive ones, and significant underprovision must be expected as small-interest nations have strong incentives to ride cheaply.

For example, Bättig and Bernauer (2009) identified free-riding as one of the problems in reducing greenhouse gas emissions to address the problem of climate change. While their results suggest that democracy, as measured by the presence of institutions, increases policy outputs related to climate change, their impact on policy outcomes is not clear. The free-rider problem among signatories to international environmental agreements can be addressed through various means, one of which is (trade) sanctions. However, whoever imposes such sanctions harms both signatories and non-signatories, so the result may not be the desired welfare increase, even if it increases the supply of GPGs (Barrett, 1997).

Another issue on the supply side is the protection of intellectual property rights, which can limit the provision of public goods on a global scale. This aspect of the role of intellectual property agreements and the privatization of public goods is a developing area of research (Brandi et al., 2010; Pogge, 2005; Maskus & Reichmann, 2004). Although the outcomes of Trade-Related Aspects of Intellectual Property Rights (TRIPS) are difficult to measure, some findings suggest that developing countries are more affected, particularly by patents on pharmaceutical and health-related products.

On the other hand, however, international solidarity in terms of financing the provision of GPGs is inherent in several international institutions. These institutions are also the main proponents of the crucial role of GPGs. In contrast to the free-rider approach, countries sometimes assume a disproportionate responsibility for financing GPGs to ensure their existence and/or sufficient volume. Funding is an important issue, especially for developing countries, so that they can also participate in the supply of GPGs. Funding is usually obtained through development assistance (Porter et al., 2008). For both reasons, i.e., to overcome the free-rider problem or to promote international solidarity in the provision of GPGs, strong international cooperation is needed, based on a formal agreement along with institutions to support it (Estevadeordal & Goodman, 2017).

5 GPGs and Sustainability

GPGs remain an important aspect of addressing many persistent issues and are as such inviolably linked to sustainable development. "Meeting our own needs without compromising the ability of future generations to meet theirs" (Keeble, 1988) is the one goal that, though perhaps sometimes overlooked, is in the background of discussions about GPGs and the need for global responses. Underprovision of GPGs, such as climate change mitigation, financial stability, global health, or cyber security, today threatens global development and, thereby, also global economic, social, and environmental sustainability (Kaul, 2019). For example, the success of the green revolution, a period of substantial agricultural development whose impact helped reduce poverty, can be attributed to heavy investment in crop research, policy support, and knowledge transfer (Pingali, 2012). Issues regarding the financing of health at the global level are prominent and have persisted for a longer period of time (McCoy et al., 2009).

The term "sustainable development" was first defined in the World Commission for Environment and Development's report *Our Common Future* (1987) as "development that meets the needs of the present without compromising the ability of future generations to meet their own needs." Still, Barbier, Markandya, and Pearce (1990) are considered as founders of the concept of sustainable development, seeing it as "the achievement of a specific set of socially desirable objectives such as fair access to natural resources, an increase in real income per capita, an improvement in health and nutrition, an improvement in education levels and sustainability and self-sustaining growth." Today, in business and policy contexts, limits to sustainability are determined by physical and natural resources, environmental degradation, and social resources. Accordingly, sustainable policies place some emphasis on the future effect of any given policy or business practice on humans, the economy, and ecology.

5.1 *SDGs and GPGs*

In 2015, United Nations member states signed the 2030 Agenda for Sustainable Development (UN General Assembly, 2015), which was expected to be a milestone in the concept of sustainable development. The 2030 Agenda adopted 17 Sustainable Development Goals (hereafter SDGs). These 17 goals are focused on economic growth, social development, and environmental protection and are universal as they concern both developing and developed countries and because they are focused on sustainability rather than mere competitiveness. SDGs are often seen as a concept that is strongly related to the context of GPGs. Namely, the introduction and implementation the 2030 Agenda and its 17 SDGs brings an opportunity to discuss the world's response to global challenges and to rethink positions on GPGs (Jenks, 2015). Similarly, Dill (2018) believes that the SDGs are about providing public goods, while Naert (2019), for example, states that several of the SDGs fall either under state-level correction of market failure, such as the health area, or are related to the need for transnational agreement, such as in the case of combating climate change or conservation of the oceans. Accordingly, with regard to SDGs the picture that emerges, in terms of provision, is a patchwork of national, subnational, and global engagement where subsidiarity should act as a guiding principle. In addition, private actors and civil society also have a role to play in the provision of these GPGs.

In Table 1.3, we focus on the global engagement part and link the four core areas of the GPGs, i.e., natural environment, health, security and food safety, and economic, social, and other conditions, to the 17 SDGs. We show examples

TABLE 1.3 Relationship between areas of SDGs and GPGs

Area of SDGs/GPGs		Natural environment	Health	Security and food safety	Economic, social, and other
1	End poverty in all its forms everywhere	early-warning system for natural disasters	developing disease treatment regimes	developing agriculture best practices	discovering scientific breakthroughs, amelioration of global crises
2	End hunger, achieve food security and improved nutrition, and promote sustainable agriculture	early-warning system for natural disasters		crop disease control, inhibiting pests	amelioration global financial and/or economic crisis
3	Ensure healthy lives and promote well-being for all at all ages		identifying virulent pathogens, eradicating infectious diseases, developing disease treatment regimes		
4	Ensure inclusive and equitable quality education and promote lifelong learning opportunities for all				addressing refuge flows, discovering scientific breakthroughs

TABLE 1.3 Relationship between areas of SDGs and GPGs (*cont.*)

Area of SDGs/GPGs		Natural environment	Health	Security and food safety	Economic, social, and other
5	Achieve gender equality and empower for all women and girls				addressing refugee flows
6	Ensure availability and sustainable management of water and sanitation for all	early-warning system for natural disasters	eradicating infectious diseases		
7	Ensure access to affordable, reliable, sustainable, and modern energy for all	curbing climate change			global network maintenance
8	Promote sustained, inclusive, and sustainable economic growth, full and productive employment, and decent work for all				amelioration global financial and/or economic crises
9	Build resilient infrastructure, promote inclusive and sustainable industrialization, and foster innovation				discovering scientific breakthroughs
10	Reduce inequality within and among countries				amelioration global financial and/or economic crises
11	Make cities and human settlements inclusive, safe, resilient, and sustainable			fostering cybersecurity, reducing transnational terrorism, maintaining world peace	developing smart city platforms and strategies

TABLE 1.3 Relationship between areas of SDGs and GPGs (*cont.*)

Area of SDGs/GPGs		Natural environment	Health	Security and food safety	Economic, social, and other
12	Ensure sustainable consumption and production patterns	protecting essential ecosystems, preserving biodiversity			preserving cultural heritage
13	Take urgent action to combat climate change and its impacts	reversing ozone layer depletion, curbing climate change			
14	Conserve and sustainably use the oceans, seas, and marine resources for sustainable development	protecting essential ecosystems			
15	Protect, restore, and promote sustainable use of terrestrial ecosystems, sustainably manage forests, combat desertification, and halt and reverse land degradation, halt biodiversity loss	protecting essential ecosystems, preserving biodiversity, curbing climate change			adopting universal regulatory practices
16	Promote peaceful and inclusive societies for sustainable development, provide access to justice for all, and build effective, accountable, and inclusive institutions at all levels			fostering cybersecurity, reducing transnational terrorism, maintaining world peace	preserving cultural heritage, addressing refugee flows

TABLE 1.3 Relationship between areas of SDGs and GPGs (*cont.*)

Area of SDGs/GPGs	Natural environment	Health	Security and food safety	Economic, social, and other
17 Strengthen the means of implementation and revitalize the global partnership for sustainable development	curbing climate change	developing disease treatment regimes	promoting institutional strengths of IOs	universal regulatory practices, global network maintenance

SOURCE: OWN WORK

of activities that support the achievement of a particular SDGs and at the same time considered GPG from a particular core GPG area. Virtually all of the SDGs require, at least to some degree, a global level of governance to address the public good nature of the goals. Several SDGs are of the interdisciplinary type, as shown by the overlapping SDG/GPG areas in Figure 1.1.

5.2 *Financing SDGs, Provision of GPGs, and Official Development Assistance*

As we explained the link between the SDGs and GPG concept, we can also relate the issues of financing the public goods and the SDGs' financing. Namely, both, the SDGs and GPGs require significant finance and often face the same non-excludability related to the free-rider issue – especially those SDGs, that can only be achieved via transnational cooperation.

The SDGs require significant increases in investment in broad-based economic transformation. The proposed approach to deal with the financing of sustainable development is called "blended finance." Blended finance is aimed at mobilizing private capital to be used as an addition to philanthropic and public development funding for strategic financing of SDGs. For development finance and philanthropic funders, Blended finance represents an opportunity to drive significant new capital flows into high-impact sectors, while effectively leveraging private sector expertise in identifying and executing development investment strategies. Blended finance has three key characteristics (World Economic Forum, 2015). First, the development finance and philanthropic funds are used to attract private capital into deals. Second, blended finance is used to finance investments driving social, environmental and economic progress. Third, financial returns for private investors are to be in line with market

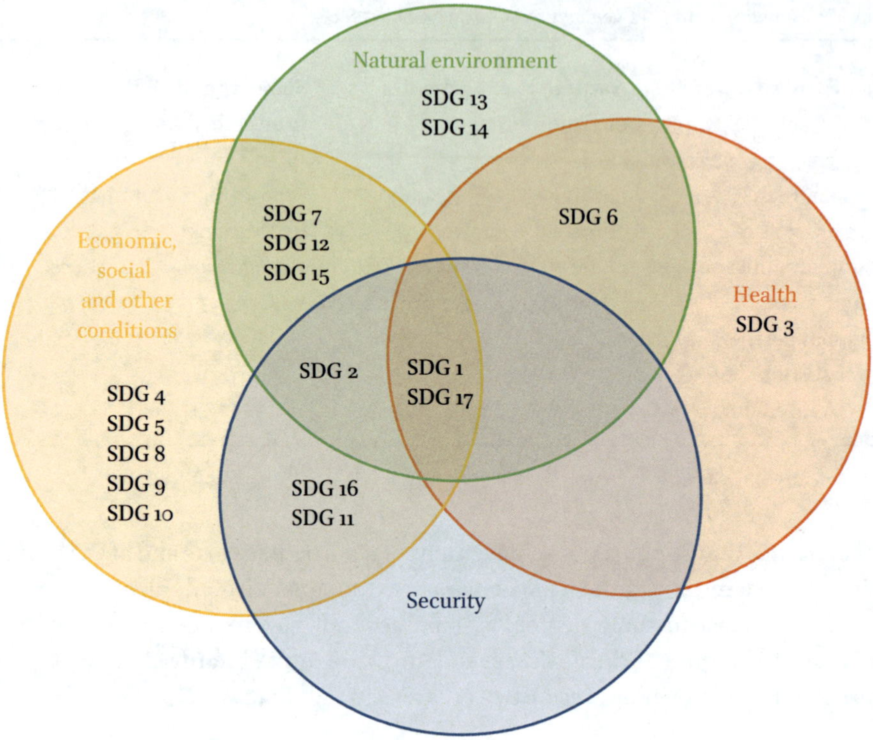

FIGURE 1.1 SDGs and GPG areas overlapping
SOURCE: OWN WORK

expectations, based on real and perceived risks. In such a financial framework, the "new ecosystem of investment for sustainable development" is key. In such a system, private actors are no longer seen as passive bystanders in the development process, nor merely as clients or contractors, but are seen as important co-investors and co-producers in development projects and programs.

Unfortunately, the reality is somewhat different. Even prior to the COVID-19 crisis, countries were already facing difficulties to finance and fulfill the ambitions of the 2030 Agenda. The US$2.5 trillion annual SDG financing gap in developing countries prior to the COVID-19 epidemic is predicted to increase due to global economic uncertainty, rising public debt, and debt servicing costs, particularly in the poorest countries. All of this puts increasing pressure on SDG funding. The gap to achieve the SDGs in developing countries increased by 56% after the outbreak of COVID-19, totaling US$3.9 trillion in 2020. However, it would take less than 1% of global finance to fill this gap (OECD, 2022).

Furthermore, another question arises about the use of official development assistance (hereafter ODA) to finance GPGs. Should the financing of GPGs be counted as ODA? Official development assistance is defined as government aid that promotes and specifically targets the economic development and welfare of developing countries. Therefore, the key point for GPGs financing to be part of ODA is who should benefit from the provision of GPGs. These are defined by the fact that they are non-rivalrous and non-excludable, rather than by a distinction based on which groups are most likely to benefit from them. Thus, there is no simple answer on the adequacy of allocation of ODA to the provision of GPGs. When the overwhelming beneficiaries of a GPG are developing countries, the answer tends to be yes, while in cases where this is much less clear, the answer tends to be no (Kenny, 2020). Another aspect is aid effectiveness; in this regard, strengthening commitments on untying ODA would increase aid effectiveness by reducing transaction costs and improving allocational efficiency, including in the case of GPG-related ODA.

There are no general statistics on the extent of ODA spent on the provision of GPGs; estimates for the share of ODA spent on GPGs available based on the OECD Creditor Reporting System range from 3.7% (Anand, 2004) and 8% (Knox, 2016) to 25% (Raffer, 1999), with this extreme range of estimates being largely due to differences in definitions. Knox (2016) reports that the most financed three broad GPG fields were environment (US$8.0 billion), global public health (US$2.1 billion) and other (i.e., non-health/non-environment) research. Reisen, Soto, and Weithöner (2008) estimated that donors spent around 30% of ODA on international public goods in 1997–2001 – half on GPGs and half on regional public goods. They also confirmed allocational trade-offs between GPG-related ODA and traditional aid but concluded that an increase in GPG spending is not likely to adversely affect the flow of aid transfers to the poorest countries.

A conceptual and practical separation of ODA and GPGs financing has been proposed (e.g., Kaul, 2019; Kaul et al., 2003;; Kenny, 2020), unless an investment brings both local (developing country) and global benefits and aid is an element of the financing mix because of local benefits. In principle, funding for GPGs such as biodiversity conservation, climate change mitigation, and related activities should be new and additional and should not come from ODA. Indeed, the concern is that by excluding general GPGs, the ODA category may exclude some expenditures that have higher return to developing countries than some expenditures included in ODA (including an inefficient technical assistance project, while excluding support for the development of a COVID-19 vaccine). This follows from the fact that ODA is explicitly not intended as a measure of all spending that brings benefits to developing countries, but rather as a measure of expenditures that are specifically motivated in terms of developing country welfare (Kenny, 2020).

6 Conclusions

The above discussion has shown that GPGs cannot be adequately and sufficiently provided by national governments acting unilaterally, and therefore cooperation among multiple countries is necessary. This requires reinforcement of existing formal arrangements as well as an updated role for the institutions to support it. Several interlinked challenges of today's world, related to environmental, technological, health, (cyber)security, economic, and geopolitical changes, have created the need for a new approach to GPGs that considers their interlinkages with the SDGs. They also call for improved effectiveness in the provision of GPGs through accountability measures aimed at increasing compliance with sustainable development and deliver better results by influencing member states' policies not only for more effective implementation but also adequate provision (private and public) for GPGs.

References

Anand, P. B. (2004). Financing the provision of global public goods. *World Economy*, 27(2), 215–237.

Barbier, E. B., Markandya, A., & Pearce, D. W. (1990). Environmental sustainability and cost-benefit analysis. *Environment and Planning A*, 22(9), 1259–1266.

Barrett, S. (1997). The strategy of trade sanctions in international environmental agreements. *Resource and Energy Economics*, 19(4), 345–361.

Barrett, S., & Dannenberg, A. (2022). The decision to link trade agreements to the supply of global public goods. *Journal of the Association of Environmental and Resource Economists*, 9(2), 273–305.

Bättig, M. B., & Bernauer, T. (2009). National institutions and global public goods: Are democracies more cooperative in climate change policy? *International organization*, 63(2), 281–308.

Baumol, W. J., & Blinder, A. S. (2015). *Economics: Principles and policy*. Cengage Learning.

Birdsall, N., & Diofasi, A. (2015). Global public goods for development: How much and what for? Center for Global Development. https://www.cgdev.org/publication/global-public-goods-development-how-much-and-what

Bostrom, N. (2013). Existential risk prevention as global priority. *Global Policy*, 4(1), 15–31.

Brandi, C., Ladenburger, C., & Pegels, A. (2010). Intellectual property rights as a challenge to providing global public goods: The cases of public health, food security and climate stability. Discussion Paper no. 17/2010, Deutsches Institut für Entwicklungspolitik (DIE).

Brundtland, G. H. (1987). Our common future: Call for action. *Environmental Conservation, 14*(4), 291–294.

Buchholz, W., & Sandler, T. (2021). Global public goods: A survey. *Journal of Economic Literature, 59*(2), 488–545. doi:10.1257/jel.20191546

Chen, C., & Zeckhauser, R. (2018). Collective action in an asymmetric world. *Journal of Public Economics, 158*, 103–112.

Coase, R. H. (1974). The lighthouse in economics. *Journal of Law and Economics, 17*(2), 357–376.

Cornes, R., & Sandler, T. (1994). Are public goods myths? *Journal of Theoretical Politics, 6*(3), 369–385.

Dill, A. (2018). *The SDGs are public goods: Costs, sources and measures of financing for development*. Policy paper to the UN Inter-agency Taskforce on Financing for Development.

Economides, G., & Philippopoulos, A. (2020). On the Provision of Excludable Public Goods-General Taxes or User Prices? CESifo Working Paper no. 8724. Center for Economic Studies and Ifo Institute for Economic Research. http://dx.doi.org/10.2139/ssrn.3740336

Estevadeordal, A., & Goodman, L. W. (2017). 21st-century cooperation, regional public goods, and sustainable development. In A. Estevadeordal & L. W. Goodman (Eds.), *21st century cooperation: Regional public goods, global governance, and sustainable development* (pp. 3–13). Routledge.

Graves, P. E. (2020). Externalities, public goods, and property rights revisited: Regulations based on traditional B – C analyses are too lax. *Journal of Environmental Economics and Policy, 9*(2), 220–226.

Hume, D. (1978). *Treatise of human nature* (L. A. Selby-Bigge, Ed.; 2nd ed.). Oxford University Press.

Jenks, B. (2015, September). From an MDG world to an SDG/GPG world: Why the United Nations should embrace the concept of global public goods. Development dialogue paper no. 15. Dag Hammarskjöld Foundation. http://www.daghammarskjold.se/wp-content/uploads/2015/10/DD-Paper-no-15.pdf

Kanbur, R. (2021, June 17). Management of global public goods: What role for international institutions? *iD4D: Sustainable Development News*. https://ideas4development.org/en/global-public-goods/

Kaul, I. (2019). Global public goods and governance for addressing Sustainability. In *The Palgrave handbook of development economics* (pp. 833–865). Palgrave Macmillan. https://doi.org/10.1007/978-3-030-14000-7_24

Kaul, I., & Mendoza, R. U. (2003). Advancing the concept of public goods. In I. Kaul, P. Conceição, K. Le Goulven, & R. U. Mendoza (Eds.), *Providing global public goods: Managing globalization*. Oxford University Press.

Kaul, I., Conceiçao, P., Le Goulven, K., & Mendoza, R. U. (2003). How to improve the provision of global public goods. Providing global public goods: *Managing globalization*, 21, 28.

Kaul, I., Grunberg, I., & Stern, M. A. (1999). Defining global public goods. In I. Kaul, I. Grunberg, & M. A. Stern (Eds.), *Global public goods: International cooperation in the 21st century* (pp. 2–19). Oxford University Press.

Keeble, B. R. (1988). The Brundtland report: "Our common future." *Medicine and War*, *4*(1), 17–25.

Kenny, C. (2020). Official development assistance, global public goods and implications for climate finance. CGD Policy Paper 188. Center for Global Development. https://www.cgdev.org/publication/official-development-assistance-global-public-goods-and-implications-climate-finance

Knox, D. (2016). Measuring aid to global public goods (GPGs): An approach to estimating funding for GPGs from providers of official development assistance. Development Initiatives Discussion Paper. https://devinit.org/wp-content/uploads/2016/07/Measuring-aid-to-global-public-goods-GPGs-Discussion-paper-July-2016.pdf

Kopiński, D., & Wróblewski, M. (2021). Reimagining the World Bank: Global public goods in an age of crisis. *World Affairs*, *184*(2), 151–175. doi:10.1177/00438200211013486

Kornek, U., & Edenhofer, O. (2020). The strategic dimension of financing global public goods. *European Economic Review*, *127*, 103423.

Maskus, K. E., & Reichman, J. H. (2004). The globalization of private knowledge goods and the privatization of global public goods. *Journal of International Economic Law*, *7*(2), 279–320.

McCoy, D., Chand, S., & Sridhar, D. (2009). Global health funding: How much, where it comes from and where it goes. *Health policy and planning*, *24*(6), 407–417.

Naert, F. (2019, May 24). Accountability issues of SDGs in a global public goods context. https://papers.ssrn.com/sol3/papers.cfm?abstract_id=3543401

OECD. (2022). *Global Outlook on Financing for Sustainable Development 2023*. OECD Publishing.

Pingali, P. L. (2012). Green revolution: Impacts, limits, and the path ahead. *Proceedings of the National Academy of Sciences*, *109*(31), 12302–12308.

Pogge, T. W. (2005). Human rights and global health: A research program. *Metaphilosophy*, *36*(1–2), 182–209.

Porter, G., Bird, N., Kaur, N., & Peskett, L. (2008, July). New finance for climate change and the Environment. Heinrich Böll Stiftung. https://cdn.odi.org/media/documents/3882.pdf

Raffer, K. (1999). *ODA and global public goods: A trend analysis of past and present spending patterns*. Office of Development Studies, Bureau for Development Policy, United Nations Development Programme.

Reisen, H., Soto, M., & Weithöner, T. (2008). Financing global and regional public goods through ODA: Analysis and evidence from the OECD creditor reporting system. In T. Addison & G. Mavrotas (Eds.), *Development finance in the global economy: The road ahead* (pp. 124–150). Palgrave Macmillan.

Samuelson, P. A. (1954). The pure theory of public expenditure. *Review of Economics and Statistics, 36*(4), 387–389. doi:10.2307/1925895

Sandler, T. (2002). Financing international public goods. In M. Ferroni & A. Mody (Eds.), *International public goods: Incentives, measurement, and financing* (pp. 81–117). Springer. https://doi.org/10.1007/978-1-4615-0979-0_4

Sandler, T., & Arce, M. D. G. (2002). A conceptual framework for understanding global and transnational public goods for health. *Fiscal Studies, 23*(2), 195–222.

Silvestre, J. (2012). *Public microeconomics: Efficiency and equity in public policy*. Edward Elgar.

Stiglitz, J. E. (1988). *Economics of the public sector*. W. W. Norton & Co.

Stiglitz, J. E. (1999). Knowledge as a global public good. In I. Kaul (Ed.), *Global public goods: International cooperation in the 21st century* (pp. 308–325). Oxford University Press.

Tan, C. (2022). Private investments, public goods: Regulating markets for sustainable development. *European Business Organization Law Review, 23*(1), 241–271.

Thöne, M., & Kreuter, H. (2020, September). European public goods: Their contribution to a strong Europe. Bertelsmann Stiftung Vision Europe Paper 3.

UN General Assembly. (2015, October 21). Transforming our world: The 2030 Agenda for Sustainable Development, A/RES/70/1. https://www.refworld.org/docid/57b6e3e44.html

World Economic Forum. (2015). *Blended finance, vol. 1: A primer for development finance and philanthropic funders*.

CHAPTER 2

The Global Governance Complex: Insights from Recent Contributions to the Definition, Measurement, and Explanation of Change

Willem Molle

1 Introduction: Aims and Ways

The main question to which authors and editors of this publication seek an answer is: How fit is the present system of global governance to respond to the considerable challenges that the system faces? This question is not new; it has been asked by statesmen and scholars ever since the world saw that globalization processes brought about the need for global governance and the first global institutions appeared. Since then a literature has developed of an overwhelming size and complexity, condensed in recent textbooks.

In order to contribute to the answering of the central question of this publication we have chosen to concentrate in this introductory chapter on three concrete sets of more concrete questions:

1. What is the scope of globalization? What was the growth of global institutions capable to deliver new global public goods? Can this be expressed in a single indicator?
2. How can these developments be explained theoretically? What are the main characteristics of the system of global governance as it has evolved up till present? And how strong is the ensuing shift in authority to IOs?
3. What are the main weaknesses of the system of global governance? How can the lack of legitimacy of existing institutions be improved? What can be done to improve the performance of institutions?

We will seek to answer these questions by using the results of recent studies that deal with the theoretical understanding, the definition of empirically observable variables, and the quantification of developments. So, the ambition of our short contribution is limited; it does not try to review all relevant studies – it just aims to give a summary of recent research results. We devote a section to each of the three sets of questions articulated above.

2 The Size and Character of Globalization

2.1 *Globalization of Human Activities*

Over the past centuries human activities have increased their geographical span from local via national to global; a process called globalization. Initially, globalization was mainly driven by economic, technological, and security developments. However, since the 1960s other factors have come to the fore, such as the environment and health. Hence the term "globalization" has got a much wider scope; it must be seen now as the intensification of cross-national interactions (such as trade and capital movements) that promote the global integration of political, security, technological, economic, environmental and sociocultural processes. Therefore, all countries in the world have become more and more interdependent on an increasing range of points (Graff et al., 2013; Baten, 2016; for definitions along these lines see among others: Dreher et al., 2008, p. 15; Held, 2014, p. 62).

There are many ways in which this increased interdependence can be illustrated. One of the early drivers of globalization has been economic policy; that is, the reduction or elimination of restrictions to international trade and to financial transactions. A common indicator to measure growth on this score is the ratio of growth of international trade compared to the growth of total GDP (WTO, 2008, p. 15). In the period 1850 to 1913 trade grew by about 4% a year, while GDP grew by about 2%. During the interwar years there was a period of stagnation, but in the decades after World War II trade increased by 8% a year while GDP grew by 5%. Since then, this differential growth has continued. As over the last half century more complete data have become available so growing trade interdependence can now be better illustrated with the change in the average ratio between total world trade and total world GDP. This indicator increased between 1960 and 2010 from about 25 to 55. Other indicators convey the same message (OECD, 2010). The liberalization of international capital movements, for instance, led to a very large increase in cross-border investment; world foreign direct investment (FDI) as percentage of GDP grew from 5% in 1980 to 25% in 2006.

In the non-economic fields, a wide array of indicators is used. In environmental matters alone the World Meteorological Organization (WMO, 2021) monitors atmospheric pollution with a range of indicators. There are many other international organizations that monitor developments by other indicators. Together this produces a wealth of information to give guidance to policy measures for emission reduction and climate change adaptation. Examples for other fields of IO activity are not hard to find. But for our purpose these example will suffice.

3 No Globalization without Institutionalization

In the beginning of globalization most transactions between traders were based on simple unwritten rules. However, the increase in interactions on the economic, technological, environmental, security, human rights, and sociocultural fields that occurred over the past could not have developed without the setting of clear, formally agreed international rules that can be enforced in some way. So, in an increasing number of fields both sovereign states and private actors have set up regimes and institutions. The diversity of situations has given rise to a set of governance forms in which actors, ranging from states to multinational corporations and civil society organizations, cooperate formally and informally to efficiently provide global public goods. Examples of such public goods are a stable regulatory environment for trade in goods, mechanisms for international conflict settlements, etc. (Reinalda, 2009; for the evolution of the socioeconomic complex, see, among others, Molle, 2008, 2014). The global governance complex is characterized by a fragmented locus of authority.

This institutional complex is formed by rule-setting organizations. They consist essentially of three types. The main ones are intergovernmental organizations (IGOs) that have states as members. The most visible of them is the United Nations complex of universal, multilateral, treaty-based intergovernmental organizations supported by their bureaucracies and implementing their policies through legally binding and enforceable rules. A second category is formed by organizations that set the standards by which a certain segment of the economy can function. Their members are often specialized technical bodies (often government departments or state enterprises). A typical case of this type was already created in the 19th century: the International Telegraph Union. Finally, a third category is formed by private standard setting organizations that are generally created under domestic law, such as internet regulators or Standard & Poor's.

Around this core of rule setter has developed a multilayered complex of partly overlapping, often competing and even conflicting entities. Many of them are non-governmental organizations (NGOs). They provide certain services (such as the Red Cross) or monitor developments (such as Amnesty International). They pursue objectives such as the ban on nuclear weapons, the safeguarding of wildlife, etc. Most of them lobby the IGOs to adopt regulation that can bring positive change in their field of concern. In order to lobby effectively, they mobilize considerable sums of money and employ increasing numbers of highly qualified staff.

3.1 *Measuring Growth of Institutions*

The growth of the number of institutions over the past centuries can be followed using the different issues of the *Yearbook of International Organizations* (Rittberger et al., 2012, pp. 66–68). During the period from 1850 to 1913 the total number of IOs grew to some 50 and the average number of members of these organizations grew to some 15. During the 1920s some 30 IOs were set up in order to cope with problems that emerged after the first World War. During the 1930s stagnation followed. But after World War II there was a boom in IO creation, in order to accommodate peacekeeping, industrial expansion, third world development, etc. In 1980 there were some 340 IOs, of which only 32 had a worldwide coverage, 50 had members spread over several continents and 255 were regional organizations.

In the last half century, the boom continued. Most of the increase in the number of IOs in recent decades are NGOs. The number of NGOs increased from some 3,400 in 1970 to some 27,000 in 2006. Many of these have a global vocation. To give an idea; around 2005 about 3,000 NGOs had consultative status in ECOSOC (United Nations Economic and Social Council). Since then, this growth has continued, but it is difficult to measure due to lack of comparability of the data. The latest *Yearbook* (2020) gives some 42,000 active international organizations, of which most are non-governmental ones. Each year some 1,200 new entries are made to the *Yearbook*.

What explains this proliferation of NGOs? The literature mentions three main causes. The first is the increase in demand; civil society has recognized that many problems need to be addressed at an international level and due to increased wealth have been able to find the money necessary to finance their activities. The second is the differentiation of interests; many NGOs operate in the same field with slightly different agendas. The third reason is the emergence of enabling technologies; the internet has made it much easier to organize and operate NGOs.

IOs once created tend to be robust and long-lived. In cases where they have outlived their original objectives they tend to use their experience to change their remit and move into an adjacent area. Yet some cease to exist. Statistics are difficult to come by. They do not permit the creation of a complete demography of IOs, but they allow us to analyze the reasons why, and under what conditions, international organizations cease to exist. An analysis over the period 1815–2016 (Eilstrup-Sangiovanni, 2021) showed that exogeneous shocks are a leading proximate cause of IO termination and that organizations that are newly created, have small memberships, and/or lack centralized structures are more likely to succumb.

3.2 *Measuring the Growth of Globalization and of Global Institutions Together*

Because of the trends depicted global governance has reached an unprecedented scope; it affects every area of policymaking. However, measuring the increase in scope is not easy. The partial economic and institutional indicators discussed in the previous sections convey only a fragmented idea of the increase in globalization. A more comprehensive indicator of globalization is needed. For a long time, its construction was precluded by the poor availability of data. Recently, this situation has changed.

Based on a very large set of data for all countries in the world for the 1970–2020 period a group of researchers has set up, refined, and updated a multidimensional index of globalization (Dreher et al., 2008; Haelg, 2019; Gygli et al., 2019). The three dimensions they used are economic, social, and political. In all three dimensions a distinction is made between de facto indicators (for instance, trade in goods in % of GDP for the economic dimension) and de jure indicators (for instance, internet access for the social dimension). In total, 43 variables are measured. On that basis weighted indices are calculated for each dimension and for the overall average. The results are very illuminating. The Index of overall globalization has steadily increased from about 40 in 1970 to about 60 in 2016. Some differences between subperiods can be distinguished. From 1970 to 1990 the index increased only moderately. Since then (the end of the Cold War) it increased dramatically up to 2008, while the growth flattened off since. One can see here the effects of the financial crisis and policy shifts of major countries. Some differences can be observed for the various dimensions, although their picture is largely in line with the overall index.

4 Defining and Measuring Shifts in Characteristics and in Authority

4.1 *A Long Development Leading to Three Streams of Thought*

The process of increasing globalization has been the subject of deep ongoing research by scholars of different disciplines. They have elaborated an impressive body of knowledge on the main questions, including why international organizations develop. In all this theoretical and empirical work, one generally distinguishes three main streams of thought that appear largely complementary. We will not go into the vast literature on the subject, but limit ourselves to cite just a recent synopsis:

> Realism explains international governance as the result of strategic choices made by independent states which exist in the absence of

> overarching authority. We concur that states are the most powerful actors in international politics and they vary widely in their power capabilities. There is, indeed, no coercive authority above states capable of sustaining international organization. Liberal institutionalism [...] [poses] the idea that states act rationally in dealing with the collective action problems produced by interdependence. This approach conceives IOs as means to reduce the transaction cost of cooperation in areas where states have overlapping interests, thereby facilitating international governance under the structural constraints imposed by anarchy. Functionalist theory is indispensable if one wishes to explain two puzzling features of international governance: Why do states delegate authority to independent IO bodies and why do states collectivise decision making in binding majoritarianism? [...] Constructivism, [a third stand of thought], explores how norms, identities, and discourse shape international cooperation. The character of international governance depends not only on its benefits, but on what the participants make of each other. Constructivism draws attention to the social fabric of international cooperation. To explain variation in international governance one needs to theorize the conditions under which the participants will be prepared to surrender some national self-rule for international shared rule. (Hooghe et al., 2019, pp. 2–5)

This overlaps largely with the synopsis made in Rittberger et al. (2012, p. 33) and Hasenclever et al. (2000).

4.2 *Main Past Trends and Present Characteristics of Global Governance*

Central in the three strands of thought given above is the idea that the increase in interactions creates the need for the effective delivering of global public goods and for compliance with international rules and norms. To that end sovereign states must give up part of their ruling power and hand over competences to international organizations. This did not occur in a same way and at the same time in all fields of emerging global public goods. So, a set of specialized idiosyncratic organizations has developed. Together, they form a global governance system that can be characterized as a multi-sectoral, multi-actor, multi-institution, multi-principle, and multi-instrument. For each of these features some major developments can be discerned.

Subjects. Collective action problems tend to lead to sector-specific organizational solutions for the creation of public goods. Different policy areas such as trade, climate change, or peacekeeping have developed differentiated governance systems. The global multi-sector system is thus not monolithic but rather segmented. Over time the issue coverage of the system has greatly increased. Today's global governance affects virtually every area of international and transnational politics. Moreover, many of the main players have increased their field of interest over time by adding flanking policies to their existing policy portfolios.[1] In each area a special type of governance complex has developed under the influence of sector-specific factors. In many areas it consists of several IOs, which leads to competition, overlaps, and conflicts between parts of the system.

Actors. The system is to a large extent supported by sovereign states that have formed international intergovernmental organizations. In some cases, other IOs are powerful actors alongside states; this applies in particular to regional organizations such as the EU that represent their interest in global for a. However, from the beginning the global governance system is far from being the exclusive prerogative of public sector bodies; it increasingly consists of a bemusing multitude of non-governmental actors, among which we find corporations, civil society organizations, advocacy groups, substate public actors, etc. All these types of NGOs have organized themselves on a global scale. There has indeed been a clear trend of an increased role of powerful non-state actors in the development of transborder governance.

Legal forms and competences. These actors work together in diverse networks being vested in a variety of legal forms. Some global governance institutions are large, treaty-based intergovernmental organizations with a strong bureaucratic support and strong instruments to enforce compliance with rules. Others are made of transnational private or hybrid arrangements. Apart from the structures with a strong formal base the need for collective action has expressed itself in a host of different flexible venues, such as regimes, forums, networks, platforms, summits, and public-private partnerships.

Principles. Cooperation becomes facilitated if partners agree on basic values and ideologies. However, even with differences on those scores, cooperation can be facilitated by formulating basic principles of conduct. Principles tend to be subject-specific. A basic set of principles concerns sovereign equality, the non-intervention of states in domestic affairs of another country. The consideration that humanity is the custodian of the global environmental patrimony has led to the adoption of the precautionary principle. In economics, the recognition of the scientific finding that free trade is advantageous has

1 "Three patterns can be discerned. First IOs have seen a secular expansion of their policy portfolios, from an average of 2.9 policies in 1950 to eight policies in 2010. Second there is less movement in IOs' core policies over time, from an average of 1.4 core policies in 1950 to 2.5 in 2010. Third and by implication, the dynamism of an IO's policy portfolio derives mostly from adding flanking policies" (Hooghe et al., 2019, p. 148).

been translated in the principle of the "most favored nation"; consequently, the trade order is often labeled as "liberal." To sustain these different substantive principles, one usually recognizes the procedural principle of multilateralism. This principle presupposes that all state actions can be justified by agreed international rules and that states in general seek long-term collective gains from cooperation and refrain from quid pro quo exchanges.

Instruments. The components of the system vary widely in power, resources, and competences from issue to issue. These differences express themselves in a wide variety of regulatory and other instruments of governance. They produce a plethora of regulations, norms, standards, etc. Over time most IOs have become more powerful and use more constraining instruments for insuring compliance with their rules, leading to a decrease in the room of maneuver of both public and private actors. Now compliance tends to rely less on obedience to formal international law, that if broken triggers sanctions and punitive actions. Much more now tends to be done thorough non-coercive soft instruments, such as monitoring, persuasion, norm diffusion, information exchange, etc.

The great diversity and multiplicity of institutional forms, cooperating partners, and instruments is very difficult to navigate for users, including the policymakers and legislators who must make them operational in their own jurisdictions.

4.3 *Measuring the Shift of Authority*

National states have handed over authority to IGOs because they believed they would benefit from the transaction; they reckoned in this way to enjoy new public goods that could not be provided on the national level. So, once the shift in authority is operated member states and their citizens comply in their own interest with supranational rules that are in everybody's interest. The trends depicted above suggest that this has been the case for an ever-increasing number of issues. Can we therefore conclude that more and more authority is transferred from the national to the international level?

To answer this question a group of researchers has attempted to measure the degree to which authority has shifted (Hooghe et al., 2019). To do so they have followed a three-stage approach. In the first stage they distinguish between two sources of authority of IOs, or ways in which authority is shifted. A first way is *delegation*: national states hand over authority to independent international bodies. After delegation these IGOs have an autonomous capacity to govern. Often the secretariat of an IGO is empowered to set the agenda and oversee implementation. More rarely states delegate powers to an international court that can deal with the consequences of non-compliance by members. A second way to hand over authority is by *pooling*. This occurs when national governments transfer independent national decision-making by collective decision-making in the framework of an IO. In this way they agree to outflank national veto power and commit themselves to decisions even if they did not agree with them.

In the second stage they translate these notions of delegation and pooling in terms of observable components. For delegation they measure the role of IOs in agenda setting, decision-making, and dispute settlement. For pooling they measure deviations from consensus in each stage in policymaking, such as constitutional reform, the budget, financial non-compliance, membership accession, and suspension.

In the third stage they quantify all components and integrate the results in a two-dimensional measure of international authority (MIA). They find that delegation has increased slightly between 1975 and 1995 to increase steeply after that up to 2010 (from 0.16 to 0.24). Pooling on the contrary did develop in a much more gradual way: from 0.29 to 0.35 in the same period (Hooghe et al., 2019, p. 148).

5 Challenges to the System: Ways to Improve it

5.1 *Contested Governance and Its Consequences*

The increase in the authority of IOs induces contestation. In the first instance, contestation comes from member states that are negatively impacted by IO decisions. They had agreed to the rules of the IO, because participating in the common public good gave them benefits. But once a particular case occurs with negative consequences for their particular interest, they will tend to devise strategies to avoid compliance with IOs' decision-making. It is not only states that are affected; in more and more cases, IO decisions also have a negative affect on the daily lives of citizens and the daily operations of business and civil society. For instance, the world economic institutional system is blamed for locking workers into low-wage activities and stimulate corporate tax evasion, leading to high wage taxes. A prominent critic in this respect has been Nobel Prize winner Joseph Stiglitz (2002). In some cases, popular and state contestation join forces. For example: the WTO has been under attack from anti-globalist popular movements and from populist governments. Consequently, it has been unable to make progress on major issues and its dispute settlement system has become non-operational.

Contestation often leads to a further fragmentation of authority in organizations that can be difficult to avoid. A case in point is the monetary/financial cluster. The anchor organization here is the IMF. The IMF has for a long time been criticized for its inadequate handling of national and international crises. This practical inadequacy has been attributed among other factors to its ideological bias. More fundamentally, its legitimacy has been criticized. Claims have been made that its decision-making is flawed due to a serious lack of representativeness: US veto power, Euro countries divided over several groups, underrepresentation of developing economies. Past attempts to repair these problems have not been successful (Hallaert, 2020). So, steps are taken to bypass the organization both in geographical and issue terms.

Japan (although an ally of the US on many fronts) and notably China (the challenger for world hegemony) together with other Asian nations have heavily criticized the IMF for its inadequate management of the latest financial crises. They have attempted to set up an Asian Monetary Fund to bypass the IMF (Narine, 2003). These attempts have until now been unsuccessful, due to the diversity of views of major partners and strong US lobbying (Hyun & Paradise, 2019).

To improve the preventive part of the global financial system the International Financial Stability Forum was created in 1998 which set up an early-warning system for crises. After the financial crisis of 2008 and the meeting of the G20 in 2009 it was transformed into the Financial Stability Board (FSB). The FSB cooperates with the IMF, the OECD, and the Bank of International Settlements on the supervision of the financial sector.

5.2 *A Systemic Dysfunction?*

This not just a problem for the IMF; almost all major IOs are heavily criticized for either lack of efficiency, institutional sclerosis, ideological infighting, duplication, excessive bureaucracy, obsolescence, inaccessibility, lack of transparency and accountability, or loss of control. Many IOs are criticized for a combination of such defaults. Populist movements and governments contest the fundamentals of the liberal international order that characterizes most of the post-World War II institutions. In that slipstream some contest all multilateralism and all concerted action for new global public good provision. They do that mainly by contesting the legitimacy of IOs.

Overshadowing these questions is a major geopolitical factor: the gradual shift in power from the US to China and the increase of the role of the largest countries in the former Third World. This tendency of increased multipolarity, which is going hand in hand with a fundamental clash of societal systems, contests the foundations of many of the constituting elements of the present global governance system.

In view of this state of affairs some observers (e.g., Hale et al., 2013) have concluded that the global governance system has come to a gridlock. Since then, this view has been found to be exaggerated. Many observers now agree that in some areas stalemates exist, but that in many other areas the system continues to provide essential global public goods (e.g., Dingwerth, 2021). However, a major effort is needed to improve the functioning of the global governance model by addressing the causes for a slipping away of the legitimacy of IOs.

In order to empirically analyze this, Zuern (2018) distinguishes between two complementary sources of legitimacy: procedure and performance. In terms of procedure IOs can refer to the generally accepted norms that they apply and to the expertise they have, and the impartiality of decisions. The term of performance translates in responsiveness to articulated needs, preferences, and effectiveness; in other words, delivering what was agreed on. Both elements have given rise to new research (Pisani-Ferry, 2018; Stephen, 2018; OECD, 2021). In the following sections we will address both improving procedural legitimacy and improving practical implementation.

5.3 *Improving Procedural Legitimacy*

Legitimacy is granted to an IGO at the moment it is set up by the fact that sovereign states have handed over authority to it (even though that authority may erode over time). Such de-legitimation may occur, for instance, due a change in the standards by which the relevant stakeholders of the IO evaluate its performance. Once a legitimacy deficit has occurred, it does hinder the development of an IO. Member states will no longer consider the IO as the proper venue for discussing and solving problems. The IO in question will have difficulty in making members comply with the rules and decisions of the IO. Naturally, under such conditions member states will shy away from the idea to entrust new tasks and responsibilities to such an organization. This can only be countered by a process of re-legitimation, for instance, by adapting the remit, governance practices, etc.

The literature on these phenomena has primarily used case studies and narratives to shed light on them. Recently attempts have been made to go beyond that. Tallberg and Zuern (2019), for instance, have conceptualized a theoretical model in which legitimacy, as the dependant variable, is influenced by three intermediate variables (public opinion, political behavior, and political communication) each operationalized by a set of concrete measurable variables. The latter are based on the quantitative results of surveys (experts or population), field experiences and content analysis of relevant documents and media texts.

The approach has delivered some promising results. One example is that IOs contested for lack of democratic control have tended to add parliamentary assemblies to their institutional setup. Another example: de-legitimation and re-legitimation processes were found to be particularly intense the higher the authority of an IO.

5.4 *Improving Performance and Governance Practice*

Another main source of legitimacy is performance. Critics agree that the performance of IOs individually and of the system collectively must be improved. Given the complexities of the global governance "system" depicted in the previous sections, one may wonder how it can function effectively. The more so in cases where it is confronted with issues that are intricately related (for instance, in international migration, where problems of economic development, security, human rights, and environmental degradation interfere). In such cases effective international policymaking and implementation requires cooperation and coordination between a range of actors. For example, humanitarian relief operations often require the coordinated efforts of global, regional, national and local, and public and private agencies. To that end, problem-based complexes of governance have been formed that have become structurally enmeshed and whose boundaries tend to be in continuous flux.

In numerous instances the expansion of the scope of international organizations has created overlap. On the one hand, the resulting conflicts between competences need to be arbitrated in order to avoid stalemates. On the other hand, numerous instances occur where existing organizations fail to address problems that go beyond their competence and require the cooperation of various specialized organizations. However, organizing the solution to both the problem of "too much" and the one of "too little" is complicated as the most concerned organizations have different rules and operating modes.

To discover a solution to the problem outlined here, the OECD (2019, 2021) has launched a voluntary partnership of some 50 secretariats of IOs to promote and discuss the conditions for greater quality, effectiveness, and impact of international rules, regardless of their substantive scope. This collective effort has led to an unprecedented collection of information on the rulemaking activities of IOs and the exchange of practices and tools on implementation, stakeholder engagement, evaluation, and coordination of international instruments. They show that overcoming fragmentation and institutional inertia, although a complicated exercise, is a feasible way forward. Efforts in this respect are beginning to produce some effects.

6 Conclusions

Over time the global governance system has grown in numbers and types of partners, size, issue coverage, intrusiveness of instruments, and complexity of operational forms. However, all IOs taken together show a considerable rise in IO authority and a shift away from national states and private organizations. This IO authority is increasingly contested, leading to a decrease in legitimacy.

Although institutional sclerosis often prevents change, many attempts are made to re-legitimate organizations and hence corroborate their authority. One avenue for this is by improving institutional design and another is by increasing governance methods. On both scores positive experiences suggest that real change is feasible.

References

Baten, J. (Ed.). (2016). *A history of the global economy, 1500 – present*. Cambridge University Press.

Dingwerth, K. (2021). Beyond gridlock: How global governance continues to shape our world. *European Review of International Studies, 8*(2), 241–253.

Dreher, A., Gaston, N., & Martens, P. (2008). *Measuring globalisation: Gauging its consequences*. Springer.

Eilstrup-Sangiovanni, M. (2021). What kills international organisations? When and why international organisations terminate. *European Journal of International Relations, 27*(1), 281–310.

Graff, M., Kenwood, A. G., & Lougheed, A. L. (2013). *The growth of the international economy, 1820–2015* (5th ed.). Routledge.

Gygli, S., Haelg, F., Potrafke, N., & Sturm, J.-E. (2019). The KOF Globalisation Index revisited. *Review of International Organizations, 14*, 543–574.

Hale, T., Held, D., & Young, K. (2013). *Gridlock: Why global cooperation is failing when it is needed most*. Polity Press.

Haelg, F. (2019). The KOF Globalisation Index – A multidimensional approach to globalisation. *Jahrbücher für Nationalökonomie und Statistik, 240*(5), 691–696. https://doi.org/10.1515/jbnst-2019-0045

Hallaert, J.-J. (2020). The tragedy of international organizations in a world order in turmoil. Policy Brief 5/2020. European Centre for International Political Economy (ECIPE).

Hasenclever, A., Mayer, P., & Rittberger, V. (2000). Integrating theories of international regimes. *Review of International Studies, 26*(1), 3–33.

Held, D. (2014). The diffusion of authority. in T. G. Weiss & R. Wilkinson (Eds.), *International organizations and global governance* (pp. 60–72). Routledge.

Hooghe, L., Lenz, T., & Marks, G. (2019). *A theory of international organization*. Oxford University Press.

Hyun, S., & Paradise, J. F. (2019, December). Why is there no Asian Monetary Fund? ADBI Working Paper Series, no. 1061. Asian Development Bank Institute.

Molle, W. (2014). *Governing the world economy*. Routledge.

Molle, W. (Ed.). (2008). *Global economic institutions: Critical writings on global Institutions* (4 Vols.). Routledge.

Narine, S. (2003). The idea of an "Asian Monetary Fund": The problems of financial institutionalism in the Asia Pacific Area. *Asian Perspective, 27*(2), 65–103.

OECD. (2010). *OECD economic globalization indicators*. Organisation for Economic Co-operation and Development.

OECD. (2019). *The contribution of international organisations to a rule-based international system*. Organisation for Economic Co-operation and Development.

OECD. (2021). *Perspectives on global development: From protest to progress*? Organisation for Economic Co-operation and Development.

Pisani-Ferry, J. (2018, October). Should we give up on global governance? *Brueghel Policy Contribution, 17*.

Reinalda, B. (2009). *Routledge history of international organizations: From 1815 to the present day*. Routledge.

Rittberger, V., Zangl, B., & Kruck, A. (2012). *International organization* (2nd ed.). Palgrave Macmillan.

Stephen, M. D. (2018). Legitimacy deficits of international organisations: Design, drift, and decoupling at the UN Security Council. *Cambridge Review of International Affairs, 31*(1), 96–121.

Stiglitz, J. (2002). *Globalization and its discontents*. Norton.

Tallberg, J., & Zuern, M. (2019). The legitimacy and legitimation of international organisations: Introduction and framework. *The Review of International Organizations, 14*, 581–606.

WMO. (2021, April 19). Climate change indicators and impacts worsened in 2020. World Meteorological Organization. https://public.wmo.int/en/media/press-release/climate-change-indicators-and-impacts-worsened-2020

WTO. (2008). *World trade report*. World Trade Organization.

Zuern, M. (2018). *A theory of global governance: Authority, legitimacy and contestation*. Oxford University Press.

PART 2

International Security: What Role Does It Play in Achieving SDGs*?*

CHAPTER 3

The Reaction of International Organizations to Global Security Challenges

Anatoliy Kruglashov

1 Introduction

We are living in a world which faces many fundamental threats and challenges. It distracts us from collective aspirations towards growing prosperity, creating more public goods, and reaching higher living standards. While international organizations (IOs) proudly announce ambitious Sustainable Development Goals, the overall picture of a global mosaic looks less optimistic, if not gloomy. In recent years, scholars, experts, civic activists, and politicians have been discussing and worrying about the rise of regional conflicts and threats of climate change, alongside efforts related to fighting poverty and unjust distribution of global wealth and resources. Then, in the last 2 years, humanity has been preoccupied with the pandemic of COVID-19, when both national and global communities were put in a very uncomfortable position of helplessness and frustration in the face of the massive spread of deadly viruses (Bengtsson & Rhinard, 2019, pp. 346–349).

Recently the global community has been confronted with kinetic security threats, and military conflicts, including full-scale wars. These make access to public goods (as they are described in the previous chapter) obstructed and constrained. As far as security and human rights are concerned, the activity of IOs, which were founded primarily to prevent conflicts and wars, should be the focus of academic scrutiny and critical analysis. The most evidence of a growing global insecurity is provided by a new stage of the Russo – Ukrainian War, launched by the Kremlin in Ukraine on February 24, 2022. It clearly means a new turn in the international order and relations. The biggest (mainly territorially) country in the world, a permanent member of the United Nations (UN) Security Council, a member of the Organization for Security and Co-operation in Europe (OSCE) and many other global and regional organizations, started an unprovoked full-scale war. This war threatens the very existence of Ukraine, which is a founding member of the UN and the biggest country in Europe. Russia is taking apart Kyiv's control territories under a severe occupational regime, expanding its territories at the expense of Ukraine, and widely applying

 | DOI:10.1163/9789004687264_005

hybrid and traditional war tools and methods. All these steps are followed by numerous military crimes, thousands of civilian victims, many cases of looting, rape, and murder committed in the temporarily occupied territories.

In this chapter, the author applies theories and concepts which are mostly developed within the realm of political science and international relations. The chapter is written based on both primary and secondary sources, including fundamental documents, such as the UN Charter, the Universal Convention on Human Rights, and others.

Structurally, the chapter is divided into four sections. The first section deals with the international community's determined search for peace and prosperity under growing tensions and confrontations. The second section of the chapter turns to the Euro-Atlantic dimension of international organizations: the first is the OSCE case, and the second one is the North Atlantic Treaty Organization (NATO). The last two sections are concerned with the European security situation. In the third section the author considers the role of the Council of Europe as a very important IO, regionally and globally. The last section examines the EU's evolution as a geopolitical actor with a certain position and responsibilities as the most important provider of security and contributor to public goods in general. Some lessons which the EU has learned after the Yugoslav Wars and Russian aggression are outlined as the most relevant to the subject of the chapter (Olech, 2019, pp. 8–9). Thus, the chapter focuses on a wide spectrum of crucial challenges and threats, as well as provides a critical analysis of the reactions of the leading IOs to them.

2 The International Community's Determined Search for Peace and Prosperity: the Question of the UN's Ability to Meet Its Goals

2.1 *Hopes and Failures of the UN*

The United Nations' activities are expected to respond to global challenges and threats. Concerning the debatable adequacy of the responsiveness of the UN to the crucial issues of global community peace and prosperity, some important points should be outlined in the broader context of global public goods distribution, and in the narrow sense of the security provision. This is a topical issue because the latter is not only an inviolable part of the former but also because public goods might be shared and accessed only under conditions of quarantined security. The UN was established after the failure of the League of Nations (dismissed later, in 1946), which had not been able to prevent the Second World War (Archer, 2001, pp. 20–22). Considering those dramatic experiences, the UN was founded to prevent a new global war (Jindal &

Dhingra, 2021, p. 51). The very danger of another world war has been well understood since the invention of the atomic bomb and its production en masse. Fears abound that a third world war would likely be the last one in the history of humanity. The UN Charter and later documents were developed to keep the peace, prevent war, and establish proper negotiations, diplomacy, regulations, moderation, and mediation among conflicting parties, states, and ethnic or religious communities in order to preserve global development and peacefully resolve issues of discord, disagreement, racism, radical nationalism, and many other problems for the sake of regional and global security and prosperity. For decades, the UN developed a massive, some would say excessive, institutional structure and capacity. This is a rightful characteristic for this unique global organization vested with the authority to handle the most important issues for the international community (Thakur, 2016, pp. 329–338). It has gradually but steadily expanded its activity into the economic sphere, addressing social prosperity (the Economic and Social Council), the fight against diseases (World Health Organization [WHO]), education and culture (United Nations Educational, Scientific and Cultural Organization [UNESCO]), migration (International Organization for Migration [IOM]), labor issues (International Labour Organization [ILO]), food security, and many others (Prosekov & Ivanova, 2018). The comprehensiveness of the UN coverage of global issues tells a story of progressive success, with IOs well represented worldwide. Indeed, the range and scope of IOs seems almost universal due to their competence and functions. Almost each recognized country is a member of the UN (now there are 194). Therefore, the UN is well known for many important proclamations and issuing concerted declarations of its goals to serve prosperity, peace, cooperation, and development worldwide. The 2030 Agenda for Sustainable Development proclaims numerous very important tasks which cover a wide variety of topical issues for humankind in general (Beisheim, 2018). But at the same time, looking at the efficiency of the UN's legal foundation and institutions via the prism of security issues, challenges, and tasks, one must acknowledge some failures and partly successful stories related to that IO in general, and its peacekeeping missions in particular (Bashota & Dugolli, 2017, pp. 98–101). For example, in the Rwanda genocide, the UN was hardly successful in preventing the very tragic deaths of more than a million victims claimed by deadly outbursts of massive, politically fueled hatred and ethnic clashes (Salim, 2021, pp. 1–2). In addition, the Mali case followed, where once again the UN was hardly impressive with the overall records of their mission (Karlsrud, 2015, pp. 45–48). The picture of the so-called "failed states" (such as Somalia, Eritrea, and Libya) remains troublesome as missions and other attempts of the UN (Della-Giacoma et al., 2016, pp. 17–21) aimed at resolving local dramas brought no considerable results. Regarding prevention of armed conflicts, even in the case of the Balkan crisis and wars of the 1990s, the consensus of the leading powers and the overall efficiency of the UN legal instruments and the course of preventing the outburst of the Yugoslav Wars are hardly successful, too. It makes sense to agree with the conclusive remarks on UN sanctions:

> Although the purposes of sanctions vary, the Security Council remains focused on coercion, which was its primary purpose in 56% of the cases, compared to 41% for constraint and 3% for signaling. Sanctions achieved their principal purpose in 19% of the cases. Sanctions were effective in coercing 10% of the time and in constraining and signaling in 27% of the cases, suggesting that sanctions might be more effective if the Council designed and imposed them for purposes other than coercion. Weighing all three purposes equally, sanctions were effective in 22% of the cases. (Biersteker et al., 2018, p. 408)

Finally, the case of Russia's war against Georgia in 2008 and the ongoing Russo – Ukrainian War since 2014 could be recalled also. These examples show the very limits of the UN's effectiveness and role in preventing and settling those conflicts, avoiding the worst-case scenario in the latter. All those cases happened despite the sophisticated institutional structure and procedural mechanisms of the UN, e.g., the General Assembly resolutions, many sittings and talks in the Security Council, a few other discussions at auxiliary bodies of that IO, the wide range of authoritative experts engaged and many conferences/debates on different issues held. Some of them have not been successfully resolved up to now.

Why did it happen? Why, given the recent very pro-Ukrainian resolutions of the General Assembly, did the Russo – Ukrainian War, which started in 2014, move to a more dangerous stage after February 24, 2022? It seems that those cases take place because the UN itself has some principal distortions and loopholes. The organization's institutes and functions are disproportionately affected by the influence of the great powers. One of the key reasons is the founding consensus of 1945, when five countries were appointed as the permanent members of the Security Council. They agreed to be a core body of the UN. That made this IO a kind of international trust, which is controlled by those principal stakeholders, namely the USA, Great Britain, France, China, and the USSR. Ironically, Russia is a self-proclaimed chief successor of the USSR. These five countries made a consensus that they have a right to be permanent members of the Security Council of the UN, and their exclusive authority, influence, and strength are legally supported and guaranteed by their veto rights. The right of veto has been often applied and used by one or another of these countries in the course of history (Salim, 2021, pp. 8–10). Intriguingly, representatives of Russia have (ab)used that right too many times. For instance, they block any attempts by Security Council members, both permanent and temporary, to discuss and find a way towards a resolution of the Russo – Ukrainian War. It is hardly an acceptable situation when a member of the UN and a permanent member of its Security Council acts as an aggressor under the agreed upon UN charter principles, thus substantially violating international law. Moreover, the same aggressor might simultaneously be able to effectively prevent any restrictive actions from the International Community, the UN, and its Security Council.

2.2 *Possible UN Reforms*

These cases explain why the UN needs thorough and comprehensive reforms, which should be centered on the role of the Security Council (Binder & Heupel, 2015, pp. 247–248). If an organization is grounded on the principle of all countries' equality, parity, and respect for any independent state as a member of the UN, the member states must exercise an equal voice and influence. In addition to the drastic division between the small and big countries, and the developed and developing countries, one has to admit evident disparity between the group of permanent member countries and the non-permanent members in the UN Security Council. For instance, Latin America and Africa are not represented in the Security Council with a decisive power or blocking power of a veto. Out of many Asian countries, only China is a permanent member of the Security Council of the UN. This corresponds to neither the economic contribution of countries to the UN budget (it ensures the material grounds for effective functioning and actions of the IO) nor to the countries' individual contribution to resolving the security, social-economic, educational, and other important problems of human existence. Undeniably, it also makes accessibility of public goods uneven. The author agrees with the following statement: "An expansion of the Security Council or the revoking of veto powers will not […] equip the UN system to fight a 'soft war.' It requires new tools and new strategies. The reforms should go beyond cosmetic changes and include all agencies and organisations working with [the] UN" (Thomas & Kumar, 2021, p. 95).

It is incompatible with the logic and spirit of the UN's mission and legal foundations that its most representative and authoritative body, the General Assembly, lacks the power to make the final decision. It does not control budgetary processes and the functioning of UN agencies, either (Janev, 2020, pp. 121–123). The General Assembly merely issues recommendations that eventually depend on the Security Council for adoption. As the core body of the UN, any move in the Security Council depends on the consensus of the five permanent members. If such a consensus is reached, the global community might expect a positive resolution of any conflict or issue. But if it fails, any one of the five can block, hinder, or even undermine the whole process of policy-making in the UN.

That is why there has been a growing anticipation and need for UN structural reforms, from the 1960s onwards (Ade-Ibijola, 2015). Different projects of reforming the UN were drafted and proposed. Key changes suggest increasing the power of the General Assembly, which is the true representative body of all the member states, and which reflects the position of the global community. The General Assembly should be the real power and ultimate body to resolve any conflict or war and to put in motion the decisive power of the UN, including the right of intervention, economic sanctions, and other measures needed to stop aggression and restore regional or global security.

Another direction of reforms is the composition and power of the Security Council. Some drafts attempt to include the representation of countries like India (Dabhade, 2022, pp. 50–68) Japan, and Germany as new permanent members. From the point of view of demography and the growing importance of India, this was a well-grounded proposal. However, that attempt failed, arousing no enthusiasm from the five principal UN stakeholders (Ade-Ibijola, 2015, pp. 138–139). It might be mentioned there was an attempt to include Japan as a new permanent member of the Security Council. As far as continental Europe is concerned, Germany is a very important stakeholder of the European order and its social and economic development. It is also an influential contributor to regional and global public goods. Yet proposals to increase its role have received the cold shoulder instead of support. Should those motions be realized, it would not resolve the problem of the exclusive privileges of the permanent members of the Security Council. Even if the countries and their representatives had supported the move to make India, Japan, and/or Germany permanent members, it would not have helped to resolve the issue of the permanent members' veto. Should the veto right be expanded to the new permanent members, it would further complicate the process of making the Security Council more democratic.

Regarding the UN Charter provision, one must accept complications of those motions being realized. This precondition influences the perspective of reforming the whole policymaking process in the UN. The veto right should be totally excluded as an instrument of the so-called "permanent members' superiority" over the Security Council and consequently the UN in general (Dadashova, 2019, p. 100). Otherwise, the international community could witness the obvious failure of the UN in preventing conflicts and resolving them. There are plenty of conflicts and they require the full attention of the UN (Chesterman, 2014).

UN reforms are inevitable and of crucial importance. They should be carried out as soon as possible. The reform agenda should have a high priority and be considered with no delay. Otherwise, the lack of timely reaction to the global challenges, including pandemics, military threats from Russia, and some alarming moves from China to establish control over Taiwan by military means, could result in a full-fledged global war with all the imaginable and predictable consequences to follow. The UN, as the most important and comprehensive global international organization, needs urgent but well-thought-out reorganization. It's the right response to the new challenging situation concerning regional and global issues. The reforms should be democratic both in the content and procedures for discussing and resolving conflictual issues. Ultimately, no state can possess privileges instead of equal rights and duties. These are the most urgent direction of changes and reforms in the UN.

3 The Euro-Atlantic International Organizations: Stormy Winds of Change

Europe and the Euro-Atlantic area are distinguished by having the dubious honor of being the starting locations for two world wars. They have shaken those regions, left behind millions of dead and wounded people, as well as ruined settlements. Furthermore, they resulted in a contradictory legacy in the collective memories of many nations there. For that reason, it is very important to analyze the Euro-Atlantic international organizations' activities and to consider to what extent those organizations are effective in preventing conflicts, resolving them, and paving a way to a stable and secure peace.

3.1 *The Origin and Development of the OSCE*

First, it is essential to touch upon the origin and evolution of the Organization for Security and Co-operation in Europe (OSCE). The process of its establishment could be observed as early as the 1970s in Détente and the Helsinki Process. The US and the USSR, the leaders of two confronting blocks, mutually recognized the importance of peaceful coexistence and the need for reduced tensions in Europe and the Euro-Atlantic space. They tried to find political solutions which would be acceptable to both camps in the framework of the Cold War era and the bipolar system of international relations (Koja et al., 2020, pp. 1–3). In some respects, the new format of Euro-Atlantic interstate dialogue and consultation contributed to the rapprochement between West and East. The OSCE itself was constituted in the early 1990s, soon after the collapse of the Warsaw Pact. It began a transformation from an important recurrent conference, a platform of political dialogue towards a new IO aimed at much wider cooperation for the engaged countries within a specific organizational and institutional structure (Herman & Wouters, 2017, pp. 7–8). It seemed to be a huge, promising IO, comprising 57 states from North America, Europe, and Central Asia (Костенко & Аметаев, 2021, pp. 48–49). The establishment of the OSCE seeded hopes of a great success and a promising beginning. The prevailing expectation was grounded in the belief that this organization would be able to play an important role in preventing conflicts, promoting cooperation among the engaged countries, and directing socioeconomic development on the three continents towards democracy, economic prosperity, and social stability.

However, after the formative years the OSCE hardly succeeded in those tasks. It did not play an important role in the prevention and resolution of conflicts in the scope of the organization's responsibility (Debuysere, 2019, pp. 250–251). The first litmus test was the context of the post-Yugoslav Wars period, where the OSCE tried its best to be as helpful as possible (Đorđević et al., 2018). Yet until the intervention of NATO, the OSCE was able to perform only a secondary role there (Simonet, 2018, pp. 284–285). It did not find a way to serve as the main platform of making peace, preventing, or managing conflict, and finding solutions for post-conflict regulation (Friesendorf, 2020).

Other conflicts where the OSCE was engaged concerned mainly the post-Soviet space. First, one has to consider the Nagorno-Karabakh case, the oldest open armed conflict in the post-Soviet space, which has been going on until now (with some aggravations in 2015 and 2020) (Guliyev & Gawrich, 2021). The role of the OSCE appeared as weak and indecisive there (Shelest, 2022, p. 14). It is also essential to recall the Moldova and Georgia cases regarding the conflicts in Transnistria, Abkhazia, and South Ossetia respectfully.Again, the author does not discover proof that the OSCE is the main actor in negotiating the acceptable approach among all the parties concerned with ending these conflicts (Mihr, 2021, pp. 8–11). Certainly, not all parties are equally concerned with productive negotiations in those conflicts. Not every one of them is interested in a fair solution to these conflicts as well. Both in the cases of Georgia and Moldova, the OSCE founded a platform for negotiation, a framework for diplomatic talks, organized different meetings, and sent monitoring missions to the regions. It has made a strenuous effort to elaborate practical recommendations for the conflicted parties for years of those protracted conflicts. Despite those efforts, regional conflicts have been unsolved until now. The position of the OSCE seems to be very low profile with no considerable outcomes achieved.

3.2 *Evaluation of the Role of the OSCE*

The driving force of the OSCE is a gradual but steady evolution from an international organization, which has been based on the idea of a peaceful coexistence of different, sometimes adversary countries with different economic systems, political regimes, and ideologies. The standards of mutual trust applied to confidence measures and cooperative approaches were advocated and supported by the organization. However, this is not satisfactory to provide peace and strengthen security in Europe and Eurasia. This became clear when the OSCE tried to interfere in the conflict in Ukraine after the illegal annexation of Crimea and the beginning of war in Donbas, both launched by Putin's Russia. The OSCE Special Monitoring Mission (SMM) to Donbas seemed to be the only IO mission that tried to observe and describe what was happening there in reality (Mihr, 2021, pp. 54–75). Because of the paradoxical situation – the offender, Russia, was an influential member of the OSCE together, with its allies, such as Belarus and Kazakhstan (at that time) – it seemed that the authority and reputation of the OSCE was compromised, resulting in lower efficacy. Not surprisingly, the IO did not achieve considerable results with its monitoring missions in Donbas (Giardullo et al., 2019, pp. 135–137). It did not make the "Minsk process" a road that led to the resolution of the conflict in Ukraine. The negotiations continued for 8 years with the assumption that they would result in positive results for Ukraine's territorial integrity and regional security. What happened instead is the opposite of those expectations. Finally, the OSCE mediation and the Minsk process were broken down by the Kremlin with the full-scale intervention in Ukraine and the launch of a new stage of the Russo – Ukrainian War on February 24, 2022. Even the staff of the OSCE SMM has suffered from the actions of the Russian occupational forces in the region under Russia's attacks, as they were not spared from violence.

These events mean that the OSCE currently remains a weak and ineffective IO regarding peacekeeping missions and the process of preventing, managing, and resolving conflicts. As Zellner rightly points out:

> Ideally, with its commitment to comprehensive, cooperative, equal, and indivisible security, it is well suited to addressing security questions of all kinds. However, the Organization has been politically sidelined and neglected to such a degree that the greater part of its agenda concerns peripheral issues, with delegations devoting most of their energy to minor battles among themselves. (Zellner, 2020, p. 33)

In general, despite the very important role the OSCE plays in dialogues involving human rights, media freedom, the development of education, gender equality, monitoring elections, etc., it failed to be an effective international organization, capable of preventing conflict, securing and guaranteeing peace, and making the countries that are the source of revisionism, aggression, or war accountable for their irresponsible and aggressive deeds. Thus, for now the future of the OSCE seems unclear.

3.3 *NATO: a Successful Survivor Despite Doubts*

Another type of international organization with authority in the Euro-Atlantic space is NATO. From the perspective of its development, NATO is much luckier compared to the OSCE. NATO came into existence as the Western countries' collective response to the Soviet and communist threat. One must keep in mind that NATO was a kind of international alliance and military block that originated in the Cold War era and was conceived within a bipolar system. Subsequently, NATO served as a counterbalance to the USSR's global domination claims with the core idea of disseminating the socialist revolution worldwide. NATO played a very important role in the Cold War era. Together with the Warsaw Pact, they were polarized balancers of the very delicate equilibrium of the two superpowers, the USA and the USSR, as well as their allies at that time. A turning point for NATO came after the collapse of the Communist Bloc, when Central Europe was undergoing a series of "velvet" revolutions, which liberated the region from communist regimes (Oztig, 2020, p. 2). When the USSR collapsed as well, the discussion about NATO's mission and the sense of its very existence reached its momentum.

The debates revolve around the key issue: Are there rational reasons for keeping up NATO's existence anymore? (Shifrinson, 2020, pp. 344–345). The assumption that those reasons are no longer valid has been swept away with the stormy waves of the Yugoslavian crisis (Ejdus & Kovačević, 2019). Soon after this, any remaining doubts were quashed by open regional conflicts in the post-Soviet space. Finally, they were destroyed by the September 11th terrorist attacks against the USA and others in some European states at the very beginning of the new millennium. These threats proved that proposals to dismiss NATO are premature and rather dangerous, both for the member states of the alliance as well as for the security system of the Euro-Atlantic area (Spohr & Hamilton, 2019, pp. 3–7).

From that moment on, NATO evolved from a military block to a political alliance with new functions and competences. The alliance has undertaken a lot of effort to cooperate with former rivals and foes, for example, establishing the Partnership for Peace program. Despite some positive steps in the early 1990s, NATO enlargement to the east of Europe was soon perceived by the Kremlin as a direct threat to Russia's national interests, security, and defense concerns (Kucharski, 2019, p. 2).

However, it is worth underlining that the new NATO member states from Central and Eastern Europe joined the Euro-Atlantic alliance of their own political will and with clear arguments in favor of such a choice. They feel insecure because of the threat of restoring Russia's power, its pretense to dominate. The Kremlin claims of being an undisputed regional leader obsessed with the idea of regaining the status of a superpower once again by any means induce growing fear in the region. The history of Estonia, Latvia, and Lithuania, as well as the experiences of many Central European countries, made them aware of the threat of Russian occupation and rule. These facts make NATO enlargement not an expansionist move but rather a fully justified reaction of the alliance toward growing revisionism, expansionism, and aggressive policy of Russia (Binnendijk & Priebe, 2019, pp. 1–2, 31–32).

Debates originated because of NATO attempts to go out of the natural geographical area of its responsibility. They concern not only NATO operations and missions to Yugoslavia, especially to Kosovo (Krivokapić, 2019). They also cover NATO missions to Libya. Operations against piracy also took place on the Indian Ocean near Somalia, and the long-standing mission of the alliance to Afghanistan. The Libyan mission was rather a failure after the dismissal and death of Qaddafi (Staack, 2018, pp. 11–12). NATO's operation against piracy (Operation Ocean Shield) involved a coalition of partners and can be evaluated as more or less effective and timely.

The most distanced NATO mission from the natural geographic area of its responsibility was its mission to Afghanistan. Obviously, despite all the efforts (Berdal, 2019), human lives, money, and other resources invested, that mission was a complete failure. One can speculate that the NATO mission to Afghanistan enforced the cooperation of member states, making it more animated and effective. The mechanism evoked because of that mission promoted solidarity and closer cooperation between NATO countries (Johnston, 2019, p. 12).

Comparing the benefits of membership for allied states, NATO is an overtly beneficial IO and military-political alliance for them. One example is the case of Turkey – Greece relations. It is evident that because of their NATO membership, both countries have (to this point) avoided engaging in a direct confrontation. Their interrelations remain tense, due to their disagreement on Cyprus and their dispute over territorial claims to some islands between them. Relations between Turkey and Greece today are closer to hostility rather than true partnership. Still, being loyal members of NATO, both countries understand their responsibilities and appreciate the benefits they receive from their membership in the alliance. Being responsible and loyal members of NATO is important to them both (despite some recent criticisms of the behavior of Turkey) (Goren, 2018).

Regarding the positions of new alliance members, especially from the former Soviet countries and the whole socialist bloc, these countries (such as Estonia, Latvia, and Lithuania) significantly benefit from NATO membership. Otherwise, they would likely fall prey to Russian expansionism very quickly (Veebel & Ploom, 2019, pp. 5–7). Recent NATO activities regarding the Russo – Ukrainian War show that, as an international organization, the alliance supports Ukraine. NATO membership has also urged some hesitant countries to be more active in their backing of Ukraine. The uneasy but still meaningful consensus of NATO countries helps it to be on guard and more effective (Klein et al., 2019).

NATO acknowledges that Russia is a direct threat, with China as a second challenge. These realities mean the NATO reinforcement of vision on global security and threats originated as a reaction to other countries. The most dangerous one is Russia (Connable et al., 2020). Still, the rise of China as a geopolitical actor may not be a direct threat (Nye, 2017), but rather a challenge for NATO solidarity and efficiency in the short term and for the foreseeable future.

NATO has witnessed some internal tensions. Old problems with the USA's centrality and tricky avoidance of military expenditure growth by other European members (Koivula, 2021, pp. 145–147) led to the progressive weakness of those countries' defensive capabilities, including the highly developed ones like France and Germany.

Regarding the Russian political threat and the growing military pressure presently approaching the eastern and southern borders of NATO, the alliance has to be more active and consolidated. It needs to move forward with reform of the organization and attract new members.

It would be reasonable to recall here the lesson of NATO's Bucharest summit in 2008 (Staack, 2018, p. 7), where the leaders of France and Germany (Olech, 2019, p. 4) – Nicolas Sarkozy and Angela Merkel, respectively – blocked the appeal of Georgia and Ukraine to enter NATO and to set up instead an action plan to eventually give them NATO membership. They argued that they did not want to see Georgia and Ukraine as new NATO members because they did not want to irritate Vladimir Putin, the leader of Russia. What followed that public statement? Russia's invasion of Georgia started the same year. Russia, for the first time in its modern history, openly used its military forces against an independent state, which was Russia's partner not only in the UN and in the OSCE, but also in the Commonwealth of Independent States (Georgia quit the organization in 2009). This example also presents an unwise solution against the necessity of fortifying NATO solidarity. To some extent, this was the move that inspired some to suspect these leaders of pro-Russian feelings or, even worse, of being disposed to defending Russia's interests for unclear reasons rather than the national interests of their own countries.

After the new stage of the Russo – Ukrainian War in 2022, NATO must reconsider its strategy regarding Russia and new prospective members from the former USSR. It is very positive that NATO promptly reacted to the appeal for membership from Finland and Sweden. This was a right and timely move which makes NATO stronger. Both countries, with their long histories of neutrality, will be protected by the alliance's collective force when their applications are accepted. NATO solidarity has in any case been confirmed. The new members could join soon, despite reservations expressed by President Recep Tayyip Erdoğan of Turkey (another NATO member) against the membership of these two countries because of their political backing of Turkish dissidents (Kurds, etc.). Notwithstanding that diplomatic turmoil, NATO found a way for a principal solution and both countries were accepted as new members unanimously. The only problem that remains is the ratification of the protocols by all the NATO member states, although hopes exist that the necessary steps can be completed without delay.

Regarding the conditions of the ongoing Russo – Ukrainian War, some priorities of NATO are visible, namely the containment and clear-cut repulsion of Russian aggression, revisionism, and retro-imperial policy. NATO needs to elaborate a new affirmative strategy and implement it as soon as possible. It should be a new efficient policy, enhancing its military and administrative capacity to act faster and stronger and to be as united as ever, securing their borders against existing and potentially emerging threats.

4 The Council of Europe's Role in Dealing with Instability

The Council of Europe (CoE) is one of the oldest post-Yalta European organizations. It became an active promoter of closer cooperation and a generator of solidarity among the European states by sharing the same values of democracy, rule of law, human rights, and respect for other principles of modern democratic lawful states (Brummer, 2012). The 1990s were a successful period for the CoE's ideals as many post-communist countries in Europe strived for membership. Practically all the countries of the former Communist bloc, including new independent European countries of the former USSR, applied for CoE membership. The inclusion of, for example, Russia, Ukraine, Moldova, and the Baltic states into the framework of the CoE promised a new era of peaceful and democratic Europe.

The value of the CoE as a gate toward the EU also played an important role. Therefore, the CoE's standards, norms, legislation, protocols, and other regulations made those countries' move toward democratic transition smoother and easier. The establishment of newly elected institutions, shaping the traditions of a judiciary addressed to the people, their needs and claims, were realized successfully. It was helpful in the promotion of the new standards of education, respect for cultural diversity, and fruitful coexistence and cooperation of different racial, ethnic, and religious communities and individuals. All of them are valuable contributions of that IO into the creation and accessibility of regional and global public goods. The 1990s, after the end of the Cold War, seemed to be a very constructive period in the contemporary history of the CoE (Stivachtis & Habegger, 2011). The moral repute and political authority of the organization was praised and respected practically by all the member countries.

Still the first abruption of this promising trend happened in Belarus with the election to the presidency of Alexander Lukashenko, when a rapid transformation took place from a very fragile and weak democratic institution to an authoritarian regime (Sahm, 2010). The process of acquiring membership to the CoE for Belarus was discontinued. It was a failure on the way towards the pan-European political homogeneity of a democratic transition.

However, this is not the only exception, as other setbacks in post-Yugoslavian countries emerged. The authoritarianism of President Franjo Tuđman in Croatia or problems with democracy in Bulgaria were obstacles as well. Even the recent spread of populism over Europe also shook and challenged democracy globally (Acharya, 2017, pp. 274–275). Again, the very concept of "illiberal democracy," which has been shared and propagated by the leading political forces in Hungary and Poland, emerged as a new challenge. All these events bring in political instability and threat cohesion inside the CoE.

The most significant impact on the CoE's efficiency and legitimacy was Putin's Russia's revisionism and expansionism. The need for a solution to the conflicts in the post-Soviet territory (wars in Georgia and in Ukraine) has complicated the organization's mission. The member states' positions were divided by their stances regarding Russia's behavior in the post-Soviet space. The outlook on all-European security issues and responsibility for maintaining peace were different too (Gawrich, 2017). While hard security issues are not the direct responsibility of the CoE, soft security is part of the organizations' responsibility.

Moreover, when the organization had been established, it neglected the issue of any means of war being acceptable and tolerated. The IO itself is rather a consequence, the instrument of preventing and resolving conflicts which were recognized as the reasons for war after the terrible experience of the two world wars in Europe. Therefore, Russia's stances toward the European standards of international relations, respect for countries' sovereignty, their free choice, their vision of the future, and their way towards the full development of democracy, contradict all of them. The CoE should have played a much more active role in resolving conflicts in the post-Soviet space much earlier.

On the contrary, the members of the CoE have been disoriented and divided regarding Russia's aggressive actions. A particularly dangerous fact is that Russia tried to corrupt the CoE by blackmailing it with its financial contribution and by seducing some member states with different manipulations in recent years. The fact that some politicians in the CoE and some of the member states' leaders tacitly accepted Russia's offer, turning blind eye to reality, deserves public criticism. In principle, these actions come close to agreeing with Russia's annexation of Crimea and with its role in the conflict in Donbas. Russia's propagandistic rhetoric and arguments that there is a civil war in Ukraine and Russia was not a part of the conflict (Mälksoo, 2018, p. 7) were-tolerated by the leadership of the CoE institutions (Committee of Ministers, Parliament, Assembly and to a lesser extent by the Council of Local and Regional Authorities). This fact makes that situation alarming. This indispensable IO, which oversees security and promotion of the high standards of democracy, rule of law, and peaceful cooperation in Europe, tacitly operated in an informal agreement with Russia, an offender, and an aggressive state. Russian policies made the situation all around the post-Soviet space dangerous and moved toward full war escalation in Ukraine. Simultaneously, the Kremlin continues its intent to make Europe disunited and weak (Karlsen, 2019, pp. 7–12).

The CoE overtly failed at preventing the aggravation of the war in Ukraine and changing Russia's political behavior. Finally, right after February 24, 2022, the CoE unanimously expelled Russia from the organization. At the same time, Russia tried to "save face" by making a gesture of withdrawing from the IO by its own choice. First, that break is pitiful for ordinary Russians. For instance, membership in the CoE excluded the use of the death penalty in its member states. It also ensured certain control over elections and the applicability of the Human Rights Court. All of that now seemed to be out in Russia's case, with long-lasting negative consequences for the prospect of democracy and the rule of law in Russia the future (Oxford Analytica, 2022). At the same time, Russia's membership is incompatible with the foundations of the CoE. The membership of the country that openly undermines the basic principles of the CoE, such as European tolerance, responsibility, cooperation, and solidarity, is not acceptable. So far, it is a timely (or maybe belated) and right decision to expel Russia from the CoE (Leach, 2022).

The CoE must learn principal lessons from the cases of Belarus and Russia and try its best to secure Europe as a space of democracy, the rule of law, peace, and solidarity. This is a crossroad in the history of the CoE, on which the direction of its future perspective will depend.

5 The EU's Evolution from an Ever-Closer Union to an Influential Geopolitical Actor

On the European Communities' way to the signing of the Maastricht Treaty and ratification by European leaders, there were continuous discussions centered on security issues. They included an increase of the EU's role and position toward regional and global security and its responsibility before the member states. The EU promoted the idea of a political union in charge of the common foreign and defense policy of the member states. These ideas were laid down as one of the three new pillars built up in the Maastricht Treaty. At the same time, that pillar comprised the idea and mechanism of intergovernmentalism rather than supranationalism regarding security and foreign policymaking. Therefore, these innovations spark further discussions about some issues, including the extent to which the EU has to develop a capacity to be an international actor in the field of foreign and security policy. What kind of guarantees and obligations should it undertake regarding member states? To what extent should it provide an elaborated institutional and legal mechanism of their interaction in those affairs? The willingness and readiness of the EU members to share out those most sensible and considerable responsibilities and delegate their sovereign rights to the supranational level of governance have been very limited. So far, the dominant role of intergovernmentalism and the exclusive position of the European Council in its Common Foreign and Security Policy (CFSP) emerged as a kind of compromise. It combines the necessity to back up the political union with some new responsibilities and competencies in the sphere of international policies and politics, and to fully secure the sovereign rights of the member states to define and to run those policies in the future.

5.1 *The EU as a Global Actor: Its Strengths and Weaknesses*

The Lisbon Treaty brought about important and beneficial legal institutional changes, thus enhancing the very capacity of the EU to act in a more consolidated way and be united in the face of various tasks of international policy and politics. The intergovernmental mechanism of decision-making prevails in the CFSP, and it limits the ability of the EU to advance as an important international player and an influential geopolitical actor. Simultaneously, it poses an obstacle and hampers setting up proactive strategies by the EU regarding global issues like the North/South division, the common efforts in fighting poverty, overcoming the post-colonial burden, etc. Those issues, intrinsically related to public goods, were recognized by the EU as a part of joint responsibility of the member states and the Union in general. In addition, the problems of uncontrolled, illegal migration affected the EU policy and relations with its neighbors (Sójka & Klasa, 2021, pp. 1611–1614), especially Northern African and Asian countries. The EU demonstrates often that it is concerned with resolving those issues. Looking at the process of their resolution, one can agree that the EU plays a very important global role and should be recognized as a principal contributor to the solution for crucial global problems such as poverty, lack of resources and support for the developing countries, the fight against organized crime, and so forth (Petkov & Krastev, 2018). The EU's reaction to climate change also earned praise for its active stance as the most devoted advocate of the concerted efforts of the international community.

However, while dealing with some hard military and security threats, the EU is less successful. Sometimes it has failed to find an appropriate solution and adequate compromise among the member states. For instance, wars in former Yugoslavia seemed to be a certain failure of Brussels regarding the breakdown of that country. The key reason is in the different positions of the member states in search of a better way to resolve those conflicts. The decisive role was given away by the EU in favor of the USA and some other international organizations, while it was primarily the EU whose member states (including Italy, Austria, and Germany) were the most affected by the consequences of those conflicts. They had to deal with flows of refugees, criminals, and other complications at the time and after the Yugoslav Wars. The EU did not face those challenges successfully.

Some other attempts at making the EU more consolidated regarding security issues appear to have finally failed. The EU hesitates a lot at times when discussing the USA's leadership in the areas of responsibility of the two important international organizations: NATO and the EU in Europe. Finally, the discussions have been closed with a compromise. Overlapping membership in organizations as well as the different concerns and visions of the European security and global agenda of conflict prevention contributed to a certain kind of redistribution of powers and competencies among NATO and the EU. So far, NATO remains the most important contributor to the hard security issues, but the EU concentrates mainly on the soft security agenda, including fighting against terrorism (Efrat et al., 2021), the illegal trade of weaponry, the prevention and resolution of regional and subregional conflicts, etc. (Bartnik, 2021, pp. 11–16). That compromise was reached at the end of the 1990s. It serves as a vantage point for drafting and implementing other attempts to make the EU a true global actor.

In the end, it makes sense to touch upon the problems of the EU aiming to reform itself. The debates are also framed with the most difficult dilemma: the choice in favor of its further enlargement or preference to solidify cohesion inside the EU. Both options are related to the EU prospect to be stronger and expansive in its activities. The failure of the constitutional process in the EU undermined the capacity of the Union to transform the integrational community into a more effective and well managed one. The proverbial characteristic of the EU as "an economic giant and political dwarf" reflects a widespread reaction to that paradox. The EU is acquiring more prominence, importance, and influence as an economic power. Still, it remains incompatible, less visible and prominent as a global political power. That situation raises a legitimate question about its governability, especially on security issues (Sperling & Webber, 2019).

A series of consecutive crises that affected the EU and the member states in recent decades was a test to the EU's powerfulness and proactive policy (Kinnvall et al., 2018, pp. 249–250). The economic crisis in 2008, the refugee crisis in 2011, the Ukrainian crisis since 2014, and Brexit after that. Optimistically, these challenges did not signify the end of the EU, of the European integration process, nor of the political union perspective. However, they have uncovered too many loopholes and weaknesses in the organization up to now (Kalniete & Pildegovičs, 2021, pp. 23–25).

5.2 *The Eastern Partnership as a Test for the EU Actors*

The very complicated nature of the European Union as a unique combination of an international organization, a confederation, and a federation, but not a state per se, makes the analysis of the EU's capacity to be a geopolitical actor a very difficult task. The external environment for the EU is growing more complicated. Since 2014, the EU has faced growing tensions with Russia. To its own surprise, it also discovered Russia's foreign policy on the eve of the Vilnius summit of the Eastern Partnership (EaP). Russia's perception of the Eastern Partnership, inaugurated in Prague in 2008 as a new program of the EU, made the Union optimistic before that time. EaP corresponds not only to the Union's vision on the Eastern European dimension of the EU's foreign and security policy. It also answers the appeals of European countries of the post-Soviet region (Crombois, 2019, pp. 90–91). This initiative was modest as to goal setting and limited with incentives and resources attained (Latoszek & Kłos, 2016). It did not correspond fully with the initial, much more ambitious ideals of the

EaP initiators, Sweden and Poland (Latoszek & Kłos, 2016), which framed the program as a kind of new open window of opportunities for aspiring countries who looked at the EU as a strategic partner, the most important ally and the closest neighbor. Three countries announced at that time that they were looking for future EU membership (Ukraine, Moldova, and Georgia, in chronological order).

The Eastern Partnership did not threaten Russia's security. Nonetheless, the Kremlin reacted as though it perceived these steps as a competition and an unacceptable challenge for Russia. Moscow initiated a full-fledged operation of threatening these countries with growing economic pressure, political intimidation, and, finally, open military attack. Before the Vilnius summit of 2013, it was expected that Ukraine, Armenia, Georgia, and Moldova would likely sign association agreements with the EU. However, drawbacks to this prospect emerged quickly. First, Armenia deserted the camp of the pro-European countries of the Eastern Partnership in favor of the Customs Union (nowadays, the Euro-Asian Union, led by Russia). Next, Ukraine faced the attempt of the government of President Viktor Yanukovych to block the European integration course of the country, withdrawing the obligation to sign the Association Agreement. Finally, only Georgia and Moldova signed the Agreement in 2013. All of this meant that it was a turning point for the geopolitical situation in the post-Soviet region (Kruglashov, 2020). Later on, the annexation of the Crimea by Russia, the war in Donbas, and the current so-called Ukrainian crisis have made Russia and the EU no longer strategic partners, as they had officially declared themselves years before. Instead, they are increasingly competitors in the geopolitical arena, full of suspicions and distrust. From February 24, 2022, onwards, almost nobody in the EU treats Russia as a reliable partner or even as a partner at all. Russia is now a principal challenger to the European order, European law, and the European value system. On the one hand, the EU is helping Ukraine in sustaining its statehood and defending its sovereignty in the face of the Russian aggression. This position and actions of the EU are very important and should be appreciated. On the other hand, the latest events of 2022 have illustrated major systemic problems in the EU. For example, the problem of the very slow policymaking process and the deficit of its internal cohesion (Juncos & Blockmans, 2018, pp. 136–138).

Furthermore, a group of so-called "Putin friends" remain a true obstacle to recognizing what the Russian regime in fact is, and what authoritarianism and neototalitarianism in Russia, Belarus, and some other post-Soviet countries means for the EU countries.

Under these circumstances, today the EU must reconsider its strategies and policymaking procedures to reinforce institutional capacity and the role of a united Europe in the region and worldwide vis-à-vis external and internal security challenges (Sperlea, 2019). Without this introspection, the EU will face many more serious and tragic moments in its development. At present, this process has become more apparent in the EU reforms and changes of policymaking procedures. It is a positive development that by supporting Ukraine and Moldova as the frontline states of Russian aggression, the EU tries to rethink its foundations, safeguard its values, and enhance the cooperation mechanisms between the member states.

Georgia, Moldova, and Ukraine applied for EU candidate status, which two of them were granted on 23 June, 2023, with the prospect of future membership. Certainly, this political solution has been colored with a lot of reservations and discussions. Still, it is very important that the EU recognizes both countries as their prospective members. That decision opens a new stage of their relations with the EU and ensures another vision of the EU regarding the Eastern European flank and the dimension of the EU's foreign and security policy.

Hopefully, the tough lessons learned in 2008, 2014, and especially in 2022 will be very carefully analyzed by the EU and the member states' leaders. The EU must be much more engaged in the resolution of existing and predictable conflicts, stimulating the member states' preparedness toward any aggressive action. It also has to strengthen the ability of the EU to be proactive and to guarantee all member states due protection in the sense of common security. Together they must be vigorous promoters of peace deals in the agenda of cooperation, prevention, and resolution of conflicts. Their responsibility in Europe and worldwide will grow substantially because all currents of global politics are of an urgent character. They should not be left unattended and postponed for further hesitation and political procrastination.

6 Conclusions

The global community is facing a situation of fearsome uncertainty, with real possibilities that the Yalta system (as a modernized continuation of the post-Westphalia system) may finally break down and fall apart. The international relations system is much closer to anarchy, rude competition, and war than ever in recent decades – it might even be defined as a "Hobbesian world" (Keohane, 2003 pp. 65–69). It can be observed that many of the international organizations are founded and claim to be proper instruments or mechanisms for securing peaceful conditions of member states' existence and perspectives. They are critically important for securing peace and cooperation, thus to be promoters and safeguards of public goods. The resolution and prevention of conflicts and the exclusion of war from the international relations arsenal are on the global agenda. Unfortunately, none of them except the relations inside IOs such as NATO and the EU are successful in realizing their statutory principles, goals, and tasks, which were the reasons and the rationale for establishing those organizations. Remedies to the weaknesses of the global community architecture are to be invented. Therefore, there is an urgent need to reform the international organizations, starting from the UN, then followed by the OSCE, and concluding with such important regional organizations as the CoE.

For various reasons, the EU and NATO are the leaders and proposers of advocating such reforms. Those reforms require some sacrifices for the self-interest of their member states to reach stable, predictable, and guaranteed peaceful conditions and resolution of conflicts in the European, Euro-Atlantic, and Euro-Asian spaces. They should lead the international community towards restoring the rule of law for all global actors worldwide.

Globally, the UN must be reformed to be unquestionably and effectively democratic, open to the member states' legitimate requests, and equitable regarding the member states' security, development, and concerns. This is a big problem and a true challenge. Yet, this is the best way to be an effective convener of the international organizations, political leaders, and the global community in general.

References

Acharya, A. (2017). After liberal hegemony: The advent of a multiplex world order. *Ethics & International Affairs*, *31*(3), 271–285.

Ade-Ibijola, A. O. (2015). The United Nations Security Council reforms and the permanent five challenge: A historical perspective. *Journal of International Studies*, 11, pp. 131–140.

Archer, C. (2001). *International organizations* (3rd ed.). Routledge.

Bartnik, R. (2021). Diagnosis of threats to the European Union's internal security. *Humanities and Social Sciences*, *28*(3), 7–18.

Bashota, B., & Dugolli, B. (2017). Transformational reforms of the UN peacekeeping system: A genealogical overview. *Analele Universită Ńii din Craiova. Istorie, Anul XXII*, *1*(31), 93–103.

Beisheim, M. (2018). UN reforms for the 2030 agenda: Are the HLPF's working methods and practices "fit for purpose"? SWP Research Paper, 9/2018. Stiftung Wissenschaft und Politik (SWP). https://nbn-resolving.org/urn:nbn:de:0168-ssoar-60443-9

Bengtsson, L., & Rhinard, M. (2019). Securitisation across borders: The case of health security cooperation in the European Union. *West European Politics, 42*(2), 346–368.

Berdal, M. (2019). NATO's landscape of the mind: Stabilisation and statebuilding in Afghanistan. *Ethnopolitics, 18*(5), 526–543. doi.org/10.1080/17449057.2019.1640508

Biersteker, T. J., Eckert, S. E., Tourinho, M., & Hudáková, Z. (2018). UN targeted sanctions datasets (1991–2013). *Journal of peace research, 55*(3), 404–412.

Binder, M., & Heupel, M. (2015). The legitimacy of the UN Security Council: Evidence from recent General Assembly debates. *International Studies Quarterly, 59*(2), 238–250.

Binnendijk, A., & Priebe, M. (2019). *An attack against them all? Drivers of decisions to contribute to NATO collective defense*. RAND Corporation.

Boulègue, M., Lutsevych, O., & Marin, A. (2018, November). Civil society under Russia's threat: Building resilience in Ukraine, Belarus and Moldova. Chatham House. https://www.chathamhouse.org/sites/default/files/publications/research/2018-11-08-civil-society-russia-threat-ukraine-belarus-moldova-boulegue-lutsevych-marin.pdf

Brummer, K. 2012). Uniting Europe: The Council of Europe's unfinished mission. *European Review, 20*(3), 403–418.

Chesterman, S. (2014). Ownership in theory and in practice: Transfer of authority in UN statebuilding operations. In D. Chandler (Ed.), *Statebuilding and intervention: Policies, practices and paradigms* (pp. 17–41). Routledge.

Connable, B., Young, S., Pezard, S., Radin, A., Cohen, R. S., Migacheva, K., & Sladden, J. (2020). *Russia's hostile measures: Combating Russian gray zone aggression against NATO in the contact, blunt, and surge layers of competition*. RAND Corporation.

Crombois, J. (2019). The Eastern Partnership: Geopolitics and policy inertia. *European View, 18*(1), pp. 89–96.

Dabhade, M. S. (2022). India's pursuit of United Nations Security Council reforms. In H. V. Pant (Ed.), *India and global governance: A rising power and its discontents* (pp. 50–68). Routledge India.

Dadashova, R. B. (2019). Perspective of reforms in context of international relations. *EPRA International Journal of Multidisciplinary Research (IJMR), 5*(10), 99–116.

Debuysere, L. (2019). Crisis responders: Comparing policy approaches of the EU, the UN, NATO and OSCE with experiences in the field. *European Foreign Affairs Review, 24*(3), 243–264.

Della-Giacoma, J., et al. (2016). *Global peace operations review: Annual compilation 2015*. Center on International Cooperation.

Đorđević, B., Glišić, M., & Dujić, I. (2018). conflict prevention and resolution under the auspices of the CSCE/OSCE after the Cold War and the Yugoslav crisis. *Review of International Affairs, 69*, pp. 25–49.

Efrat, A., Friedman, M., Hirsch-Hoefler, S., & Magen, A. (2021). *Report on the relationship between terrorist threats and governance conditions in the European Union.*

RECONNECT (Reconciling Europe with Its Citizens through Democracy and Rule of Law). https://reconnect-europe.eu/wp-content/uploads/2021/06/D11.3.pdf

Ejdus, F., & Kovačević, M. (2019). Penetration, overlay, governmentality: the evolving role of NATO in the Western Balkan security dynamics. *Journal of Intervention and Statebuilding, 13*(5), 566–580.

Frantsuz, A. (2020). Central and Eastern Europe: The globalization process, and hybrid threats, viewed through political and legal aspects. *Ukrainian Policymaker, 6*(6), 24–31.

Friesendorf, C. (2020). The OSCE in Central Asia: Debating police-related activities. In Institute for Peace Research and Security Policy at the University of Hamburg (Ed.), *OSCE Insights 2020: Corona, War, Leadership Crisis* (pp. 13–28). Nomos Verlagsgesellschaft. doi:10.5771/9783748922339-01

Gawrich, A. (2017). A bridge with Russia? The parliamentary assemblies of the OSCE and of the Council of Europe in the Russia – Ukraine crisis. In S. Stavridis & D. Jančić (Eds.), *Parliamentary Diplomacy in European and Global Governance* (pp. 156–173). Brill/Nijhoff.

Giardullo, C., Dorn, W., & Stodilka, D. (2019). Technological innovation in the OSCE: The Special Monitoring Mission in Ukraine. In *OSCE Yearbook*.

Goren, N. (2018, January). The NATO/US – Turkey – Russia strategic triangle: Challenges ahead. CISSM Working Paper. Center for International and Security Studies at Maryland. https://cissm.umd.edu/sites/default/files/2019-07/NatoUSRussiaTurkeyStrategic011518.pdf

Guliyev, F., & Gawrich, A. (2021). OSCE mediation strategies in Eastern Ukraine and Nagorno-Karabakh: A comparative analysis. *European Security, 30*(4), pp. 569–588.

Herman, O., & Wouters, J. (2017, December). The OSCE as a Case of Informal International Lawmaking. GGS Working Paper no. 192. Leuven Centre for Global Governance Studies.

Jackson, N. (2019). Deterrence, resilience and hybrid wars: The case of Canada and NATO. *Journal of Military and Strategic Studies, 19*(4), 104–125.

Janev, I. (2020). Recommendation for reforms of the co-ordination in the UN system. *International Journal for Social Science Studies, 8*(3), 116–123.

Jindal, N., & Dhingra, A. (2021). Democracy, security and UN reforms. *Politico, 13*(1), 51–60.

Johnston, S. A. (2019). NATO's lessons. *Parameters – US Army War College Quarterly, 49*(3), Article 4. https://press.armywarcollege.edu/cgi/viewcontent.cgi?article=2771&context=parameters

Juncos, A. E., & Blockmans, S. (2018). The EU's role in conflict prevention and peacebuilding: Four key challenges. *Global Affairs, 4*(2–3), 131–140.

Kalniete, S., & Pildegovičs, T. (2021). Strengthening the EU's resilience to hybrid threats. *European View, 20*(1), 23–33.

Karlsen, G. H. (2019). Divide and rule: Ten lessons about Russian political influence activities in Europe. *Palgrave Communications, 5*(1), 1–14.

Karlsrud, J. (2015). The UN at war: Examining the consequences of peace-enforcement mandates for the UN peacekeeping operations in the CAR, the DRC and Mali. *Third World Quarterly, 36*(1), 40–54.

Keohane, R. O. (2003). Hobbes's dilemma and institutional change in world politics: Sovereignty in international society. In R. O. Keohane, *Power and Governance in a Partially Globalized World* (pp. 77–101). Routledge.

Kinnvall, C., Manners, I., & Mitzen, J. (2018). Introduction to 2018 special issue of European Security: "Ontological (in)security in the European Union." *European Security, 27*(3), 249–265.

Klein, R. M., Lundqvist, S., Sumangil, E., & Pettersson, U. (2019, November). Baltics left of bang: The role of NATO with partners in denial-based deterrence. *Strategic Forum, 301*. Institute for National Strategic Studies.

Koivula, T. (2021). Carry that weight: Assessing continuity and change in NATO's burden-sharing disputes. *Defense & Security Analysis, 37*(2), 145–163.

Koja, C., Raunig, F., & Strohal, C. (2020, October). OSCE at 45: A new spirit of Helsinki. Policy Paper no. 1. Liechtenstein Institute on Self-Determination at Princeton University. https://oar.princeton.edu/bitstream/88435/pr1rv5v/1/October_2020_OSCE_at%20_45.pdf

Костенко, О., & Аметаев, Д. (2021). Современная деятельность ОБСЄ в сфере миротворчества. *International Independent Scientific Journal*, 31, 48–52.

Krivokapić, B. (2019). The NATO bombing of Yugoslavia (1999) 20 years later – The problems of legality, legitimacy and consequences. In N. Vuković (Ed.), *David vs. Goliath: NATO war against Yugoslavia and its implications* (pp. 19–56). Institute of International Politics and Economics.

Kruglashov, A. (2020). Eastern Partnership vis-à-vis challenges and doubts. *Studia i Analizy Nauk o Polityce, 1*, 65–78.

Kruglashov, A. (2021). Eastern Partnership in the system of European (in)security. *Materialele Conferinței științifico-practice internaționale "Spaţiul european de securitate: provocări, oportunităţi, perspective de integrare."* http://Materialele_conferintei_stiintifico-practice_internationale_11_ocombrie_2019_IRIM-with-cover-page-v2.pdf

Kucharski, L. (2019). *Russian multi-domain strategy against NATO: Information confrontation and US forward-deployed nuclear weapons in Europe*. Technical Report no. LLNL-TR-767588. Lawrence Livermore National Lab (LLNL). https://doi.org/10.2172/1635758

Latoszek, E., & Kłos, A. (2016). The Eastern Partnership as a new form of the European Union's cooperation with the third countries. *Studia z Polityki Publicznej, 3*(4 (12)), 177–194.

Latoszek, E., & Kłos, A. (2016). The role of Poland in financing reforms in the countries of the Eastern Partnership. In C.E. Pacheco Amaral, G. Gabrichidze, I. Horga, A. Kruglashov, E. Latoszek, M. Pachocka, V. Cucerescu (Eds.). *EU Relations With Eastern Partnership: Strategy, Opportunities and Challenges*, Chisnau-Chernivtsi-Tbilisi, 77–110.

Leach, P. (2022, March 17). A time of reckoning? Russia and the Council of Europe [blog post]. *Strasbourg Observers*. https://strasbourgobservers.com/2022/03/17/a-time-of-reckoning-russia-and-the-council-of-europe/

Mälksoo, M. (2018). Countering hybrid warfare as ontological security management: The emerging practices of the EU and NATO. *European Security*, *27*(3), 374–392.

Mihr, A. (2021). *Between peace and conflict in the East and the West: Studies on transformation and development in the OSCE region*. Springer Nature.

Nechaeva-Yuriychuk, N. (2010). The frozen conflicts influence on security and energy stability in Black Sea region. In S. Yılmaz (Ed.), *Proceedings of the Third International Symposium on Strategy and Security Studies, 15–16th April 2010: The energy security* (pp. 212–215). Beykent University.

Noonan, J. (2023). Ukraine conflict as a case of the political contradictions of contemporary imperialism. *International Critical Thought, 13*(1), 1–21.

Nye, J. S., Jr. (2017, January/February). Will the liberal order survive? The history of an idea. *Foreign Affairs, 96*.

Olech, A. (2019). Determinants for the international security: Membership of Ukraine in NATO. *International Relations Review, 6*, 1–22.

Oxford Analytica. (2022). Russia exits European court but faces war crimes probe. *Expert Briefings*. https://doi.org/10.1108/OXAN-ES268028

Oztig, L. I. (2020). The transatlantic alliance in the Age of Trump. *Global Change, Peace & Security*, *32*(3), 297–315.

Petkov, M., & Krastev, D. (2018). Pumps for the action on the European Union in the scope of the European agenda on security. *IJASOS – International e-Journal of Advances in Social Sciences*, *4*(11), 448–454.

Prosekov, A. Y., & Ivanova, S. A. (2018). Food security: The challenge of the present. *Geoforum*, *91*, 73–77.

Renz, B. (2019). Russian responses to the changing character of war. *International Affairs*, *95*(4), 817–834.

Rudyi, N., Makarchuk, V., Zdrenyk, I., & Prodan, I. (2021). Democratic state-legal regime: Twenty-First Century threats. *Amazonia Investiga, 10*(44), 288–294. doi.org/10.34069/AI/2021.44.08.28

Sahm, A. (2010). Belarus at the crossroads? Institute for Peace Research. https://ifsh.de/file-CORE/documents/yearbook/english/09/Sahm-en.pdf

Salim, B. G. F. H. (2021, June). A more responsive United Nations Security Council: Necessary reforms. PKSOI Paper. Peacekeeping and Stability Operations Institute (PKSOI).

http://pksoi.armywarcollege.edu/wp-content/uploads/2021/12/A-More-Responsive-United-Nations.pdf

Shelest, H. (2022). From soft security to hard security in the Black Sea Region – Does the OSCE fit? *Security and Human Rights, 32*(1), 106–120. https://doi.org/10.1163/18750230-bja10008

Shifrinson, J. R. (2020). NATO enlargement and US foreign policy: The origins, durability, and impact of an idea. *International Politics, 57*(3), 342–370.

Simonet, L. (2018). The OSCE and NATO: Side by side in a turbulent world. *OSCE Yearbook: Yearbook on the Organization for Security and Co-operation in Europe (OSCE), 23*, 279–313.

Sójka, W., & Klasa, M. (2021). Poland's border as external border of the European Union – Contemporary threats and challenges. In *Сборник: Доклади от Годишна Университетска Научна Конференция, 27–28 Май 2021 Година* (pp. 1604–1638). Издателски комплекс на НВУ "Васил Левски."

Sperlea, M. (2019). European Union internal security – Setting up security conditions against threats for the coming years. *Social-Economic Debates, 8*(2), 1–6.

Sperling, J., & Webber, M. (2019). The European Union: Security governance and collective securitisation. *West European Politics, 42*(2), 228–260.

Spohr, K., & Hamilton, D. (2019). *Open door: NATO and Euro-Atlantic security after the Cold War*. Brookings Institution.

Staack, M. (2018). *Russia, the European Union and NATO: Is a "new normal" possible?* Verlag Barbara Budrich.

Stivachtis, Y. A., & Habegger, M. (2011). The Council of Europe: The institutional limits of contemporary European International Society? *European Integration, 33*(2), 159–177.

Thakur, R. (2016). *The United Nations, peace and security: From collective security to the responsibility to protect*. Cambridge University Press.

Thomas, S., & Kumar, M. (2021). Reforms in reframed world: Can UN survive with a change of guards? *Politico, 13*(1), 85–96.

Veebel, V., & Ploom, I. (2019). Are the Baltic States and NATO on the right path in deterring Russia in the Baltic? *Defense & Security Analysis, 35*(4), 406–422.

Warner, J., & Boas, I. (2019). Securitization of climate change: How invoking global dangers for instrumental ends can backfire. *Environment and Planning C: Politics and Space, 37*(8), 1471–1488.

Weinlich, S., et al. (2022). New rules, same practice? Analysing UN development system reform effects at the country level. Discussion Paper no. 3/2022, Deutsches Institut für Entwicklungspolitik (DIE). https://doi.org/10.23661/dp3.2022

Zellner, W. (2020, November). Using the OSCE more effectively – Ideas and recommendations. Institute for Peace Research and Security Policy at the University of Hamburg (IFSH). https://epub.sub.uni-hamburg.de/epub/volltexte/2021/128436/pdf/20210301_USING_THE_OSCE_MORE_EFFECTIVELY.pdf

CHAPTER 4

The Role of International Organizations in Global Migration Governance: Sustainable Development as a Strategy for Extending Global Public Goods

Leiza Brumat, Diego Caballero Vélez and Marta Pachocka

1 Introduction

This chapter explores how and why sustainable development (SD) is used by international organizations (IOs) as a strategy for boosting international cooperation on migration, increasing the likelihood of providing global public goods (GPGs). Global public goods and institutional approaches have acknowledged that international governance institutions help to overcome collective action problems (Coleman 1988; Ostrom, 1990; Putnam, 1993). Following this argument, we show that IOs deliberately seek to strengthen cooperation on migration by including fragmented issues related to human mobility in other policy areas. This is a strategy for overcoming the absence of a comprehensive international migration regime.

The literature on GPGs demonstrates that the convergence of states' preferences in a certain policy area is crucial for the provision of such goods and that this eventually leads to more robust forms of global governance (Kok et al., 2011; Olson, 1965). IOs play a key role in the provision of GPGs because they facilitate cooperation among states by increasing access to information and by providing "technical" and more "neutral" expertise (Martin & Simmons, 1998). The expert and "neutral" role played by IOs, in turn, helps to overcome the reluctance to cooperation and finding common interests.

The literature on global migration governance has argued that some types of governance can have public goods characteristics. This means that the existence of common norms, rules, and procedures in certain policy areas can produce non-excludable and non-rivalrous benefits (Betts, 2011; Chand & Markowski, 2018; Hollifield, 2012; Suhrke, 1998). However, there are different classifications of the diverse "types" of migration governance through the public goods theory. We build from Betts (2003), Suhrke (1998), and Thielemann (2013) to argue that refugee protection is a global public good because granting international protection to refugees has benefits for all states, even for those that do not provide this protection. This approach helps us to better understand how and

DOI:10.1163/9789004687264_006

why the United Nations (UN) Sustainable Development Goals (SDGs) are strategically "used" by IOs to implement refugee governance policies at the global level. The UN SDGs are a global framework for governance that is perceived as legitimate by the international community and whose benefits could have global reach, contributing to the development of GPGs.

The implementation of the refugee protection regime results in benefits and costs for states. The costs can reduce the complementarity of states' interests (Betts, 2011; Chand & Markowski, 2018; Hollifield, 2012; Suhrke 1998). States follow the calculations and measurements of the potential benefits, as well as the costs of providing protection to forcibly displaced persons. Many times, these calculations may result in states' preferences against international cooperation. In addition to this, the adoption and implementation of international regimes for human mobility have a significant impact on states' sovereignty, and for this reason, states have historically been reluctant to cooperate and to adopt global-level agreements in this agenda (Betts, 2011; Geiger & Pécoud, 2014). However, by agreeing on a common set of standards, the SDGs establish some basic international norms for human mobility. How and why did states agree on adopting these global-level norms on human mobility? What is the role that IOs have played in this process?

It has been widely acknowledged that in the 2030 SDG Agenda, migration is fragmented and referred to in several areas (Crush, 2019; Guild, 2021; Piper, 2017). This is because, given states' reluctance to include one goal on migration, IOs have included migration in several SDGs. The primary goal of this strategy is to broaden the opportunities for cooperation in the highly contested area of global governance, where the convergence of preferences is usually low. By shedding light on the role of IOs in including migration in the SDG agenda, we make two main contributions. First, we expand the literature on global migration governance and on the role of IOs by showing how and why these organizations seek to enhance such global governance as a way of strengthening the fragmented global migration regime as a global public good. Second, we contribute to the debates on international cooperation and the SDGs by looking at the migration agenda.

This chapter is divided into three main sections. In the first one, we explain the crucial role played by IOs in the production of GPGs in the area of migration. In Section 2, building from collective action and constructivist theories, we address how the development and provision of GPGs works in highly contested policy areas such as migration. Section 2 begins by explaining the main characteristics of global migration governance, i.e., its fragmentation and overlaps, overlaps and states' unwillingness to cooperate in the area. In relation to this, Section 2.1 suggests that refugee protection can be seen as an impure global public good. Section 3 shows the way in which migration was included in the UN SDG Agenda and then provides two empirical examples that illustrate how and why two IOs, the United Nations High Commissioner for Refugees (UNHCR) and the European Union (EU), strategically use the SDGs to enhance cooperation on migration and asylum as they seek to improve the provision of global and regional public goods. We conclude with a summary of the key findings and propose future lines of research.

2 The Role of IOs in the Provision of GPGs in Highly Contested Policy Areas

The scholarship on international cooperation identifies the provision of GPGs and the costs and benefits that arise from them as comprising a core element for understanding states' motivations to engage in international cooperation (see Kaul et al., 1999; Kaul et al., 2003). Collective action failure is more likely to happen in highly contested policy areas. For instance, it is frequently the case that in the area of environmental protection, domestic interests such as economic protectionism prevail, and collective action fails. As we explain below, this is also the case in migration. International cooperation and successful collective action in highly contested areas is more likely to happen when certain domestic and international factors combine. On the domestic side, states may choose to cooperate and seek solutions at the international level when they fail to provide public goods at the national level (Betts, 2009; Caballero Vélez & Pachocka 2021; Kaul et al., 2003). On the international side, IOs can be key agents for the promotion of international cooperation and for achieving successful collective action. IOs, which are actors with a relatively high degree of autonomy and legitimacy in their areas of expertise, manage the agenda, adoption, and provision of GPGs, and states ultimately collaborate with such provision.

In this analysis, we consider that public goods are socially constructed and, consequently, their costs and benefits are perceived by states and constrained by institutions (see Betts, 2009; Roberts, 2017, 2019; March and Olsen, 1989). In other words, the identification of a public good as such is a political decision and its provision at the international level depends on the implementation of rules set by the specific international policy regime in a certain policy area. States are more likely to provide GPGs if the perceived utility gained from the public good is high (Roberts, 2019). Conversely, if states' perceived utility is low, there probably will be an underprovision of GPGs. The divergent preferences for the provision of a public good may lead to a lack of consensus on a certain issue and this eventually results in the fragmentation of the issue and in the underprovision of the public good in question (Kok et al., 2011, p. 16). As we explain in this chapter, this is what happens in the case of migration, which, due to its transnational nature, can be addressed from a global public goods perspective.

GPGs are goods whose effects go beyond state borders. They provide non-rivalrous and non-excludable benefits to citizens of more than two countries and in more than two different world regions. The costs and benefits produced by GPGs can spill over transnationally and can have effects at the global level (Sandler, 2006). With their "technical" and more "neutral" expertise, IOs are key in "transnationalizing" public goods, particularly in a highly contested area such as migration. One example of this is the set of international security standards for travel documents (passports). After these standards were adopted, IOs assisted many developing countries in complying with the new security measures and, in turn, this assistance resulted in these countries expanding their capacities for issuing travel documents, which ultimately contributed to facilitating human mobility worldwide (see Andrijasevic & Walters, 2010).

The SDGs can be conceptualized as GPGs due to the global reach of their potential benefits (Huck, 2021; Estevaeordal & Goodman, 2017). The SDGs are a set of objectives that, together, provide a policy framework for governance actors to achieve a more sustainable future and cope with global challenges (Huck, 2021). Their wide acceptance by the international community and the key role of IOs in their implementation provides them with legitimacy and a normative dimension. Indeed, some IOs, such as UN specialized agencies with specific expertise, have the role of "custodian" agencies of certain SDGs. In the fields of migration and refugees, these agencies are the International Organization for Migration (IOM) and the UNHCR. However, it is also the case for some highly institutionalized IOs with a strong regional reach, such as the European Union (EU), which develops its own sustainable development and migration political agendas and corresponding sectoral policies. In addition, conceptualizing the SDGs as GPGs allows for a better measurement of the impact of the policy framework adopted by IOs (Huck, 2021). As we expand on this concept below, these aspects are crucial in migration and displacement, where disagreements are frequent and collective action is rare.

3 Global Migration Governance and the Production of Public Goods

Governance is both a structure and a process (Börzel, 2016; Levi-Faur, 2012). Governance structures are the formal and informal institutions and the actor constellations that govern an issue area. Institutions are norms, rules, and procedures aimed at the provision of collective (public) goods and common rules (Börzel & Van Hüllen, 2015, p. 5). Governance processes consist of the interaction between the actors who design governance institutions. The dynamics of these interactions are shaped by, but also contribute to, shaping actors' choices and preferences (Börzel, 2016; Levi-Faur, 2012, p. 7). Governance structures and processes are inherently linked because institutions constitute arenas for social coordination and interaction and promote specific modes of coordination (Börzel, 2016). The governance concept addresses the processes of governing "beyond the state" that can occur at a transnational level and can have effects at the global, national, regional, and local levels (Geddes, 2021). Indeed, "global" governance is defined not by the level of government but by the effects that governance institutions and processes have on the behavior of states and other transnational actors (Betts 2011, p. 4). Global migration governance does not only happen in international forums, such as UN summits, it can also happen and have effects on people's daily lives by, for example, expanding or constraining their opportunities for obtaining a regular migratory status in a foreign country. For these reasons, "regional" governance is a form of global governance (Brumat et al., 2021). This definition highlights the importance of the structural relations between states, institutions and non-political actors in the governance of international migration.

At the global level, there is no international migration regime, no single institutionalized framework that regulates states' responses to human mobility. This means that states retain a significant degree of autonomy in determining their migration political agendas and corresponding public policies. Global migration governance is characterized by overlapping and fragmented legislation and regimes with different degrees of institutionalization that regulate diverse aspects of migration and different "types" of mobile populations (Hollifield, 2012; Geddes, 2021). The overlapping and fragmented character of global migration governance has powerful effects on individuals' access to rights and mobility (Mau et al., 2012) because these overlapping norms basically create "categories" of persons who have differential access to mobility rights, as different groups of individuals (Cresswell, 2010). For example, there are different mobility rights for "forced" and "voluntary" migrants, and among these, there are many categories, including students and highly qualified workers, but there are also different mobility rights for family members of non-nationals residing in states other than their native one and at the same time, there are different definitions of family (see Geddes et al., 2020). This fragmentation and overlap, as well as the lack of an all-encompassing "global migration regime," act as incentives for promoting ad hoc cooperation and preventing states from achieving wider common consensus. Another example of this fragmentation is so-called environmentally induced migration, which is not regulated in any multilateral norm within the fragmented international migration regime. There is a general consensus that the number of environmental migrants is increasing and will continue to grow yearly (Pachocka & Sobczak-Szelc, 2018). However, there is no precise global estimate of the number of people affected and no consensus on forecasts in this regard.

There are several explanations for the reluctance to cooperate and to agree on a more comprehensive global migration regime. One of these explanations affirms that states' interests are non-complementary because most international migrants reside in Global North countries, so the adoption of global standards has a larger effect on a small number of more developed countries (Pécoud, 2021). Other explanations point at nationalist tendencies (Triandafyllidou, 2021) and sovereignty concerns (Newland, 2010) and yet others focus on the reliance of informal workers with low wages in a large sector of the economy (Pécoud, 2021).

For the purposes of this analysis, we assert that the combination of the wide range of states' interests, ideas. and cost/benefit perceptions about each different "type" of migration results in fragmentation of global migration governance.

3.1 *Refugee Protection as an Impure Public Good*

It has been argued that the (fragmented) global migration governance structures have public goods characteristics (Betts, 2011; Chand & Markowski, 2018; Hollifield, 2012; Suhrke, 1998). Following this argument, some scholars have initiated a heuristic framework based on the innate economic properties of public goods (their publicness or cost-benefit calculus) of the different "types" of migration (see Betts, 2011; Suhrke, 1998; Thielemann, 2018). Betts (2011) identifies the existing global regimes that address different migration "types" and classifies them as specific public goods. These migration types are refugee migration as a public good, irregular and low-skilled migration as a club good, and high-skilled labor migration as a private good.

According to Betts (2011), refugee governance can be seen as a public good, meaning that states can receive non-excludable and non-rivalrous benefits from developing common norms and standards in this area of governance. However, it also means that the free-riding problem may emerge. By irregular and low-skilled migration governance being a "club good," Betts means that the benefits emerging from collective action are non-rivalrous but can be excludable. For example, high-skilled migration governance has excludable and rivalrous benefits for the states that host high-skilled migrants in their territories because, in this case, states perceive private benefits from high-skilled migration (Betts, 2011).

Surhke's seminal article (1998) showed the public nature of refugee protection. Following her argument, states face a double dilemma in situations of massive displacement crises: on the one hand, states are willing to accept refugees for moral/humanitarian reasons but, on the other hand, they seek to reduce the security costs of receiving them into their territories. Further developing this humanitarian–security dichotomy, scholars have identified other benefits such as prestige (Barbou des Places & Deffains, 2003), political stability (Thielemann, 2018) and security (Thielemann & Dewan, 2006). The mentioned benefits can be non-rivalrous because, when a country provides refugee protection to a certain group, spillover to other countries persists (Thielemann, 2018).

Another important characteristic of refugee protection as a public good is the free-riding question (Thielemann & Dewan, 2006). If one state relocates refugees to its territory, other states may perceive benefits from that, without contributing to refugee protection. In migration and refugee protection, in particular, non-cooperation and collective action failure are quite frequent because, as stated above, states' preferences in the area are often divergent. The free-riding problem raises the question of the degree of publicness of refugee protection because the provision of refugee protection by one state may generate excludable benefits for others (see Betts 2003). The degree of publicness is also related to the degree of pureness of refugee protection. "Pure" public goods are unusual because most public goods generate private benefits (Sandler, 1977), so impure public goods partially satisfy one or both of the primary public goods characteristics (non-rivalry and non-excludability). In recent years, scholars have investigated the impure public nature of refugee protection. These investigations conclude with the fact that from granting refugee protection, partial excludable and rivalrous benefits may emanate (see Betts, 2003; Roper & Barria, 2010; Thielemann & El-Enany, 2010). Refugee protection is an impure good because it confers private benefits (Caballero Vélez & Pachocka, 2021, p. 6). This happens because the different "degrees of publicness" generate multiple benefits for different states. For instance, some states that provide humanitarian protection to refugees receive some private benefits, such as international prestige and economic growth. These partial benefits are excludable to the states that grant the status of refugees.

4 Global Migration in the 2030 UN Agenda

Many studies have addressed the relationship between migration and the SDGs, and a large part of this literature has acknowledged the relative "absence" and the marginalization of migration as an SDG (Guild, 2021; Pécoud, 2021; Crush,

2019; Piper, 2017; Sivakumar & Rajan, 2022). There is one goal that is directly related to migration: Goal 10.7 calls for the facilitation of "orderly, safe, regular and responsible migration and mobility of people, including through the implementation of well-managed migration policies." As noted by Guild (2021, p. 358), SDG 10 is aimed at the reduction of inequality within and among countries and, in that context, goal 10.7 is "something of an outlier" in SDG 10. This goal was admittedly a response to the IOM's requests (Ashutosh & Mountz, 2011). SDG 10 also served as a basis for the 2016 New York Declaration that eventually led to the adoption of the two global compacts, the Global Compact for Migration (GCM) (UNHCR, 2022a) and the Global Compact on Refugees (GCR) (UNHCR, 2022b), in 2018. Harrington (2019) stresses that global governance mechanisms and IOs, in particular, are "at the heart" of SDG 10, as enshrined in Goal 10.6, which calls for international institutions to "ensure enhanced representation and voice for developing countries in decision-making in global international economic and financial institutions in order to deliver more effective, credible, accountable and legitimate institutions" (UNGA, 2015, p. 21). Furthermore, the relevance of IOs in the implementation of Goal 10 is crucial because such implementation relies on expertise, coordination and oversight (Harrington, 2019), which are the key roles and tasks that comprise IOs' agency and legitimacy.

The 2030 SDG Agenda emphasizes migrant rights and safeguarding livelihoods. The implementation of the SDGs is a high priority on the international agenda (Guild, 2021). This, together with the fact that other issues on the agenda, especially development, have greater chances of facing less opposition and thus limitations for cooperation and reaching agreement (Guild, 2021, pp. 361–362), which increases the likelihood of countries perceiving a wider set of benefits in the adoption of public goods in the area of development. Development policies can be framed as a form of "managerial" global migration governance. Managerial migration governance (Pécoud, 2021) aims at conciliating diverging interests on migration because the apparently "technical" content of such policies increases its "neutral" appearance, its legitimacy and, finally, the likelihood of it being approved (Brumat, 2020). Together, these factors explain the "linking" of migration to other SDGs and other global governance agendas.

As we show in this chapter, IOs are aware that states' interests are more likely to converge in the SD agenda rather than the migration agenda (see Guild, 2021; Crush, 2019). As a result, many IOs have actively included migration onto their SD agendas in order to broaden the opportunities for cooperation on migration, as we illustrate in the section below.

4.1 *Including Migration in the SDG Framework: the Cases of the UNHCR and the EU*

4.1.1 The UNHCR

How do IOs include international migration governance in the SDGs to develop a more global migration regime? As mentioned above, refugee protection can be seen as an impure public good and therefore this section focuses on the case of the UNHCR. When mapping the most important intergovernmental organizations (IGOs) and their bodies/agencies responsible for managing forced migration, the UNHCR has remained a key actor since the mid-20th century. This is legally established in the UNHCR Statute (UNHCR, 1950), whose Article 1 states that UNHCR

> shall assume the function of providing international protection, under the auspices of the United Nations, to refugees who fall within the scope of the present Statute and of seeking permanent solutions for the problem of refugees by assisting Governments and, subject to the approval of the Governments concerned, private organizations to facilitate the voluntary repatriation of such refugees, or their assimilation within new national communities.

The crucial role of the UNHCR is reinforced by the fact that the only category/type of international migrants with a binding legal definition are refugees, as defined in Article 1A of the Convention Relating to the Status of Refugees from July 28, 1951 (usually referred to as the 1951 Geneva Convention) (UNGA, 1951), in conjunction with the Protocol Relating to the Status of Refugees from January 31, 1967 (usually referred to as the 1967 New York Protocol) (UNGA, 1967).

Article 8 of the Statute clearly indicates that the UNHCR should provide protection to refugees falling under its competence. The first two ways in which the UNHCR should do so are particularly relevant because they include "promoting the conclusion and ratification of international conventions for the protection of refugees, supervising their application and proposing amendments thereto" and "promoting through special agreements with Governments the execution of any measures calculated to improve the situation of refugees and to reduce the number requiring protection" (UNHCR Statute, Articles 8a–b). So, the UNHCR's mandate includes a crucial transnational issue: how to protect refugees and ensure appropriate international standards through common legal and policy frameworks for their safe reception in host countries. The implementation of this overarching task within the specific functions of the UNHCR can be carried out in the context of achieving the SDGs. Linking refugee protection with SDG implementation is even more important in the context of changing international migration flows and an increasingly challenging and complex geopolitical context.

If we look at refugee migration as a component of the broader category of forced migration (also including displacement caused by natural or human-made disasters) (see IOM, 2019), it should be noted that, in many cases, forced migrations are a large-scale and relatively permanent, long-term phenomenon (Pachocka & Sobczak-Szelc, 2018). As illustrated by recent UNHCR data, these features have intensified in recent years – the total number of people forcibly displaced (internally within the same territory or internationally) as a result of persecution, conflict, violence, human rights violations or events seriously disturbing public order increased from 38.54 million in 2011 to 89.32 million in 2021 worldwide (UNHCR, 2022a). In absolute numbers, the most dramatic increase in just one decade was in the number of IDPs (by nearly 31 million), and to a lesser extent in the number of refugees under UNHCR's mandate (by almost 12 million). Moreover, these numbers are likely to increase significantly by the end of 2022 due to the humanitarian crisis in Ukraine caused by the full-scale Russian invasion and aggression against this country since late February.

All this requires a rethinking of forced migration governance within international migration governance, including addressing the needs of migrants and receiving communities and considering the interests and capacities of host countries. Given the reluctance of states to adopt global norms on migration mentioned above, changing the international legal framework in this field (e.g., the 1951 Geneva Convention) to adapt it to the current circumstances seems to be an enormously difficult task. Instead, as seen above, given the perceived utility and legitimacy of development as a global public good, it seems much more feasible to act through the implementation of the SDGs.

The increasing scale, regularity, and persistence of forced migration can be understood as a rapidly and systematically increasing number of forced migrants to a relatively high level on specific migration routes in different regions of the world (e.g., migration from the MENA region to Europe, and specifically to the EU, within the Mediterranean). In light of the increasing numbers of forced migrants in some countries (e.g., Syrian asylum seekers and refugees in Turkey or Lebanon), many states, particularly in the Global South, face the challenge of ensuring appropriate and sustainable conditions for their everyday life, often in the medium to long term. In the cases of sudden increases in forced displacement, this raises challenges for their capacities of providing such public goods due to the costs that these states face for receiving and hosting large groups of people who entered the country in a short period of time.

Only in recent years have we seen an important step towards the development and implementation of a comprehensive, systemic, multi-dimensional, and multi-actor response to the current challenges of refugee migration governance at the international level. On December 17, 2018, the UN General Assembly adopted Resolution A/RES/73/151 affirming the UNHCR-led Global Compact on Refugees and its importance as "a representation of political will and ambition of the international community to operationalize the principle of burden and responsibility sharing, to mobilize the international community as a whole, and galvanize action for an improved response to refugee situations" (UNHCR, 2018b). The GCR follows the overall refugee response framework set out in Annex I of the New York Declaration for Refugees and Migrants, adopted by the General Assembly on September 19, 2016 (A/RES/71/1) (UNHCR, 2018a).

In the New York Declaration, states sought to address migration in general terms, as identified in the SDGs but, due to pressure from the UNHCR and some states, the states finally decided to adopt two separate Compacts: one for Migrants and one for Refugees (Klein Solomon & Sheldon, 2018; Betts, 2018). UNHCR and some governments were concerned about the possible reduction of protection provisions in case that both migration and asylum were addressed together in one global agreement (Klein Solomon & Sheldon, 2018). As Betts (2018) notes, UNHCR followed a strategy of "self-preservation," as it tried to prevent the international refugee regime based on the 1951 Geneva Convention from being undermined in any form because that would also affect UNHCR's mandate (Betts, 2018). As a result of these negotiations, the GCM adopts and develops the principles of "safe, orderly and regular" migration of SDG 10.7.

Even if the GCR is not legally binding and does not legally and institutionally restructure the system of international refugee protection, it provides an important framework based on the political will of various stakeholders for a new approach to managing large-scale refugee situations in line with existing international refugee law (see Gammeltoft-Hansen, 2018). The GCR includes four interlinked and interdependent objectives, including easing pressures on host countries, enhancing refugee self-reliance, expanding access to third-country solutions, and supporting conditions in countries of origin for return in safety and dignity, the achievement of which will be possible thanks to "the mobilization of political will, a broadened base of support, and arrangements that facilitate more equitable, sustained and predictable contributions among States and other relevant stakeholders" (United Nations, 2018b, p. 4). The Global Compacts are relevant for many reasons, but mainly because they give content to the common framework adopted in SDG 10.7 and because they define common norms and standards and a common framework for implementation for migration and refugee protection. This common framework and standards include some goods with potentially non-excludable and non-rivalrous characteristics for people on the move. For instance, all states agreed that migrants and refugees should have access to basic services regardless of their legal status (Kainz et al., 2020). The GCR directly refers to the 2030 Agenda for Sustainable Development framework and strives to link the implementation of the GCR goals with the SDGs. Development challenges concern both the root causes of forced migration and the sustainable reception of refugees in host communities. UNHCR went a step further and made it clear how the GCR and SDGs converge, showing the contribution of the GCR to all 17 specific Goals (except 14) and their relevant Targets (UNHCR, 2022d). Thus, both UN agendas – in refugee migration management and sustainable development – are entirely related, and their implementation is jointly conditioned.

Indeed, given the controversies that arose during the negotiation process of the GCR and especially the GCM (see Espinoza et al., 2018), some governments in their national implementation plans avoid mentioning the Global Compacts and instead refer to the SDGs (Kainz et al., 2020). This is because, as mentioned above, the development agenda is perceived as more legitimate and less controversial than the migration and asylum agenda. Recent studies acknowledge that the GCR (and the GCM) has expanded international migration and asylum policy agendas and pushes some countries into acting in some policy areas in which they had not been active previously (Kainz et al., 2020; Triggs & Wall, 2020). One example is Canada, whose refugee and asylum governance structures were already in line with both Compacts. The GCR and GCM implementation process led Canada to evaluate the performance of the existing policies and check what was potentially missing (Kainz et al., 2020).

The fact that the UNHCR is the "custodian" agency of global refugee governance and that the GCR's underlying legal and normative basis is binding international law (the 1951 Geneva Convention) made its implementation quicker than the GCM (Kainz et al., 2020). Indeed, the UNHCR's political leadership was key for the adoption and for the implementation of the GCR through its organizational culture of strategic thinking and political entrepreneurship (Betts, 2018).

As a result of both the UNHCR's role and the GCR's legitimacy, crucially framed as part of the sustainable development agenda, thousands of pledges were made as part of the GCR implementation, particularly in the areas of burden and responsibility sharing (Triggs & Wall, 2020). Many of these pledges came from countries and other actors who have not traditionally played a relevant role in refugee governance (Triggs & Wall, 2020). Some GCR goals have been prioritized over others by most countries. In practice, the most popular ones are strengthening international cooperation and investing in asylum and protection capacities, both of which create avenues for expanding protection and for generating non-rivalrous and non-excludable benefits. The less popular objectives include increasing employment opportunities for refugees in third countries and increasing efforts to track missing migrants (Kainz et al., 2020).

According to the GCR's mechanism for tracking the implementation of pledges made at the Global Refugee Forum, the total number of pledges was 1,636 at the end of July 2022; 53% of the pledging entities were states, followed by Civil Society Organizations (CSOs) with 24% and IOs at 12%. Among the IOs pledges, those which involved the UNHCR (34% of all entities in this category) prevailed (UNHCR, 2022c). Eight pledges had the status of "fulfilled" and they covered such issues as cooperation and support on restoring refugee family links, FAO/UNHCR cooperation on sustainable agricultural livelihoods for refugees and other persons of concern to UNHCR in Eastern and Central Africa, support for refugee children, or strengthening the refugee status determination (RSD) procedure in the Republic of Ecuador. As we can see, these pledges are related to a wide range of issues, from material and/or technical support to legal and policy aspects, including issues dedicated to individual countries and regions, so they effectively link asylum and forced migration to a broad range of other policy areas. This shows the enormous potential of various actors, including IOs, to influence migration governance through the implementation of specific projects in line with the SDGs.

4.1.2 The European Union

Cooperation on asylum and refugees, together with external border control and irregular migration, is the most developed area of EU migration policy (Geddes et al., 2020). Refugee protection is the cornerstone of the EU's asylum policy. In general, from the legal perspective, three basic components of EU migration policy – three specific/sectoral EU policies – are asylum (international protection) policy, immigration policy, and policy on border checks (border management) (Pachocka & Caballero Vélez, 2022; Caballero Vélez & Pachocka, 2021). They are part of the EU's area of freedom, security, and justice, which is subject to shared competences between the EU and its member states (Article 4(2)(j) TFEU), which means that both parties "may legislate and adopt legally binding acts in that area" (Article 2(2) TFEU), in line with the principle of subsidiarity (Pachocka & Caballero Vélez, 2022). The legal basis and general framework for EU asylum policy is rooted in EU primary law: Articles 67(2), 78 and 80 of the Treaty on the Functioning of the European Union and Article 18 of the EU Charter of Fundamental Rights. This is expanded and detailed by EU secondary law and supplementary sources, such as unilateral acts of law (e.g., directives, regulations), international agreements, and case law of the Court of Justice of the EU (CJEU) (Pachocka & Caballero Vélez, 2022).

The process of EU-level harmonization of asylum policy began in the 1990s. The basis of the Common European Asylum System (CEAS) was defined in 1999 with the twofold objective of harmonizing policies in the short term with the ultimate goal of establishing a common asylum procedure and uniform legal status of international protection throughout the EU. The rationale behind this was that the creation of a common market and a common political space where internal borders were inexistent and required an integrated response to migration (Geddes et al., 2020, pp. 115–118). To do this, the EU developed five policy instruments:

1. The Dublin regulation, which determines which state is responsible for examining asylum claims
2. Common standards of reception of asylum seekers, set out in the Reception Conditions Directive
3. Common procedures for the examination, granting and withdrawal of protection, defined in the Asylum Procedures Directive
4. Common criteria to qualify for refugee status or subsidiary protection, included in the Qualifications Directive
5. Mechanisms for temporary protection and assistance to respond to sudden and high numbers of arrivals, established in the Temporary Protection Directive (Geddes et al., 2020, pp. 116–117) and used for the first time in 2022 to provide a legal status to forced migrants from Ukraine

Despite these policy and legislative efforts, harmonization remained incomplete. The uneven implementation, together with highly asymmetrical costs for member states and wide divergence in the ideas that drive policy adoption and implementation on asylum has led to the CEAS having both restrictive elements and a strong protection framework (see Geddes et al., 2020). This uneven policy implementation, in many states, is not compatible with EU asylum, and migration law, the EU Charter of Fundamental Rights and the UN Global Compact on Refugees (Carrera et al., 2021; Pachocka & Caballero Vélez, 2022). So, to overcome this problem and to strengthen the Common European Asylum System (CEAS), on 23 September 2020, the European Commission (EC) launched the New Pact on Migration and Asylum (NPMA) as a follow-up to the previous EU migration strategy expressed in the EC's European Agenda on Migration (EAM) from May 13, 2015 (Pachocka & Caballero Vélez, 2022). The NPMA's main goal is to set up a common European framework for the management of migration and asylum policy (Carrera et al., 2021). As the EC stated in the introduction to its new strategy:

> Key societal challenges faced by the world today – demography, climate change, security, the global race for talent, and inequality – all have an impact on migration. Policy imperatives such as free movement in the Schengen area, safeguarding fundamental rights, ensuring security, and filling skills gaps, all call for an effective migration policy. The task facing the EU and its member states, while continuing to address urgent needs, is to build a system that manages and normalizes migration for the long term and which is fully grounded in European values and international law. (EC, 2020)

One of the most important aspects of the Pact linked to the UN SDGs is the implementation of the UN GCR. The Pact implicitly refers to "sustainable protection" providing an "end-to-end approach needed to make migration management in Europe fair, efficient and sustainable" (EC, 2020). By including this reference to sustainable protection, the Pact provides a clear case of how the EU implements some elements of the UN SDGs in its legislation. From a public goods perspective, the implementation of sustainable development in asylum policy could help in overcoming the lack of cooperation in the provision of refugee protection. This could be witnessed the case with the temporary relocation scheme of 2015–2017 for asylum seekers from Italy and Greece during the migration and refugee management crisis in the EU (see Pachocka & Caballero Vélez, 2022).

As refugee protection is covered by the scope of the EU asylum policy, which is subject to shared competence under EU law (Article 4 TFEU), as explained above, member state governments include/adopt the European legal framework into national legislation in different ways depending on the type of legal document, e.g., a directive or regulation or other form, to make it coherent across the EU as much as possible.

So far, under current legal and policy settings, this situation renders ineffective provision of refugee protection by the EU, as reflected during the challenges related to the implementation of the relocation scheme in 2015–2017. Consequently, as we assert in this chapter, the implementation of the UN Global Compacts can be seen as an attempt by the EU to overcome divergences on policy costs between the member states.

5 Conclusions

This chapter has shown how and why IOs actively include forced migration on the SDG agenda to broaden the possibilities of increasing international cooperation on the topic and eventually providing GPGs. Global migration governance is highly fragmented and consists of overlapping regimes that address different aspects of human mobility, or different migration "types." In this challenging context, UNHCR and IOM actively pushed for the adoption of two separate international agreements, the GCR and the GCM, within the framework of the SDGs implementation because the global sustainable development agenda is more legitimate, and less controversial, than the (forced) migration agenda. By doing so, the possibilities of providing GPGs such as more equal rights for refugees and asylum seekers, increased labor opportunities, and more international solidarity are increased. The UNHCR, the "custodian agency" of the international refugee regime, played a key role in linking the GCR to the SDGs and continues to play a crucial role in the implementation of this action, actively linking issues such as sustainable livelihoods to the global asylum agenda. We have also shed light on the way in which the EU New Pact on Migration and Asylum is framed and includes elements of the UN Global Compact for Refugees, which builds from the UN Sustainable Development Goals. Importantly, some relevant aspects of the Pact, such as the external dimension of the EU, put emphasis on the importance of treating migration in a "sustainable manner." We suggest that EU member states would be more willing to adopt and internalize the Pact if migration and asylum are more closely linked to the SDGs. By applying a public goods approach to migration and asylum governance, we can observe that EU member states have similar incentives when cooperating in the field of SDGs and, at the same time, those similar incentives can be translated to the migration and asylum policy agenda. This would reduce the perceived costs and facilitate the provision of refugee protection.

Future research that explores the roles of other IOs, such as the International Labour Organization (ILO) or the United Nations Development Programme (UNDP), whose mandate does not directly include (forced) migrants, could shed further light on the linkage processes and the mechanisms used by IOs to provide GPGs and enhance global migration governance.

References

Andrijasevic, R., & Walters, W. (2010). The International Organization for Migration and the international government of borders. *Environment and Planning D: Society and Space, 28*(6), 977–999. https://doi.org/10.1068/d1509

Ashutosh, I., & Mountz, A. (2011). Migration management for the benefit of whom? Interrogating the work of the International Organization for Migration. *Citizenship Studies, 15*(1), 21–38. https://doi.org/10.1080/13621025.2011.534914

Barbou des Places, S., & Deffains, B. (2003). Cooperation in the shadow of regulatory competition: The case of asylum legislation in Europe. *International Review of Law and Economics, 23*(4), 345–364. https://doi.org/10.1016/j.irle.2003.07.001

Betts, A. (2003). Public goods theory and the provision of refugee protection: The role of the joint-product model in burden-sharing theory. *Journal of Refugee Studies, 16*(3): 274–296. https://doi.org/10.1093/jrs/16.3.274

Betts, A. (2009). *Protection by persuasion: International cooperation in the refugee regime*. Cornell University Press.

Betts, A. (2011). *Global migration governance*. Oxford University Press.

Betts, A. (2018). The global compact on refugees: Towards a theory of change? *International Journal of Refugee Law, 30*(4), 623–626. https://doi.org/10.1093/ijrl/eey056

Börzel, T. A. (2016). Theorizing regionalism: Cooperation, integration and governance. In T. A. Börzel & T. Risse (Eds.), *The Oxford handbook of comparative regionalism* (pp. 41–63). Oxford University Press.

Börzel, T. A., & Van Hüllen, V. (2015). Towards a global script? Governance transfer by regional organizations. In T. A. Börzel & V. van Hüllen (Eds.), *Governance transfer by regional organizations: Patching together a global script* (pp. 3–21). Palgrave Macmillan.

Brumat, L. (2020). Four generations of regional policies for the (free) movement of persons in South America (1977–2016). In G. Rayp, I. Ruyssen, & K. Marchand (Eds.), *Regional integration and migration governance in the Global South* (pp. 153–176). Springer International. https://doi.org/10.1007/978-3-030-43942-2_7

Brumat, L., Geddes, A., & Pettrachin, A. (2021). Making sense of the global: A systematic review of globalizing and localizing dynamics in refugee governance. *Journal of Refugee Studies, 35*(2), 827–848.

Caballero Vélez, D., & Pachocka, M. (2021). Producing public goods in the EU: European integration processes in the fields of refugee protection and climate stability. *European Politics and Society, 22*(1), 1–18. https://doi.org/10.1080/23745118.2020.1791458

Carrera, S., Vosyliute, L., Brumat, L., & Feith Tan, N. (2021). Implementing the United Nations Global Compact on Refugees? Global asylum governance and the role of the European Union. Policy Brief 2021/26. Migration Policy Centre/Schuman Centre of Advanced Studies, European University Institute.

Chand, S., & Markowski, S. (2018). ANZ–Pacific migration governance system. *International Migration, 57*(5): 294–308. https://doi.org/10.1111/imig.12524

Coleman, J. S. (1988). Social capital in the creation of human capital. *American Journal of Sociology, 94*, 95–120.

Collignon, Stefan. (2017). *The governance of European public goods*. Palgrave Macmillan.

Cresswell, T. (2010). Towards a politics of mobility. *Environment and Planning D: Society and Space, 28*(1), 17–31. https://doi.org/10.1068/d11407

Crush, J. (2019). Achieving the Sustainable Development Goals. In S. Dalby, S. Horton, R. Mahon, & D. Thomaz (Eds.), *The problem with international migration and sustainable development* (pp. 85–99). Routledge. https://doi.org/10.4324/9780429029622-6.

Deutschmann, E. (2020). Visualizing the regionalized structure of mobility between countries worldwide. *Socius* 6(January): 2378023120958564. https://doi.org/10.1177/2378023120958564

Espinoza, M. V., Hadj-Abdou, L., & Brumat, L. (2018, December 7). Global compact for migration: What is it and why are countries opposing it?" *The Conversation.* http://theconversation.com/global-compact-for-migration-what-is-it-and-why-are-countries-opposing-it-106654

Estevadeordal, A., & Goodman, L. W. (Eds.). (2017). *21st century cooperation: Regional public goods, global governance, and sustainable development.* Routledge.

European Commission (EC). (2020). Communication from the Commission to the European Parliament, the Council, the European Economic and Social Committee and the Committee of the Regions on a New Pact on Migration and Asylum (COM/2020/609 final).https://eur-lex.europa.eu/legal-content/EN/TXT/?uri=COM%3A2020%3A609%3AFIN

European Union. (2016). Consolidated versions of the Treaty on European Union and the Treaty on the Functioning of the European Union. (2016/C 202/01). https://eur-lex.europa.eu/legal-content/EN/TXT/?uri=celex%3A12016ME%2FTXT

Fuest, C., & Pisani-Ferry, J. (2019). A primer on developing European public goods. EconPol Policy Report 16). European Network of Economic and Fiscal Policy Research (EconPol). https://www.econpol.eu/sites/default/files/2019-11/EconPol_Policy_Report_16_2019_EuropeanPublicGoods-v2.pdf

Gammeltoft-Hansen, T. (2018). International cooperation on migration control: Towards a research agenda for refugee law. *European Journal of Migration and Law,* 20(4).

Geddes, A. (2021). *Governing migration beyond the state: Europe, North America, South America, and Southeast Asia in a global context.* Oxford University Press.

Geddes, A., Hadj Abdou, L., & Brumat, L. (2020). *Migration and mobility in the European Union.* Palgrave Macmillan.

Geiger, M., & Pécoud, A. (2014). International organisations and the politics of migration. *Journal of Ethnic and Migration Studies, 40*(6), 865–887. https://doi.org/10.1080/1369183X.2013.855071

Guild, E. (2021). Why the Sustainable Development Goals? Examining international cooperation on migration. In C. Dauvergne (Ed.), *Research handbook on the law and politics of migration* (pp. 355–368). Edward Elgar. https://www.elgaronline.com/view/edcoll/9781789902259/9781789902259.00037.xml

Harrington, A. R. (2019). Global governance and the Sustainable Development Goals. In S. Dalby, S. Horton, R. Mahon, & D. Thomaz (Eds.), *Achieving the Sustainable Development Goals: Global governance challenges* (pp. 240–254). Routledge.

Hollifield, J. F. (2012). Migration and international relations. In M. R. Rosenblum & D. J. Tichenor (Eds.), *The Oxford handbook of the politics of international migration*. Oxford University Press.

Huck, W. (2021). The UN Sustainable Development Goals and the governance of global public goods: The quest for legitimacy. In M. Iovane, F. M. Palombino, D. Amoroso, & G. Zarra (Eds.), *The protection of general interests in contemporary international law* (pp. 344–362). Oxford University Press. https://doi.org/10.1093/oso/9780192846501.003.0015

IOM. (2019). Glossary on migration. International Organization for Migration (IOM). https://publications.iom.int/system/files/pdf/iml_34_glossary.pdf

Kainz, L., Banulescu-Bogdan, N., & Newlandm, K. (2020, December 10). The divergent trajectories of the global migration and refugee compacts: Implementation amid crisis [blog post]. *Migration Policy Institute*. https://www.migrationpolicy.org/research/divergent-trajectories-global-migration-refugee-compacts

Kaul, I., Conceição, P., Le Goulven, K., & Mendoza, R. U. (2003). Why do global public goods matter today?" In I. Kaul, P. Conceição, K. le Goulven, & R. U. Mendoza (Eds.), *Providing global public goods: Managing globalization* (pp. 2–20). Oxford University Press.

Kaul, I., Grunberg, I., & Stern, M. A. (1999). Defining global public goods. In I. Kaul, I. Grunberg, & M. A. Stern (Eds.), *Global public goods: International cooperation in the 21st century* (pp. 2–19). Oxford University Press.

Klein Solomon, M., & Sheldon, S. (2018). The global compact for migration: From the Sustainable Development Goals to a comprehensive agreement on safe, orderly and regular migration. *International Journal of Refugee Law, 30*(4), 584–590. https://doi.org/10.1093/ijrl/eey065

Kok, M., Brons, J., & Witmer, M. (2011). A global public goods perspective on environment and poverty reduction: Implications for Dutch foreign policy. PBL Netherlands Environmental Assessment Agency. https://www.pbl.nl/sites/default/files/downloads/A-global-public-goods-perspective-on-environment-and-poverty-reduction-555075001.pdf

Levi-Faur, D. (2012). From "big government" to "big governance"? In *The Oxford handbook of governance*, edited by D. Levi-Faur (pp. 3–18). Oxford: Oxford University Press.

March, J. G., & Olsen, J. P. (1989). *Rediscovering institutions*. Free Press.

Martin, L. L., & Simmons, B. A. (1998). Theories and empirical studies of international institutions. *International Organization, 52*(4), 729–757. https://doi.org/10.1162/002081898550734

Mau, S., Brabandt. H., Laube, L., & Roos, C. (2012). *Liberal states and the freedom of movement: Selective borders, unequal mobility*. Palgrave.

Newland, K. (2010). The governance of international migration: Mechanisms, processes, and institutions. *Global Governance, 16*(3), 331–343.

Olson, M. (1965). *The logic of collective action: Public goods and the theory of groups*. Harvard University Press.

Ostrom, E. (1990). *Governing the commons: The evolution of institutions for collective action*. Cambridge: Cambridge University Press.

Pachocka, M., & Caballero Vélez, D. (2022). Exploring migration challenges in Europe after 2014: What is the direction of EU migration management and policy?" Unpublished chapter submitted for review.

Pachocka, M., & Sobczak-Szelc, K. (2018). Migracje przymusowe [Forced migration]. In M. Lesińska & M. Okólski (Eds.), *25 wykładów o migracjach* [25 lectures on migration] (pp. 334–351). Scholar.

Pécoud, A. (2021). Narrating an ideal migration world? An analysis of the Global Compact for safe, orderly and regular migration. *Third World Quarterly, 42*(1), 16–33.

Piper, N. (2017). Migration and the SDGs. *Global Social Policy, 17*(2), 231–238. https://doi.org/10.1177/1468018117703443

Putnam, R. (1993). What makes democracy work? *National Civic Review, 82*(2), 101–107.

Ratha, D. (2016). *Migration and Remittances Factbook 2016*. 3rd ed. The World Bank. https://doi.org/10.1596/978-1-4648-0319-2

Roberts, J. C. (2017). What do rules do? Making room for rationality in constructivist thought. In H. D. Gould (Ed.), *The art of world making: A Festschrift in honor of Nickolas G. Onuf* (pp. 80–90). Routledge.

Roberts, J. C. (2019). *Constructing global public goods*. Lexington Books.

Roper, S. D., & Barria, L. A. (2010). Burden sharing in the funding of the UNHCR: Refugee protection as an impure public good. *Journal of Conflict Resolution, 54*(4), 616–637. doi:10.1177/0022002710364131

Sandler, T. (1977). Impurity of defence: An application of the economics of alliances. *Kyklos, 30*(3), 443–460. https://doi.org/10.1111/j.1467-6435.1977.tb02203.x

Sandler, T. (2006). Regional public goods and international organizations. *Review of International Organization*, 1(1), 5–25.

Sivakumar, P., & S. Rajan, I. (Eds.). (2022). *Sustainable Development Goals and migration*. Routledge.

Suhrke, A. (1998). Burden-sharing during refugee emergencies: The logic of collective versus national action. *Journal of Refugee Studies, 11*(4), 396–415. https://doi.org/10.1093/jrs/11.4.396

Thielemann, E. (2018). Why refugee burden-sharing initiatives fail: Public goods, free-riding and symbolic solidarity in the EU. *Journal of Common Market Studies, 56*(1), 63–82. https://doi.org/10.1111/jcms.12662

Thielemann, E., & Armstrong, C. (2013). Understanding European asylum cooperation under the Schengen/Dublin system: A public goods framework. *European Security, 22*(2), 148–164. https://doi.org/10.1080/09662839.2012.699892

Thielemann, E, & Dewan, T. (2006). The myth of free-riding: Refugee protection and implicit burden-sharing. *West European Politics, 29*(2), 351–369.

Thielemann, E., & El-Enany, N. (2010). Refugee protection as a collective action problem: Is the EU shirking its responsibilities? *European Security, 19*(2), 209–229. https://doi.org/10.1080/09662839.2010.531708

Triandafyllidou, A. (2021). The global governance of migration: Towards a "messy" approach. *International Migration, 60*(4), 19–27. https://doi.org/10.1111/imig.12931

Triggs, G. D., & Wall, P. C. J. (2020). "The makings of a success": The global compact on refugees and the inaugural Global Refugee Forum. *International Journal of Refugee Law, 32*(2), 283–339. https://doi.org/10.1093/ijrl/eeaa024

UNGA. (1951). Convention relating to the status of refugees, 28 July 1951. United Nations General Assembly. https://www.refworld.org/docid/3be01b964.html

UNGA. (1967). Protocol relating to the status of refugees, 31 January 1967. United Nations General Assembly. https://www.refworld.org/docid/3ae6b3ae4.html

UNGA. (2015). Resolution adopted by the General Assembly on 25 September 2015 (A/Res/70/1). United Nations General Assembly. https://www.un.org/en/development/desa/population/migration/generalassembly/docs/globalcompact/A_RES_70_1_E.pdf

UNHCR. (1950). Statute of the Office of the United Nations High Commissioner for Refugees: General Assembly Resolution 428 (V) of 14 December 1950. United Nations High Commissioner for Refugees. https://www.unhcr.org/en-us/protection/basic/3b66c39e1/statute-office-united-nations-high-commissioner-refugees.html

UNHCR. (2018a). The New York Declaration for Refugees and Migrants: Answers to frequently asked questions. United Nations High Commissioner for Refugees. https://www.unhcr.org/en-lk/584689257.pdf

UNHCR. (2018b). Resolution adopted by the General Assembly on 17 December 2018. United Nations High Commissioner for Refugees. https://www.unhcr.org/en-us/excom/unhcrannual/5c4088f44/resolution-adopted-general-assembly-17-december-2018.html

UNHCR. (2022a). Figures at a glance. United Nations High Commissioner for Refugees. Accessed August 15, 2022. https://www.unhcr.org/figures-at-a-glance.html

UNHCR. (2022b). The global compact on refugees: Digital platform. United Nations High Commissioner for Refugees. Accessed August 15, 2022. https://globalcompactrefugees.org/article/global-compact-refugees

UNHCR. (2022c). Pledges & contributions: The global compact on refugees: Digital platform. United Nations High Commissioner for Refugees. Accessed August 15, 2022. https://globalcompactrefugees.org/channel/pledges-contributions

UNHCR. (2022d). The Sustainable Development Goals and the Global Compact on Refugees: Working together to ensure that refugees and host communities are not left behind. United Nations High Commissioner for Refugees. Accessed August 15, 2022. https://www.unhcr.org/5efcb5004

United Nations. (2018a). Global compact for migration. International Organization for Migration (IOM). Accessed August 15, 2022. https://www.iom.int/global-compact-migration

United Nations. (2018b). Global compact on refugees. https://globalcompactrefugees.org/sites/default/files/2019-12/Global%20compact%20on%20refugees%20EN.pdf

CHAPTER 5

Public Goods at Risk: The Crisis of the Rule of Law in the European Union in Light of the Violation of the Fundamental Rights of LGBT Persons

Angela Maria Romito and Aleksandra Szczerba

1 Introduction

The purpose of this chapter is to examine the rule of law crisis in the European Union, using the examples of Polish and Hungarian actions violating the fundamental rights of LGBT persons[1] and to evaluate the efficiency of the institutional mechanisms under EU law to respond to these actions. The issue is not simply theoretical since the recent controversies emerging from human rights and rule of law backsliding in Poland and Hungary have turned this question to one of the core issues of the European project and are critical to the Union's legitimacy.

The analysis particularly considers the approaches adopted by the EU institutions to the protection of the rule of law as the backbone of any modern democratic system. The threat to equality and respect for the dignity and human rights of individuals as core values of the EU will be illustrated with two examples. The first is the "LGBT ideology-free zones" in Poland. The second is the recent law adopted in Hungary that limits access for individuals under 18 to content that promotes or portrays the "divergence from self-identity corresponding to sex at birth, sex change or homosexuality." Consequently, the first section of this chapter provides an overview of the existing EU mechanisms which aim to guarantee the rule of law and, along with it, fundamental rights. The next section analyzes the EU response to Polish and Hungarian anti-LGBT actions[2]. Finally, in the conclusion the adequacy of the EU's use of financial sanctions to protect EU foundational values will be assessed.

The analysis in this chapter is made in the context of public goods theory. In the view of the authors, both categories under scrutiny, i.e., the rule of law and

1 "LGBT" is used in this chapter as an acronym for lesbian, gay, bisexual, transgender persons, and any other persons of diverse sex, diverse sexual orientation, or diverse gender.
2 Reflecting the state of the art as to the date of the submitting the chapter in April 2022.

human rights (including the right to non-discrimination), may be considered as public goods (Enderle, 2021, pp. 148–158).

2 Rule of Law and Non-Discrimination: Basic Characteristic of the EU Legal System

The concepts of the rule of law and fundamental rights may be said to be dynamic if not "famously elusive" concepts, whose boundaries remain relatively unclear. It is clear, however, that the two concepts – together with democracy – are intrinsically linked with each other in a triangular relationship (European Commission European Parliament, 2014): the absence of democracy is a clear violation of human rights and the respect of the rule of law is the prerequisite for their protection. In other words, democracy relates to the involvement of the people in the decision-making process in a society; human rights seek to protect individuals from arbitrary and excessive interference with their freedoms and liberties and to secure human dignity; the rule of law promotes democracy by limiting and independently reviewing the exercise of public powers.

Therefore, the rule of law constitutes the backbone of every modern constitutional democracy and respect for it is integral to and necessary for any democratic society. Not surprisingly, therefore, it has become a dominant organizational paradigm of modern constitutional law and is commonly recognized as a key principle at national and international levels to regulate the exercise of public power (European Commission, 2014, p. 2).

The rule of law – considered as an overarching notion, encompassing various legal concepts – is central both to the national constitutional orders of European States and to the EU, as respect for it is one of the requirements to join the European Union (Preambles to the Treaty, Article 2 of Treaty on European Union (TEU), and 49 Charter of Fundamental Rights of the EU).[3]

3 It has therefore played a significant role in the enlargement process of the EU. The so-called Copenhagen criteria (which include compliance with the values in Article 2 TEU), were established in 1993 as a means of assessing whether Candidate States were eligible to accede to the EU, including the rule of law. That notwithstanding, problems arise since no similar method exists to supervise adherence to these foundational principles after accession. In the literature this has been referred to as the "Copenhagen dilemma." It was only 2021 that, for the first time, the European Union Court of Justice (in *Repubblika v Il-Prim Ministru*, Case C-896/19 ECLI:EU:C:2021:311) established the principle of "non-regression" according to which member states cannot fall beneath the minimum standard of compliance with the Article 2 TEU values which they reached in the course of the

2.1 *Rule of Law: Looking for a Definition*

The rule of law is commonly referred to, but it is seldom defined (Magen, 2016). At first, it seems to be a self-evident and self-explanatory concept: in every legal system, the law must be the rule and without rule of law, rights remain lifeless paper promises. Beside such a tautological definition, at closer inspection it is a complex, flexible, and contested concept, which can be defined in different ways depending on the historical and institutional context. As a first and general approximation, the rule of law ensures that all public authorities act within the constraints of law, in accordance with the values of democracy and fundamental rights, and under the control of independent and impartial courts (Craig, 1997).[4]

Although it has become a global ideal and aspiration, internationally there is still no shared notion: it appears in several treaties but also in soft law; the Venice Commission[5] first addressed the issue in a report adopted in 2011 and it reached the conclusion that the rule of law was indefinable (Craig, 2017; Bartole, 2020). It therefore took a pragmatic and empirical approach and concentrated on identifying the core elements of the rule of law by enumerating its common features in a checklist intended as a comprehensive tool to assess the degree of respect for the rule of law in each state.[6]

In the EU, even before its formal recognition in the founding Treaties, the value of the rule of law was repeatedly affirmed by the Court of Justice of the European Union (CJEU) since 1986.

---

pre-accession exercise, making them suitable for European Union membership (Leloup, M., Kochenov, D., & Dimitrovs, A. 2021).

4 From an academic point of view, at the heart of the struggle for conceptualization of the rule of law lies a fundamental choice between what has been variably called "formal" and "substantive," "negative" and "positive," or "rule-book" as opposed to "rights-based" narrow ("thin") and comprehensive approaches ("thick"). Formal, or thin, conception focuses rather on procedural safeguards of the law, due process principles, and evidence rules, and more generally to all the conditions necessary for law to restrict sheer arbitrariness in the use of public power. In a thick, or "democratic rule of law," conception, laws enshrine and protect political and civil liberties as well as procedural guarantees: the rule of law cannot be divorced from political morality, fundamental rights, or democracy.

5 The Venice Commission, officially named the European Commission for Democracy through Law, is the Council of Europe's advisory body on constitutional matters (see http://www.venice.coe.int/WebForms/pages/?p=01_Presentation). See also the European Commission for Democracy through Law (Venice Commission) Rule of Law Checklist.

6 Those core elements are the principle of legality, which implies that the legislative process is transparent, accountable, democratic, and pluralistic; legal certainty, which requires that the rules be clear and predictable and cannot be changed retroactively; the prohibition of arbitrariness of the executive power; equality before the law; and judicial review that is independent and effective, including as regards respect for fundamental rights.

The first judicial reference to the rule of law in the EU was made in the judgment *Les Verts v Parliament* (Case 294/83, ECLI:EU:C:1986:166, para. 23),[7] which referred to the EU as a "Community based on the rule of law inasmuch neither its member states nor its institutions can avoid a review of the question whether the measures adopted by them conform with the basic constitutional charter, the Treaty." Since then, multiple references have been made to the rule of law in the Treaties: at the beginning, these references were largely symbolic, however, subsequent and successive treaty amendments reinforced the constitutional significance of the rule of law and made it clear that this principle was a part of a bigger "package" together with human rights and democracy.

Rule of law has been further clarified by the European Commission (EC) in its Communication to the European Parliament (EP) and the Council of March 11, 2014, "A New EU Framework to Strengthen the Rule of Law" (European Commission, 2014). The EU definition draws on principles set out in the case law of the CJEU and of the European Court of Human Rights (ECHR) and reports written by the Venice Commission. According to the EC, the rule of law entails compliance with the six legal principles that stem from the constitutional traditions common to most European legal systems and define the core meaning of the rule of law within the context of the EU legal order in accordance with Article 2 TEU, namely, the principle of legality, of legal certainty, prohibition of arbitrariness, of equality before the law, of independent and effective judicial control also as regards the respect for fundamental rights.[8]

2.2 *The EU's Current Toolbox*

Several different mechanisms exist at EU levels which aim to protect, safeguard, and promote the rule of law (and fundamental rights and democracy). These include legally binding mechanisms such as Article 7 TEU and the

7 The approach applied by the Court in the judgment was rather formal as this concept was attached mainly to legality. For an analysis of this judgment and its importance as regards the principle of the rule of law in the EU legal framework, see Lenaerts, 2010, 304.

8 The EU Commission's understanding of the rule of law is similar to the understanding of the Venice Commission, but a number of minor differences may be highlighted: the European Commission specifies that it is the executive branch of government that shall be prohibited from demonstrating arbitrariness, whereas the Venice Commission makes no such restriction; the EU Commission refers to fundamental rights while the Venice Commission refers to human rights; and the European Commission leaves out non-discrimination as a component of the rule of law. However, it can be interpreted that equality before the law encompasses non-discrimination. The CJEU and the ECtHR have stated that the abovementioned principles are not purely formal and procedural requirements, but that they are the vehicle for ensuring compliance with and respect for democracy and human rights. Hence, the rule of law may be said to be a constitutional principle with both formal and substantive components.

traditional jurisdictional procedures, in addition to non-binding (or soft law) tools, including annual reports prepared by EU institutions covering matters related to EU values.

A variety of actors tend to be involved in these mechanisms, with different competences and mandates: not only the political and jurisdictional EU institutions and member states but also civil society. The selected EU tools to protect the rule of law are described below.

2.2.1 Article 7 TEU

Article 7 TEU is the only specific EU provision dedicated to the protection of EU values in the EU member states. It is unique in that it established the procedures for stating the threat of a breach of EU values by a member state, the existence of such a breach, as well as a possible sanctioning mechanism to bring the recalcitrant member states back to compliance, while not being confined by the general EU competence limitations. In fact, in the same norm there are two distinct procedures – the preventive mechanism (Article 7(1) TEU),[9] and the reactive one (Article 7(2)–(3) TEU): both are independent from each other, as they aim to address two different situations, so that the sanctions mechanism can be triggered without going through the preventive mechanism, and the preventive mechanism does not necessarily entail any sanctions.

While the preventive mechanism, set out in Article 7(1) TEU, can be activated only where there is a "clear risk of a serious breach" of Article 2 TEU by a member state, Article 7(2) TEU provides for the eventual adoption of sanctions in a situation where a "serious and persistent breach" by a member state has been established by the European Council. The activation of the preventive mechanism is aimed at sending a warning signal to an offending member state and places the EU institutions under an obligation to maintain constant surveillance. Under the preventive mechanism, the European Council has a discretionary power to determine whether there is a clear risk of a serious breach of the EU fundamental values, that is, excluding "purely contingent risks from the scope of the preventive mechanism."[10]

---

9 On December 20, 2017, the Commission adopted a reasoned proposal for a Council decision on the determination of a clear risk of a serious breach of the rule of law by Poland (procedure 2017/0360(NLE), and on September 12, 2018, Parliament adopted a resolution under Article 7(1) TEU, calling on the Council to establish a clear risk of a serious breach of EU values by Hungary (procedure 2017/2131(INL)).

10 To make such determination, the following conditions have to be met: (1) proposal by one-third of the member states, by the Parliament or by the Commission; (2) the assent of the Parliament (i.e., a two-thirds majority of the votes cast, representing a majority of its members); and (3) a majority of four-fifths of the Council's members.

In order to apply the "sanctioning" mechanism laid down in Article 7(2) TEU, the breach of EU values must be serious and persistent and must therefore go beyond individual violations of fundamental rights, the rule of law, or other values laid down in Article 2 TEU. This mechanism has two phases: (1) determination of the existence of a serious and persistent breach of EU values by a member state – by unanimity of the European Council after the consent of the EP has been obtained; and (2) suspension of member state rights deriving from the Treaties, including (but not limited to) voting rights (Article 7(3) TEU). As the Council in the preventive mechanism, the European Council has also a wide margin of discretion to determine the existence of a serious or persistent breach under the sanctioning mechanism. Once the European Council has determined the seriousness and persistence of the breach, it enjoys discretion as to the choice of sanctions to be imposed and may even decide not to impose sanctions, but it is not obliged to do so.

The abovementioned procedure shows that the decision to apply Article 7 TEU is in practice almost impossible to use, not only because of the relative incertitude considering what constitutes "a clear risk of a serious breach" or "a serious and persistent breach," but also for the natural reluctance of the European Council and Council to act against one of the member states.

The fact that the procedure has essentially a highly political nature has also led to the EU being criticized for an apparent lack of political will to effectively uphold EU fundamental values (Besselink, 2017).

Despite the extreme political difficulty in reaching the required majority for activating the mechanism mentioned above, it has a very serious impact both externally and internally: on the one hand, it is likely to discredit the member state on the international scene; on the other, serious consequences can also occur within that country because the activation of the procedure pursuant to Article 7 TEU could trigger social and political reactions against the national government. Moreover, the mechanism may also produce relevant juridical effects: firstly, referring to Protocol (no. 24), on asylum for nationals of member states of the European Union,[11] and, secondly, with regard to the European Arrest Warrant (EAW) procedure that can be suspended in the event

11 The asylum application made by a citizen of a member state cannot be taken into consideration in another member state since each EU member state must consider itself a safe country of origin in terms of the level of protection of fundamental rights and freedoms. However, if the procedure referred to Articles 7(1) or 7(2) of the TEU has been initiated in respect of the member state of which the applicant is a national, that Country is no longer considered a safe country and the application for asylum of its citizen may be taken into consideration or declared admissible for processing by another member state. See CJEU case C-411 e 493/10, ECLI:EU:C:2011:610; case C-394/12, ECLI:EU:C:2013:813.

of a serious and persistent violation by the State of the principles enshrined in the TEU[12] (Villani, 2020).

2.2.2 Legally Binding Tools

The legal procedure may be instigated for protecting EU values are those enshrined in the Treaties. First of all, the Commission is empowered to commence infringement proceeding before the CJEU (pursuant to Article 258 of the Treaty on the Functioning of the European Union [TFEU]) in order to have a binding declaration that a member state has violated the EU law in a way that threatens the EU rule of law.[13] It is strengthened by a financial penalty imposed upon a member state for non-respect of a judgment rendered at the end of an infringement procedure (Article 260(2) TFEU). As a critical remark, it has to be specified that infringement actions are understood to allow for the investigation of specific violations of EU law on a case-by-case basis only and cannot be used to investigate a situation of systemic violation of EU values.

In addition, independent and impartial courts are active guardians of the rule of law, and such a view is presented in the ECJ's decisions on the preliminary ruling procedure: Article 267 TFEU has been largely used by the national judges to assess the conformity of specific national measures with EU law.[14] It is an instrument of indirect control on the correct interpretation of the rules of European law and the validity of the rules of secondary legislation which guarantees the respect of fundamental rights and the rule of law in the member state: the ECJ's ruling is not only binding on the individual referring national court, but as a precedent contains an authoritative interpretation of EU law, binding on all member states and their authorities. It has to be noted, however, that the judicial control exercised by the Court of Justice – when it concerns the respect of the values listed in Article 2 TEU – is still limited to the "material" sphere of EU law: this means that the jurisdiction of the Court is relevant only

---

12 See the Council Framework Decision 2009/299 of February 26, 2009, thereby enhancing the procedural rights of persons and fostering the application of the principle of mutual recognition to decisions rendered in the absence of the person concerned at the trial and case C-404/15 e C-659/15 PPU, ECLI:EU:C:2016:198; case C-554/14, ECLI:EU:C:2016:835.

13 The action taken by the Commission in the infringement procedures can be launched by the Commission only where these concerns constitute, at the same time, a breach of a specific provision of EU law. See the cases CJEU, C-286/12 ECLI:EU:C:2012:687, C-192/18, ECLI:EU:C:2019:924, and Case C-619/18, ECLI:EU:C:2019:531.

14 Specifically in Poland, see CJEU Joined Cases C-585/18, C-624/18 ECLI:EU:C:2019:982 and C-625/18 ECLI:EU:C:2019:982; Joined Cases C-558/18 and C-563/18 ECLI:EU:C:2020:234.

when the case in question falls within the "scope of application of EU law" (Pech & Kochenov, 2021).[15]

2.2.3 Monitoring Procedures

Specifically in case of a suspected breach of the rule of law by a member state, the "political" European institutions can activate "monitoring procedures" which do not give rise to legally binding effects.[16] This includes a temporary mechanism, set up in 2007 (for Bulgaria and Romania only) called a "cooperation and verification mechanism"; the annual Council rule of law dialogues, set up since December 2014, in the General Affairs Council, to be prepared by Coreper based on the principles of objectivity, non-discrimination, and equal treatment of all member states;[17] and the "rule of framework" (pre-Article 7 procedure), introduced by the Commission in 2014, providing a space for structured dialogue with member states suspected of rule of law breaches (Kochenov & Pech 2015).[18] The key element is the political persuasion.

Moreover, Article 70 TFEU allows the Council, on a proposal from the Commission, to adopt measures for collaboration between the Commission and the member states to conduct so-called "peer reviews" or evaluations of member state implementation of the EU policies in the area of freedom, security, and justice (AFSJ). From the perspective of the protection of Article 2 TEU values, the peer review mechanism can be used to carry out evaluations of member states' compliance in all of these matters related to the broad area mentioned above which might contribute to assess the situation of democracy, rule of law, and fundamental rights at the national level (Andersen, 2014; Moxham & Stefanelli, 2013; Hirsch-Ballin, 2015).

---

15 The Court of Justice itself considers that the provision of Article 2 is not sufficient to confer the competence to review the respect of the values contemplated by the member states, but that, for this purpose, it is necessary to identify a link between the same values, in particular the rule of law, and matters already belonging to the scope of EU law.

16 The so-called "soft law" mechanisms can themselves be divided between two categories: there are soft law mechanisms of a general scope which aim to address all member states equally, and soft law mechanisms of limited scope, either because they address a specific topic (fundamental rights, corruption, and effectiveness of justice systems) or because they address a specific country (the Cooperation and Verification mechanism).

17 The peer-to-peer dialogues on the rule of law are conducted on a non-partisan and evidence-based approach and without prejudice to the principle of conferred competences, as well as the respect of national identities of member states.

18 The framework encompasses three stages: assessment, recommendation, and follow-up by the Commission.

Although the specific tool is mentioned among the juridical one, it lacks enforceability since it results in non-binding recommendations and judicial review is therefore not possible.

In addition, due to the EU's worsening rule of law crisis and, more broadly, the unprecedented and expanding attempts by some national authorities to organize the systemic undermining of the EU's shared foundational values, a new process of prevention has been established by the Commission as of 2020: the rule of law mechanism. It provides a process for an annual and inclusive dialogue between the EC, the Council, and the EP together with member states as well as national parliaments, civil society, and other stakeholders on the rule of law.

The key element of the new tool is the early identification of challenges in order to find solutions with the broad and mutual support of stakeholders (including the Council of Europe and the Venice Commission). Differently from the previous mentioned tools, the annual *Rule of Law Report*[19] and the preparatory work with member states are the foundation of this new process, since they are a basis for discussions in the EU as well as a measure to prevent problems from emerging or deepening further. In this way, the purpose of prevention prevails over that of monitoring.

Finally, a new tool is at the disposal of the EU to combat violations of the rule of law in its member states: Regulation 2020/2092 adopted by Parliament and Council on December 16, 2020 (Łacny, 2021). The Regulation introduces a general conditionality regime to protect the EU budget in the event of breaches of rule of law principles (the so-called "rule of law conditionality," that is, a conditionality governing access to European funds). To achieve this goal, the Council, acting on a proposal from the Commission, may adopt safeguard measures, such as the suspension of payments, which are charged to the EU budget, or the suspension of the approval of one or more programs financed by the EU budget. The EU can withhold payments to member states if the violation of the rule of law in the said member state sufficiently directly affects the EU's budget or its financial interests.[20] The rationale for these measures is that

19 It takes the form of 27 country chapters and an umbrella report presenting an overview of the situation of the rule of law situation across the EU; it monitors significant developments, both positive and negative, relating to the rule of law in member states and focuses on four pillars: the justice system, the anti-corruption framework, media pluralism, and other institutional issues related to checks and balances.

20 See Articles 4 to 6 of the Regulation Rule of Law Conditionality for Access to European Funds. Following the Commission's proposal to activate the mechanism, the Council would have 1 month (or 3 months in exceptional cases) to vote on such a measure, possibly approving it by qualified majority. The Regulation provides that measures against the

respect for the rule of law is a prerequisite for sound financial management and effective financing of the EU.[21]

Some have considered this to be a necessary instrument and a substantial success, above all because it would apply not only to "direct" violations of the rule of law in the use of European funds (such as, for example, in cases of fraud or corruption), but also to systemic violations of the principles of the rule of law (such as, for example, the independence of the judiciary), should they affect the management of funds.

Others, on the other hand, have strongly criticized it, on the grounds that once again the Union has failed to play an effective constitutional role in protecting the values on which it is founded, and has instead turned its attention to its own economic and financial interests and the disbursement of funds.[22] This implies that breaking European values is not sufficient motivation to take action against those responsible, but that there must be a real economic damage, quantifiable and only then "tangible" (Fiscaro, 2019; Halmai, 2019; Kirst, 2021). It seems that the regulation has "hollowed out" the rule of law from a constitutional principle to an expedient policy tool.

2.3 *Public Good Under Scrutiny: the Principle of Non-Discrimination in the EU Legal Order*

The principle of equality and, along with it, the right to equality/non-discrimination are part of the foundation of the rule of law in the EU legal system. They are both, at the same time, EU values. What is important for further consideration is that both non-discrimination and the rule of law may be understood to be public goods (Szczerba-Zawada, 2017).

The principle of equality is the value on which the European Union is founded (Article 2 TEU) and one of the objectives of the EU and its member states (Article 3 TEU). It places a valid obligation on the EU which in defining and implementing its policies and activities shall aim to combat discrimination based on sex, racial or ethnic origin, religion or belief, disability, age or sexual orientation (Article 10 TFEU) as well as to eliminate inequalities, and to promote

member state must be concluded within a maximum of 7 to 9 months from the violation of the rule of law.

21 See the Preamble of the Regulation.

22 On February 16, 2022, the ECJ delivered an important ruling on the rule of law conditionality regulation in the two cases of *Hungary v Parliament and Council* (C-156/21) and *Poland v Parliament and Council* (C-157/21), fully dismissing Hungary's and Poland's actions for annulment against the general regime of conditionality. Their main objection was based on the fact that the disbursement of funds should depend on virtuousness in their use, rather than compliance with the rule of law.

equality, between men and women (Article 8 TFEU) and on the member states – each of them shall ensure that the principle of equal pay for male and female workers for equal work or work of equal value is applied (Article 157(1) TFEU). They are obliged also to fully implement the EU equality legislation adopted on the basis of Article 19 TFEU. The body of the latter is exemplified by the Framework Employment Directive (Directive 2000/78/EC) against discrimination at work on grounds of religion or belief, disability, age or sexual orientation and the Gender Recast Directive (Directive 2006/54/EC) on the implementation of the principle of equal opportunities and equal treatment of men and women in matters of employment and occupation. Under the Charter of Fundamental Rights of the European Union (CFR) – that has the same legal value as the Treaties (Article 6(1) TEU) – everyone is equal before the law (Article 20 CFR). The CFR also guarantees freedom from discrimination, stating that any discrimination based on any ground, including sex, shall be prohibited (Article 21 CFR). Article 23 CFR prescribes that equality between men and women must be ensured in all areas, including employment, work, and pay, and confirms the entitlements of the addresses of the Charter to adopt the positive actions.

The normative power of the EU as a promoter of equality and non-discrimination as a public good is realized through the sanctions imposed on the member states in case of a violation of the equality principle. The failure by member states, including Poland, to fulfill their obligations under the equality principle may give rise to a variety of consequences at the EU level, also in connection with the rule of law protection mechanisms. In the next section they are analyzed using, as examples, Polish and Hungarian anti-LGBT laws and resolutions.

3 EU Legal Response to Polish and Hungarian Anti-LGBT Actions

3.1 *The Polish "LGBT Ideology-Free Zone"*

Almost a hundred local authorities in Poland adopted anti-LGBT resolutions. These anti-LGBT resolutions cover two types of acts: resolutions of regional governments (taking place at different levels)[23] declaring "LGBT ideology-free zones" and adopting a "local government charter of the rights of the family." Not all of them are identical, but they all are homophobic in their wording, suggesting that the so-called "LGBT ideology" was a threat to traditional Polish values, particularly the idea of family based on marriage between a woman

23 In Poland there is a three-tier division in local government: voivodship (*województwo*), county (*powiat*), and municipality (*gmina*).

and a man. They pledge to fight "political correctness" and "homo-propaganda" and to "prevent [...] the early sexualization of Polish children." They also urge local governments to withhold funding from NGOs and projects considered not to support these values (Florczak, 2022; Adamczewska-Stachura, 2021).

The consequences exceed the purely rhetorical dimension. This is clear in light of the results of the 2020 LGBTI Survey II conducted by the European Union Agency for Fundamental Rights that reveal an increasing intolerance and violence in Poland towards its LGBT minority. It is exemplified by the highest percentage of respondents reporting experiences of physical or sexual attacks due to being LGBT in the past 5 years in Poland across the Union (15%) or avoiding of holding hands in public with a same-sex partner for fear of being assaulted, threatened, or harassed (58%). What is most striking is the high percentage of LGBT respondents in the EU-28+ (83%) who do not believe the Polish government's combat against prejudice and intolerance has been effective (Fundamental Rights Agency, 2020). These results must be perceived through the prism of more and more complex application of the means of legal protection against progressive rule of law backsliding, enabling Polish authorities to apply discriminatory legal instruments to limit LGBT minority rights more easily (Grabowska-Moroz & Wójcik, 2021).

Not surprisingly, resolutions of this content and results turned out to be non-compliant with the EU value of non-discrimination safeguarded by EU law and policies. As a result of their normativization, the EU member states are obliged to fully respect the EU value of equality and to observe the right to equal treatment and non-discrimination enshrined in numerous EU legal acts. Despite this obligation, discrimination against lesbian, gay, bisexual, transgender, and intersex people persist throughout the EU, taking various forms, including the anti-LGBT declarations of some Polish municipalities. As such, they constitute a threat to the EU rule of law as in a union of law public actors at any level cannot declare itself free from "LGBT ideology." The opposite course of action in Poland resulted in numerous steps undertaken by the EU institutions aimed at protecting the European public goods: equality and rule of law.

3.1.1 The European Parliament and the "LGBT Ideology-Free Zones"

Against the situation at stake the EP – using soft law instruments – called for the protection of LGBT persons' rights and for the adoption of a comprehensive, permanent, and objective EU mechanism on the rule of law and fundamental rights.

The resolution of December 18, 2019, on public discrimination and hate speech against LGBT people, including "LGBTI free zones" (European Parliament, 2019), underlined the urgent need for such a mechanism. The EP reiterated the need for an impartial and regular assessment of the situation with regard to the rule of law, democracy, and fundamental rights in all the member states and called on the EC and the Council to use all the tools and procedures at their disposal to ensure the full and proper application of Treaty principles and values, such as infringement procedures, budgetary procedures, the rule of law mechanism, and the Article 7 procedure. The EC was also summoned by the EP to monitor fundamental rights violations in the framework of its announced rule of law review cycle, assess whether Poland has failed to fulfill an obligation under the Treaties and whether it should deliver a reasoned opinion on the matter, in accordance with Article 258 TFEU, monitor the use of all EU funding streams, including EU Structural and Investment Funds, and to hold regular dialogues with national, regional, and local authorities to remind stakeholders of their commitment to non-discrimination and that such funds may under no circumstances be used for discriminatory purposes and to take concrete measures to address clear and direct breaches of anti-discrimination rules, in particular, the prohibition of the instruction to discriminate under Directive 2000/78/EC, by local councils adopting regulations that attack LGBT rights (European Parliament 2019).

This confirms the wide range of different tools at the disposal of the EU – from political through financial to legal ones – as described briefly earlier in this chapter, which might be used to protect the EU public goods – the rule of law and human rights, especially – right to non-discrimination. Nevertheless, the EP kept underlining the meaning of the procedure envisaged in Article 7 TEU to protect the rule of law against the situation in Poland.

The resolution of September 17, 2020, on the proposal for a Council decision on the determination of a clear risk of a serious breach by the Republic of Poland of the rule of law (European Parliament, 2020) referred to the deterioration of human rights protection in Poland, typified by the declarations of zones free from so-called "LGBT ideology" and the adoption of "regional charters of family rights," discriminating in particular against LGBTI peoples. The Parliament stated that along with a malfunctioning of the legislative and electoral system and problems with the independence of the judiciary and the rights of judges, this amounts to a systemic threat to the values of Article 2 TEU and constitutes a clear risk of a serious breach thereof. Hence, the EP called on the Council to use the procedure under Article 7(1) TEU to its full potential by addressing the implications of the Polish government's action for all the principles enshrined in Article 2 TEU, including democracy and fundamental rights. It also called on the EC to make full use of the tools available to it, to address a clear risk of a serious breach by Poland of the values on which the Union is founded, in particular, expedited infringement procedures and applications for interim measures before the Court of Justice, as well as budgetary tools (European Parliament, 2020).

The EP repeated its call on Article 7 TEU as well as any other tools at the disposal of the EU institutions, including infringement procedures, the Rule of Law Framework, and the conditionality mechanism in order to address violations of the fundamental rights of LGBTIQ people everywhere in the Union, including Poland, in the resolution of March 11, 2021, on the declaration of the EU as an LGBTIQ Freedom Zone (European Parliament, 2021). In the context of the public goods analyzed in this chapter, the EP highlighted that the backlash against LGBT people is often coupled with a broader deterioration in the situation of democracy, the rule of law, and fundamental rights (European Parliament, 2020).

3.1.2 The European Commission and the "LGBT Ideology-Free Zones"

The EC confirmed that anti-LGBT zones in Poland are on a collision course with the EU legal order as they may violate EU law regarding non-discrimination on grounds of sexual orientation. LGBTQI-free zones (in essence, humanity-free zones) have no place in the "Union of equality," as declared by President of the EC Ursula von der Leyen in her speech on September 16, 2020 (European Commission, 2020b).

The issue of "LGBT ideology-free zones" turned out to be particularly relevant in the context of EU cohesion policy. In its letter dated May 27, 2020, addressed to marshals of several Polish voivodeships, the EC recalled the obligation stemming from the principle of equal treatment and non-discrimination for authorities managing EU funds. The EC pointed to Article 6 of Regulation (EU) no. 1303/2013 requiring that operations supported by European Structural and Investment Funds (ESIF) must comply with applicable EU law, including respect for Article 2 of the TEU as well relevant provisions of the CFR as well as to Article 7 of the Regulation (EU) no. 1303/2013, obliging member states to take appropriate steps to prevent any discrimination based on sex, racial or ethnic origin, religion or belief, disability, age or sexual orientation, during the preparation and implementation of ESIF programs. In the Commission's view, the adoption branding LGBTI community postulates as "ideology" and declaring their territories as "LGBT unwelcome," put into question the capacity of these regional managing authorities to ensure compliance with the horizontal principle of non-discrimination in the implementation of ESIF programs. What is important in the perspective of the aim of this chapter, the Commission highlighted that declaring "LGBT free" or "LGBT unwelcome" territories, workplace, or services constitutes an action that is against the values set out in Article 2 TEU rights (European Commission, 2020a).

As the situation did not change, in July 2021 the EC decided to launch infringement procedure under Article 258 TFEU against Poland related to equality and the protection of fundamental rights, and in particular in response to the declaration of "LGBT ideology-free zones." In the Commission's view the Polish authorities failed to fully and appropriately respond to its inquiry regarding the nature and impact of this type of discriminatory resolutions against LGBT persons voted by several Polish regions and municipalities (INFR(2021)2115).

Being worried that the principle of non-discrimination in the implementation of ESIF was not ensured by the regional and local authorities which adopted anti-LGBT resolutions, the EC, in a letter of September 3, 2021 referring to the instigated infringement procedure, encouraged authorities of regions that declared themselves as "LGBT ideology-free zones" to undertake any possible corrective measures with regard to the resolutions in order to eliminate the risk that the fundamental values enshrined in Article 2 TEU as well as provisions of the Charter of Fundamental Rights are violated. Therefore, the EC put on hold the REACT-EU program amendments in relation to relevant regional operational programs (European Commission, 2021b).

Apparently, the risk of loss of EU funding seemed to be – at least partially – an effective incentive: some local authorities withdrew their anti-LGBT resolutions. Nevertheless, as long as some of the anti-LGBT declarations have not been revoked, the problem still exists.

3.2 *The Hungarian Case*

The EC's determination to use all available instruments to defend the core EU values of equality and respect for individual dignity and human rights has resulted in the instigation of infringement procedures to protect the right not to be discriminated against. This can be seen in letters of formal notice sent to Hungary in two cases.

The first one addresses a law adopted on June 23, 2021, which stipulates a number of discriminatory measures in Hungary. In particular, the law prohibits or limits access to content that promotes or portrays the so-called "divergence from self-identity corresponding to sex at birth, sex change or homosexuality" for individuals under 18. As Hungary failed to explain why the exposure of children to LGBTIQ content as such would be detrimental to their well-being or not in line with the best interests of the child, the Commission found this action to violate many EU norms. In particular, this includes the violation of human dignity (Article 1 of the Charter), freedom of expression and information (Article 11), the right to respect of private life (Article 7), as well as the right to non-discrimination (Article 21). As the EC highlighted explicitly, because of the gravity of these violations, the contested provisions also violate the values laid down in Article 2 TEU.

The second Hungarian case in which the EC decided to apply Article 258 TFEU concerns the obligation set by the Hungarian Consumer Protection Authority on the publisher of a book for children presenting LGBTIQ people to include a disclaimer that the book depicts forms of "behaviour deviating from traditional gender roles." In terms of equality principle, the EC found this as discrimination based on sexual orientation. As Hungary did not justify the restriction of the right to non-discrimination as enshrined in Article 21 of the Charter, the Commission has decided to send Hungary a letter of formal notice.

It must be pointed out that in those cases, differently from the ones referred to Poland, the rule of law conditionality would not be applied, since – as Commissioner Jourova explained – this mechanism allows the EU to suspend or limit a member state's access to EU funding in the event of a violation (of the rule of law) that has a "sufficiently direct" impact on the EU budget, particularly in cases of corruption and tax evasion.

The abovementioned examples illustrated that the new mechanism of protection of LGBT+ persons emerged under which Article 258 TFEU may be used a tool of defense of the EU core value of equality and discrimination in the context of the rule of law and other EU values (INF_21_3440).

4 Conclusions

As the above-mentioned examples show, the crisis of the rule of law – marked by several infringement procedures instigated by the EC against Poland as well as against Hungary – goes hand in hand with the decline in the level of protection of human rights, especially the right to non-discrimination. It must be highlighted that action of all public authorities within the limits set by law, in accordance with the values of democracy and fundamental rights, including the right to non-discrimination and under the supervision of an independent and impartial judge constitutes the merit of the rule of law. Threat to any of these components implies – inevitably – erosion of the latter principle.

To prevent transmitting this destructive trend to the EU level and to protect the EU rule of law being a public good in the community based on law, the EU undertook several steps. It proved that despite the body of EU instruments and processes to uphold Article 2 TEU values, the effectiveness of the EU actions requires the adoption of "hard" financial instruments. This has twofold consequences. Firstly, it shows that the EU public goods (such as right to non-discrimination) might be priced. Secondly, it shows that the conditionality mechanism, linking EU funds to the rule of law, is in fact a tool of last resort to convince member states to fully comply with EU values. In the process of creating an ever closer union among the peoples of Europe, the economic union has gained axiological foundation.

Note: A. M. Romito, Associate Professor of European Union Law at the University of Bari Aldo Moro, is the author of Sections 2, 2.1, and 2.2 of this chapter. A. Szczerba, Associate Professor at the Jacob of Paradies University in Gorzów Wielkopolski, is the author of Sections 2.3 and 3. The introduction and the conclusions express the views of both authors. The writing of this chapter has been funded by the European Union under the project "Between Hate and Equality: The EU as a Guard of Human Rights and Non-discrimination" (EUHatEq), project no. 101047948. The views and opinions expressed here are those of the authors only and do not necessarily reflect those of the European Union or the European Education and Culture Executive Agency (EACEA). Neither the European Union nor the granting authority can be held responsible for them.

References

Adamczewska-Stachura, M. (2021, January 13). Combating "anti-LGBT" resolutions in Poland: Stories from behind the scenes [blog post]. *Equinet*. https://equineteurope.org/combating-anti-lgbt-resolutions-in-poland-stories-from-behind-the-scenes/

Bartole, S. (2020). *The internationalisation of constitutional law: A view from the Venice Commission*. Hart Publishing.

Besselink, L. (2017). The bite, the bark and the howl: Article 7 TEU and the rule of law initiatives. In A. Jakab & D. Kochenov (Eds.), *The enforcement of EU law and values: Ensuring member states' compliance* (pp. 128–144). Oxford University Press.

Craig, P. (1997). Formal and substantive conceptions of the rule-of-law: An analytical framework. *Public Law*, 467–487.

Craig, P. (2017). Transnational constitution-making: The contribution of the Venice Commission on Law and Democracy. *UC Irvine Journal of International, Transnational, and Comparative Law*, 2, 57–85.

Council of the European Union. (2000, November 27). Council Directive 2000/78/EC of 27 November 2000 establishing a general framework for equal treatment in employment and occupation.

Enderle, G. (2021). *Corporate responsibility for wealth creation and human rights*. Cambridge University Press.

European Commission. (2014, March 19). Communication from the Commission to the European Parliament and the Council: A new EU Framework to strengthen the rule of law. COM(2014) 158 final/2.

European Commission. (2020a). Responsibility of the Managing Authorities and beneficiaries of EU cohesion policy funds to comply with the principle of non-discrimination based on sexual orientation and gender identity. EMPL/REGIO/JC/db (2020)8845638.

European Commission. (2020b). State of the Union 2020 – President von der Leyen's speech. https://ec.europa.eu/info/strategy/strategic-planning/state-union-addresses/state-union-2020_en

European Commission. (2021a). Infringement decisions – INFR(2021)211. Retrieved April 21, 2022. https://ec.europa.eu/eurostat/data/database

European Commission. (2021b). Responsibilities of the regional Managing Authorities to provide comprehensive answers to the letter of formal notice of 14 July 2021 and to undertake corrective measures. REGIO/MG/(2021)6136636.

European Parliament. (2000, December 7). Charter of Fundamental Rights of the European Union. https://www.europarl.europa.eu/charter/default_en.htm

European Parliament. (2019, December 18). European Parliament resolution of 18 December 2019 on public discrimination and hate speech against LGBTI people, including LGBTI free zones (2019/2933(RSP)).

European Parliament. (2020, September 17). European Parliament resolution of 17 September 2020 on the proposal for a Council decision on the determination of a clear risk of a serious breach by the Republic of Poland of the rule of law (COM(2017)0835 – 2017/0360R(NLE)).

European Parliament. (2021, March 11). European Parliament resolution of 11 March 2021 on the EU's declaration as an LGBTIQ Freedom Zone (2021/2557(RSP)).

European Parliament & Council of the European Union. (2006, July 5). Directive 2006/54/EC of the European Parliament and of the Council of 5 July 2006 on the implementation of the principle of equal opportunities and equal treatment of men and women in matters of employment and occupation (recast).

European Parliament & Council of the European Union. (2013, December 17). Regulation (EU) no. 1303/2013 of the European Parliament and of the Council of 17 December 2013 laying down common provisions on the European Regional Development Fund, the European Social Fund, the Cohesion Fund, the European Agricultural Fund for Rural Development and the European Maritime and Fisheries Fund and laying down general provisions on the European Regional Development Fund, the European Social Fund, the Cohesion Fund and the European Maritime and Fisheries Fund and repealing Council Regulation (EC) no. 1083/2006. Arts. 6, 7, in OJ L 347, 20.12.2013, pp. 320–469.

European Parliament & Council of the European Union. (2020, December 16). Regulation (EU, Euratom) 2020/2092 of the European Parliament and of the Council of 16 December 2020 on a general regime of conditionality for the protection of the Union budget, OJ L 433, 22.12.2020.

European Union. (2012, October 26). Treaty on the Functioning of the European Union. *Official Journal of the European Union*, C 326/47.

Fiscaro, M. (2019). Rule of law conditionality in EU funds: The value of money in the crisis of European values. *European Papers, 4*(3), 695–722.

Florczak, A. (2021). Reakcja instytucji Unii Europejskiej na strefy anty-LGBT+ w Polsce. In B. Orłowska, A. Szczerba, & K. Wasilewski (Eds.), *Od stereotypów do nienawiści. Hejt w perspektywie interdyscyplinarnej* (pp. 125–150). Akademia im. Jakuba z Paradyża w Gorzowie Wielkopolskim.

Fundamental Rights Agency. (2020). A long way to go for LGBTI equality. https://fra.europa.eu/en/publication/2020/eu-lgbti-survey-results

Grabowska-Moroz, B., & Wójcik, B. I. (2021). Reframing LGBT rights advocacy in the context of the rule of law backsliding Intersections. *East European Journal of Society and Politics, 7*(4), 85–103. https://doi.org/10.17356/ieejsp.v7i4.852

Halmai, G. (2019). The possibility and desirability of rule of law conditionality. *Hague Journal on the Rule Law, 11*, 171–188.

Hirsch-Ballin, E. (2015). Mutual trust: The virtue of reciprocity – Strengthening the acceptance of the rule of law through peer review. Tilburg Law School Legal Studies Research Paper Series, no. 14/2015.

Kirst, N. (2021). Rule of law conditionality: The long-awaited step towards a solution of the rule of law crisis in the European Union? *European Papers, 6*(1), 101–110.

Kochenov, D. (2017). The *acquis* and its principles: The enforcement of "law" versus the enforcement of "values" in the European Union. In A. Jakab & D. Kochenov (Eds.), *The enforcement of EU law and values* (pp. 9–27), Oxford: Oxford University Press.

Kochenov, D., & Pech, L. (2015). Monitoring and enforcement of the rule of law in the EU: Rhetoric and reality. *European Constitutional Law Review, 11*(3), 512–540. doi:10.1017/S1574019615000358

Łacny, J. (2021). The rule of law conditionality under Regulation no. 2092/2020 – Is it all about the money? *Hague Journal on the Rule of Law, 13*, 79–105. https://doi.org/10.1007/s40803-021-00154-6

Leloup, M., Kochenov, D., & Dimitrovs, A. (2021, June). Non-regression: Opening the door to solving the "Copenhagen dilemma"? All the Eyes on Case C-896/19 *Repubblika v Il-Prim Ministru*. Working Paper no. 15. Reconnect. https://reconnect-europe.eu/wp-content/uploads/2021/06/WOP15_June2021.pdf

Lenaerts, K. (2010). The basic constitutional charter of a community based on the rule of law. In M. Poiares Maduro & L. Azoulai (Eds.), *The past and the future of EU law: The classics of EU law revisited on the 50th anniversary of the Rome Treaty* (pp. 295–315). Oxford: Hart Publishing, 304.

Magen, A. (2016). Cracks in the foundations: Understanding the great rule of law debate in the EU. *Journal of Common Market Studies, 54*(5), 1050–1061. doi:10.1111/jcms.12400

Moxham, L., & Stefanelli, J. (2013, November 15). Safeguarding the rule of law, democracy and fundamental rights: A monitoring model for the European Union. Bingham Centre for the Rule of Law.

Pech, L. (2016). The EU as a global rule of law promoter: The consistency and effectiveness challenges. *Asia Europe Journal, 14*(1), 7–24. http://hdl.handle.net/10.1007/s10308-015-0432-z

Pech, L., & Kochenov, D. (2021). Respect for the rule of law in the case law of the European Court of Justice: A casebook overview of key judgments since the Portuguese Judges case. Swedish Institute for European Policy Studies (SIEPS). https://ssrn.com/abstract=3850308

PART 3

Multilateral Trade: How Do International Organizations Use It To Foster a More Sustainable World?

CHAPTER 6

Trade as a Tool of Sustainable Development in the Context of Regulatory Systems Created by International Organizations (WTO, OECD)

Lenka Fojtíková

1 Introduction

Trade as an economic activity has a long history which is connected with forming civilization, establishing towns, and creating individual states. In the modern era, nations are more closely linked than ever before through trade in goods and services, flows of money, and investment in one other's economies. Free trade and capital flows enable countries to produce and sell more through national borders and to compete with one other in the world markets. Although international competition results in lower costs and prices, the growing production and trade can also have a negative impact on the environment and human life. On the other hand, trade reinforces international cooperation and contributes to a peaceful coexistence among nations. As international trade plays an important role in the development of many countries, on the multilateral level the process of trade liberalization is governed by some international organizations. There are in particular two international organizations, namely the World Trade Organization (WTO) and the Organisation for Economic Co-operation and Development (OECD), which currently contribute to the achievement of the Sustainable Development Goals through international trade.

The aim of this chapter is to show the main problems in the trade liberalization process with focus on three areas of trade that represent the most sensitive areas of multilateral negotiations: agricultural trade, services trade, and intellectual property protection. The main hypothesis is that trade liberalization, which is carried out under the WTO multilateral framework and supported by the OECD, contributes to sustainable development in the world. The main contribution of this chapter is that it gives the current view on the role of the WTO and the OECD in achieving sustainable development via trade liberalization processes.

The empirical verification of the fulfillment of the main tasks of the WTO and the OECD in the field of trade liberalization has the character of qualitative research, and is carried out using secondary sources, including scientific articles, official reports, and statistical data

The content of this chapter is structured along three sections. Section 1 points out some economic and environmental aspects of globalization. Section 2 introduces the role of the WTO and the OECD in achieving environmental sustainability. Section 3 depicts the endeavors as well as difficulties that arise from the current WTO negotiations in agricultural trade, trade in services, and intellectual property protection with focus on the environment. The chapter ends with the presentation of some conclusions.

2 Economic and Environmental Aspects of Globalization

Economic globalization speeded up processes in the world economy and contributed to the economic development of many countries. During the last several decades some developing countries[1] (such as China, India, Brazil, South Korea, and some others) became the largest economies and the leading exporters and importers of goods and services in the world. Because of trade, millions of people can produce to export, and, thus, increase their consumption. Besides these positive phenomena, which are the result of interdependencies between production, consumption, and job creation, however, the expansion of production and trade resulted in growing environmental problems, such as air, water, and soil pollution, global warming, declining biodiversity, overpopulation, waste disposal, ocean acidification, deforestation, water scarcity, acid rain, ozone layer depletion, and public health issues. For example, Robalino and Herrera (2010), who analyzed the interface between trade and deforestation, found out that deforestation was affected by agricultural output prices, deducing that trade affects these prices as well as the deforestation rates. Empirical evidence confirms that increases in the agricultural and timber process lead to an increase in deforestation in Mexico, Tanzania, Thailand, Brazil, Costa Rica, Australia, and Brazil (Robalino & Herrera, 2010). Thus, growing production and pressure on raw materials consumption can have a negative impact on the environment, health of people, and the quality of life.

Another example is the world's fastest-growing sea corridor, the Northern Sea Route. This project has economic, but also ecological consequences. Although it will bring benefits for some economies due to the reduction of

1 The classification of UNCTADStat distinguishes two main groups of regions, i.e., developing and developed regions, based on the development status in accordance with the United Nations' Standard country or area codes for statistical use (the M49 standard).

distance among countries, it may have detrimental effects on the environment, such as increasing emissions into the air, the increasing release of oil through spills, or introducing invasive alien marine species (Dellink et al., 2017).

In general, the liberalization of trade and investment flows contributed to the geographical fragmentation of production, which also increased trade with components produced in different parts of the world. The predominant part of the world production, especially in the manufacturing sector, is currently internationalized through global value chains (GVCs), in which every country or region specializes on the production of a piece or component. It leads to "trade in tasks"[2] that adds value along the production chain. Thus, international trade is created by countries that participate in these GVCs as a source of raw materials, manufacturing countries that make and process them, and those that export the final goods to be consumed. Complex GVCs are the opportunity for many countries on different economic levels to participate in world trade. However, it is important to ensure GVCs themselves are environmentally and socially sustainable (Okonjo-Iweala, 2022).

A typical case of this phenomenon is a developing Asia. On the one hand, it is the largest recipient of foreign direct investment (FDI), accounting for more than half of the global FDI (UNCTAD, 2021b), and East Asia is the main industrial "factory" in the world, clearly illustrated in trade statistics. Between 1948 and 2020 the share of Asia in world merchandise exports increased from 14 percent to more than 36 percent (WTO, 2021b), especially due to the Chinese trade expansion. The important role of Asia in world trade has also been obvious in the time of COVID-19. In 2020, while global trade declined in volume terms by 5.3 percent, Asia's merchandise trade was only down by 0.5 percent (WTO, 2021b). On the other hand, Asia is a region that accounts for about 60 percent of the world population, and has many environmental problems. For example, of the top 40 most polluted cities in the world, 37 are in South Asia. Overall, it contributes to around 11 percent of all deaths, and approximately 40 million disability-adjusted life years in South Asia (World Bank, 2021). However, air pollution as well as water pollution is not a localized phenomenon. It is transported across borders, and its effect spreads to places far away from the source. Thus, these global problems require global solutions through international organizations, such as the World Trade Organization and the Organisation for Economic Co-operation and Development.

Another issue arises from the fact that different ecological and work standards and claims on achieving sustainability in the individual countries also

2 This new paradigm was first used by Princeton University economists Gene Grossman and Esteban Rossi-Hansberg (Grossman & Rossi-Hansberg, 2006).

have an impact on the country's competitiveness. As Low, Marceau, and Reinaud (2011) state, when an industry in one country assumes additional costs in order to reduce greenhouse gas emissions and those same industries in other countries incur lesser (or zero) costs, this may affect geographical patterns of investment, production, and trade, but emission will not be reduced, but only shifted to another country or region. The results of a study, which was focused on the economic consequences of climate change, show that despite being negatively affected by climate damages, a region may increase its competitiveness if other competitors for a certain market are more severely damaged, or there is a move to specialize in the production of other goods (Dellink et al., 2017).

On the whole, the world production and consumption are increasing, the living standards are improving and the populations are becoming better off, but these developments also create new demands on the environment and depleted natural resources. As the OECD projected, between 2017 and 2060 the resources used will nearly double from 89 to 167 gigatons (Yamaguchi, 2021), and with respect to the prospect of a world population of 9 billion by 2050, we need to produce and consume more sustainably and foster innovation. Elms and Low (2013) state that besides ecological aspects, social inequality within and between societies is an important element of sustainability as well. They argues that, although governments have a major role in these matters, little success is shown in fostering cooperation in which governments can advance common policies, with respect to the stalled Doha negotiations in the WTO, in climate change negotiations, and in discussion over a new international financial architecture (Elms & Low, 2013).

Although trade is the fuel of economic globalization, and usually has a direct impact on the environment by increasing pollution or degrading natural sources, it can also be the driver of environmental sustainability. For example, the support of a circular economy makes resource use more sustainable. In this vein, the results of Steinfatt's (2020) analysis show that besides resource savings, circular economy brings environmental outcomes, trade, and economic diversification.

The effect of trade on the environment is, thus, dual. On the one hand, trade liberalization may lead to specialization in pollution-intensive activities in some countries if environmental policy stringency differs across countries. On the other hand, trade liberalization enables countries to get new technologies that make local production cleaner. In addition, as a country is more integrated within the world economy through GVCs, its exports become more exposed to environmental standards created by the leading importers. However, the positive or negative effects of trade on the environment can also have an opposite impact, i.e., from the environment to trade. This impact can been seen, for example, when the results of climate change (extreme weather and rising sea levels) have a negative impact on maritime shipping, which accounts for around 80 percent of global trade by volume (OECD, 2022).

Thus, the cooperation on the creation of a suitable institutional framework, which would protect the environment but not create new barriers to trade, is desired at the local, regional, national, and international levels. In this context, Jansen and Keck (2004) argue that in theory the WTO law provides the appropriate tools to ensure rulings that are consistent with economic thinking, but economists usually have imperfect knowledge of the precise welfare effects of the different types of environmental policies. In practice, therefore, it is questionable whether economists are able to give adequate guidance to legal experts when it comes to the evaluation of national environmental policies (Jansen & Keck, 2004). Thus, the development of a set of trade and environmental indicators by the OECD in order to analyze the relationship between domestic environmental regulations and international policies is essential to better understand the interactions between trade and environmental policies (Garsous, 2019). In terms of the WTO, Low, Marceau and Reinaud (2011) state that the existing GATT and WTO rules were not drafted to address climate change problems and policies.

From the focused analysis of the link between sustainability and trade or trade policy in the abovementioned literature, this chapter considers sustainability as a complex issue, and verifies the theory of public goods in the fulfillment of tasks by the WTO and OECD in the field of the liberalization processes in order to foster a more sustainable world.

3 The Role of the WTO and the OECD in Achieving Environmental Sustainability

The WTO as well as the OECD are both international organizations that propound the idea of open markets for trade and investments around the world in order to achieve sustainable development.

The OECD was the first international organization that established the Joint Working Party on Trade and Environment in 1991, i.e., a standing body to examine trade and environmental issues and to develop discussion on different levels around evidence-based analysis concerning the environment, such as the reform of fossil fuel subsidies. The OECD, as a long-standing partner of the United Nations (UN), also contributes to achieving the Sustainable Development Goals (SDGs)[3] which were adopted by the UN General Assembly in September 2015 by a wide range of policy tools, analytical work and dialogue platforms. In 2016, the OECD issued an action plan in which it introduced how it would support the achievement of the 2030 Agenda for Sustainable Development launched by the United Nations in 2015. The action plan determines, among other things, the implementation of the OECD Guidelines for Multinational Enterprises as well as related guidance on responsible supply chains, the dissemination of the updated OECD Policy Framework on Investment, which helps countries to improve their investment climates, and the support of market opening as well as trade facilitation initiatives (OECD, 2016).

In order to share national experience in the implementation of the 2030 Agenda, annual meetings of the OECD Council and Partners as well as international organizations are held. The last meeting took place in 2021 in virtual format with over 65 participants. It discussed the role of tax in delivering SDGs, the importance of private investment to foster progress towards SDGs, and the budget process and public procurement to accelerate progress on SDGs.

In the WTO, the discussion about the optimal use of the world's resources in accordance with the objective of sustainable development and seeking both to protect and preserve the environment started during the GATT rounds of negotiations in 1970. After the establishment of the WTO in 1995, the issue of sustainable development was introduced in the Preamble of the Marrakesh Agreement establishing the World Trade Organization. Thus, the environmental goals were to be achieved in compliance with the multilateral trade principles on which the WTO exists. This means that the fundamental principles of non-discrimination, transparency, and predictability create the framework for the WTO members to implement measures in order to achieve environmental goals.

Regardless of the non-discrimination rule, Article XX of the General Agreement on Tariffs and Trade (GATT) enables the WTO members in a specific situation to adopt measures that are inconsistent with the non-discriminatory principle but necessary to protect human, animal or plant life or health, or related to the conservation of exhaustible natural resources. The phrase "exhaustible natural resources" was interpreted broadly to include not only mineral or non-living resources, but also endangered living spaces. Like GATT, the General Agreement on Trade in Services (GATS) contains general exceptions in Article XIV, which covers environmental concerns. Besides the two pillar agreements, GATT and GATS, other multilateral agreements also include

3 Many of the 17 SDGs and the associated 169 targets involve long-standing trade-related issues, such as the reform of government support for fisheries or fossil fuels.

the right to adopt appropriate measures to protect human, animal or plant life or health and environment.

In connection with discriminatory treatment, in the history of GATT and the WTO environmental policies were the subject of only nine panel proceedings from a total of 356 disputes (from 1995 to 2020) involving the examination of environmental measures or human health-related measures. The countries most often accused of abusing Article XX of GATT were the United States, and members of the European Communities/European Union.

Recording environmental-related notifications and measures in the WTO contributes to transparency and avoiding discriminatory treatment. In 2021, the WTO members submitted 827 environmental-related notifications, which was 16.7 percent of the total submitted notifications (WTO, 2022). Since 1997, there has been a sustained increase in the number of environmental-related notifications to the WTO. The share of environmental-related notifications as a percentage of all notifications more than doubled over the same period albeit with year-on-year fluctuations (see Figure 6.1). The predominant part of environmental-related notifications was related to the Technical Barriers to Trade (TBR) Agreement. Thus, in the period 2009–2020 more than 62 percent of the total environmental-related notifications was covered by the TBR Agreement (WTO, 2022). Figure 6.1 depicts the total number of environmental-related notifications (the left axis) in the period 1997–2020 for which data are available, and the proportion of environmental-related notifications to the total number of notifications (the right axis).

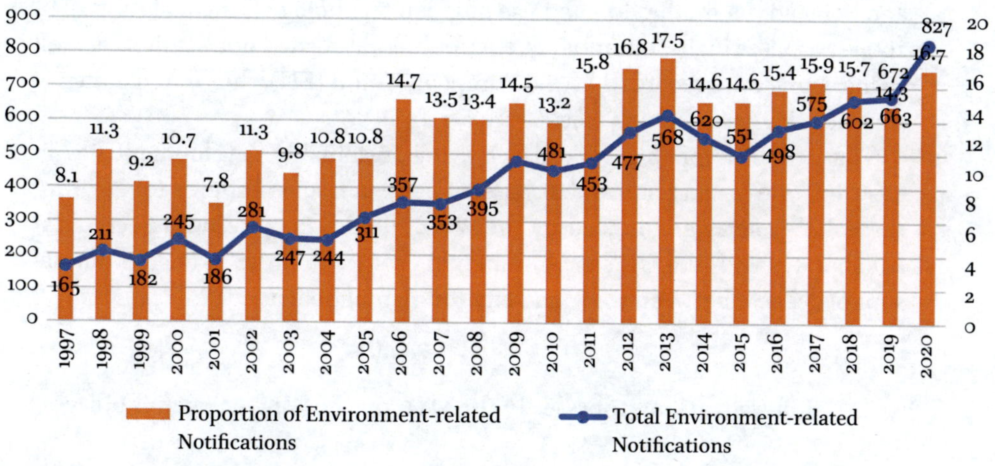

FIGURE 6.1 Environmental-related notifications in the WTO in 1997–2020

SOURCE: OWN ELABORATION, DATA FROM THE WTO ENVIRONMENTAL DATABASE (WTO, 2022)

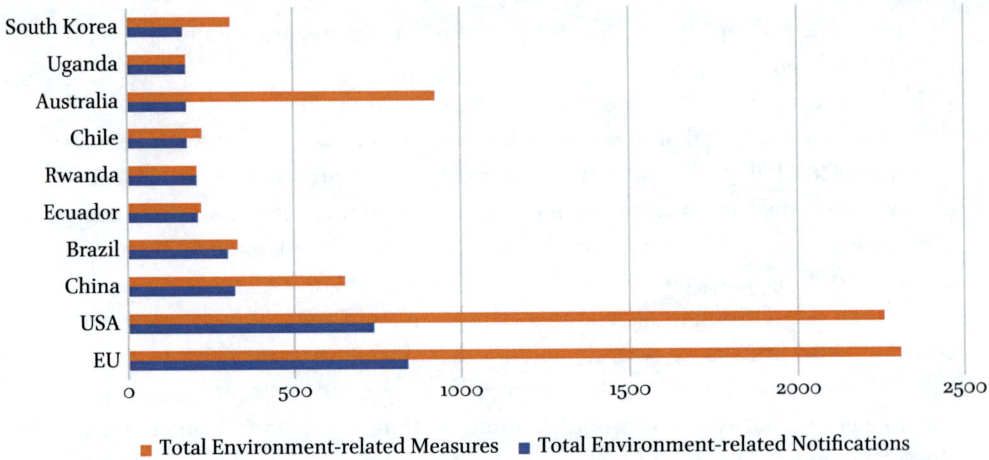

FIGURE 6.2 Top 10 WTO members by environmental-related notifications and measures in 2009–2020
SOURCE: OWN ELABORATION, DATA FROM THE WTO ENVIRONMENTAL DATABASE (WTO, 2022)

Besides notifications, the Committee on Trade and Environment recorded 14,604 environmental-related measures that were introduced by the WTO members in the period 2009–2020. The Committee receives data about environmental-related measures from regular Trade Policy Reviews, which enables the Committee to understand how the WTO members are addressing environmental challenges through specific trade policy measures. For example, the Trade Policy Review of Malaysia in 2017 showed that the Malaysian government encouraged R&D, promoted small and medium-sized enterprises (SMEs), and boosted the production and use of green technology (Lim et al., 2020). In 2009–2020, the highest number of environmental-related notifications as well as measures were recorded by the European Union (EU), the United States of America (USA) and China (see Figure 6.2).

Thus, the role of the WTO in achieving sustainable development lies in ensuring rule-based trade and discussing trade measures adopted for environmental objectives announced by the WTO. In addition, the WTO Secretariat collaborates with the UN's environmental entities in order to ensure mutual supportiveness between trade and environmental policies.

4 Liberalization Processes in the WTO on the Way to Sustainability

The WTO as a supporter of free trade plays an especially important role in ensuring market access for environmental goods and services. In the era of the WTO, the first environment-specific discussion was opened in the Doha Round of trade negotiations, which was launched in 2001. In Doha, the WTO members received a mandate to negotiate certain areas focused on trade and environment, particularly the relationship between the multilateral trade agreements governed by the WTO and those of other agencies. These negotiations are managed by the Trade and Environmental Committee under Special Sessions.

On this base, in July 2014 a group of WTO members started negotiations in order to establish the Environmental Goods Agreement (EGA). The main idea of the EGA was to promote trade in key environmental products, such as wind turbines and solar panels to help achieve environmental and climate goals. The agreement was negotiated among 18 participants representing 46 WTO members (see Figure 6.3), benefiting all WTO members on the most favored nation (MFN) basis.

Although the EGA negotiations only covered about one-third of the WTO members, the participants accounted for the majority of global trade in environmental goods, which more than doubled to US$1,260 billion between 2003 and 2016, namely due to renewable energy plants that accounted for about 35 percent of exported environmental goods. In relative terms, the share of

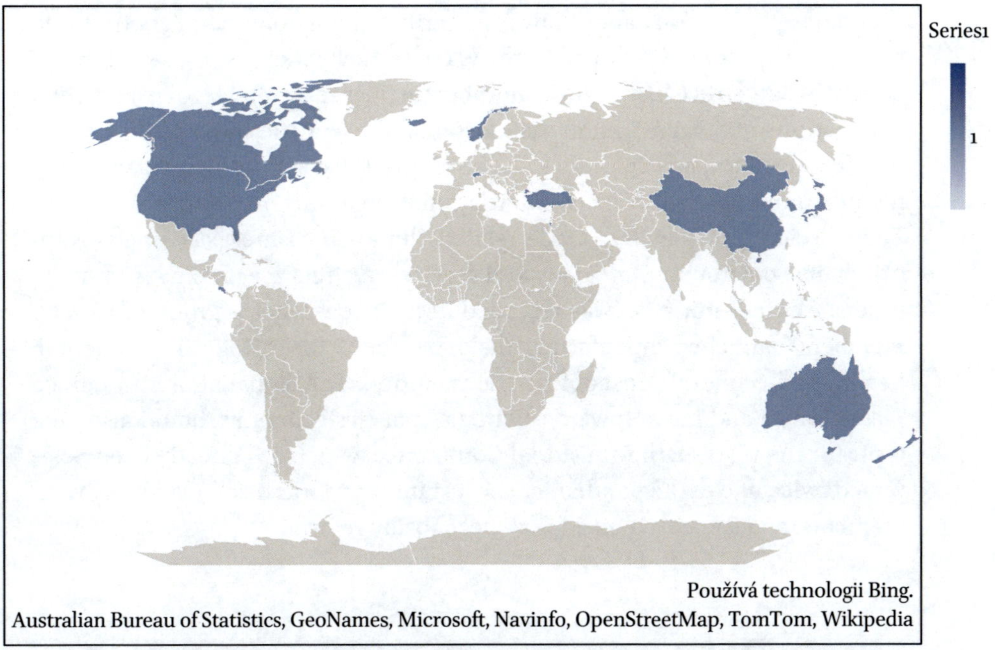

FIGURE 6.3 Negotiator countries of the environmental goods agreement

Note: The negotiators of the EGA were Australia, Canada, China, Costa Rica, European Union, Hong Kong (CH), Iceland, Israel, Japan, South Korea, New Zealand, Norway, Singapore, Switzerland, Liechtenstein, Chinese Taipei, Turkey, and United States.

SOURCE: OWN ELABORATION

trade in environmentally related goods in global trade grew from 7.2 percent to 8.1 percent (OECD, 2022).

Commitments to reduce bound tariffs on those goods to zero was based on the APEC List of 54 Environmental Goods. In the period 2001–2016, 18 rounds of negotiations took place, especially in Geneva. Participants held a discussion on product coverage and the EGA text in various configurations. In 2015, the negotiations already included a list of roughly 650 product groups of the Harmonized System, and discussions were held in small groups that included the key proponents and opponents of each product (Global Affairs Canada, 2014). Although constructive talks were held, the participants were not in a position to close the EGA negotiations, which were suspended at the end of 2016. Regardless of the unsuccessful negotiations, the average tariffs applied to the imports of environmental goods in the OECD countries declined from 1.7 percent in 2003 to 0.8 percent in 2016. Tariffs in countries outside the OECD area were significantly higher, but also declined from 7.4 percent to 4.1 percent at the same time (OECD, 2022). However, tariffs on renewable energy goods and heat pumps remained on a high level, i.e., between 10 and 14 percent (Okonjo-Iweala, 2022).

Besides negotiations about lowering tariffs on environmental goods, three new initiatives were developed in the WTO. In November 2020, 50 WTO members of a large diversity, whose number increased to 71 in 2021, launched negotiations about environmental sustainability on the basis of structured discussions. The participants of the structured discussion include the business community, civil society, international organizations, and universities. They discuss topics such as trade-related climate measures, sustainable supply chains, environmental goods and services, a circular economy, and many others. Another initiative was recorded in June 2021 when a group of 16 WTO members[4] launched an informal dialogue about the rising environmental, health, and economic costs of plastic pollution. The global efforts to reduce plastic waste and move towards a circular plastics economy should also be a topic for the WTO's 12th Ministerial Conference, which has already been postponed twice due to the pandemic. The last initiative was developed by 45 WTO members, and is focused on a fossil fuel subsidy reform.

4 The group of 16 WTO countries includes Australia, Barbados, Cabo Verde, Canada, the Central African Republic, China, Ecuador, Fiji, the Gambia, Jamaica, Morocco, New Zealand, Switzerland, Thailand, and the United Kingdom (WTO, 2021a).

4.1 *The Liberalization of Agricultural Trade*

The liberalization of agricultural trade has belonged to the most sensitive areas of multilaterally led negotiations for decades. The restart of the negotiations began in early 2000 under a mandate set out in Article 20 of the WTO Agreement on Agriculture. Besides the liberalization of agricultural trade, the agreement mentioned that talks should consider other objectives, such as food security and the protection of the environment. These issues are also covered by the WTO Agreement on Sanitary and Phytosanitary Measures. The agreement enables members to adopt sanitary and phytosanitary measures for environmental purposes, but should not create unnecessary obstacles to trade, should not discriminate between members, and measures should be adopted in a transparent way. Thus, the role of the WTO lies in making markets more sustainable, stable, and predictable through trade rules. Trade talks could also improve the competitiveness and resilience of producers, and food security for consumers. Moreover, the WTO trade negotiations could contribute to a more effective allocation of scarce global resources, such as reducing the levels of agricultural supports that are connected with greenhouse gas emissions, and thus mitigate the negative impact of climate changes.

The current agricultural negotiations are held in the frame of the Doha Round that was launched in 2001. Agriculture is a part of a "single undertaking," which means that all areas of negotiations will be finalized as a whole package. As a result, while the objectives of the trade talks were set in 2001, the WTO members reached progress especially in the trade talks at the 2013 Bali Ministerial Conference and the 2015 Nairobi Ministerial Conference. The farm trade package, which was agreed at the Ministerial Conference in Bali in 2013, includes facilitating imports that are allowed under tariff rate quotas, reflecting the various needs of developing countries and granting them some exemptions. The Nairobi package includes the commitments of the WTO members such as to abolish agricultural export subsidies and set new rules for other forms of farm export support, which went hand in hand with the UN's Sustainable Development Goals, namely SDG 2.[5] However, some countries consider the Nairobi Decision as "unfinished business" with respect to various measures which can have similar effects on trade comparable to those of export subsidies. Moreover, although export subsidies were abolished, the area of domestic support remains the most crucial topic in the agricultural negotiations until now.

---

5 SDG 2 deals with the end of starvation, achieving food security and improved nutrition, and promoting sustainable agriculture.

Regardless of the fact that particular progress in the farm trade talks was reached at the Bali and Nairobi Ministerial Conferences, persistent gaps between the negotiating positions among the WTO members continue to exist. The current agricultural negotiations focus on seven topics, such as domestic support, market access, export competition, export prohibitions and restrictions, and the area of cotton. The other two areas include negotiations on a new special safeguard mechanism and talks on public stockholding programs for food security purposes. Both areas of these negotiations cover the special issues of developing countries, such as allowing them to temporarily increase tariffs in the event of a sudden surge in import volumes or price depression, and to apply farm subsidy rules at government-set prices.

The 2030 Agenda for Sustainable Development, namely SDG 14.6, aims to prohibit certain forms of fisheries subsidies which would contribute to overcapacity and overfishing by 2020.

Public spending has contributed to a situation where nearly half of the global marine fish stocks are overfished, threatening the livelihoods of 260 million people (Okonjo-Iweala, 2022). Although the WTO plays an important role in this issue, the deadline which was set by the 2030 Agenda was not performed and negotiations have continued until now. The Ministerial Declaration from the WTO's 11th Ministerial Conference includes the decision to conclude negotiations and adopt an agreement on fisheries subsidies reflecting the UN Sustainable Development Target 14.6, namely to prevent illegal, unreported, and unregulated fishing. The draft agreement on fisheries subsidies was submitted by the WTO negotiators in November 2021 for consideration by the WTO ministers at the 12th Ministerial Conference in Geneva in December 2021. Although the draft text covers all negotiated topics, including specific provisions for least developed countries (LDCs) members as well as technical assistance and capacity building assistance to developing countries, it does not represent the final text. The main reason is that many disagreements remain in the individual negotiation groups (see Table 6.1). In addition, the 12th Ministerial Conference was postponed due to the COVID-19 pandemic developments to June 2022. The Ministerial Decision of 17 June 2022 has only confirmed the need to continue the negotiations to make recommendations to the 13th WTO Ministerial Conference for additional provisions that would achieve a comprehensive agreement on fisheries subsidies.

With respect to the fact that the WTO currently has 164 members with different interests, finding compromise solutions in trade talks is often very difficult. Thus, countries create coalition groups that speak with one voice using a single coordinator or negotiating team in the WTO practice. Table 6.1 shows the main groups engaged in agricultural negotiations held under the WTO framework. The overview of the negotiation groups indicates some facts: besides the

TABLE 6.1 WTO agricultural negotiation groups

Groups	Description	Issues	WTO members
ACP	African, Caribbean, and Pacific countries with preferences in the EU	Agricultural preferences	62
African Group	African members and observers of the WTO	General	44
Asian Developing Members	Asian developing WTO members	General	35
Land-locked Developing Countries	Informal group of land-locked developing countries	General	26
Mercosur	Common Market of the Southern Cone, a customs union	General	4
G-90	African Group + ACP + LDCs	General	72
LDCs	Least developed countries	General	35
SVEs	Small, vulnerable economies	General	32
Article XII Members	A group composed of members that joined the WTO after 1995	General	23
Low-income economies in transition	A group is seeking to secure the same treatment as LDCs	Agriculture	3
Cairns group	A coalition of agricultural exporting nations lobbying for agricultural trade liberalization	Agriculture	19
Tropical products	A coalition of developing countries seeking greater market access for tropical products	Agriculture	8
G-10	A coalition of countries lobbying for agriculture to be treated as diverse and special because of non-trade concerns	Agriculture	9
G-20	A coalition of developing countries pressing for an ambitious reform of agriculture in developed countries with some flexibilities for developing countries	Agriculture	23
G-33	A coalition of developing countries striving to undertake limited market opening in agriculture	Agriculture	47
Cotton-4	A West African coalition seeking cuts in cotton subsidies and tariffs	Agriculture	5
Pacific Group	Developing country members of the Pacific Islands Forum	General	6

SOURCE: WTO (2022)

agricultural aspect, the negotiation groups usually reflect geographical coverage, they are of different sizes and predominantly represent the interests of developing countries.

The main exporter as well as importer of agricultural products is the European Union (EU). In 2020, the EU shared by more than 36 percent in the world agricultural exports and by about 32 percent in the world agricultural imports. Besides the EU, the USA, China, Brazil, Canada, Indonesia, Thailand, Mexico, India, and Argentina are also among the top ten agricultural exporters. The list of the top ten agricultural importers is a little bit different; it includes the EU, China, the USA, Japan, the United Kingdom, Canada, South Korea, Russia, Mexico, and India. However, except for India, the other countries are also among the leading exporters and importers of food. All these leading exporters and importers shared in the world agricultural and food trade by more than 70 percent in 2020 (WTO, 2021a). This probably explains why these countries are only sporadic participants in the WTO agricultural coalition groups.

4.2 *Liberalization of Trade in Services with Focus on the Environment*

As Sauvage and Timiliotis (2017) state, there are strong complementarities between environmental goods and the provision of services, because numerous services are essential to the proper delivery and functioning of environmental equipment. As trade in environmental goods has lowered the price of cleaner technologies, it appears that trade in environmental services could lower the cost of environmental protection (OECD, 2022). Thus, negotiations about removing barriers to trade in goods should be accompanied by liberalization in trade in services.

Environmental services represent one of the broad 12 service sectors which are qualified in the Services Sectoral Classification List (the W/120 Classification List). The Classification List is based on the UN's Central Product Classification, which also distinguishes four environmental subsectors:

- Sewage services (A)
- Refuse disposal services (B)
- Sanitation and similar services (C)
- Other environmental services (D)[6]

However, the scope of what has the character of environmental related services is the subject of long-term discussions, and also many other services not

6 Other environmental services include the cleaning of exhaust gases, noise abatement services, nature and landscape protection services, and other environmental protection services which correspond to the four other environmental service subsectors identified in the UN's Provisional Central Product Classification (WTO, 2022).

classified as environmental have environmental use. For example, repair or preservation can play an important role in the installation and functioning of environmental facilities. Thus, for removing barriers to trade, especially non-tariff barriers, a better identification of environmental-related services would be desirable.

In principle, the so-called core environmental services, such as wastewater treatment and solid-waste management, are public goods. They have several specific characteristics, i.e., they benefit all members of society, they are non-excludable and non-rivalrous from consumption. They require large-scale investment, and, thus, they are managed and financed by public utilities or a few large multinational companies from developed countries. Besides infrastructure environmental services, specialized small firms can also provide non-infrastructure environmental services, such as consulting, legal services, accounting services, etc. This is also an opportunity for small suppliers from developed as well as developing countries. Thus, besides trade liberalization, the privatization of the suppliers of environmental services is important as well.

Trade in environmental services has gained significance in recent years, particularly in connection with global challenges, such as climate change, resource depletion, and waste generation. Moreover, the development of new technologies has also contributed to the growth of this sector, with new areas of trade negotiations dealing, for example, with the circular economy transition.

In the WTO, the General Agreement on Trade in Services (GATS) modifies trade in environmental services. The GATS sets rules for trade in services based on non-discriminatory treatment. Like Article XX of GATT, paragraph (b) of the GATS allows the WTO members to adopt policy measures that would normally be inconsistent with the GATS if it is necessary to protect human, animal or plant life or health. However, these measures should not result in arbitrary or unjustifiable discrimination and should not constitute hidden protectionism.[7]

The liberalization of services is generally carried out through members' commitments. Every WTO member has a national schedule, which includes two types of commitments, i.e., horizontal and specific commitments accepted through services sectors and subsectors corresponding to the W/120 Classification List. While horizontal limitation[8] is applied across all sectors and often refers to a particular mode of supply (see Table 6.2), specific

7 The GATS also determines six types of quantitative restrictions, including limitations on types of legal entity and on foreign equity participation.

8 Horizontal limitations include limitations on real estate ownership or lease, foreign equity limitations, economic needs tests, residency or nationality requirements for directors,

TABLE 6.2 Examples of services provided by WTO modes of supply

Mode	Description	Example
1 – Cross-border trade	From the territory of one member into the territory of any member	A company monitors and diagnoses its wind turbines from one foreign-based remote operations center.
2 – Consumption abroad	In the territory of one member to the service consumer of any other member	An engineer travels abroad to further his or her knowledge of energy efficiency through a course organized by foreign experts.
3 – Commercial presence abroad	By a service supplier of one member, through commercial presence in the territory of any other member	A firm establishes several subsidiaries abroad to provide environmental consulting and engineering services locally.
4 – Temporary presence of natural persons abroad	By a service supplier of one Member, through the temporary presence of natural persons of member in the territory of any other member	Experts in a particular environmental domain travel abroad to train local staff or conduct repairs.

SOURCE: SAUVAGE AND TIMILIOTIS (2017)

commitments deal with only a particular service, and specify the levels of market access and national treatment. When a member receives a commitment in a sector or subsector it must indicate for each mode of supply what limitations it maintains on market access. Practical examples of the four modes of supply through which services are traded in the WTO framework with focus on the environmental industry are introduced in Table 6.2.

The WTO negotiations about trade liberalization in the environmental sector began in January 2000 under the Council for Trade in Services. Between 2000 and 2002, seven WTO members (Australia, Canada, Cuba, Colombia, EU, Switzerland, and the US) submitted negotiation proposals. Besides proposals to ensure market access for environmental services, these countries proposed to broaden the sectoral classification of environmental services to bring the

discriminatory minimum capital requirements, technology transfer requirements, and the obligation to train nationals.

W/120 Classification List into line with the current practice in trade in services. For example, the European Union and Switzerland proposed a more diversified classification with the creation of seven environmental subsectors, which would increase the possibility for the WTO members to make commitments. The USA highlighted the importance of liberalizing core environmental services along with those that are related (namely under business services, construction services, and distribution services). However, the WTO members have not agreed so far to formally modify the classification of environmental services. In addition, the last report about the results of the WTO's negotiations in environmental service sectors was published by the Trade Negotiations Committee in 2010.

In parallel to these negotiations, the environment has been a part of the Doha negotiations which focused on the reduction or elimination of tariff and non-tariff barriers to environmental goods and services. It has been included in the Doha Declaration (WTO, 2001). After the 2005 Hong Kong Ministerial Conference, a group of 23 WTO members submitted a plurilateral request on environmental services to a group of 20 other members. This collective request included commitments for high levels of market access across all environmental service subsectors, in the four modes of supply.[9]

However, compared with other sectors, such as tourism, financial services, or telecommunications, the level of commitments has remained modest (WTO, 2022). As of January 1, 2022, 59 WTO members (counting the EU with 25 members as one[10]) had made commitments in at least one environmental service subsector. Specifically, 52 members have accepted commitments for sewage services, 50 members for refuse disposal services, 51 members for sanitation and similar services, and 51 members for other environmental services. Although many empirical studies have confirmed a detrimental effect of protectionism on trade (for example, Sauvage & Timiliotis, 2017), the reason for only small progress that was recorded in these negotiations can be related to the fact that developed countries have a higher interest in the liberalization of environmental services than developing countries.[11]

9 Although environmental negotiations have taken place on a plurilateral base, the outcomes of these negotiations are applied on the MFN basis, i.e., to all WTO members in compliance with the WTO rules.

10 Although the EU has had 27 members since 2021, the WTO database introduced commitments for the EU with 25 members in January 2022.

11 The developed countries which managed the top 50 environmental companies are the main consumers and suppliers of environmental services, and developing countries are net importers of environmental services (WTO, 2010).

4.3 *Intellectual Property Protection and Sustainability*

Intellectual property rights (IPRs) can be defined as the rights given to people over the creations of their minds (Cosbey, 2000). They are legally enforceable and are granted by the state to owners of IPRs. They specify a time period during which other producers may not copy the innovators' inventions, giving them the possibility to cover the costs coupled with the innovations and invest in new research. The argument for IPRs protection is that without the protection of new inventions, there would be less innovation. It is cheaper to manufacture drugs, computer software, etc. than to develop them. Intellectual property protection, thus, has legal, economic, and social aspects.

While the World Intellectual Property Organization (WIPO) promotes and protects intellectual property across the world through the administration of international treaties that deal with a wide variety of intellectual property issues, the WTO, on the one hand, promotes effective and adequate protection of IPRs, and, on the other hand, ensures that measures and procedures to enforce IPRs do not become barriers to trade. With respect to the fact that IPRs also have an impact on trade and sustainability,[12] cooperation among the WTO, the WIPO, and the World Health Organization (WHO) is needed. While the topic of IPRs from the point of view of different international organizations is described in more detail in Chapter 14, in this part of the monograph we focus solely on the WTO trade liberalization in light of the Sustainable Development Goals.

The WTO Agreement on Trade-Related Aspects of Intellectual Property Rights (hereafter the TRIPS Agreement) states, in particular, that "the protection and enforcement of IPRs should contribute to the promotion of technological innovation and to the transfer and dissemination of technology." In relation to the environment, the TRIPS Agreement (2017) sets certain inventions ineligible for patenting in order to protect human, animal or plant life or health, and to avoid serious harm to the environment. While plants, animals, etc., can be excluded from patenting, plant varieties as well as microorganisms, etc., have to be eligible for protection either through patents or another specific system, or a combination of the two. The discussion about this topic and

12 Cosbey (2000), in an examination of the effects of the TRIPS Agreement on the sustainable development in developing countries, states that the strengthening of IPRs embodied in the TRIPS Agreement will have varied effects on innovation in different countries. Developing countries that have a healthy domestic capacity for research and development and strong management and marketing skills may benefit from stronger IPR laws in terms of increased domestic innovation. Those that do not may be hampered by TRIPS in their ability to develop such capacity through the necessary imitation stage of development.

the need to modify the TRIPS Agreement began in 1999 in the TRIPS Council, and has continued under the Doha Round framework. The debate currently has the form of informal consultations chaired by the WTO director-general and focuses especially on the relation between the TRIPS Agreement and the UN's Convention on Biological Diversity.

The topic of IPRs also gained significance at the WTO Ministerial Conference in Doha in 2001, especially with a focus on public health. As a result of the negotiations, a separate declaration to the TRIPS Agreement set the possibility to adopt appropriate measures necessary to protect public health. In this vein, the Declaration confirmed the governments' right to use the agreement flexibilities, in particular, compulsory licensing and parallel importing. This means that generic versions of the patented product can be locally manufactured or imported without the authorization of the patent holder (WTO et al., 2020). The decision to remove the final patent obstacles to cheap drug imports was accepted by the WTO members in 2003, and was replaced by a Protocol amending the TRIPS Agreement, which took effect in 2017. In practice, it waives the countries' obligation under the provision of the TRIPS Agreement, which says that production under compulsory licensing must be predominantly for the domestic market. Removing obstacles in production and drug export expresses the fact that public health problems resulting from HIV/AIDS, malaria, and other epidemics are global problems with impacts on human society, and take development issues fully into account. As a result, thanks to the transition period under the TRIPS Agreement, which currently exempts LDCs from implementing patent protection for pharmaceutical products, generic manufactures in Bangladesh have begun producing a generic version of remdesivir against the threat of COVID-19, which is patented in a number of other countries (WTO, 2020).

Besides public health, the flexibilities in the TRIPS Agreement could also be applied in other areas in order to contribute to sustainable development in the world. For example, some developing countries negotiating climate change issues have argued that flexibilities are significant for getting access to green technology. At the 14th Global Forum for Food and Agriculture in January 2022, Pauman (2022) emphasized the important role of trade in ensuring efficient agricultural production and in providing access to technologies needed to improve soil management.

Thus, international trade can contribute to sustainable development through the WTO negotiations, which have two directions, i.e., negotiations about lowering tariffs on environmental goods and using the TRIPS flexibilities for getting better access to technologies.

5 Conclusions

Although international organizations, such as the WTO and the OECD, have a long tradition in supporting free trade and sustainability, the real achievements of trade negotiations led on the multilateral level within the Doha Development Round are not visible enough. The analysis of trade negotiations in the WTO in the area of agricultural trade shows "a grey area" more than real progress in trade negotiations. This means that the main topics, such as domestic support, market access, export competition, and restrictions, have been negotiated for more than 20 years. In the area of services trade the technical issue that is connected with the classification of services has been negotiated since 2000, and also the level of members' commitments remains low in comparison with other sectors. The only limited success was achieved in technological transfer in the area of public health, but other areas for flexibilities in the TRIPS Agreement remain open for discussion. The main reason for the stagnation in the negotiations is the single-undertaking approach that the WTO members approved within the Doha Round in 2001. As the interests of the WTO members are different and making compromise solutions is difficult, a single undertaking among 164 WTO members is impossible. Moreover, the trade policy of the individual members usually varies under the influence of their domestic policy priorities.

The plurilateral initiatives under the WTO framework show the fact that only a limited number of members is interested in trade liberalization. Thus, although trade can contribute to sustainable development in many ways, the multilateral negotiations are not effective. Therefore, the hypothesis that trade liberalization, which is carried out under the WTO multilateral framework and supported by the OECD, contributes to sustainable development in the world, has not been confirmed. The growing number of environmental-related notifications in the WTO can, on the one hand, show a transparency in trade, but, on the other hand, the environmental-related measures can be the source of "green protectionism" in the form of non-tariff barriers. In addition, the data about tariffs on the imports of environmental goods declined although the EGA was not signed by the WTO members.

Although the OECD grants analytical support in the form of data for negotiations on trade and environment and the WTO ensures transparency in trade, progress in multilateral trade negotiations is very small. Thus, progress in environmental negotiations in the WTO can be achieved by a complex reform of the WTO, which would bring changes in the multilateral system. Besides the modernization of the WTO functioning, it would also be desirable to solve new aspects of trade that are the result of economic globalization. In this vein, some

WTO members, such as the EU, Japan, etc., have already submitted proposals for a WTO reform towards a sustainable and effective multilateral system. Besides this, personal changes in the WTO Secretariat occurred as well. Thus, the reform of the WTO is a topic for the upcoming 12th Ministerial Conference. If these negotiations are without results, it will again reduce the credibility of the WTO. Moreover, the mistrust in the WTO is followed by the growing activities of countries through regional trade agreements. However, global problems, which deal with achieving sustainable development, need global solutions.

References

Cosbey, A. (2000, September 7). Sustainable development effects of the WTO TRIPS Agreement: A focus on developing countries. Institute for Agriculture & Trade Policy. https://www.iatp.org/documents/sustainable-development-effects-of-the-wto-trips-agreement-a-focus-on-developing-countries

Dellink, R., Hwang H., Lanzi, E., & Chateau, J. (2017, April 29). International trade consequences of climate change. OECD Trade and Environmental Working Papers, no. 2017/01. Organisation for Economic Co-operation and Development. https://www.oecd-ilibrary.org/docserver/9f446180-en.pdf?expires=1641130278&id=id&accname=guest&checksum=1130DF14258290E5DBBF1DCE33F6EF09

Elms, K. D., & Low, P. (2013). *Global value chains in a changing world.* Fung Global Institute, Nanyang Technological University & WTO. https://www.wto.org/english/res_e/booksp_e/aid4tradeglobalvalue13_e.pdf

Garsous, G. (2019, March 1). Trends in policy indicators on trade and environment. OECD Trade and Environmental Working Papers, no. 2019/01. Organisation for Economic Co-operation and Development. https://www.oecd-ilibrary.org/docserver/b8d2bcac-en.pdf?expires=1641290974&id=id&accname=guest&checksum=45B95EC9FF05799A6ACF28A597303937

Global Affairs Canada. (2014, July 8). Joint statement regarding trade in environmental goods. Government of Canada. https://www.international.gc.ca/trade-agreements-accords-commerciaux/topics-domaines/env/joint-statement-goods-declaration-commune-biens.aspx?lang=eng

Grossman, G. M., & Rossi-Hansberg, E. (2006). The rise of offshoring: It's not wine for cloth anymore. In *Proceedings – Economic Policy Symposium – Jackson Hole* (pp. 59–102). Federal Reserve Bank of Kansas City. https://www.princeton.edu/~erossi/RO.pdf

Jansen, M., & Keck, A. (2004, January). National environmental policies and multilateral trade rules. WTO Working Paper, no. ERSD-2004-01. World Trade Organization. https://www.wto.org/english/res_e/reser_e/ersd200401_e.htm

Lim, A. H., Mathur S., & Suk, G. (2020, March 24). Trade and environment: What can we learn from trade policy reviews? WTO Staff Working Paper, no. ERSD-2020-06. World Trade Organization. https://www.wto.org/english/res_e/reser_e/ersd202006_e.pdf

Low, P., Marceau, G., & Reinaud, J. (2011, January 12). The interface between the trade and climate change regimes: Scoping the issues. WTO Staff Working Paper, no. ERSD-2011-1. World Trade Organization. https://www.wto.org/english/res_e/reser_e/ersd201101_e.pdf

OECD. (2016, December 13). Better policies for 2030: An OECD action plan on the Sustainable Development Goals. Organisation for Economic Co-operation and Development. https://www.oecd.org/dac/Better%20Policies%20for%202030.pdf

OECD. (2022). *OECD Work on Trade and the Environment: A Retrospective, 2008–2020*. Organisation for Economic Co-operation and Development. https://www.oecd.org/trade/topics/trade-and-the-environment/

Okonjo-Iweala, N. (2022, January 28). DG Okonjo-Iweala tells sustainability conference "trade is part of the solution to challenges we face" [blog post]. World Trade Organization. https://www.wto.org/english/news_e/news22_e/dgno_28jan22_e.htm

Paugam, J. M. (2022, January 28). DDG Paugman underscores important role of trade for food security, sustainable land use [blog post]. World Trade Organization. https://www.wto.org/english/news_e/news22_e/ddgjp_28jan22_e.htm

Robalino, J., & Herrera, L. D. (2010, January). Trade and deforestation: A literature review. WTO Working Paper, no. ERSD-2010-04. World Trade Organization. https://www.wto.org/english/res_e/reser_e/ersd201004_e.pdf

Sauvage, J., & Timiliotis, C. (2017, May 9). Trade in services related to the environment. OECD Trade and Environment Working Papers, no. 2017/02. Organisation for Economic Co-operation and Development. https://www.oecd-ilibrary.org/docserver/dc99bf2b-en.pdf?expires=1642331537&id=id&accname=guest&checksum=54B681EB5301498DBD32E0B39620F3A8

Steinfatt, K. (2020, June 23). Trade policies for a circular economy: What can we learn from WTO experience? WTO Staff Working Paper, no. ERSD-2020-10. https://www.wto.org/english/res_e/reser_e/ersd202010_e.pdf

UNCTAD. (2021a). Developing and developed regions. United Nations Conference on Trade and Development. Retrieved January 30, 2022. https://unctadstat.unctad.org/en/Classifications/DimCountries_DevStatus_Hierarchy.pdf

UNCTAD. (2021b). *World investment report 2021: Investing in sustainable recovery*. United Nations Conference on Trade and Development. https://unctad.org/system/files/official-document/wir2021_en.pdf

World Bank. (2021, July 27). Breathing uneasy: Regional response to air pollution in South Asia. Retrieved January 17, 2022. https://live.worldbank.org/breathing-uneasy-regional-response-air-pollution-south-asia

WTO. (2001, November 14). The Doha Declaration explained. World Trade Organization. Retrieved January 30, 2022. https://www.wto.org/english/docs_e/legal_e/legal_e.htm.

WTO. (2010). Background note on environmental services. World Trade Organization. https://docs.wto.org/dol2fe/Pages/SS/directdoc.aspx?filename=Q:/S/C/W320.pdf&Open=True

WTO. (2017). Agreement on Trade-Related Aspects of Intellectual Property Rights (as Amended on 23 January 2017). World Trade Organization. Retrieved January 17, 2022. https://www.wto.org/english/docs_e/legal_e/31bis_trips_01_e.htm

WTO. (2020). Short answers to big questions: On the WTO and the environment. World Trade Organization. https://www.wto.org/english/res_e/booksp_e/envirqapublication_e.pdf

WTO. (2021a). Informal dialogue on plastics pollution and environmentally sustainable plastic trade. World Trade Organization. Retrieved January 22, 2022. https://www.wto.org/english/news_e/news21_e/ega_21jun21_e.htm

WTO. (2021b). *World Trade Statistical Review 2021*. World Trade Organization. https://www.wto.org/english/res_e/statis_e/wts2021_e/wts2021_e.pdf

WTO. (2022). Environmental database. World Trade Organization. Retrieved January 4, 2022. https://edb.wto.org

WTO. (N.d.). Trade and environment. World Trade Organization. Retrieved January 14, 2022. https://www.wto.org/english/tratop_e/envir_e/envir_e.htm

WTO, WIPO, & WHO. (2020). *Promoting access to medical technologies and innovation*. World Trade Organization, World Intellectual Property Organization, and World Health Organization. https://www.wto.org/english/res_e/booksp_e/extract_who-wipo-wto_2020_e.pdf

Yamaguchi, S. (2021, February 19). International trade and circular economy – Policy alignment. OECD Trade and Environment Working Papers, no. 2021/02. https://dx.doi.org/10.1787/ae4a2176-en

CHAPTER 7

The International Trade System in the Concept of Global Public Goods: Principles of Export Credit Functioning in WTO and OECD Regulations

Piotr Stolarczyk

1 Introduction

The growing importance of international trade for world development is undeniable. Trade is an increasing share of the world's GDP. The importance of trade increases with the liberalization of international trade rules. Countries compete for a share in world trade perceiving it as a tool for stronger economic development, setting up special mechanisms for national export support, inter alia, by providing financing through special agendas and state-owned institutions (so-called export credits). State actions aimed at export support may lead to disruption of international trade rules and distort the competitiveness of traded goods and services (export and import). This is the main reason why the national systems of export credit support need to be regulated on the international level. Two international organizations, the World Trade Organization and the Organisation for Economic Co-operation and Development, set the legal framework for the principles of export credit support provided by all international trade actors. The rules ensure the retention of the basic characteristics of global public goods (GPGs), that they are non-excludable and non-rivalrous.

As generally accepted, public goods are both non-excludable and non-rivalrous. In other words, they are goods from the consumption of which no one can be excluded, and therefore their provision remains in the domain of the state. The process of globalization has given rise to a new category of goods which transcend national borders and which are characterized by collective consumption on a global scale. Research conducted by Inge Kaul in 1999 became crucial in the development of the concept of GPGs (Kaul et al., 1999).[1] In light of the considerations that have been made so far, it can be assumed that GPGs are a specific type of public good that have become internationalized

1 For more on the theory of global public goods (GPGs), see Chapter 1.

DOI:10.1163/9789004687264_009

as a result of globalization, while retaining the basic characteristics of public goods (i.e., non-excludable and non-rivalrous). GPGs, apart from goods such as security, health, and a clean environment, also include an open and non-discriminatory system of international trade.

The institution that provides public goods is the state, which creates its supply through taxation and ensures open consumption by all market participants. At the international level, however, there are no institutions that can play a commensurate role. The benefits of consuming GPGs are geographically dispersed and spread over time, making it more difficult to provide (and finance). It seems that the entities that can take the most effective actions in the context of managing GPGs are international organizations.

Of special interest to the author are the rules defining the principles of financing global trade (so-called export credits and export insurance[2]). There are two important organizations responsible for setting up the regulatory framework for all the export credit and insurance principles, namely the World Trade Organization (WTO) and the Organisation for Economic Co-operation and Development (OECD).[3]

It is worth emphasizing that 80% of world trade requires some form of financing (Napiórkowski & Stolarczyk, 2018; Antras & Fritz Foley, 2011). In this context, the non-discriminatory nature of the rules specifically related to financing trade is one of the fundamental conditions for its sustainable development. The WTO and the OECD have long emphasized the crucial importance of companies' access to finance for trade development. The studies confirm the positive impact of trade financing on the volume of international trade (Napiórkowski & Stolarczyk, 2018; Manova & Zhang, 2012; Chor & Manova, 2012; Auboin, 2009). The value of insurance was used as a proxy for the amount of financing. Therefore, it was established that the higher the value of export insurance to a given country, the higher the value of international trade in that country.

Export credits, which are a special form of foreign trade financing insured by state agencies, can also be a tool of foreign policy. They can be used, for example, to encourage export in directions considered by the government to be strategic. They can also be used to support selected industries in the economy (Dewit, 2001). Ahn et al. (2011) showed that the decline in US exports was greater in sectors more dependent on external financing. Amiti and Weinstein (2011) emphasize the relationship between export sales of companies and the

2 Export financing takes the form of either export credit insurance, export credit, or official development assistance.

3 For more about trade liberalization under the WTO and OECD rules, see Chapter 3.

possibility of obtaining external financing and the condition of the banking sector. Similar conclusions were drawn by Felbermayr and Yalcin (2013), who describe exports in individual sectors of the German economy in their model, Egger and Url (2006), who examine the foreign trade of Austria, Janda (2014), who analyzes the situation in the Czech Republic, and Bricogne et al. (2010), in their study of France. In a broader sense, companies using financial products show higher sales and employment than export companies that do not use them (Felbermayr et al., 2012).

The analysis is based on the tests of both WTO and OECD regulations, which, in the author's opinion, relate to the rules of financing international trade. In the context of issues concerning trade finance rules, these regulations, as the author shows, are inextricably linked, forming a coherent whole. The starting point for the analysis is the definition of the essence of international organizations in the context of GPGs.

In the next section the relevant provisions of the Agreement on Subsidies and Countervailing Measures, the Agreement on Agriculture, and the OECD Consensus are analyzed.

2 The Background of Institutionalization of International Trade as a GPG

Created in 1947, the General Agreement on Tariffs and Trade (GATT) was a treaty regulating trade policy.[4] Its main task was to liberalize trade. GATT pursued its objectives through so-called negotiating rounds, which mainly concerned the abolition of non-tariff barriers and lowering tariffs. The WTO is a continuation of GATT. It was established in 1994 in Marrakech within the framework of the so-called Uruguay Round of GATT. The WTO commenced its activities on January 1, 1995. The objectives of liberalizing international trade in goods and services and protecting equal access to the global market remained unchanged.

The removal of trade restrictions, including the lowering of tariffs, was accompanied by a dynamic increase in international competition which domestic enterprises had to face. As trade liberalization progressed, the struggle for foreign markets became more intense. Under such conditions, it became important, especially for open economies, firstly, to address the issue of available export support instruments and those allowed by international

4 Agreement signed in Geneva in 1947. GATT entered into force on January 1, 1948.

regulations. Secondly, it was essential to maintain the shape of regulations which ensure the non-discriminatory nature of global trade and, at the same time, unrestricted access to the global market of goods and services. This concerns not only the principles of maintaining tariff or non-tariff barriers but also issues related to the use of export subsidies in various forms, including export credit financial support instruments. Entities of different market power (countries or companies) are brought together by the global market. An important goal of regulations is to ensure equal opportunities for all entities, taking into account their position on the global market. Regulations that create barriers to the cross-border movement of goods and services have the effect, firstly, of restricting market access; in other words, they introduce an element of discrimination against exporters/importers from different countries and against companies operating in internal markets. Secondly, these barriers affect all market participants on both the demand (buyer) and supply (seller) side (Napiórkowski & Stolarczyk, 2018).

The WTO is a regulator of GPGs, namely open and non-discriminatory international trade. The WTO also acts as a watchdog guarding respect for the established rules of the game. It is worth noting that WTO member countries account for 98% of world trade (Berthelot, 2019). In 2020 global trade constituted 50% of world GDP, whereas in 2010 it was 60% (World Bank, n.d.).[5] Exports account for more than a quarter of global income. International trade (including exports) is therefore a key aggregate of world income and a determinant of its growth. In this context, the principles governing world trade and the role played in this area by the WTO seem to be of crucial importance. It should also be emphasized that the shape of regulations (WTO decisions) has a huge impact on sustainable development of the world. Striving for sustainable development is one of the fundamental principles of the WTO. The system of preferential rules and special trade policy measures introduced for less developed countries aims at facilitating access to the world trade system and a fuller and more equal use of economic benefits resulting from the liberalization of trade exchange. The author devotes particular attention to this issue.

The second organization analyzed in this chapter is the Organisation for Economic Co-operation and Development (OECD). The OECD is an international organization of 38 highly developed countries. It was established by the Convention on the Organisation for Economic Co-operation and Development, signed in Paris on December 14, 1960. The OECD works out the "rules of the game" in international economic relations and introduces standards of

5 In 2010 it was 60 percent.

operation (best practices) in individual areas of the economy. An area of special attention are the OECD's activities in the field of sustainable international trade. The OECD defines the rules for providing financing (so-called export credits) for cross-border trade contracts. The role of the OECD in the context of the uninterrupted functioning of GPG is identical to that of the WTO. The written standards that financial institutions are required to follow are designed to put participants in the international trading market on an equal footing, so that those with a weaker capital position (or from less developed countries) can participate fully in global trade. In sum, there is a close relationship between WTO and OECD regulations in the area under analysis. Proceeding in accordance with the OECD principles sanctions the WTO rules.

3 Principles of Export Credit Functioning in WTO and OECD Regulations

3.1 *WTO Regulations*

As a general rule, the WTO, which replaced GATT,[6] introduced the prohibition of export subsidies that distort international trade. The rules concerning subsidies were already introduced under c and then extended to industrial products in the Agreement on Subsidies and Countervailing Measures (SCM Agreement) and to agricultural commodities in the Agreement on Agriculture (AoA). Both agreements are part of the treaties establishing the World Trade Organization.

This sections is structured as following. Analysis of the SCM Agreement constitutes the first subsection, where author provide definition of subsidies, rules on prohibited subsidies, and export credit and insurance as a form of subsidy. The SCM Agreement defines subsidies that are not prohibited. The second subsection introduces briefly the main rules concerning the subsidies under AoA. Export credit rules under the OECD Agreement are described in last subsection.

3.1.1 The SCM Agreement

The SCM Agreement refers to subsidies, as defined (Berthelot, 2019)[7] in Article 1 (of the Agreement), which are specific to a particular enterprise, a group of enterprises or an industry as defined in Article 2. Support, which falls within the definitions indicated in Article 1 and Article 2, is prohibited under Article 3.[8]

6 It was established in 1994 in Marrakech as part of the so-called Uruguay Round of GATT. It came into effect on January 1, 1995.
7 There is a ongoing criticism of the definition perceived to be unfair for developing countries.
8 Further comment below.

According to Article 1, a subsidy exists if the following conditions are met. Firstly, a government or any other public body provides funds ("financial contribution") in any form whatsoever. Secondly, it constitutes a benefit to a specific recipient.

The main principle is that "if the granting authority, or the legislation pursuant to which the granting authority operates, explicitly limits access to a subsidy to certain enterprises, such subsidy shall be specific." Thus, if a subsidy is specifically limited to a single trader, a group of specific traders, a specific industry or economic sector, certain undertakings located in a specific geographical region,[9] it shall be considered a specific subsidy. This is set out in Article 2, which introduces criteria necessary to determine whether a subsidy as defined in Article 1 is specific to a particular enterprise. According to Article 2, "the use of a subsidy program by a limited number of certain enterprises, the predominant use of subsidies by certain enterprises, the granting of disproportionately large subsidies to certain enterprises, and the manner in which discretion has been exercised by the granting authority in the decision to grant a subsidy."[10]

It should be noted that even if a subsidy is not formally restricted, but a disproportionate share of the funds is allocated to a certain group of entities, such a subsidy may be considered specific. Of course, this does not mean that in all similar situations, the above will determine the specificity of the subsidy. What is important is that the criteria or conditions for obtaining a subsidy are objective, so that if they are fulfilled, the subsidy can automatically be granted.[11]

The next step is to verify the "financial contribution" under Article 1, i.e., to check whether it is provided by the government and whether it constitutes a benefit to the recipient.

The term "government" should be interpreted broadly. It refers not only to public authorities or government agencies but also to all entities that are directly or indirectly controlled by the state. This includes state-owned companies as well as the central bank. The term "financial contribution" includes a broad catalogue of forms of financial support that is provided by the state treasury. They include:

1. Donations, loans, and credits (including export credits) or capital contributions granted by the government that are a direct flow of funds

---

9 Article 2 (a).

10 Article 2 (c).

11 Article 2.1. "if the granting authority, or the legislation pursuant to which the granting authority operates, establishes objective criteria or conditions governing the eligibility for, and the amount of, the subsidy, provided that eligibility is automatic, that such criteria or conditions are strictly adhered to, and that they are clearly spelled out in an official document so as to be capable of verification."

2. Potential flows of funds or transfers of liabilities, e.g., in the form of loan guarantees
3. Tax exemptions granted to entrepreneurs, such as tax credits (e.g., reduction of the CIT rate or exemption from part of the tax)
4. The provision of goods and services by the government other than in the form of general infrastructure or the purchase of goods and services from a particular enterprise by the government

Financial support can be direct and indirect. Indirect is the use of private entities in which there is no government involvement to provide a "financial contribution" that constitutes a benefit and is specific to the enterprise in question. This happens when a government induces a private bank to grant a preferential loan to a designated enterprise. Article 1(iv) of the Arrangement on Officially Supported Export Credits states that "a government makes payments to a funding mechanism, or entrusts or directs a private body to carry out functions which would normally be vested in the government and the practice, in no real sense, differs from practices normally followed by governments" (OECD, 1978). In addition, within the meaning of Article XVI of GATT, a subsidy is also any form of income or price support which could lead to an increase in exports or a reduction in imports. It should be noted that this wording includes export support systems in the form of insurance and export credits.

The second condition for the existence of "subsidies" is the existence of a benefit from the provision of the "financial contribution." A benefit must be deemed to exist where the recipient obtains better conditions for the financial contribution provided than it could obtain on the market.

The determination of whether there is a benefit can create room for interpretation. A good example of a "financial contribution" is a credit provided by a development bank (e.g., an export bank) to a private entity. In order to determine the existence of a "benefit" and thus qualify a credit as a subsidy under Article 1(1), the parameters of the credit itself must be verified. If it is determined that the credit is made available on terms more favorable than those available in the banking market (private commercial banks), then it should be considered that the entity obtained a benefit under the provided "financial contribution."

Article 14 of the SCM Agreement sets forth the guidelines for the calculation of the amount of a subsidy in terms of the benefit to the recipient. The remainder of Article 14 applies analogous logic to equity instruments[12] granted by a government and an examination of the benefit that could potentially

12 Article 14 (a).

arise from the provision of goods or services and the purchase of goods by the government.[13]

Export subsidies are prohibited under Article 3. The text of the article refers to Annex I of the Agreement, which lists a set of export subsidies. The list is not exhaustive and is to be considered as an illustrative list of measures and instruments that constitute prohibited export subsidies used by countries. The list consists of 12 examples. It is understood that subsidies provided in the form indicated in Annex I are prohibited.

The prohibited export subsidies include the following: direct subsidies to a firm or industry dependent on export activity; exemptions, remissions, or deferrals of direct or indirect taxes as well as reductions in the tax base; foreign exchange deductions; the application of more favorable freight and shipping charges to exported goods than to domestic cargo; the remission or refund of shipping charges; and the provision by governments or their agencies of goods or services for use in the production of exported goods on terms more favorable than for production destined for the domestic market.

The first point refers to the provision of export guarantees or insurance provided by governments directly or through government-controlled institutions. When granting support in the form of guarantees or insurance, attention shall be given to the pricing conditions of the guaranteed products offered. The price of a guarantee or insurance policy shall not be set at a level that is insufficient to cover the long-term costs and damages associated with the products offered.[14]

The second point refers explicitly to the granting of export credits by governments or by financial institutions controlled by or acting on behalf of governments. Export credits cannot be granted at a price below the one which can be obtained on the market. In order to verify the level of interest rates, the cost of borrowing on international capital markets and the main parameters of the credit, such as the tenor of the credit, shall be taken into account. Export credits cannot cover costs incurred by exporters or financial institutions in obtaining the credits either.[15]

It should be borne in mind that the prohibition of export subsidies may result from both de jure regulations and de facto situations. A de jure prohibition of export subsidies is verified on the basis of the regulations. In order to prove the use of prohibited export subsidies by a country, it is sufficient to indicate the text of the regulation introducing the subsidy in question. In the

13 Article 14 (d).
14 Annex I of the Agreement (Agreement on Subsidies and Countervailing Measures).
15 Ibidem.

context of our subject matter, it is particularly important to trace the way in which the WTO assesses the granting of export credits. A credit granted at preferential rates may or may not be considered an export subsidy. When examining a credit for the existence of an export subsidy, the WTO may take into account the type of information requested by the bank in the credit application, the criteria for granting the credit, or the content of the credit agreement concluded between the bank and the company.

Attention is drawn to whether the bank obtains information on the export activity of the company as part of the information necessary to apply for financing. Requiring data on, e.g., export sales or anticipated export sales, may constitute grounds for verifying whether the credit in question is an export subsidy.

At the stage of application for a credit by an entrepreneur, it is important whether the criteria for granting financing refer to or depend on current or future export activity. Where a credit agreement takes into account covenants that relate to the export activity of the borrower, the presence of such provisions may constitute grounds for verifying whether the credit in question is an export subsidy. An example of a contractual obligation that meets this condition may be an obligation for the debtor to export a given volume of production or to generate a portion of the proceeds from the sale of products abroad. Conversely, a credit agreement may prohibit the sale of all or a given proportion of production in the country. These provisions may be analyzed in the context of the size and absorption capacity of the domestic market. Where a credit agreement sets minimum sales limits and, at the same time, an insufficiently absorptive domestic market, the sales target can be regarded as an implicit export target. This would be a sufficient indication to start verifying whether the credit is not an export subsidy.

Subsidies that do not qualify as prohibited subsidies under Article 3 of the Agreement[16] may also be subject to sanctions if they cause "adverse effects," which are defined in Article 5 of the Agreement, according to which "no Member should cause, through the use of any subsidy referred to in paragraphs 1 and 2 of Article 1, adverse effects to the interests of other Members" (Table 7.1).

Where the term "serious prejudice" is defined in Article 6 of the Agreement. For example, serious prejudice may occur in the event of a reduction in liabilities towards the state, whether through direct cancellation of debt or the granting of subsidies for debt repayment.[17] The text of the same article also lists the observed effects that may indicate the existence of serious prejudice to

16 Consistent with the analysis presented above.
17 Article 6 (d) of the Agreement.

TABLE 7.1 Adverse effects as defined by the agreement on subsidies and countervailing measures

Agreement on subsidies and countervailing measures, Article 5, adverse effects
(a) injury to the domestic industry of another Member;
(b) nullification or impairment of benefits accruing directly or indirectly to other Members under GATT 1994 in particular the benefits of concessions bound under Article II of GATT 1994;
(c) I serious prejudice to the interests of another Member

SOURCE: AGREEMENT ON SUBSIDIES AND COUNTERVAILING MEASURES

the interest of a country. It is pointed out that the import of products into the country is hindered or the product is pushed out of the market, that the price of products is reduced when the price of similar imported goods is higher, that sales are made at a loss due to the low price, that there is a significant increase in the production of a given good on the international market compared to the average share over the previous 3 years.[18]

The agreement also identifies situations where the restrictions and practices in question will not have adverse effects. For example, these are external events beyond control, i.e., force majeure, including transport disruptions, natural disasters, or strikes. Within the content of the same article, there are also internal elements, such as technical standards in force in the importer's country, which the foreign supplier is unable to meet.[19]

Apart from subsidies that are not specific according to Article 2,[20] the Arrangement allows, as non-sanctioned subsidies, support for research and development,[21] aid for regions that are lagging behind,[22] and support for environmental protection.[23] In the case of support for research and development, Article 8 of the Agreement lists the following costs to which support should be limited: personnel costs, costs of equipment, materials, consultancy, and overheads directly related to the research carried out. Support for regions is limited to regions fulfilling the relevant economic development criteria. The

18 Article 6.3 of the Agreement.
19 Article 6.7 of the Agreement.
20 Article 8.1.
21 Article 8.2 (a).
22 Article 8.2 (b).
23 Article 8.2 (c).

economic criteria relate to the level of GDP[24] and the unemployment rate[25] (Article 8.2 b). Environmental support is limited to aid that fulfills specific criteria, such as the amount of the costs incurred and the fact that the aid is one-off and proportional to the expected effects.[26]

3.1.2 WTO Rules Provide Special Treatment for Developing Countries

It is understood that subsidies can play an important role in stimulating the economic development of less developed countries. The rules relating to these countries are less restrictive than the general rules.[27]

The ban on export subsidies does not apply to the following:

1. Least developed countries (LDCs) as classified by the United Nations.[28]
2. Developing countries with a GDP per capita level of less than US$1,000 per year. These are: Bolivia, Cameroon, Congo, Ivory Coast, the Dominican Republic, Egypt, Ghana, Guatemala, Guyana, India, Indonesia, Kenya, Morocco, Nicaragua, Nigeria, Pakistan, the Philippines, Senegal, Sri Lanka, and Zimbabwe.[29]
3. Other developing countries which are treated differently from the general regime.[30]

This treatment is linked to the implementation of specific programs.

In summary, 49 WTO member countries are excluded from the application of the general rules prohibiting the maintenance of export subsidies, and 32 of these countries are on the UN list of LDCs. Table 7.2 shows the countries that receive special treatment under the Arrangement and therefore are not affected by the export subsidy ban. The exemption from the need to apply the general rules is not temporary.

This specific rule aims to assist the poorest countries in gaining the full access to the global trade system. On the one hand, the WTO maintains a non-discriminatory system of international trade as a general rule and stays in line with the principles of the GPG and, on the other hand, facilitates access for the least developed members to international trade market. By supporting their

24 GDP/capita must not be higher than 85% of the average for the territory.
25 The unemployment rate exceeds 110% of the average rate for the territory.
26 Article 8.2 (c).
27 Article 27 of the Agreement.
28 Annex VII (a) of the Agreement.
29 Countries are listed in accordance with the content of Annex VII (b) of the Agreement. The Dominican Republic, Guatemala, and Morocco have so far been removed from the list, having exceeded a certain level of GDP/capita.
30 For a period of 8 years from the date of the Agreement, i.e., until 2002.

TABLE 7.2 Countries receiving special treatment under WTO rules

Countries to which exemptions apply	
Annex VII paragraph (a) – Least developed countries	**Annex VII, paragraph (b) – Developing countries fulfilling the development criterion**
Angola	Bolivia
Bangladesh	Cameroon
Benin	Congo
Burkina Faso	Ivory Coast
Burundi	Egypt
Cambodia	Ghana
Congo	Guyana
Djibouti	Honduras
Chad	India
Central African Republic	Indonesia
Gambia	Kenya
Guinea	Nicaragua
Guinea-Bissau	Nigeria
Haiti	Pakistan
Lesotho	Philippines
Madagascar	Senegal
Malawi	Sri Lanka
Maldives	Zimbabwe
Mali	
Mauritania	
Mozambique	
Burma	
Nepal	
Niger	
Rwanda	
Senegal	
Sierra Leone	
Solomon Islands	
Tanzania	
Togo	
Uganda	
Zambia	

Note: Senegal is on both lists. The status has changed since 2000. Senegal was included in the list of least developed countries.

SOURCE: WORLD TRADE ORGANIZATION, UNITED NATIONS

development, the WTO fosters the concept of sustainable development of the world.

The third group of countries are developing countries for which an exemption from the rules is foreseen for a period of 8 years from the entry into force of the Arrangement. This temporary derogation from the Arrangement's export subsidy rules is conditional, depending on the relationship between the instrument used and the development needs of the applying country.[31] Article 27.4 of the Agreement also allows for an exemption period of more than 8 years, subject to approval with clear justification of the necessity of the subsidy and its relation to "economic, financial and developmental" needs.[32] Of the 22 countries which applied for an extension of the Article 27.4 waiver period, the WTO granted waivers to 21 countries.[33] In July 2007, an extension of the exemption from the Agreement on Subsidies and Countervailing Measures until the end of 2013 was approved, with a two-year phase-out period until the end of 2015.[34] Finally, on October 23, 2012, the Committee on Subsidies and Countervailing Measures confirmed the validity of the exemption until the end of 2013. The programs run by the countries mainly concerned free trade areas and tax instruments (tax incentives).

Developing countries also benefit from the so-called *de minimis* levels for the subsidies applied. This means that all exporters from developing countries are, by law, treated better than producers from other countries. Article 27.10 of the Agreement sets out the maximum levels of subsidies that will not be subject to sanctions. According to this Article, "any countervailing duty investigation of a product originating in a developing country member shall be terminated as soon as the authorities concerned determine that:

- the overall level of subsidies granted upon the product in question does not exceed 2 per cent of its value calculated on a per unit basis; or
- the volume of the subsidized imports represents less than 4 per cent of the total imports of the like product in the importing Member, unless imports from developing country Members whose individual shares of total imports represent less than 4 per cent collectively account for more than 9 per cent of the total imports of the like product in the importing Member. (Article 27.10)

31 Article 27.4 of the Agreement.

32 Article 27.4 of the Agreement.

33 WTO Ministerial Conference, Doha, November 9–14, 2001.

34 Countries are required to present plans for phasing out support instruments.

Table 7.3 is a summary of the Arrangement's treatment of developing countries' export activities. There are three groups of developing countries with slightly different treatment in terms of export subsidies: least developed countries, countries whose level of development exceeds the minimum specified in the regulations, and other countries that can benefit from the designated minimum level of subsidies.

TABLE 7.3 Summary of the application of Article 3.1

Article 3.1. (a) of the agreement prohibiting the use of export subsidies			
Least developed countries Annex VII a	**Developing countries with GDP/capita below US$1,000 Annex VII b**	**Developing countries with GDP/capita below or above US$1,000**	**Other developing countries**
Exemption from Article 3.1 (a)	Exemption from Article 3.1 (a)	No exemption from Article 3.1 (a), except for countries according to Article 27.4 Temporary exemption	Full application of Article 3.1 (a) taking into account Article 27.10
Angola, Bangladesh, Benin, Burkina Faso, Burundi, Cambodia, Congo, Djibouti, Chad, Central African Republic, Gambia, Guinea, Guinea-Bissau, Haiti, Lesotho, Madagascar, Malawi, Maldives, Mali, Mauritania, Mozambique, Myanmar, Nepal, Niger, Rwanda, Senegal, Sierra Leone, Solomon Islands, Tanzania, Togo, Uganda, Zambia	Bolivia, Cameroon, Congo, Ivory Coast, Dominican Republic, Egypt, Ghana, Guatemala, Guyana, India, Indonesia, Kenya, Morocco, Nicaragua, Nigeria, Pakistan, Philippines, Senegal, Sri Lanka and Zimbabwe	Antigua and Barbuda, Barbados, Belize, Costa Rica, Dominican Republic, El Salvador, Fiji, Grenada, Guatemala, Jamaica, Jordan, Mauritius, Panama, Papua New Guinea, St. Kitts and Nevis, St. Lucia, St. Vincent, Grenada, Uruguay	

SOURCE: OWN ELABORATION

3.1.3 The Agreement on Agriculture

The Agreement on Agriculture contains important provisions from the point of view of the tightness of the system aimed at limiting export subsidies.[35] Article 10 deals explicitly with the prohibition of circumvention. It follows from the wording of the article that "export subsidies not listed in paragraph 1 of Article 9 shall not be applied in a manner which results in, or which threatens to lead to, circumvention of export subsidy commitments."

The next paragraph of Article 10(2) is devoted to a form of support that was not mentioned before, namely export credits and insurance. The intention is to regulate the system of export support in the form of the abovementioned financial instruments. "Members undertake to work toward the development of internationally agreed disciplines to govern the provision of export credits, export credit guarantees or insurance programs and, after agreement on such disciplines, to provide export credits, export credit guarantees or insurance programs only in conformity therewith."[36]

The Agreement on Agriculture also provides for differential treatment for the least developed countries. The reduction commitments adopted in the Agreement do not apply to the poorest countries.[37] The remaining developing

---

35 The Agreement on Agriculture is the basic document that governs international trade in agricultural commodities. The content of the Agreement was determined during the negotiations of the GATT Uruguay Round, which took place between 1986 and 1994, the latter being the date of the creation of the WTO. This document addresses issues in three basic areas, namely: access to one's own market for foreign products beyond the level of protection; the system of support for one's own market; and the system of export subsidies. An important achievement of the Uruguay Round is the replacement of most non-tariff instruments by tariff instruments and the establishment of a maximum level of own market protection and the use of export subsidies. Subsequent rounds of negotiations aimed at further liberalization of trade. In 2001, agricultural negotiations began as part of the ninth negotiating round, known as the Doha Round. In the following years, talks were held within the framework of the Ministerial Conference in Cancun (2003) and then the Ministerial Conference in Hong Kong (2005). Among the most important postulates of the Conference in Hong Kong, attention is drawn to the further reduction of the level of agricultural support. The draft declaration includes agreements concerning the reduction of export subsidies aimed at an increase in trade liberalization. Attention was drawn to the reduction of all export support instruments, including export credits, guarantees, and export credit insurance granted for a period of 180 days. The lengthy process of negotiating trade liberalization, which often ends in a lack of agreement among WTO members, is due to several important elements that are worth noting. The agricultural sector is often a very sensitive subject in many countries. Each country pursues a policy of protecting and strengthening its domestic agriculture for economic, social, and political reasons. Agricultural commodities are a product which can be traded quite easily.

36 Article 10.2 of the Agreement.

37 Article 15.2.

countries with a low level of economic development have been given flexibility to meet their reduction commitments for 10 years. This principle is derived from a similar approach as in the case of the poorest countries' exemption from the rules of applying to the limitations of export subsidies. It aims to create an opportunity for weaker economies to take full advantage of the GPG, which is the system of international trade.

3.2 *Characteristics of Export Credit Provision and Export Guarantees Under the OECD Arrangement*

The aim of the Arrangement is to increase transparency in offering export credit support by various countries, creating a level playing field, and, ultimately, to limit the use of export subsidies in the form of export credit. The main idea is to give special guidelines for export credit support schemes present in different countries, the use of which ensures compliance with the international rules.

The rules governing the granting of export credits are set out in Annex I of the Arrangement. As a general rule, it is prohibited to grant export credits at a price below the one offered by the market. The Arrangement makes an exception to this rule in the same paragraph. Subsidies provided in the form of export credits are not prohibited if they are provided under the terms of the Arrangement on Officially Supported Export Credits (OECD Consensus). Consistency with the OECD Consensus must be applied to all export credit parameters set out therein.

The Arrangement on Officially Supported Export Credits was signed in 1978 within the OECD Group on Export Credits.[38] It is worth noting that the principles set out in the OECD Consensus have been accepted by both the WTO and the EU (Council of the European Union, 1998). The Arrangement applies to all capital goods and services export from OECD countries.[39] They concern rules for insurance and long-term credit with repayment terms above 2 years. In the case of short-term insurance not regulated by the OECD, it is specified within the EU that support is only possible if exports are directed to the so-called high-risk countries because then the risks (commercial and political) are classified as non-marketable.[40] The above principles must be respected by institu-

38 Arrangement on Officially Supported Export Credits: http://www.oecd.org/trade/topics/export-credits/arrangement-and-sector-understandings/.

39 This is one of the biggest challenges that the regime faces and applies only to OECD countries.

40 The rules were introduced to address the problem of unauthorized state aid and to ensure a level playing field for companies from different countries where export finance support systems exist.

tions providing financial support for exports. This includes both insurers and development banks or dedicated financial institutions such as export banks and export credit agencies (ECA) (Drummond, 1997; Stephens, 1998; Chauffour et al., 2010; Dinh & Hilmarsson, 2012). The main purpose of the provisions is to create a framework for non-distortive export credit, so that exporters compete on price and product quality rather than on financing terms. These rules clearly protect less wealthy actors (countries) by creating a level playing field to compete in terms of the quality of products or services provided.

The OECD Arrangement introduces minimum parameters for export credits to be officially backed by government-guaranteed insurance. These insurances significantly improve the risk profile of financed projects, which may translate into lower prices and their wider accessibility. In other words, the insurance increase competitiveness of export project (support export). The aforementioned parameters set a maximum financing range of up to 85% of the contract, which introduces the need for the foreign buyer to make a payment of at least 15% of the contract value. The permissible repayment period depends on the risk classification of the importer's country. In the case of rich countries in the so-called Category I, it is 8.5 years, while in the case of exports to poorer countries in the so-called Category II, it is 10 years. The regulations also introduce the possibility of a longer period for the so-called project finance, which is set out in Annex X. These rules apply to the so-called long-term loans with a repayment period of at least 2 years. The repayment of the principal of the credit is either straight-line amortization (equal installments) or non-standard, but with an appropriate weighted average length of credit (WALoc). The maximum grace period allowed is 6 months.

The OECD Arrangement gives special treatment to projects financing marine vessels, nuclear power plants, civil aircraft, renewable energy projects, green projects aiming at the mitigation of climate change, rail transport, and coal-fired power plants. In recent years, the OECD has supplemented the Arrangement with rules governing environmental and social requirements relating to transactions covered with export credit. Separate rules also apply to tied aid loans. It is worth noting, that by introducing the rules of different treatment, the OECD may effectively affect world trade flows. Making the financing rules more flexible for selected sectors (e.g., renewable energy or important social projects), the OECD creates incentives for the financial market, to facilitate the access of financing and, consequently, support specific key projects. The influence of the OECD by creating adequate provisions is notable. It results from the close interdependence of financing and world trade.

4 Conclusions

International trade plays an extremely important role in world economic development. Exports are often called the engine of economic growth. The scale of their significance is confirmed in the statistics of global GDP. The data show a consistent increase in the importance of countries' openness to cross-border exchange of goods and services and an increasing share of world income generated from trade in total world income. The value of exports – goods only – amounted to US$19 quintillion in 2019. To ensure the sustainable development of the world, issues concerning an open and, above all, non-discriminatory system of international trade become crucial, i.e., a system which ensures equal opportunities to benefit from the effects of global economic growth, taking into account differences in income of individual countries, i.e., participants of the system.

The focus of the analysis was on the export support instruments, i.e., export credits. Assuming that financing is of key importance for trade, special attention should be paid to the conditions of granting such loans in order to eliminate practices leading to privileging one of the parties to the transaction that is the basis for the international trade development as a GPG.

The World Trade Organization is the key body that upholds respect for openness and elimination of discriminatory practices in international trade. The WTO introduced the prohibition of export subsidies, i.e., instruments that distort competition in the international exchange of goods and services, as a basic principle. The regulations define the parameters for which practices become prohibited. In a clear way, the regulations also define situations in which existing subsidies are not prohibited. In the regulations concerning prohibition of forbidden subsidies, exemptions for countries with a lower level of income/development are also introduced. The author has analyzed one of the export support instruments, i.e., export credits. Assuming that financing is of key importance for trade, special attention should be paid to the conditions of granting such loans in order to eliminate practices leading to privileging one of the parties to the transaction what is the basis for the international trade development as a GPG. The intention of OECD regulations is to ensure fair competition in this area as one of the elements moving the global economy towards the fulfillment of the Sustainable Development Goals.

Both organizations ensure to retain the basic characteristics of GPGs – that are non-rivalrous and non-excludable in relation to international trade.

References

Ahn, J., Amiti, M, & Weinstein, D. E. (2011). Trade finance and the great trade collapse. *American Economic Review, 101*(3), 298–302.

Amiti M., & Weinstein D. E. (2012). Export and financial shocks. *Quarterly Journal of Economics, 126*(4), 1841–1877. https://doi.org/10.1093/qje/qjr033

Antras P., & Fritz Foley, C. (2011). Poultry in motion: A study of international trade practices. NBER Working Paper, no. 17091. National Bureau of Economic Research.

Auboin, M. (2009, June 5). Boosting the availability of trade finance in the current crisis: Background analysis for a substantial G20 package. Policy Insight no. 35. Centre for Economic Policy Research. https://cepr.org/system/files/publication-files/103051-policy_insight_35_boosting_the_availability_of_trade_finance_in_the_current_crisis.pdf

Berthelot, J. (2019, January 9). Rebuilding the WTO for a sustainable global development. Alternatives Agroécologiques et Solidaires (SOL). https://www.wto.org/english/forums_e/ngo_e/rebuilding_the_wto_for_a_sustainable_global_development_9_january_2019_e.pdf

Bricongne, J.-C., Fontagné, L., Gaulier, G., Taglioni, D., & Vicard, V. (2010, September). Firms and the global crisis: French exports in the turmoil. European Central Bank Working Paper, no. 1245. https://www.ecb.europa.eu/pub/pdf/scpwps/ecbwp1245.pdf

Chauffour, J., Soylemezoglu, A. I., & Saborowski, C. (2010, January). Trade finance in crisis: Should developing countries establish export credit agencies? Policy Research Working Paper. World Bank. http://doi.org/10.1596/1813-9450-5166

Chor, D., & Manova, K. (2012). Off the cliff and back: Credit conditions and international trade during the global financial crisis. *Journal of International Economics, 87*(1), 117–133.

Council of the European Union. (1998). EU Council Directive of 7 May 1998 on harmonization of the main provisions concerning export credit insurance rules for transactions with medium and long-term cover. https://eur-lex.europa.eu/legal-content/en/TXT/?uri=CELEX:31998L0029

Dewit, G. (2001). Intervention in risky export markets: Insurance, strategic action or aid? *European Journal of Political Economy, 17*(3), 575–592. http://doi.org/10.1016/S0176-2680(01)00046-5

Dinh, T. Q., & Hilmarsson, H. Þ. (2012). Private sector export to emerging market economies during times of crisis: How can export credit agencies help? *Review of International Comparative Management, 13*(1), 167–180.

Drummond, P. F. N. (1997, March). Recent export credit market developments. IMF Working Paper. https://www.imf.org/external/pubs/ft/wp/wp9727.pdf

Egger, P., & Url, T. (2006). Public export credit guarantees and foreign trade structure: Evidence from Austria. *World Economy, 29*(4), 399–418. http://doi.org/10.1111/j.1467-9701.2006.00790.x

Felbermayr, G. J., & Yalcin, E. (2013). Export credit guarantees and export performance: An empirical analysis for Germany. *World Economy, 36*(8), 967–999. http://doi.org/10.1111/twec.12031

Felbermayr, G. J., Heiland, I., & Yalcin, E. (2012, July). Mitigating liquidity constraints: Public export credit guarantees in Germany. CESifo Working Paper no. 3908. Center for Economic Studies and Ifo Institute for Economic Research. https://www.cesifo.org/en/publications/2012/working-paper/mitigating-liquidity-constraints-public-export-credit-guarantees

GATT. (1947). General Agreement on Tariffs and Trade. https://www.wto.org/english/docs_e/legal_e/gatt47.pdf

Janda, K. (2014, March 4). Czech export credit agencies and their market power. MPRA Paper no. 54097. https://mpra.ub.uni-muenchen.de/54097/

Kaul, I., Grunberg, I., & Stern, M. A. (Eds.). (1999). *Global public goods: International cooperation in the 21st century*. Oxford University Press.

Manova, K., & Zhang, Z. (2012). Export prices across firms and destinations. *Quarterly Journal of Economics, 127*(1), 379–436. https://doi.org/10.1093/qje/qjr051

Napiórkowski, T., & Stolarczyk, P. (2018). Rola kredytu eksportowego jako czynnika determinującego sprzedaż międzynarodową na przykładzie wybranych krajów UE [The role of export credit as a determinant of international sales on the example of selected EU countries]. *Studia Europejskie – Studies in European Affairs, 2*, 169–185.

OECD. (1978). Arrangement on Officially Supported Export Credits, with later amendments. Organisation for Economic Co-operation and Development. http://www.oecd.org/trade/topics/export-credits/arrangement-and-sector-understandings/

Samuelson, P. (1955). Diagrammatic exposition of a theory of public expenditure. *Review of Economics and Statistics, 37*, 350–356.

Stephens, M. (1998). Export credit agencies, trade finance and South East Asia. IMF Working Paper, WP/98/175.

World Bank. (N.d.). Database Trade (% of GDP) – Data.

WTO. (1995a). Agreement on Agriculture. World Trade Organization. https://www.wto.org/english/res_e/booksp_e/agrmntseries3_ag_2008_e.pdf

WTO. (1995b). Agreement on Subsidies and Countervailing Measures. World Trade Organization. https://www.wto.org/english/docs_e/legal_e/24-scm.pdf

CHAPTER 8

The Role of EU Trade Agreements in Light of the Sustainable Development Goals

Aleksandra Borowicz and Rasa Daugėlienė

1 Introduction

Although the expansion of international trade over the past few decades has brought economic and societal benefits across the globe, it has also at times failed to address the accompanying adverse social, environmental, and even economic impacts (United Nations, 2021). In the post-WWII period world trade agreements were established mainly as free trade agreements and customs unions. In the wake of WWII the European Economic Community became the leading player on the global trade scene. Later, the advent and rapid spread of globalization brought about changes to the nature of trade agreements. It should be stressed that this resulted in much more complex agreements involving the opening of international borders. The nature of international trade has changed in the last decades. "Steadily declining costs of trade and information and telecommunications have permitted firms to geographically splinter their 'production lines,' designing international supply chains that allocate different parts of the production process to firms in different countries" (Hoekman, 2014). The EU, along with the WTO, has retained the dominant role in terms of shaping the global order. Trade agreements regulate not only the trade in goods and services, but also aspects of capital flow, labor law, and social or environmental (ecological) objectives. The latter are nowadays regarded as global public goods.

The chapter aims to analyze selected features of European Union (EU) trade policy in relation to the Sustainable Development Goals (SDGs), with a particular focus on trade relations with third countries. This has grown in significance since the H declared regional trade agreements (RTAs) and international organizations (IOs) to be the key fixtures in international trade relations. The study constitutes a new scientific approach to the global challenges as trade is considered a global public good.

The chapter will focus on the EU as a case study to verify what role the EU plays in terms of international trade and its response to global challenges. It is key to emphasize that the UN focuses on a specific tool, namely Voluntary

 | DOI:10.1163/9789004687264_010

Sustainability Standards (VSS), which comprise certification schemes, labeling programs, and private standards. It is stressed, in contrast to some WTO statements, that "VSS aim to make global value chains, from producer to consumer, more sustainable by considering social and environmental requirements in the production process" (United Nations, 2021). In first section, "Trade as global public good in the context of the SDGs," the chapter identifies linkages between the SDGs and EU trade policy through numerous indices. In order to demonstrate the specificity of the EU's international trade, which is based on agreements with the WTO, we seek to systematize the existing tariff and non-tariff trade barriers in the second section, "The holistic approach to trade policy by the European Union." We aim to show the complexity of international trade conditions in public goods which need to be revised to promote sustainability rather than hamper international trade. The last section, "The EU mechanism for the implementation of trade agreements in relation to the SDGs," gives an overview and space for critical debate on the role of the EU as an international organization in the creation of a multilateral trade regime in the context of the SDGs through the trade channel.

2 Trade as a Global Public Good in the Context of the SDGs

Trade, which is considered one of the components of globalization, has contributed to the prosperity of nations. The benefits seen by states stem from the effective usage of comparative advantages in the area of goods and services production. Since WWII exports of merchandise grew almost 290-fold from 1948 (US$59 billion) to 2020 (US$17,070 billion) (WTO, 2021c). Globalization has given rise to new challenges in terms of global supply chain organization and consumption, as well as a revolution when it comes to environmental and social impacts (Wiedmann & Lenzen, 2018). The ongoing post-World War II liberalization, which resulted in a huge surge in trade and diversification of production, has led to the emergence of fragmented global value chains (GVCs) in the world economy. The goal of global players such as IOs is to ensure that GVCs contribute to sustainable development, as the negative consequences of trade can involve not only environmental but also social aspects, such as widening socioeconomic inequalities between developed and developing countries (Xu et al., 2020).[1]

1 For more on globalization, the economy, and the environment, see Chapter 6.

The 2030 Agenda for Sustainable Development (further referred to as Agenda 2030) of the United Nations constitutes the most important and comprehensive global sustainable development agenda for the future. It is known for its far-reaching and ambitious vision with its 17 Sustainable Development Goals (SDGs) and 169 targets that are listed as part of the so-called "universal policy agenda." The 17 SDGs within Agenda 2030 can be divided into five areas. These include people, planet, prosperity, peace, and partnership. The SDGs, in comparison with the Millennium Development Goals (MDGs), challenge the definition of the root cause of poverty and promote a universal global approach to development (Servaes, 2017). In order to counteract the WTO claim that the development of international trade contradicts the ideas of sustainability, this chapter supports the definition of Agenda 2030, namely that international trade is "an engine for inclusive economic growth and poverty reduction." Carried out in accordance with the principles of humanity and justice, it definitely contributes to the promotion of sustainable development. In order to become a "sustainable engine," one of the increasingly applied approaches is to internalize social, economic, and environmental concerns in international trade. This can be done by many different means and policy instruments and tools (United Nations, 2021).

International trade as a global public good means that benefits or costs are shared equally and nobody can be excluded from the trade effects. Globalization, which has also affected the process of liberalization of international trade, is the carrier of the effects of trade at the same time (Ocampo, 2016). According to the WTO, international trade can be deemed a global public good on the basis of the following features:

- *Non-rivalry*: the value of the system increases simultaneously to increased participation.
- *Non-excludability*: in the global world multilateral trading system affects all and is universal and potentially open to all. (Secretariat of the International Task Force on Global Public Goods, 2006)

International trade is considered to be a channel for the delivery of SDGs. The impact of trade on sustainable development has been extensively described in the literature. The international trade structure has demonstrated that the developed (and, consequently, more powerful) countries are better equipped to absorb the generated waste material. As a result, there exists unequal distribution of hazards and pollution connected with all stages of global production chains: starting from extraction, production, throughout the consumption to disposal (Givens et al., 2019; Jorgenson, 2016). This creates room for debate on the influence of the EU on the international trade regime and the liberalization of trade so strongly argued for in the WTO forum.

It should be noted that countries are the main partner for SDGs implementation; however, Agenda 2030 underlines the importance of regional organizations in terms of the fulfillment of the SDGs. Through their role as translators, supportive bodies, coordinators, and monitoring bodies, Agenda 2030 becomes more viable and increases the capabilities of nations to follow global goals. Some of the SDGs, such as 1. No poverty, 2. Zero hunger, 9. Industry, innovation and infrastructure, 11. Sustainable cities and communities, clearly prove the need for close and in-depth cooperation between individual nations. Furthermore, the global goals set up in Agenda 2030 need to be translated into actions on the national level, which requires adapting the goals into unique national contexts. To best meet the challenges, the cooperation and exchange of good practices and know-how is of paramount importance. Finally, IOs constitute significant players in the monitoring systems and can react to delays or deviations (Marx et al., 2021).

To link the SDGs with trade, the United Nations Statistical Commission (UNSC) has approved six indicators within the following SDGs (ITC et al., 2022).[2] Trade orientation among the SDGs concerns the following four: 2. Zero hunger; 8. Decent work and economic growth; 10. Reduced inequalities; 17. Partnerships for the goals. Trade policies must meet the challenges of SDGs and regional trade agreements are one of the leading tools available to global partners like the EU. In case of trading goods, with a special focus on agricultural goods, the costs are higher for emerging markets and developing economies (EMDEs) than in advanced economies (IMF et al., 2017).

The provisions of EU trade policy shall be analyzed in the context of the following targets set in Agenda 2030, as they correspond directly to particular aspects of trade:

- 2.b Correct and prevent trade restrictions and distortions in world agricultural markets, including through the parallel elimination of all forms of agricultural export subsidies and all export measures with equivalent effect, in accordance with the mandate of the Doha Development Round.
- 8.a Increase Aid for Trade support for developing countries, in particular least developed countries, including through the Enhanced Integrated Framework for Trade-related Technical Assistance to Least Developed Countries.

2 The SDG Trade Monitor was created in order to evaluate the progress on the path to SDGs by global partners and to allow different groups of professionals (such as policymakers and researchers) to analyze the synergies between SDGs and trade.

- 10.a Implement the principle of special and differential treatment for developing countries, in particular least developed countries, in accordance with World Trade Organization agreements.
- 17.10 Promote a universal, rules-based, open, non-discriminatory and equitable multilateral trading system under the World Trade Organization, including through the conclusion of negotiations under its Doha Development Agenda.
- 17.11 Significantly increase the exports of developing countries, in particular with a view to doubling the least developed countries' share of global exports by 2020.
- 17.12 Realize timely implementation of duty-free and quota-free market access on a lasting basis for all least developed countries, consistent with World Trade Organization decisions, including by ensuring that preferential rules of origin applicable to imports from least developed countries are transparent and simple, and contribute to facilitating market access. (ECOSOC, 2016)

The international trade regime is a sum of processes initiated in many countries within the WTO or the EU or any other IOs or regional trade agreements. European implementation of the trade policy impacts the European market and increases policymaking interdependence between countries in the long term. It seems that trade fulfilled by EU states is becoming a key component of sustainable development. The more holistic approach to trade presented by the EU will undoubtedly contribute to achieving the SDGs.

3 The Holistic Approach to Trade Policy by the European Union

One of the key documents that determines the EU's trade policy in the coming years is *Trade for All: Towards a More Responsible Trade and Investment Policy*, which charts a new course for the European trade and investment policy. The EU has taken up the challenge of becoming the largest foreign direct investor and the most important location for foreign direct investment (FDI). The idea is to foster an environment conducive to trade and investment for consumers, workers, and companies alike. It puts the spotlight on the effectiveness of policy to deliver opportunities to society and addresses challenges such as the value-chain economy or digitalization. Secondly, the process of trade negotiations must meet the challenge of transparency. Thirdly, EU trade policy needs to promote core values, such as sustainable development or human rights (European Commission, 2014). The document also proposes a strategy based on sustainability pillars and refers to the obligations resulting from the Paris Agreement on climate change. The role of the new trade policy strategy is to translate the ambitious goals connected with sustainable development into trade agreements with third countries (WTO, 2021b, p. 178).

In 2019 the European Commission proposed six strategic goals, which essentially correspond to the challenges set in Agenda 2030, i.e.: the European Green Deal; an economy that works for people; a Europe fit for the digital age; Promoting our European way of life; Stronger Europe in the world; New push for European democracy. The agenda proposed by the EC for 2019–2024 by its president, Ursula von der Leyen, refers to Agenda 2030 and the SDGs (see Table 8.1).

There is nothing new about the strong focus of EU member states on reforming their economies towards sustainable development. The overall score proposed by the UN, representing total progress towards all 17 SDGs, shows that among the countries with the highest score, 9 out of 10 belong to the EU. The highest scorers include Finland (85.9%); Sweden (85.61%) and Denmark (84.86%) (Sachs et al., 2021). At the same time, the EU as a whole has an overall score of 71.4% (Sustainable Development Solutions Network & Institute for European Environmental Policy, 2021).

TABLE 8.1 Priorities of the EC and links with the SDGs

EC priorities 2019–2024	**SDGs**[a]																
	1	**2**	**3**	**4**	**5**	**6**	**7**	**8**	**9**	**10**	**11**	**12**	**13**	**14**	**15**	**16**	**17**
European Green Deal						(X)	X	X	X		(X)	(X)	X				X
An economy that works for people	X	X	X	(X)	X	(X)	(X)	X	X	X	(X)						X
Europe fit for the digital age								X	X							X	X
Promoting our European way of life					X					X						X	
Stronger Europe in the world																X	X
New push for European democracy					X					X						X	

Note: [a] Brackets indicate a possible positive impact on the SDGs through a given priority.

SOURCE: LATOSZEK AND BOROWICZ (2022)

The holistic approach of the EU to trade policy is influenced by the following facts:

1. The EU itself is a regional trade agreement, and the member states have treated trade (or, in broader terms, economic aspects) as a focal point of European integration since the inception of the European Community.
2. The EU, as an international organization and a global leader in the political, social and economic domain, views developing countries as partners to which it is open and accepts the existence of asymmetries in the trade liberalization process by proposing a conditional regime, the Generalised System of Preferences (GSP).
3. The EU is a key member of the WTO and upholds the rules as an ultimate value in the area of trade.
4. As a member of the UN, the EU is one of the IO signatories to Agenda 2030, regarding EU cooperation and the EU's role in the area of global governance as its responsibility.

In 1970, the ratio of world trade to GDP stood at 26.01% while in 2020 it reached 51.57%. In comparison, the trade-to-GDP ratio in the European Union was 39.89% in 1970 and amounted to 85.58% in 2020 (down from 92.18% in 2019) (World Bank, 2022). In 2020, the European Union's share of global merchandise exports reached 31%, and of imports 28.8% (WTO, 2021c). In 2019, EU exports (internal and with non-EU countries) were responsible for more than 62 million jobs worldwide. In the EU alone, it generated employment of 38.1 million jobs. The last 10 years have seen an increase of 11 million jobs (Rueda-Cantuche et al., 2021).

EU trade policy that ensures social justice, respect for human rights, high labor standards, and high environmental standards is one of the tools to achieve the SDGs. The analysis of the priorities reveals that the priority "Stronger Europe in the World" emphasizes the EU's role as a champion in a rules-based global order, with a firm focus on activating the EU as a strong partner in the world. In its priorities, the EU wants to achieve global leadership status that ensures the highest standards of climate, environmental, and labor protection both internally and externally (European Commission, 2022). These two dimensions are intertwined and push the EU towards achieving the SDGs on trade.

EU trade policy is directed towards third countries and its economic dimension is described in the Treaty on European Union (TEU) in Article 21 as one of the facets of external relations. Consequently, EU trade policy is not simply about trade liberalization; it goes much further (European Commission, 2018; Leblond & Viju-Miljusevic, 2019). As mentioned above, EU trade policy falls under the exclusive competence of the EU and as such the European Commission plays a leading role in its development. The EU defines trade policy as one of the channels for delivering sustainable development through trade agreements, special incentives for developing countries, and trade and development policies.

Contemporary agreements signed by the EU with third countries cover issues related to sustainable development. According to the data presented on the official websites of the European Commission, the agreements that include at present trade and sustainable development provisions are those concluded with Canada, Central America, Colombia, Peru and Ecuador, Georgia, Japan, Mercosur, Mexico, Moldova, Singapore, South Korea, Ukraine, and Vietnam.

The reformulated GSP scheme has been targeted at least developed countries (LDCs) since 2012.[3] The objective of the asymmetry underlying the GSP is to enable developing countries to access the European market by reducing customs duties on their products. The GSP is based on an approach that creates opportunities for developing countries to gain access to the common market and its consumers. The system is based on conditionality and exerts pressure on third countries to propose and implement changes in the economic (adaptation to the requirements of European customers, compliance with European quality, safety or environmental standards) and social (implementation of changes in market work, protection of human rights or education) fields. In the political dimension, this requires the creation of a climate for negotiations, but also the implementation of good practices in the area of good governance or reducing the level of corruption. Trade policy is indirectly linked to the implementation of the EU's development policy, the objective of which is to support the countries most in need (Jaszkiewicz & Latoszek, 2013).

In 2018, the European Commission published a mid-term evaluation of GSP which outlines its economic, social, and political effects. The GSP system based on the asymmetry of relations with developing and least developed countries has resulted in an increase in the dynamics of exports and imports in GSP countries between 2011 and 2016. In selected industry sectors such as footwear, clothing, machinery, and mechanical equipment, which constitute the largest group of products imported by EU member states from outside the EU, the growth reached a high level of 24.5%. This compares with an increase of only 6.5% between 2011 and 2013. Countries benefitting from the standard GSP scheme recorded the highest export diversification, while Everything but Arms (EBA) countries continue to have the least diversified export structure. The GSP scheme is seen as a catalyst for change in the economic, political, and social

3 The reform was introduced on the basis of Regulation (EU) no. 978/2012 of the European Parliament and of the Council on October 25, 2012, implementing the scheme of generalized tariff preferences and changing Council Regulation (EC) no. 732/2008, OJ L 303, October 31, 2012: 1.

spheres in member states, with cooperation under the scheme affecting the environment and quality of life, and as such contributing to progress towards the SDGs through its trade policies. According to the Commission's report, the GSP has a significant impact on non-economic spheres such as the protection of human rights, good governance, or the Social Progress Index (SPI). This illustrates the process of interdependence between EU trade policy and the fulfillment of Agenda 2030 commitments. At the same time, the impact generated by international trade reveals global spillovers from EU trade policy.

4 The EU Mechanism for the Implementation of Trade Agreements in Relation to the SDGs

The trade channel, which is covered by trade agreements between the EU and third countries, obliges both parties to adhere to the following principles in line with the SDGs (European Commission, 2020):
- Follow international labor and environment standards and agreements
- Effectively enforce their environmental and labor laws
- Not deviate from environmental or labor laws to encourage trade or investment, and thereby preventing a "race to the bottom"
- Sustainably trade natural resources, such as timber and fish
- Combat illegal trade in threatened and endangered species of fauna and flora
- Encourage trade that supports tackling climate change
- Promote practices such as corporate social responsibility
- Promote sustainable public procurement
- Remove barriers to trade and investment in renewable energy

The Lisbon Treaty extended the European Parliament's competence to negotiate trade agreements. Indeed, the European Parliament has in fact become a "veto player" as it has gained the competence to approve each and every agreement. The national level in the EU is informed about ongoing developments in the agreements through the Trade and Sustainable Development Expert Group. At the same time, the area of investment has come under the exclusive competence of the EC under EU trade policy, which stems from the Lisbon Treaty (Rudloff & Laurer, 2017).

The implementation of EU trade agreements also involves civil society representatives in the form of an advisory group who have the opportunity to discuss various aspects of the sustainable development agenda in trade agreements. The chapters related to sustainable trade and development are considered to become essential elements of the "new generation" trade agreements. In 2018, the EC proposed a 15-point action plan to review the effectiveness of improving trade agreements. The proposed plan was reformulated into four principles: Working Together, Enabling Civil Society, Delivering, and Communicating and Transparency. The idea was to transform EU trade policy in terms of both processes and outcomes.

This action plan resulted in the publication of a *Comparative Analysis of TSD Provisions for Identification of Best Practices to Support the TSD Review* in September 2021 (LSE Consulting, 2021). The analysis included a selection of 11 trade agreements with OECD countries (Canada, Japan, South Korea, Singapore, and the UK); developing countries (Central America, Colombia/Peru/Ecuador, and Vietnam); and countries that are part of the EU Eastern Partnership and are implementing Deep and Comprehensive Free Trade Areas (DCFTAs) as part of their Association Agreements with the EU (Georgia, Moldova, and Ukraine). In most agreements, trade and sustainable development objectives such as labor, environment, and cross-cutting issues are attached as a single chapter. However, agreements such as the EU-Canada Comprehensive Economic and Trade Agreement (CETA) contain three chapters, and the EU–UK Trade and Cooperation Agreement (TCA) differs significantly from other structures due to the specificity of the existing relationship between the parties (LSE Consulting, 2021).

The analysis presented by LSE Consulting focuses on 11 agreements with various third countries. The detailed scope of the agreements is divided into the following areas (Velut et al., 2022):

- Specific environmental issues covered by EU free trade agreements (FTAs).

  All the agreements covered by the survey contain a protocol and appendices focusing on environmental aspects. All agreements directly address the following issues: climate change, renewable energy, fisheries and forest protection. Biodiversity is covered in 10 agreements – only the EU–Singapore Free Trade Agreement does not contain any specific provisions in this regard. In the area of illegal trade in rare species and genetic resources, including traditional knowledge, nine agreements incorporate such provisions. In the case of air pollution (five agreements) and the ozone layer (five agreements), most provisions are based on cooperation between the parties involved.
- Explicit reference to multilateral environmental agreements (MEAs).[4]

4 Within this area MEAs taken into consideration:: United Nations Framework Convention on Climate Change (UNFCCC); Kyoto Protocol to the United Nations Framework Convention on Climate Change (Kyoto Protocol); Paris Agreement; Montreal Protocol on Substances that Deplete the Ozone Layer (Montreal Protocol); Convention on Biological Diversity (CBD); Nagoya Protocol on Access to Genetic Resources and the Fair and Equitable Sharing of Benefits Arising from their Utilization to the Convention on Biological Diversity (Nagoya Protocol); Convention on International Trade in Endangered Species of Wild Fauna and

The UN Framework Convention on Climate Change (UNFCCC) and the Kyoto Protocol are referred to in 10 agreements (in addition to the EU–Canada Protocol). The Paris Agreements are included in four FTAs between the EU and Japan, Singapore, Vietnam, and the EU–UK agreement. The CBD can be found in nine agreements and a reference to the Montreal Protocol in three. The Nagoya Protocol is included in two agreements (with Vietnam and the UK). The Basel Convention is included in two agreements: a free trade agreement with Colombia, Peru, and Ecuador and another with Central America.

- Environmental regulatory sovereignty and exceptions.

  All agreements leave it to the parties to define their own environmental provisions and to modernize their policies in this direction.
- Reference to international labor standards.

  All 11 agreements contain chapters on the standards outlined in the ILO Convention. Of all agreements, three do not cover occupational health and safety (FTAs with South Korea, Japan, and Vietnam); two agreements cover minimum wage and labor inspection (CETA and EU–UK); four cover aspects related to migrant workers' rights (EU–Colombia/Ecuador/Peru, CETA, Vietnam, and EU–UK).
- Explicit reference to international labor instruments.
- Parties to all agreements agreed to add chapters on international labor instruments in the form of a commitment to the objectives of ILO conventions.
- Other social commitments.
- In the area of social commitments, gender and corporate social responsibility/responsible business conduct (CSR/RBC) promotion are included. CSR/RBC promotion is included in all agreements, while gender is included in nine – the agreements with Colombia/Ecuador/Peru and CETA do not address the following category.
- Labor regulatory sovereignty.
- The parties have retained the right in all agreements to adapt labor and social aspects to national law.
- Trade and sustainable development (TSD) provisions on implementation: intergovernmental mechanisms; role of international organizations; civil society participation.

An intergovernmental committee was set up to monitor the level of implementation of all FTAs. Regular cooperation and exchange of information on the progress of the TSD chapters are essential for success. In the case of Ukraine, Georgia and Moldova, there is a need to align national instruments

Flora (CITES); Waste management; Basel Convention on the Control of Transboundary Movements of Hazardous Wastes and Their Disposal (Basel Convention).

on employment, social and environmental policies with those of the EU. All agreements signed with the Eastern Partnership countries provide for close cooperation to build labor market capacity.

All agreements underline the need for assistance from international organizations such as the ILO or the MEA. The role of such involvement is to promote deeper co-operation and coherence, but also to consult and analyze different tasks. The new nature of the FTAs reveals an openness to the public. All 11 agreements include different aspects of civil society involvement in monitoring implementation at national and supranational levels. Depending on the agreement, this takes the form of a civil society forum or a subcommittee. The EU–UK agreement ensures representation of workers, employers and civil society organizations in cooperation on trade-related aspects of labor policy.

The context of WTO membership exerts a powerful influence on the shape of EU trade policy. The nature of EU trade policy measures depends on multilateral negotiations within the WTO system. The EU as an international organization is a member of the WTO, but at the same time each member state is a member of the WTO. The predominant objective of the WTO is to guarantee free trade, with some exceptional exemptions in cases of threats to food security or depletion of resources and people. The main principle of the WTO is non-discrimination or most favored nation (MFN). Within the WTO, the EU is committed to establishing the rules of the multilateral world trading system and negotiates its own bilateral trade agreements with third countries (as mentioned in the above section). WTO members can set tariffs, which cannot exceed national (local) taxes. Anti-dumping duties can be applied when goods are exported at a lower price than the price at which they are sold for domestic consumption in the exporting country (dumping). Despite the desire to develop free trade, WTO member states retain the right to protect themselves with export tariffs.

It is generally accepted that the objectives of the EU Common Market have been achieved by:

- Abolishing customs restrictions as well as import and export quantitative restrictions.
- Abolishing other measures that had an equivalent effect on trade between member states.
- Applying the same trade policy and common customs tariff to third countries.
- Removing obstacles to the free movement of services, capital and labor.
- Applying a common agricultural and transport policy.
- Pursuing a competition policy that seeks to protect the market from competitive distortions.

However, these measures are only applied in the EU internal market; that is to say, in trade with EU member states. Other measures (tariff barriers) are applied in trade with third countries. Many of these tariffs are "frozen" by the WTO. It is assumed that the efficiency of international trade depends on many conditions and characteristics. One of the most important of these is the differentiation of trade barriers (tariff and non-tariff). Those countries that are more transparent in reporting their regulations appear to be more restrictive (Chen & Novy, 2012). Theory has shown that there are many ways to classify trade barriers (European Commission, 2021a; WTO, 2021a; Daugėlienė, 2016). The traditional classification of trade barriers includes tariff and non-tariff measures or barriers (Benz & Jaax, 2022). Figure 8.1 depicts possible tariff and non-tariff barriers introduced by developed countries to protect the domestic market from foreign competition.

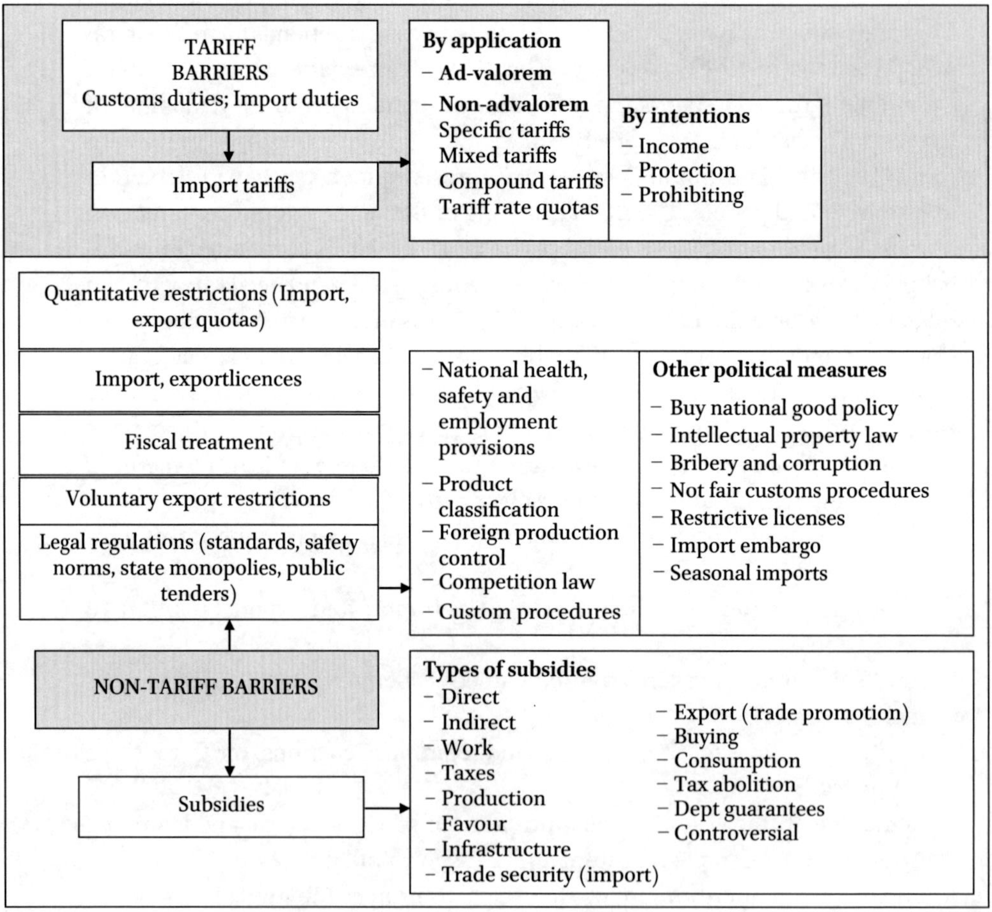

FIGURE 8.1 Structure of tariff and non-tariff trade barriers

SOURCE: AUTHOR'S CONSTRUCTION BASED ON DAUGELIENE, (2014); WTO (2021); EUROPEAN COMMISSION TARIC (2022)

The first group comprises tariff barriers (customs and import duties) – import or export tariffs, which are categorized according to their application (ad valorem; specific or mixed import tariffs) or their purpose (e.g., income, protective or prohibitive). Tariff barriers can be applied depending on the underlying purpose of their application. This means that governments may have different objectives when they impose import tariffs. One of them may be to increase revenues from international trade. Secondly, in order to protect domestic infant industries from foreign players, they apply various quotas as well as substantial tariffs on export goods. Prohibitive import tariffs are usually so high that no imports are economically viable.

The second category includes non-tariff barriers. Since most of the world's developed countries (members of the WTO and the European Union with its introduction of free movement of goods) radically reduced tariffs, more attention has been paid to non-tariff barriers. Due to their intrinsic heterogeneity, non-tariff barriers are categorized into several relatively more homogeneous subgroups (Li & Beghin, 2012). Health and safety measures and technical standards – including sanitary and phytosanitary measures, technical barriers to trade, competition rights, customs clearance procedures and other standards – are often singled out as policies among other non-tariff measures. They affect the scope of trade controversially. Technical standards and regulations have both trade-impeding effects by raising the costs incurred by exporters and comparable demand-enhancing effects by certifying quality and safety to consumers. Li and Begin (2012), after conducting their study, found that agriculture and the food industry tend to be more impeded or less enhanced by technical tariffs than other sectors.

In conclusion, non-tariff barriers can be divided into seven large groups. These include, for example, quantitative restrictions (import and export quotas); import and export licenses; fiscal treatment; voluntary export restrictions; legal regulations (norms, safety standards, state monopolies, public tenders); subsidies; other policy measures (such as "buy national goods policy"; intellectual property rights; bribery and corruption; unfair customs procedures; restrictive licenses; import embargoes; seasonal imports) (Daugėlienė, 2016).

The EU maintains tariffs in most product groups at the same (or very close to) levels negotiated in the WTO. For agricultural and food products, the EU plays a key role in agricultural liberalization.[5] The global trend is to reduce the level of tariffs, but at the same time an increase in tariffs on food products was observed between 2002 and 2019 (Figure 8.2).

In 2019, around 63% of imports into the EU market were zero-duty. The tariff structure applied by the EU remains stable. The simple average MFN tariff

5 For more on the liberalization of the agriculture trade, see Chapter 6.

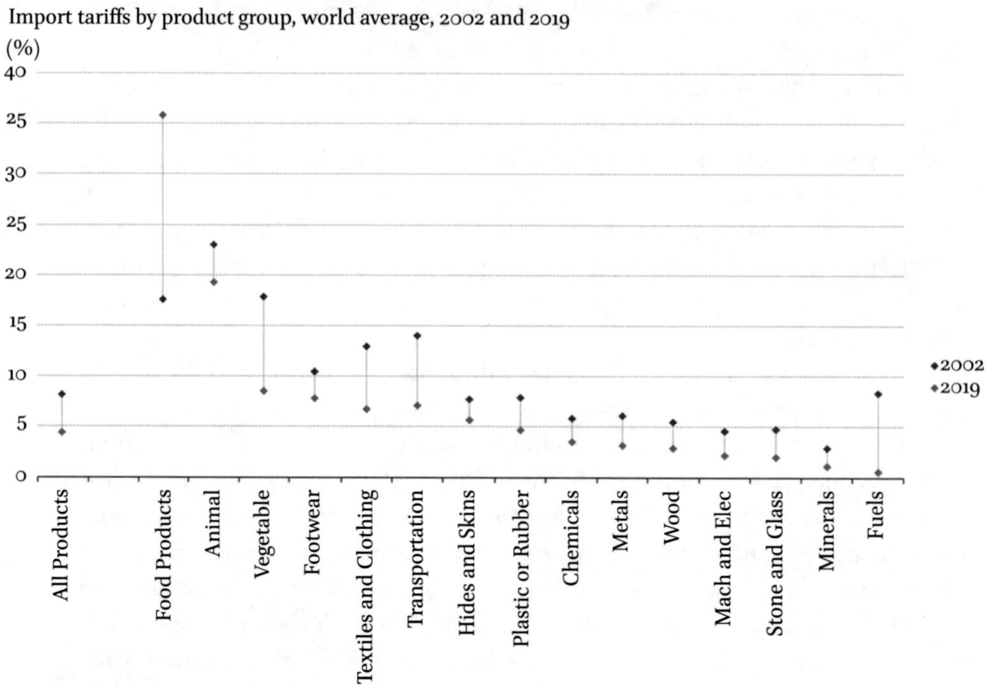

Note: trade-weighted average for effectively applied tariffs.
Source: World Bank, WITS (World Integrated Trade Solution)

FIGURE 8.2 Import tariffs by product group, world average, 2002 and 2019 (%)
SOURCE: HTTPS://EC.EUROPA.EU/EUROSTAT/STATISTICS-EXPLAINED/IMAGES/2/2A/IMPORT_TARIFFS_BY_PRODUCT_GROUP%2C_WORLD_AVERAGE%2C_2002_AND_2019.PNG

rate remains at 6.3%. The applied MFN rates are broadly identical or close to the WTO bound rates. In the agricultural sector, tariffs are well above WTO rates with an average of 14.2 %. In sectors such as fish and fishery products and clothing, the highest protective rates remain at 11.8% and 11.6%. It is worth noting that the WTO underlines that the EU maintains an active role in terms of subsidies and state aid through the EU budget and member states' national budgets. At the same time, this is driven by the modernization objectives needed to protect the environment (World Trade Organization, 2019).

In 2021, the EU initiated a discussion on the reform of the WTO. One of the arguments against the current nature of the WTO is that trade is an opportunity because of its undeniable impact on economic development. At the same time, the EU emphasizes the leading role of the WTO in creating a balanced multilateral trading system. The WTO has done much for millions of people, helping to lift them out of poverty and reduce inequality between nations. The EU suggests that the crisis in effective governance at the WTO stems from the ongoing conflict between the US and China, which is being settled outside the organization. The EU proposes a stronger engagement within the WTO to contribute to the achievement of the SDGs, and as such notes the lack of such joint engagement and the setting of common goals in the shape of a reform of the WTO rulebook, which should correspond to the challenges of the modern world, such as digitalization and climate challenges, by establishing new rules on digital trade, services, and investment. The WTO shall add to the new rules those that are applicable and help to reduce the degree of state intervention in trade. While reforming, the WTO should focus on modernizing the rules on competitive neutrality: subsidies, state-owned enterprises, forced technology transfers and domestic regulation. Notably in the area of fishery subsidies, there is an observed need to finalize negotiations so as to send a signal to all members that the WTO has the inherent strength to propose and effectively implement multilateral agreements. Moreover, fishery subsidies would signal that the WTO keeps the SDGs at the heart of its agenda. The EU emphasizes in its proposal the need to deepen cooperation on SDGs related to decent work and gender equality, so that trade liberalization contributes to meeting these goals. In the EU's trade policy, but also in its priorities for the coming years, this issue is present in both external and internal relations. What is very intriguing is that the EU, in its relations with developing countries, including the LDCs, suggests that trade should be seen as an opportunity for these countries to integrate into the global economy (inclusive impact of trade) and therefore the WTO is not doing enough to integrate these countries into the global economy. The proposed reform also addresses the problem of governance, monitoring and functioning of the WTO (European Commission, 2021b).

5 Conclusions

The European Union is undoubtedly a major player when it comes to influencing the global trading regime. The EU is one of the leaders in the export and import of goods and services. At the same time, it pursues an active trade and development policy towards third countries. The EU considers trade to be a fundamental element of global development and a tool for the integration of developing countries, including LDCs, into the world economy, proposing a trade regime based on the GSP. Still, the EU is deeply committed to achieving the SDGs, which have been incorporated into the EU priorities for 2019–2024 and provide a roadmap for the years ahead. EU member states support the achievement of climate neutrality, but at the same time, in the EU, trade is perceived as providing leverage for greater business competitiveness and a better life for European citizens. The impact of trade on the internal market (EU firms, number of jobs generated inside and outside the EU) and on the integration of developing countries into the global economy plays a significant role.

The nexus between trade and the SDGs is evident in bilateral agreements between the EU and third countries. A review of trade policy has shown that most agreements have one section dedicated to the Sustainable Development Goals. In the case of GSP, positive impacts in LDCs have been observed in areas such as human rights, good governance, and environmental protection.

There are contentious issues between the EU and the WTO on trade liberalization in the context of tariffs in the agricultural sector, as the EU maintains much higher tariffs than those proposed by the WTO. The second issue involves state aid. The EU proposes a more comprehensive approach to public intervention in trade, while the WTO argues that the EU broadly supports a wide range of actors and sectors through the common budget. An approach in trade policy that includes the preparation of mid-term reviews reveals the EU's efforts in implementing the SDGs in bilateral agreements, on the one hand, and the efforts of third countries in reaching global goals, on the other. The EU appears to be an international organization that considers trade to be a global public good and treats it as one of the tools for building a resilient economy.

Tight cooperation between the WTO and the EU is a prerequisite for securing the multilateral trade regime as a global public good in relation to the SDGs. Equitable benefit sharing between countries in terms of social and economic impact is critical to protecting stable trade development in the context of the SDGs. Since 2019 in the wake of the COVID-19 pandemic, protectionism may seem like an enticing prospect, but all theories from classical theory onwards clearly indicate that free trade can result in the building and subsequent development of a comparative advantage. Despite the undeniable gains of trade, it is important to consider how the parties involved share and develop these gains (Mendoza & Bahadur, 2002). The aim should be to prevent market failure and its spillovers, as well as asymmetry in access to information or incomplete information (Rudloff & Laurer, 2017).

References

Benz, S., & Jaax, A. (2022). The costs of regulatory barriers to trade in services: New estimates of ad valorem tariff equivalents. *Economics Letters, 212* doi:10.1016/j.econlet.2021.110057

Chen, N., & Novy, Y. (2012, February 12). On the measurement of trade costs: Direct vs. indirect approaches to quantifying standards and technical regulations. http://www2.warwick.ac.uk/fac/soc/economics/staff/academic/novy/wtr.pdf

Daugėlienė, R. (2016). Nature of trade policy between Lithuania and Russia: A study on the application of trade barriers in the period of 2007–2014. *Journal of Economics and Management Research, 4–5*, 41–58. https://www.lituanistika.lt/content/74927

ECOSOC. (2016, December 15). Report of the Inter-agency and Expert Group on Sustainable Development Goals. E/CN.3/2017/2*. United Nations Economic and Social Council. https://unstats.un.org/unsd/statcom/48th-session/documents/2017-2-IAEG-SDGs-E.pdf

European Commission. (2014). *Trade for all: Towards a more responsible trade and investment policy.* Publications Office of the European Union.

European Commission. (2018). President Jean Claude Junker's State of the Union. https://ec.europa.eu/commission/presscorner/detail/en/SPEECH_18_5808

European Commission. (2020). Sustainable development. https://ec.europa.eu/trade/policy/policy-making/sustainable-development/

European Commission. (2021a). Trade barriers. https://trade.ec.europa.eu/access-to-markets/en/content/trade-barriers

European Commisssion. (2021b). Reforming the WTO. Towards a Sustainable and Effective Multilateral Trading System. https://knowledge4policy.ec.europa.eu/sites/default/files/NG0221300ENN.en_.pdf

European Commission. (2022). A stronger Europe in the world. https://ec.europa.eu/info/strategy/priorities-2019-2024/stronger-europe-world_en#policy-areas

Givens, J. E., Huang, X., & Jorgenson, A. K. (2019). Ecologically unequal exchange: A theory of global environmental in justice. *Sociology Compass, 13*(5), e12693. https://doi.org/10.1111/soc4.12693

Hoekman, B. (2014). Supply chains, mega-regionals and multilateralism: A road map for the WTO. RSCAS Working Papers. European University Institute.

IMF, WB, & WTO. (2017). *Making trade and engine of growth for all: The case for trade and for policies to facilitate adjustment.* International Monetary Fund, World Bank, and World Trade Organization. https://sdgtrademonitor.cdn.prismic.io/sdgtrademonitor/9cc023ad-6083-48bd-90df-029bec2249b5_041017joint-wto-wb-imf-trade-paper.pdf

ITC, UNCTAD, & WTO. (2022). *SDG Trade Monitor.* International Monetary Fund, United Nations Conference on Trade and Development, and World Trade Organization. https://sdgtrade.org/en/

Jaszkiewicz, M., & Latoszek, E. (2013). Polityka rozwojowa Unii Europejskiej. Geneza, ewolucja,zasady funkcjonowania. In E. Latoszek & M. Proczek (Eds.), *Polityka rozwojowa. Rola organizacji międzynarodowych w zwalczaniu ubóstwa na świecie* (pp. 171–211). Oficyna Wydawnicza Szkoły Głównej Handlowej w Warszawie.

Jorgenson, A. (2016). The sociology of ecologically unequal exchange, foreign investment dependence and environmental load displacement: Summary of the literature and implications for sustainability. *Journal of Political Ecology, 23*(1). https://doi.org/10.2458/v23i1.20221

Latoszek, E., & Dugiel, W. (2018). The EU's common trade policy: Implementation of the concept of sustainable development and free trade in the era of de-globalization processes? *Studia Europejskie – Studies in European Affairs, 4*, 23–44.

Latoszek, E., & Borowicz A. (2022). Wdrożenie celów zrównoważonego rozwoju a jednolity rynek cyfrowy w kontekście nauki, technologii i innowacji. In M. Gorynia, J. Kuczewska, & A. Z. Nowak (Eds.), *Polskie przedsiębiorstwo na jednolitym rynku europejskim. Wyzwania współczesności*. PWE.

Leblond, P., & Viju-Miljusevic, C. (2019). EU trade policy in the twenty-first century: Change, continuity and challenges. *Journal of European Public Policy, 26*(12), 1836–1846. https://doi.org/10.1080/13501763.2019.1678059

Li, Y., & Beghin, J. C. (2012). A meta-analysis of estimates of the impact of technical barriers to trade. *Journal of Policy Modeling, 34*(3), 497–511. https://doi.org/10.1016/j.jpolmod.2011.11.001

LSE Consulting. (2021). *Comparative analysis of TSD provisions for identification of best practices to support the TSD review*. https://trade.ec.europa.eu/doclib/docs/2021/september/tradoc_159810.pdf

Marx, A., Pertiwi, S. B., Depoorter, C., Hoornick, M., Mursitama, T. N., Otteburn, K., & Arnakim, L. Y. (2021). What role for regional organizations in goal-setting global governance? An analysis of the role of the European Union and ASEAN in the Sustainable Development Goals. *Global Public Policy and Governance, 1*(4), 421–445. https://doi.org/10.1007/s43508-021-00027-6

Mendoza, R., & Bahadur, C. (2002). Toward free and fair trade: A global public good perspective. *Challenge, 45*(5), 21–62. doi:10.1080/05775132.2002.11034175

Ocampo, J. A. (2016). *Global governance and development*. Oxford University Press.

Rudloff, B., & Laurer, M. (2017, January 1). The EU as global trade and investment actor – The times they are changin'. Working Paper RD EU/Europe. Research Division EU/Europe Stiftung Wissenschaft und Politik, German Institute for International and Security Affairs. https://www.swp-berlin.org/publications/products/arbeitspapiere/IO_trade_EU.pdf

Rueda-Cantuche, J. M., Piñero, P., & Kutlina-Dimitrova, Z. (2021). *EU exports to the world: Effects on employment*. EUR 30875 EN. Publications Office of the European Union. doi:10.2760/245264

Sachs, J., Kroll, C., Lafortune, G., Fuller, G., & Woelm, F. (2021). *Sustainable Development Report 2021*. Cambridge University Press.

Secretariat of the International Task Force on Global Public Goods. (2006). *Expert Paper Series Four: International Trade*.

Servaes, J. (2017). *Sustainable development goals in the Asian context*. Springer. https://doi.org/10.1007/978-981-10-2815-1

Sustainable Development Solutions Network & Institute for European Environmental Policy. (2021). *Europe sustainable development report 2021. Transforming the European Union to achieve the Sustainable Development Goals*. https://s3.amazonaws.com/sustainabledevelopment.report/2021/Europe+Sustainable+Development+Report+2021.pdf

United Nations. (2021). *The Sustainable Development Goals Report 2021*. https://unstats.un.org/sdgs/report/2021/The-Sustainable-Development-Goals-Report-2021.pdf

Velut, J., Baeza-Breinbauer, D., De Bruijne, M., Garnizova, E., Jones, M., Kolben, K., & Zamparutti, T. (2022). *Comparative analysis of trade and sustainable development provisions in free trade agreements*. LSE Consulting. https://trade.ec.europa.eu/doclib/docs/2022/february/tradoc_160043.pdf

Wiedmann, T., & Lenzen, M. (2018). Environmental and social footprints of international trade. *Nature Geoscience*, *11*(5), 314–321. https://doi.org/10.1038/s41561-018-0113-9

World Bank. (2022). *Trade (% of GDP) – European Union*. https://data.worldbank.org/indicator/NE.TRD.GNFS.ZS?locations=EU

WTO. (2019). *Trade policy review of the European Union*. World Trade Organization. https://www.wto.org/english/tratop_e/tpr_e/s395_e.pdf

WTO. (2021a). *International trade and market access data*. World Trade Organization. http://www.wto.org/english/res_e/statis_e/statis_e.html

WTO. (2021b). *World trade report 2021: Economic resilience and trade*. World Trade Organization. https://www.wto.org/english/res_e/booksp_e/wtr21_e/00_wtr21_e.pdf

WTO. (2021c). *World trade statistical review 2021*. World Trade Organization. https://www.wto.org/english/res_e/statis_e/wts2021_e/wts21_toc_e.htm

Xu, Z., Li, Y., Chau, S. N., Dietz, T., Li, C., Wan, L., & Liu, J. (2020). Impacts of international trade on global sustainable development. *Nature Sustainability*, *3*(11), 964–971. https://doi.org/10.1038/s41893-020-0572-z

PART 4

Financial Stability and GDP in World Bank, IMF, and EU Activities

CHAPTER 9

The World Bank: A New Narrative for New Challenges?

Ewa Latoszek and Andrzej Latoszek

1 Introduction

Increased globalization over the last decades, occurring in parallel with rapid economic growth in middle-income countries, has increased the sense of economic, social, and ecological interdependence while intensifying concerns over a growing list of global problems. Nowadays global public goods (GPGs) as such and sustainable growth concern all stakeholders, including international organizations and rich and poor countries. Moreover, the current economic and social situation poses the greatest challenge to international development cooperation and the aid system since World War II.

The spread of communicable diseases (especially the COVID-19 pandemic), the multilateral trade and financial system structure of today, the impact of climate change, international security etc. clearly illustrate the urgency of concerted global actions of all actors in international relations, with the World Bank/World Bank Group (WB/WBG) at the forefront.

The contribution of this chapter to the main objective of this monograph is that it provides the current view on the role of the World Bank in fostering sustainable growth in the world via increasing its involvement in the management and production of global public goods parallel to its statutory activities focused on planned financial support for member states. The main aim of this section is to analyze and suggest ways in which the World Bank can strengthen its abilities in GPGs production to assist member states to meet their development objectives together with sustainable growth goals. The basic question that should be answered in these analyses refers to the backgrounds of changes that took place in World Bank priorities over the decades and the ways in which this organization is able to combine its main statutory aims with delivering GPGs to foster sustainable growth.

The crisis and challenges of today have among others resulted in a particularly painful widening of the gap between the financial needs of developing countries and the actual possibilities of financing them by the main actors in international relations. Unfortunately, this process may be more difficult

DOI:10.1163/9789004687264_011

than ever as the economic crisis resulting from the pandemic and the war in Ukraine has hit both developed and developing countries, i.e., traditional aid donors as well as recipients. Regardless of this, the World Bank underlines that it has a number of comparative advantages over other institutions: a global presence, a repository of best practices, financial acumen, leadership in global public goods, and an established role as an international development catalyst. According to Vikram Nehru, former World Bank chief economist for East Asia, while the Bank has always represented a tiny share of public investments in most countries, its strength comes from leveraging its lending with ideas.

This chapter is organized as follows. A brief introduction defines the research problem and covers the aim and research questions. Section 1 deals with the structure of the WBG, its main statutory goals, and the role of the International Bank for Reconstruction and Development in the WBG, as well as changes in its policy priorities that took place over the decades. Section 2 depicts the endeavors as well as difficulties connected with the WB policy towards GPGs, their management, production, and distribution, with special attention to the influence of the crisis caused by the pandemic. In Section 3 the backgrounds of WB finances are discussed, as well as the trends of some new financial instruments. Finally, the conclusion sums up the chapter and elaborates the answers to the research questions.

2 World Bank Group: Structure and Priorities

The World Bank Group (WBG) has always played a special role in the process of contributing its knowledge and financial support to less developed countries and regions, as well as taking part in collective actions of other international organizations on GPGs.

The WBG is made up of five organizations:
- International Bank for Reconstruction and Development (IBRD)
- International Development Association (IDA)
- International Finance Corporation (IFC)
- Multilateral Investment Guarantee Agency (MIGA)
- International Centre for Settlement of Investment Disputes (ICSID)

The largest and oldest institution in the WBG is undoubtedly the International Bank for Reconstruction and Development, which began its activity in 1945. The World Bank is not a bank in the strict sense of the word. It is the largest and most well-known development bank in the world, which in addition is an observer in the United Nations Development Group. The original goal of the IBRD was to finance the reconstruction and development of member states by facilitating capital investment for productive purposes, including the reconstruction of economies destroyed during the war and the adaptation of their productive capacities for peaceful purposes as well as stimulating their development through the provision of loans, guarantees, risk management products, and advisory services. The activities of the World Bank are based on the provision of the following functions: providing financial assistance, performing fiduciary functions for private and public institutions from member states, providing advisory and analytical services and, in recent years, carrying out activities aimed at strengthening their development capacity to increasing their welfare through poverty reduction, development financing,[1] providing loans for the development of health-care and education systems, advanced good quality infrastructure, and environment protection[2] (World Bank, 2007a).

In the 1950s, the priority of the IBRD was the development of broadly understood infrastructure by granting loans for projects such as the construction of dams, power grids, irrigation systems, and roads. In the next decade – the 1960s – loans were aimed mainly at restructuring agriculture and solving the problem of poverty and malnutrition. In the 1970s, attention was focused on health and education, i.e., on general aspects of hygiene, prevention, broadly understood health, fighting illiteracy, better access to education. In the 1980s, the IBRD's attention was focused on new financial instruments aimed at stabilizing the economies of less developed countries. The new element in the Bank's policy was also inviting experts from various fields, who supported the Bank with their knowledge in different areas, including in the field of national economic stability. In the 1990s, more attention was paid to social life and the role of the individual in society, cultural heritage, and also to the issue of climate change, which at that time was becoming the most important global public good in the world (Gutner, 2016, pp. 211–215). In 1991, the WBG formed the Global Environment Facility (GEF) to promote environmentally friendly and sustainable economic development (Independent Evaluation Group, 2013). After the 1992 Earth Summit in Rio, GEF became a separate institution (in legal terms it is still a part of the World Bank), being the greatest public funder for projects aiming to globally improve environmental conditions, bringing together 182 countries in collaboration with international

1 Financial assistance includes direct financing of specific investment projects and programs, co-financing of loans from various sources, guarantees for borrowings, and assistance in obtaining loans by member states. The IBRD and IDA mainly provide financing for two types of operations: investment project financing and development policy financing.

2 The last element includes, among others, initiatives to support economic growth and poverty reduction programs, such as global and regional programs, the Global Development Learning Network, the Global Development Network, and the Global Knowledge Partnership.

institutions, civil society organizations and the private sector to solve global environmental problems while supporting domestic sustainable development initiatives. Moreover, the World Bank received authorization to administer the Green Climate Fund, which is an operating unit of the UN Framework Convention on Climate Change (UNFCCC), thus confirming its authorization and capabilities to produce and manage GPGs. At that time the World Bank also became the trustee of the Adaptation Fund established under the 1997 Kyoto Protocol, which maintained that the Fund would be financed with a 2% trading fee for carbon dioxide emissions allowances under the Clean Development Mechanism. The funds thus raised were supposed to bring ample benefits to developing countries by increasing the funds to foster sustainable development because of financing projects for the countries to reduce exhaust gases emission into the atmosphere. This was a novel approach to finance, albeit seriously defective for several reasons, including an objection on the part of potential beneficiaries who fear such a policy may, in their case, reduce the pace of their economies' growth. Hence, with varied attitudes of the signatory states of the Kyoto Protocol, the Adaptation Fund become a non-credible financing source (Evans & Davies, 2015, pp. 63–64).

In the first decade of the 21st century, the World Bank's policy focused on delivering to beneficiaries the financial support and knowledge to solve problems related to state governance. In 2000, for the first time, the IBRD also indicated directly and assessed its place in GPGs production (Narayan et al., 2018, pp. 200–208). One of the first basic documents on the WB's role in the production of GPGs was also prepared during this period as a joint background report of the WB/IMF (World Bank, 2007b). Notwithstanding, the strategy sparked criticism for focusing mainly on the existing traditional lending operations of the WBG, with just a little indication of something "new" (Birdsall, 2012). For the IBRD, as a primarily country-focused development institution, the key became its ability to work consensually with partner countries combining national development priorities and global public goods (World Bank, 2001). The Critical Ecosystem Partnership Fund (CEPF) established in 2000 by the GEF, the European Union, the government of Japan, L'Agence Française de Développement, Conservation International, and the World Bank is an example of a global program that provided financing and technical support to non-governmental organizations (NGOs) and private sector partners in order to protect important ecosystems with a significant impact on local, regional, and global development. To date, the program has provided grants to support over 3,000 projects globally, ranging from US$20,000 (small grants) to US$150,000 (large grants).

The second decade of the 21st century, i.e., the period between 2010 and 2019, was a time of focusing on so-called big data and the flow of personal data. This is the most common topic concerning not only the data flow of the most important global institutions, but also the security of citizens and the problem of government surveillance (World Bank Group, 2021).

New circumstances of the regional and global situation since 2020 have brought about adjustments in emphasis, instruments, and responses based on GPGs production. And so in the current decade, the main objectives of the World Bank Group cover human capital, the environment,[3] smart cities, equality for women,[4] threats and armed conflicts, and pandemics (HIV, Ebola, malaria, SARS, COVID).

3 The Role of the World Bank in Promoting Global Public Goods

Building on the Samuelsonian public goods theory, there is a proposition that multilateral institutions, such as the World Bank, should undertake the mission of providing global public goods. The World Bank is often considered the most qualified institution for this task. Such a proposal has solid theoretical and practical foundations, as an organization whose mission are sustainable development and global prosperity is promoting the idea of GPGs ever more audaciously. The GPGs themselves have become an important constituent of the Bank's strategies (Ravallion, 2016). It is also beyond doubt that the World Bank still mainly provides private goods and resolves the problems of its beneficiaries, while global hazards are only becoming more conspicuous in its policy. Still, many researchers of the problem find it is necessary to analyze the Bank's actions from three perspectives, i.e., nationally, regionally, and globally (Kaul & Grunberg, 2016, p. 27). Such a holistic approach to the World Bank shows that its actions undertaken at particular levels are complementary and thus contribute to producing GPGs by giving the Bank's members an opportunity to solve global problems. Hence, it may be concluded that certain programs and products offered by the Bank, be it to one country only, should be considered a

3 The environment includes financing of renewable energy, forest management, rural protection, and development of approx. US$200 billion for the years 2021–2025, while natural disasters reduce consumption by about US$520 billion per year.

4 According to IBRD data, in 2019 alone 130 million girls in the world did not take up education, and 13 million were married off before the age of 18. See https://www.worldbank.org/en/who-we-are/ibrd (retrieved December 10, 2021).

contribution to GPGs by the so-called spillover effect. This is because normally lending-based activities carried out by less developed countries also impact other countries of the region, and often of the world. For instance, a loan given to an African country to fight malaria may consequently stabilize health conditions regionally or globally, and it is connected with measures undertaken by other organizations, e.g., the WHO, in this area, which ultimately makes the good a cumulated GPG. In turn, many economists are of the view that in practice, the Bank's production of GPGs is still too marginal, as the institution mainly focuses on specific problems of member states rather than global issues. However, despite critical and prudent opinions of numerous experts (Ravallion, 2016), some researchers find that the World Bank Group (IDA, in particular) itself is a GPG (Kanbur, 2002, p. 24).

Undoubtedly, numerous products and services rendered by the Bank are not only of a local, but also regional and global nature. This is because the World Bank offers innovative financial solutions, including financial products (loans, guarantees, and risk management products), as well as access to knowledge and advisory services for governments on a domestic and regional level. It finances investment projects across all the sectors and provides technical support and expertise at each stage of a project. IBRD resources not only provide the borrowing countries with the required financing, but they are also a tool for a global transfer of knowledge and technical assistance. Advisory services in the area of sovereign debt and assets management support governments, official sector institutions, and developmental organizations in building transparent and stable institutions that guarantee protection and strengthening of the public finance management system, the improvement of the investment climate, the elimination of bottlenecks, and state enhancement. IBRD support also includes preference interest long-term lending for the most disadvantaged member states, as well as public and private business entities (on receiving government guarantees), and technical assistance. All the above are aimed at combating poverty, being a public anti-good, and financing sustainable development by supporting such social life areas as health care, education, environmental protection, and infrastructure development. In return, however, the countries which benefit from the said support are required to undertake important political and economic measures, such as combating corruption, the growth of democracy, or the expansion of the private sector. Over the consecutive decades of its operations, the World Bank passed plans for the reconstruction and development of the world, plans allowing for global economic, social, and political changes, while the financed projects were to help implement the plans. Accordingly, the researchers basically agree that while the Bank's specific programs and products target member states, most of them may and should be considered as a contribution to the production and management of GPGs because of the abovementioned "spillover effect" of the provided lending (Kenny et al., 2018, p. 12). Simultaneously, only certain activities of the World Bank may be considered core activities from a GPG production perspective. Trust funds managed by the Bank are a flagship example in this respect, which is elaborated later on in the next part of this section (Aramonte & Avalos, 2020). Experts maintain that the following are the most important GPGs with respect to their significance for development and dependence on assistance financing:

- Overseeing, controlling, and fighting communicable diseases
- Sustainable management of cross-border natural resources, such as the atmosphere, forest and marine ecosystems, fresh water, and fishery
- Knowledge creation for development

Conceptually, what should be deemed as the purest form of activities classified as GPGs in the World Bank are research and research findings published globally over the internet, publishing data, reports, and a variety of scientific and expert studies. This is because the IBRD is one of the world's most prominent development research centers and a knowledge "bank" employing the world's best experts who create tools to support development, such as the Doing Business project (provided objective measures of business regulations and their enforcement), the *World Development Report* (an annual report providing in-depth analysis of a specific aspect of economic development), the Development Gateway (an interactive portal for sharing information on development and poverty reduction); AIDA (a complex database on developmental projects), and DG Market (an international database on the World Bank's procurement procedures).

While researching the World Bank in the sense of its impacting sustainable development and the production of GPGs, it is vital to remember that the world used to be a completely different place 80 years ago than it is now. In the early 21st century the Bank took interest in global public goods, and it made the provision of global public goods strategic. It is beyond doubt that the Bank's involvement in partnerships, as well as regional and global programs, varied, and with varying outcome. Some of the effects were significant achievements indeed. Should the bank change radically and become a "global institution addressing the global challenges of the future through global collective action" (Birdsall & Subramanian, 2007)? The World Bank may and should play an important role in providing such global public goods that pursue its main goal of reducing poverty and thus improving global prosperity. Moreover, the IBRD is engaged in actions that concern, among others, climate change and solving the problem of global warming, monitoring, and supervision of the relevant agreed measures undertaken, as well as initiating steps for enhancing

R&D with regards to new technologies for poor countries. Climate change is included in the greatest investment program being part of the environmental portfolio the World Bank (and possibly the world) has undertaken in terms of providing GPGs. In the years 2010 to 2021, a significant portion of the World Bank's Country Assistance Strategies (CASs) and Country Partnership Frameworks (CPFs) concerned climate change. A good example of environmental a GPG initiative is the Global Partnership founded in 2012 to raise US$1.5 billion for the world's overfished, polluted, and warming oceans, to double the number of protected marine areas, and to rebuild fish stocks. It is a coalition of governments, NGOs, scientists, and businesses committed to mobilizing at least US$300 million in catalytic financing to leverage another US$1.2 billion from businesses, NGOs, and other institutions (Evans & Davies, 2015, p. 64).

So as to face up to the challenge, the Bank is taking up numerous initiatives aimed at linking its own development agenda to global public goods (World Bank, 2020a). Currently, there is in fact no single institution responsible for providing global public goods on a worldwide scale. For instance, the Global Polio Eradication Initiative is managed by the WHO, but it is also financed from other intergovernmental sources. Global attempts to prevent climate change are coordinated under a UNFCCC umbrella agreement. The impact of international marine transportation on the environment is solved in agreements negotiated by members of the International Marine Organization. The list is long. The point is, however, that various public goods imply various problems, require various technical expertise and are of varying importance for various country groups. Thus, it is not possible for the World Bank to accept the role proposed by Birdsall and Subramanian (2007), and it is not obviously necessary. Many of these organizations work very effectively to produce global public goods. Hence, leaving these issues up to some selected organizations only could, in practice, result in numerous errors. Concomitantly, the World Bank must not just stand by only because the global efforts in some impact area of a given GPG are the responsibility of other organizations or because some management or supply measures have failed (Kopiński & Wróblewski, 2021).

To summarize, given the current trends in the global economy the Bank will need to work with partner countries combining national development priorities with regional and global concerns. According to the World Bank Framework of 2007 (World Bank, 2007a) this requires the Bank to undertake activities in the following areas:

1. Enhance cooperation with partner countries on the integration of country priorities and global/regional public goods. Management will explore how best to ensure a more systematic treatment of global public goods at the country-level, working collaboratively with partner countries and building on the Bank's diversified tools of country assistance.

2. Strengthen its capacity for advisory services and lending related to global and regional public goods. To be credible in its advice, the Bank will continue to upgrade its staff expertise in areas of emerging priority and better align Regions and Networks in implementing the global public goods agenda.
3. Participate strategically in global partnerships. Partnerships are an important instrument for pursuing critical global public goods objectives, and the Bank has many vehicles to participate in global initiatives. The major challenge is selectivity, to ensure that the Bank achieves the greatest impact from its interventions. Management sees a need to explore the coherence of the Bank's large trust fund portfolio in support of global partnerships and to identify gaps in critical priorities.
4. Explore new financing modalities for global public goods. Building on recent experiences (for example with the International Financing Facility for Immunization and joint IBRD/IFC-funded projects), Management will continue to support new financing instruments, particularly if they help to address market failures (as in low-carbon investments) and if they contribute to leveraging private resources in the infrastructure, energy and health sectors. Such instruments should be pursued for global public goods activities that fill extraordinary and critical gaps in innovation, that provide major incentives for collective action, and those that would have a catalytic impact on other sources of funds.
5. Continue to promote informed debate on global issues, and advocate constructively for developing countries. In particular, the Bank should contribute to: (i) a durable and equitable framework to reduce greenhouse gas emissions; and (ii) a successful conclusion of the Doha Round of trade negotiations.
6. Increase action at the regional level. Concentrating on regional approaches to regional and global public goods may be a more relevant operational approach in some problem areas – such as water, energy, transport and health – and is likely to continue to gain in importance. The Bank can assist in developing common regulatory frameworks and shared financing options, and will enhance lending for multi-country investments addressing global public goods at the regional level. (World Bank, 2007a, pp. v–vi)

4 World Bank Financing of GPGs

The operations of the World Bank chiefly rest on providing financial assistance. The World Bank's funds derive from member states' contributions, repayment of loans incurred earlier on and from the issue of bonds on global capital markets. The initial capital is share capital, with the largest portion of the Bank's funds coming from global financial markets. In this way, it was possible to obtain more than US$500 billion to be provided to member states in loans aiming to alleviate poverty and improve global prosperity, from the Bank's inception to 2021.

As a financial institution, since 1959 it has continued to be AAA rated by rating agencies. Hence, it is by far easier for the Bank to incur low-cost loans and offer average-GDP developing countries access to capital on convenient terms. This, in turn, helps to pursue development projects in a more sustainable manner. Investors perceive the Bank's bonds as quality securities, and IBRD financing often attracts financing from private sources. The funds that the Bank obtains yearly as profit from equity and non-significant credit margins cover the World Bank's operating costs and make up the reserve to enhance its annual balance sheet and secure yearly transfer of funds to the IDA for the poorest member states. The Bank's financial strength rests on the support it has from its shareholders, as well as on an array of financial policies and practices. An effective credit policy and experience in finance and risk management have enabled the World Bank to maintain capital liquidity, diversify its financing sources, and use a portfolio of liquid investments to meet the financial obligations and mitigate risk, including credit and market risk (Beegle & Christiaense, 2019, pp. 247–267). Borrowers may adapt the repayment terms to their needs and debt management capabilities as the loans offered bear fixed and variable interest in many currencies. However, borrowers typically prefer loans denominated in American dollars and the euro. The IBRD also supports its borrowers by providing them with access to risk management tools, such as derivative instruments, including FX swaps and interest rate caps (World Bank, 2019). To conclude this topic, it is difficult to discriminate between actions to support member states and those creating global public goods, while discussing the activities of the World Bank. This is because they may be complementary, as it is often so that a single project combines domestic support with a regional or global component. However, in order to play a more comprehensive role in providing GPGs, the Bank, next to the measures shown, also needs resources primarily dedicated to promote and supply so-called core global public goods. To date, the Bank was chiefly based on trust funds and short-term pilot programs in this area. Generally speaking, they were created by rich Bank members who also took care of the financial side, while the Bank was their administrator and not an institution that impacted their form, purpose, or consumption. It is all the more so that they have so far made up relatively minor funds pools, not integrated with the Bank's budget, albeit fully dependent on their donors, with the beneficiaries actually being fully dependent on their founders. The Bank's authorities estimate that approximately US$600 million are spent annually under trust funds for GPG-related actions (Birdsall & Morris, 2016, pp. 5–10). This means that merely 10% of funds fuel, to varying degrees, international or global issues. The World Bank manages and coordinates around 3,000 trust funds by providing accounting, legal, financial, and technical support (World Bank, 2020b). The most renowned and the largest funds the World Bank is involved in are the following: the Global Environmental Facility (GEF, est. 1992), the Climate Investment Fund (CIF, est. 2008), the International Finance Facility for Immunizations (IFFIm, est. 2006) together with the Gavi, the Vaccine Alliance (est. 2000 as the Global Alliance for Vaccines and Immunization), the Global Partnership (est. 2012) or the Consultative Group on International Agricultural Research (CGIAR, est. 1971), the Extractive Industries Transparency Initiative (EITI, est. 2004). Many other, smaller mechanisms have also been created, such as the Critical Ecosystem Partnership Fund (2000), the Global Crop Diversity Trust (2004), the Global Concessional Financing Facility (GCFF, est. 2016), a considerable number of health-sector product development partnerships, such as the Medicines for Malaria Venture (late 1999) and the Drugs for Neglected Diseases Initiative (2003); pilot "pull" mechanisms, such as the Pneumococcal AMC (Advance Market Commitment) vaccination initiative (2006) and the Results Initiative (2012); and World Bank – led mechanisms, such as the Extractive Industries Transparency Initiative (2002) and the State- and Peace-Building Fund (2008). The World Bank Group has also mounted the largest crisis response in its history to help over a hundred low- and middle-income countries fight the health, economic, and social impacts of COVID-19 with its commitments for the 12-month period of fiscal year 2021 totaled US$98.8 billion, including spending for GPG to achieve a more sustainable world and to better protect the poor through digital economy (aimed at building financial sector resilience and resilience in value chains as well as universal, affordable, and high-quality infrastructure), more effective, resilient, and equitable education rebuilding existing systems to be more effective, and investing in remote learning, saving lives, and securing food. Coordination and cooperation – including with the IMF, multilateral development banks, UN agencies, foundations, parliamentarians, the private sector and CSOs – have been key to the WBG crisis response. Close coordination with the IMF throughout the crisis has enhanced debt sustainability analysis, helped countries manage debt vulnerabilities and fiscal space, supported fiscal reforms, and ensured consistency of public spending and policies with macroeconomic stability. Close cooperation with the UN is particularly important in order to provide support to countries and vulnerable communities across the humanitarian – development – peace nexus. Safeguarding global public health requires boosting capacity to stem the spread of the virus everywhere – including in fragile settings and refugee communities. The Bank launched the Health Emergency Preparedness and Response Multi-Donor Fund to complement WBG support and extend vital aid on health emergency preparedness and the response for COVID-19 and future epidemic outbreaks – including to member countries not in good standing with the IDA, the West Bank and Gaza, and Jordan and Lebanon for the benefit of Syrian refugees. The HEPRTF, and any future associated trust funds under that umbrella, have provided an initial amount of up to US$500 million to support countries to prevent, respond to, and mitigate the impact of COVID-19 and future epidemic outbreaks (World Bank, 2021).

To summarize, it should be emphasized that establishing trust funds and grants, whatever the above said defects they may have, enables expanding the operations of the IBRD, in particular in response to natural and other types of disasters, as well as to finance innovations (World Bank, 2020a). Thanks to them, the World Bank Group is able to provide practically instant support whenever the creditworthiness of countries suffering such problems is inadequate. Partner programs are increasingly more often used to engage partners from the non-governmental and private sector, as well as to combine their knowledge and capital with the WBG's capabilities regarding the provision of pro-development solutions in beneficiary states. As in the case of IDA resources, within the framework of the World Bank, the funds belong to a so-called development finance instrument (DFI), which is managed by the Bank's Vice President of Development Finance. The structure aims to create and popularize business programs, trust funds and partner programs. The unit helps to develop and manage business operations related to the Bank's partnership and trust funds. It is a link between external and internal clients as regards the development of program strategy, policy, and management. What is more, the DFI facilitates the creation of trust funds. In the realm of partner relations, it helps to maximize resources from current and new development partners. The unit is in charge of strategic high-profile consultations between the World Bank Group and its development partners (IBRD, 2021). Owing to these consultations, the unit supports actions to identify common development priorities and understand the options offered by various financing channels within the World Bank Group. The DFI also facilitates coordination among the World Bank's business units by way of early and regular reporting on fundraising actions.

Given the rising interest in sustainable development policy, GPG production, as well as new global challenges emerging (such as pandemics, the war in Ukraine, and mass migration), it seems highly likely that the production and financing of GPGs will continue to increase robustly in absolute terms. Nevertheless, the funds' origin remains a problem, as the donors, particularly under current circumstances, are unwilling to devote increasing funds to this purpose. It means that the production of GPGs is financed at the cost of the remaining, domestic development assistance. Researchers of the problem show that GPG expenses under multilateral development assistance rose from 5 in 2010 to around 18 in 2019. Still, it needs to be pointed out that the data is not very precise, as the construction of a systematic and regular system of computing the share and structure of the assistance given to GPGs has failed over the years, be it globally, on a particular donor country level, or that of multilateral institutions that spend ample funds under development assistance for this purpose.

5 Conclusions

The mission of the World Bank Group is to enhance security and prosperity of the population by reducing poverty and fostering sustainable development in developing countries, while the main instruments of its policy are loans, guarantees, analytical works, and technical assistance. Undoubtedly, from its very inception, the WBG has contributed to a high level of progress in fighting poverty on a global scale. The World Bank itself, which the many years of its operations testify, is a global institution with almost universal membership and, principally, with a global mission to reduce poverty in the world, to protect the environment and redress the damage humans have inflicted over the last few dozen years. This is because the challenges are still valid and have even deepened, including on account of the world encompassing the pandemic or the war in Ukraine. Around 20% of people in the world are still living on less than US$1 a day, and 46% – on less than US$2; over 3 million people (including 2 million children) are dying each year from diseases for which vaccines exist, 30,000 people are dying every day from hunger, and more than 113 million children do not go to school. There are still insufficient funds to help the poorest. On a yearly average, the official development assistance (ODA) amounts globally to around US$110 billion a day, while US$1,000 billion annually is spent on the military and over US$20 billion annually is spent to feed domestic animals in the US and in Europe. As the World Bank provides lending to the governments of developing countries to finance development projects, economic reforms, and technical assistance, it has to evaluate project applications with respect to whether the project will help the beneficiary country economy, whether it will favor the world's poorest regions and increase the opportunities for such social groups as youth and women, how it will impact the environment in the long term, whether it can be financed from other sources, and whether the state will be able to continue actions carried out as part of a project once the Bank's financing is over. It is also for this reason that, in line with the mandate's objectives, the actions of the WBG are subjected to the needs of particular member states. Such an assumption largely impacts the scope and directions of providing GPGs by the WBG. More funds are needed to finance the purpose: if no additional sources are employed, member states will receive less assistance funds and will compromise their own development goals. Therefore, paradoxically, it is the poorest countries that in practice oppose to such a policy of the World Bank the most, arguing that the money they deserve is being taken away from them. As mentioned before and as the World Bank's practice to date shows, trust funds should be the best instruments providing the production of GPGs. However, their usefulness depends on how rich they are. As they are still regrettably not affluent enough, they are confined to just a certain group of countries. On the other hand, however, it is important to highlight that the current global governance landscape has given rise to a unique political vacuum. In the face of increasing threats of nationalism and related challenges around the world, institutions like the World Bank are being called upon to play a critical role in addressing these issues. For over 20 years, the focus of the Bank's work in global public goods has been on five areas endorsed by the Development Committee in September 2000: preserving the environment, controlling communicable diseases, strengthening the international financial architecture, enhancing developing countries' participation in the global trading system, and creating and sharing knowledge relevant for development (IMF/World Bank,2000). To meet such expectations, its engagement should be consistent with its development mandate and relative strengths to assist countries in achieving sustainable development and increasing their welfare through the production of GPGs. It follows that the operations of the World Bank should be based on financing investment projects which, in the long term, will be important for and favor not only selected countries, but also global development. Therefore, the Bank along with other organizations (including the Global Environmental Facility) should ensure that funds are made available and wisely invested. Other actions of the World Bank with respect to providing GPGs include investments in tropical medicine research, supervision over communicable diseases, and the development of global common resource management institutions. Initiating efforts for international security by "cutting off" Russia from credit and any forms of support with respect to the assault on Ukraine is an example of the World Bank's involvement in GPG management and production.

The Bank may and should do more in all these areas. This implies that a comprehensive review of the Bank's policy is necessary to channel its strategy towards better coordination of the Bank's present policy with the broadly understood goals of providing global public goods to promote development and security. The Bank's involvement in this respect has been of an on-and-off nature so far, often in response to a crisis or inspired by third parties. The Bank's overall involvement in the production of GPGs should be more strategic. More ideas should be generated internally. The focus should be on policies and projects that complement the Bank's core operations, which largely involve domestic lending. The programs and strategies the Bank creates should also point to external partners.

References

Aramonte, S., & Avalos, F. (2020, April 14). The recent distress in corporate bond markets: Cues from ETFs. *BIS Bulletin, 6*. https://www.bis.org/publ/bisbull06.pdf

Beegle, K., & Christiaensen, L. (2019). *Accelerating poverty reduction in Africa*. World Bank. https://openknowledge.worldbank.org/handle/10986/32354

Birdsall, N. (2012, July). The World Bank and climate change: Forever a big fish in a small pond? CGD Policy Paper 007, Center for Global Development. https://www.cgdev.org/sites/default/files/1426335_file_Birdsall_Big_Fish_Small_Pond_final_0.pdf

Birdsall, N., & Morris, S. (2016). multilateral development banking for this century's development challenges: Five recommendations to shareholders of the old and new multilateral development banks. Center for Global Development. https://www.cgdev.org/sites/default/files/multilateral-development-banking-report-five-recommendations.pdf

Birdsall, N., & Subramanian, A. (2007, October). From World Bank to world development cooperative. CGD Essay. Center for Global Development. https://www.cgdev.org/sites/default/files/14625_file_WorldDevCooperative.pdf

Creswell, J. W., Plano Clark, V. L., Gutmann, M. L., & Hanson, W. E. (2003). Advanced mixed methods research designs. In A. Tashakkori & C. Teddlie (Eds.), *Handbook of mixed methods in social and behavioral research* (pp. 209–240). Sage.

Evans, W. J., & Davies, R. (2015). *Too global to fail: The World Bank at the intersection of national and global public policy in 2025*. World Bank.

Gutner, T. (2016). *International organizations in world politics*. Sage/CQ Press.

IBRD. (2021, June 30). Management's discussion & analysis and financial statements. International Bank for Reconstruction and Development. https://thedocs.worldbank.org/en/doc/9e6e5c7c885899cba176dd6e1409cbeb-0040012021/original/IBRD-Financial-Statements-June-2021.pdf

IMF/World Bank. (2000). Poverty reduction and global public goods: Issues for the World Bank in supporting global collective action (DC/2000-16). Development

Committee (Joint Ministerial Committee of the Boards of Governors of the Bank and the Fund On the Transfer of Real Resources to Developing Countries).

Independent Evaluation Group. (2013). *The World Bank Group's partnership with the Global Environment Facility.* World Bank.

Kanbur, R. (2002). IFI's and IPG's: Operational implications for the World Bank. Paper prepared for the G24 Technical Group Meeting, Beirut.

Kaul, I., & Grunberg I. (2016). *Global public goods.* Edward Edgar.

Kenny, C., Snyder, M., & Pate, D. (2018). Measures of global public goods and international spillovers. Working Paper 474, Center for Global Development.

Kopiński, D., & Wróblewski, M. (2021). Reimagining the World Bank: Global public goods in an age of crisis. *World Affairs, 184*(2), 151–175. https://doi.org/10.1177%2F00438200211013486

Narayan, A., Van der Weide, R., Cojocaru, C., Lakner, A., Redaelli, S., Gerszon Mahler, D., Ramasubbaiah, R. G. N., & Thewissen, S. (2018). Fair progress? Economic mobility across generations around the world. International Bank for Reconstruction and Development/World Bank.

Ravallion, M. (2016). The World Bank: Why it is still needed and why it still disappoints. *Journal of Economic Perspectives, 30*(1), 77–94. doi:10.1257/jep.30.1.77

World Bank. (2001). *World development report 2000/2001: Attacking poverty.* Oxford University Press.

World Bank. (2007a, September 28). Global public goods: A framework for the role of the World Bank, Development Committee (Joint Ministerial Committee of the Boards of Governors of the Bank and the Fund On the Transfer of Real Resources to Developing Countries), DC2007-0020.

World Bank. (2007b). *A guide to the World Bank* (2nd ed.). International Bank for Reconstruction and Development/World Bank.

World Bank. (2019, June). *Management's discussion & analysis and financial statements.* http://pubdocs.worldbank.org/en/625641565356285634/IBRD-Financial-Statements-June-2019.pdf

World Bank. (2020a). *Engaging with investors on environmental, social, and governance (ESG) issues: A World Bank Guide for sovereign debt managers.*

World Bank. (2020b). *Poverty and shared prosperity 2020: Reversals of fortune.* doi:10.1596/978-1-4648-1602-4

World Bank. (2021). *Annual report 2021.* doi:10.1596/978-1-4648-1778-6.

World Bank Group. (2020). *Modified cash basis trust funds: Report of internal control over financial reporting & combined statements of receipts, disbursements and fund balance.* http://www.worldbank.org/

World Bank Group. (2021). *World development report 2021: Data for better lives.* doi:10.1596/978-1-4648-1600-0

CHAPTER 10

IMF Activity Supporting International Financial Stability and Sustainable Development

Magdalena Proczek

1 Introduction

The International Monetary Fund (IMF) ensures the stability of the international financial and economic system by controlling, regulating, and assisting its members. The IMF conducts ongoing bilateral and multilateral surveillance of member countries' financial and economic policies, which is an important part of the IMF's work to sustain the development and manage global public goods. In the process of surveillance and regulation, the Fund identifies potential risks to macroeconomic and financial stability. It also identifies necessary adjustments and, where necessary, assists member countries in preparing along with implementing adjustment and recovery programs, which is often combined with the provision of financing during the period of implementation of the programs and technical assistance.

The aim of this chapter is to present the IMF as an international governmental organization, which works to ensure stability and sustain the development of member states together with the global economy. The International Monetary Fund is an international organization, which creates global public goods such as financial stability on a national and international scale and provides financial and technical assistance to member states for the implementation of the Sustainable Development Goals. This task is reflected in the structure of the chapter, which consists of an introduction, three main sections, and a conclusion. The three sections cover the International Monetary Fund as an international governmental financial organization, international financial stability as a global public good and a priority for IMF operations, and the engagement of the IMF in achieving the Sustainable Development Goals.

Nowadays, global state-of-the-art includes an in-depth discourse on the stability of the financial system. This issue has been analyzed by, among others, Minsky (1992), Crockett (1997), Fidrmuc and Schardax (1999), Trichet (2000), Padoa-Schioppa (2002), Large (2003), Schinasi (2004), Allen and Wood (2006), Heiko and Čihák (2007), Shirakawa (2012), Mitrović Mijatović (2013), and Morgan and Pontiens (2014). In turn, research on the creation of international

DOI:10.1163/9789004687264_012

financial stability by the IMF has recently been carried out by Lastra (2011), Ciobanasce (2012), Zamorski and Lim (2013), Taylor (2015), Gallego et al. (2018), Bhasin and Gupta (2018), Gao and Gallagher (2019), and Pandey (2020). Therefore, it seems justified – especially from the perspective of contemporary global threats such as the COVID-19 pandemic or the war in Ukraine – to question the contemporary role of the IMF to sustain the development and management of the global public good which is international financial stability. Therefore, the research problem posed in this way requires the presentation of the IMF's role in more detail. This is the main objective of this chapter.

In sum, the chapter is a study of the issues selected by the author and does not pretend to exhaust the full extent of the subject. Including all issues concerning the IMF's activities for ensuring stability and sustainable development of member states and the global economy would undoubtedly exceed the scope of the proposed analysis.

2 The International Monetary Fund as an International Governmental Financial Organization

The IMF was created in order to recreate the international financial architecture after the Second World War. Its establishment was decided in July 1944, but formally the Fund began functioning on 27 December 1945, when 29 countries – members of the founding conference in Bretton Woods – ratified the Articles of Agreement (Vreeland, 2007, p. 5). The IMF Statute is based on the American plan, or rather the concept of H. D. White, according to which the balance of payments of the member states should be achieved by conducting an adequate economic policy, to which the countries participating in the Bretton Woods Conference committed. The inclusion in the IMF Statute of the principles of functioning of the monetary system determined the central position of this organization in the international financial system and care for its stability through control, regulation, and assistance to its members.

From the very beginning of its existence, the organization has been working for the stabilization of the international financial system, especially the system of exchange rates and international payments, as a tool and, at the same time, a category of global public goods classified by Stiglitz (2003). The objectives of the IMF's activities, which are formulated in Article I of the IMF's Statute, therefore include (IMF, n.d.-a):

1. Promoting international monetary cooperation through the establishment of a permanent organization providing a mechanism for consultation and interaction in international monetary relations.

2. Pursuing sustainable development and an increase in the volume of international trade, fostering the growth of employment and real income as well as the development of the productive resources of member countries.
3. Ensuring exchange rate stability, maintaining regulated monetary relations among IMF members, and avoiding the use of competitive currency devaluation.
4. Supporting the establishment of a multilateral clearing system for current transactions and removing foreign exchange restrictions that hamper the development of international exchanges.
5. Placing general resources of the IMF at the disposal of member countries in periods requiring balance of payment adjustments, without measures which could negatively impact the economies.
6. Reducing the length of imbalance periods in IMF member countries' balance of payments.

In fulfilling its statutory objectives, the IMF simultaneously performs three basic functions:

1. Controlling: it supervises its members' observance of the established rules of activity related to monetary policy, international payments, and currency convertibility.
2. Regulatory: it is a platform for multilateral negotiations and cooperation for the regulation of international monetary and financial relations.
3. Operational: it puts the necessary financial resources at the disposal of member countries and provides technical assistance mainly for equalizing and maintaining the balance of payments.

The International Monetary Fund is a specialized organization within the United Nations system. However, it has its own structure and financial resources, and its cooperation with the UN takes place under a separate agreement. The organization currently covers almost all countries in the world. It has 190 members (IMF, n.d.-g). The IMF, like any international governmental organization, conducts activities for the implementation of which it needs financial resources. The financing of the Fund's activities, including the implementation of the objectives of sustainable development with the use of global public goods – international financial stability – is possible thanks to its resources and borrowed money. These include: payments of member countries to the share capital (the so-called member quotas or shares, that is, national currencies, special drawing rights [SDRs], and gold), income from deposits, and financial operations. The Fund also raises money by borrowing on the financial markets. From its member shares, borrowed resources, and income from lending operations, the IMF pursues external activities, i.e., the creation of a global public good (such as international financial stability) and provides financial along with the technical assistance to member countries in support of the Sustainable Development Goals.

3 International Financial Stability as a Global Public Good: a Priority for IMF Operations

3.1 *The Concept of International Financial Stability*

The concept of international financial stability has changed its original meaning over the years of IMF operations. Initially, the term was equated with financial stability, understood as price stability or the non-existence of inflation or deflation. The literature emphasizes the link between financial and exchange rate stability and draws attention to the dynamics of contemporary financial processes. Many definitions include stability as the absence of instability or disorder. Mishkin believes that financial stability is "a state in which there is no financial crisis." Therefore, ensuring stability is primarily associated with preventing financial crises and mitigating the effects of crises (Mishkin, 1991). On the other hand, the Bundesbank defines financial stability as "a state in which the financial system effectively performs its key functions, such as resource allocation, risk sharing, payment settlement, and is able to do so in the face of shocks, stress situations and periods of fundamental change" (Deutsche Bundesbank, 2003, p. 8). In turn, for Schinasi,

> financial stability is a situation in which the financial system is able to perform its three basic functions simultaneously. First, the financial system is efficient and smoothly facilitates the intertemporal allocation of resources from savers to investors and the allocation of general economic resources. Second, future financial risk is identified and appraised accurately and is relatively well managed. Third, the financial system is in a condition that allows it to absorb financial and economic shocks in an efficient and comfortable manner. (Schinasi, 2006, p. 82)

Defining financial stability by paying attention to the components of the financial system and identifying the stability of the financial system as the stability of markets and financial institutions is proposed by Mitrović Mijatović (2013). The mechanisms facilitating the maintenance of international financial stability, which as mentioned earlier is a global public good, are supervision, regulation, but also financial and technical assistance from the International Monetary Fund.

The monitoring of financial, exchange rate, and economic policies is an important part of the IMF's work in balancing development and managing global public goods in fulfilling its monitoring function. Indeed, financial, exchange rate, and economic stability are both national and global public goods.

3.2 *Surveillance Activities*

The IMF's surveillance activities are governed by the IMF's Statute, which defines the responsibilities of both member countries and the Fund itself. According to the Statute, each member undertakes obligations concerning the conduct of monetary, exchange rate, and economic policies, in particular those that promote economic growth and ensure financial stability, and entrusts the Fund with the surveillance of the fulfillment of its obligations concerning exchange rate policy and the financial system and makes the reliable information necessary for the surveillance available to the organization. In turn, the IMF undertakes to exercise control over the international financial and monetary system with a view to ensure its effective functioning, particularly its stability. The Fund's surveillance function is carried out through surveillance at the national level (so-called bilateral surveillance: IMF – state) and at the global level (multilateral surveillance).

The translation of the provisions of Article IV of the IMF's Articles of Agreement into concrete IMF surveillance activities takes place through decisions on surveillance, which set the direction of the activities. They are supplemented by guidance notes, which specify the principles for the preparation of surveillance analyses. In particular, the IMF is currently conducting analyses of the potential impact of domestic economic policies on the spillover environment and of financial stability issues, including external stability, particularly with regard to two aspects – exchange rates and capital flows. These activities are intended to ensure that the IMF is able to monitor members' external activities more effectively, engage member countries in constructive dialogue, and promote global economic and financial stability.

The Fund also carries out activities to promote global financial stability and sustainable development, particularly in support of employment growth and a better understanding of countries' development prospects. These are mainly tasks related to five priorities: the integration and deepening of risk analysis and extrapolation, macro-financial surveillance, increased attention to structural policies (including labor market issues), consistent policy recommendations and expert advice from the Fund, and transparent IMF – member country dialogue (IMF, 2014).

The IMF carries out surveillance of the economic and financial policies of member countries and of the international financial and monetary system using a range of analytical surveillance instruments. Policy advice to members is provided in reports presenting the results of surveillance analysis. These are recommendations that, in the Fund's point of view, promote domestic and international financial and macroeconomic stability. These recommendations are often the result of the Fund's cooperation with other international institutions, notably the International Bank for Reconstruction and Development. This cooperation and the issuing of recommendations and regulations to member states by the Fund are carried out by the organization as part of its regulatory function.

Today, the IMF's bilateral surveillance and regulatory instruments are:

1. Reviews of economies under Article IV of the Statute: are a key instrument of IMF surveillance activities. They are mandatory for member countries and take place annually or on a biennial basis. During the review the risks to a country's internal and external stability are identified. The review concludes with an IMF report containing an assessment of the country's current economic situation.
2. Financial systems reviews: aim to stabilize financial systems in member countries, in particular to identify the strengths and risks of the financial system, the quality of the regulatory and supervisory framework, to identify ways to manage key risks, and to analyze its stability and crisis resilience.
3. Reviews of the consistency of national financial standards, codes and good practices with international standards: are an analysis and assessment of the member states' compliance with international standards and codes in various areas, which include, among others: accounting, anti-money laundering and counter-terrorist financing, banking supervision, transparency of financial and monetary policy, and payments systems. (IMF, n.d.-k)

In turn, when it comes to the IMF's multilateral surveillance and regulation, these include the following instruments (IMF, n.d.-j):

1. World Economic Outlook (WEO): presents an analysis of the current situation of the world economy and prospects for its development as well as analyses of the most important current problems of the world economy. Spillovers and international interactions are examined.
2. Regional Economic Outlook (REO): are prepared on the basis of WEO reports for: Sub-Saharan Africa, Asia and the Pacific, Europe, the Middle East and Central Asia, Asia and the Pacific and the Western Hemisphere area (USA and Canada and Latin America and the Caribbean).
3. Global Financial Stability Report (GFSR): presents analysis on the most important current issues in global financial stability. It includes analyses

of credit, market, and liquidity risks, with particular reference to the situation in emerging markets.

4. Fiscal Monitor (FM): contains analyzes of the public finance sector. The report analyzes – from a national perspective – the impact of the crisis on fiscal policy and the sustainability of public finances.
5. External Sector Report (ESR): analyzes global external developments and provides multilateral assessments of the world's largest economies, representing over 90% of global GDP. The report includes: an overview chapter that emphasizes multilateral issues and discusses the risks and policies needed to reduce excessive imbalances; an analytical chapter that covers topics relevant to the analysis of external sector dynamics and adjustment mechanisms; and a final chapter that details the assessment of each economy considered.

During the surveillance and regulatory process, the Fund identifies potential risks to macroeconomic and financial stability and identifies necessary adjustments. The primary objective of surveillance and regulation is thus to promote sustainable development using global public goods, both domestically and internationally. At the same time, if necessary, the IMF supports member countries in the preparation and implementation of adjustment and recovery programs, which is often combined with the provision of financing during the implementation period of the programs and technical assistance.

3.3 *IMF's Provision of Financial Resources*

Today, as part of its operational function, the IMF provides financial resources to member countries essentially in the form of a repayable loan. The Fund aids members both from its own and borrowed resources. Loans are granted in the form of sales of foreign currencies to countries in exchange for their own currencies, with an obligation to reverse the transaction at a specified date (Dicks-Mireaux, et al., 2000, p. 504). The loan is granted based on an agreement with the Fund, which, depending on the financial instrument concerned, may be general or preferential.[1]

The assistance made available by the IMF shall in principle be proportional to the country's contribution to its capital stock. Obtaining financing is preceded by negotiations between the member and the Fund on the terms and conditions of the adjustment program, the amount of the loan and the choice of the financial instrument to be supported. The proposal of the country concerned is presented in the form of a Letter of Intent. Upon approval

1 IMF preferential assistance will be discussed later in this chapter.

of the agreement, funds are transferred on the basis of loan tranches. The disbursement of each subsequent tranche usually takes place after the IMF has assessed the effectiveness of the implementation of the adjustment program by the respective borrower and is usually disbursed on a quarterly basis. The above procedure provides the Fund with an opportunity to influence the effectiveness of structural reforms aimed at improving the economic situation of the country applying for financing. In accordance with the IMF decision of March 24, 2009, the upper limit for loans is now 200% of the value of a country's contribution to capital per year and no more than 600% in total. Occasionally the Fund may, after an individual assessment of the situation in the recipient country, increase the maximum limits (IMF, 2009).

The scope of contemporary IMF lending assistance includes the following non-preferential facilities available to all member countries (IMF, n.d.-e):

- *Stand-by Arrangement* (SBA) is the International Monetary Fund's primary lending facility and represent the first option to assist member states in case of balance of payments needs. The SBA facility is designed to help countries resolve short- and medium-term balance of payments problems. The length of the SBA is usually between 12 and 24 months, but not more than 36 months. The loan is repaid within 3.25 to 5 years from the start of the program. SBAs can be used on a precautionary basis, where countries do not borrow approved amounts, but retain the option to do so if conditions deteriorate. The SBA provides flexibility with respect to the timing of IMF disbursements, with the possibility to accelerate them if necessary.
- *The Extended Fund Facility* (EFF) was established in 1974 to help countries resolve medium- and long-term balance of payments problems that have structural impediments requiring fundamental economic reform. Extended Fund Facility (EFF) programs are longer than the SBA, but usually no longer than 3 years at the time of approval, with a maximum extension of an additional year when necessary. However, a maximum period of 4 years is also allowed at the time of approval in order to restore macroeconomic stability and to adequately ensure the member state's ability and capacity to implement deep and lasting structural reforms. The EFF loan matures between 4.5 and 10 years after the start of the program.
- *The Flexible Credit Line* (FCL), available since 2009, is designed for countries with very strong macroeconomic fundamentals and credible economic policies and is useful for both crisis prevention and resolution. The FCL is granted at the request of a member if certain eligibility criteria are met (ex ante conditionality). The duration is 1 or 2 years (with a periodic review of continued eligibility after 1 year) and the loan repayment period is the same as for the SBA. Unlike the SBA/EFF, the use of funds available under the FCL

line is not subject to ex post conditionality, as countries meeting the FCL eligibility criteria are expected to implement appropriate macroeconomic policies. It is possible to draw on the credit line at any time after activation or to treat it as precautionary.

- *The Precautionary and Liquidity Line* (PLL) has been an IMF supplementary lending facility since 2011 to flexibly meet the needs of member countries with sound macroeconomic fundamentals but with certain vulnerabilities that prevent them from using the FCL. A PLL may be granted at the request of a member country if the member meets certain eligibility criteria (ex ante conditionality), with ex post conditionality also lying if available funds are drawn down. PLL contracts can last for 6 months or 1 to 2 years.
- *The Rapid Financing Instrument* (RFI) provides rapid and easily accessible financial assistance to member states facing acute balance of payments needs without the need for a full adjustment program. The RIF applies, inter alia, in cases of urgent needs, including those resulting from commodity price shocks, natural disasters, post-conflict situations and emergency situations resulting from fragility. Financial assistance provided under the RIF is subject to the same financing conditions as for the SBA. A member country requesting emergency assistance is required to cooperate with the IMF in its efforts to resolve balance of payments problems and to outline the general economic policies it proposes to pursue.

The assistance placed at the disposal of members by the Fund is, therefore, aimed at helping individual countries overcome balancc of payments problems, improve their macroeconomic and financial situation, and provide them with conditions for sustainable development, both economically and socially. Nowadays, the IMF's priority is also to prevent crises and to promptly mitigate their consequences for international stability. The pursuit of this goal manifests itself, inter alia, in the increasingly frequent granting of credit to countries in need in excess of the exceptional access amount and in taking precautionary steps, i.e., the use of precautionary loans on offer. In addition, there have also been changes related to the conditions for borrowers. The Fund now seeks to optimize these conditions so that they meet the objectives of IMF's activity (Edwards & Hsieh, 2011, p. 79).

3.4 *The Specific Case of Ukraine*

Ukraine is the IMF's largest borrower. In the years 1994–1995, it used a loan of US$763.1 million under the Systemic Transformation Facility to sustain its balance of payments. It was the only program that was implemented in its entirety.

In the next 3 years, annual stand-by programs for a total amount of US$1.9 billion were implemented, supporting the exchange rate of the national currency, and stabilizing the transition from centrally planned economy to a free market. However, in March 1998, the IMF suspended the program due to the failure of the government to deal with the budget deficit and the money supply. Since 1998, Ukraine has become a beneficiary of the Extended Fund Facility, using only slightly more than half of the funds (US$1.19 billion out of US$2.6 billion) allocated in 1998–2002 to increase the foreign exchange reserves of the National Bank of Ukraine.

In the following years, until the crisis on world financial markets in 2008, the cooperation between the IMF and Ukraine was based on the principles of technical support. For the fourth time, it benefited from financial assistance under the Emergency Financing Mechanism in 2008 to the amount of US$16.5 billion, of which it received US$10.6 billion in three tranches (64% of the allocated amount). This program was replaced in 2010 by a new 2.5-year program of US$15.1 billion, of which US$3.39 billion had been used by 2013 (22.5%). The sixth stage of IMF support started in 2014 after the approval of a new stand-by loan.

However, due to the economic and political crisis caused by the Russian aggression, Ukraine used only 26% of this amount, and in 2015 this loan was replaced with a 4-year EFF program (US$8.7 billion). In 2018, a new EFF program for Ukraine was adopted for a period of 14 months and an amount of US$3.9 billion, which was completed on February 17, 2020. After difficult negotiations (and the fulfillment of two conditions – the adoption of the banking law and the law on trade in agricultural land) on June 9, 2020, the IMF and the Ukrainian authorities resumed their cooperation by signing an 18-month stand-by agreement of US$5.04 billion to help counter the negative effects of the COVID-19 pandemic, restore the balance of payments, and carry out further structural reforms.

It should be noted that the cooperation between the IMF and Ukraine is conditional. The partners agree on the effects expected from Ukraine after the end of the next aid program. The IMF assesses the implementation of the suggested reforms and decides on the level of their effectiveness. The requirements set by the IMF from program to program are becoming more and more difficult to meet in a short time, which translates into a low level of use of the allocated funds by Ukraine.

The main goal of Ukraine's cooperation with the IMF so far has been to stabilize the Ukrainian financial system, carry out structural reforms, and create the foundations for sustainable economic growth. However, the funds were mainly used to cover the budget deficit or sustain the balance of payments. Due to late fulfillment of obligations and unused tranches under loan agreements, Ukraine pays the so-called commitment fee.

Nevertheless, the requirements set by the IMF are in line with the planned reforms. At the same time, the funds at the disposal of the IMF are cheaper than commercial loans or money obtained from the issuance of Eurobonds, and the government has managed to implement socially unpopular reforms that have been blocked for many years by oligarch groups or the Ukrainian society. Ukraine's cooperation with the IMF also offers the possibility of obtaining financing from other international institutions, such as the World Bank, EBRD, EIB, as well as from countries and organizations, e.g., from the USA, EU, Germany, Canada, China (Drabczuk, 2021). As a result of Russia's aggression in Ukraine, the IMF made another US$1.4 billion available to Ukraine as part of the RFI.

3.5 *Technical Assistance*

In addition to its surveillance, regulatory, and financial assistance activities, the IMF provides technical assistance for stability and sustainable economic development, which is a very important complement to the organization's activities. IMF technical assistance can take many forms, such as educational assistance or staff training, advice, workshops, seminars on fiscal, monetary and exchange rate policies, regulation and supervision of financial systems, statistics, and legal frameworks. It aims at strengthening members' capacity to plan and implement sound economic policies, and at contributing to the effectiveness of member countries' economic reforms and adjustment programs (IMF, n.d.-f, p. 53). Technical assistance is provided from Headquarters in Washington, through a network of regional technical assistance centers, trust funds and IMF collaborators. Depending on the nature of the assignment, support is in the form of staff missions from Washington or from regional offices for a limited period, or in the form of visits by experts or advisors for periods ranging from a few weeks to several years (IMF, n.d.-m). As regards training activities, the IMF Institute offers courses and seminars every year, as well as online courses. This assistance is aimed at enhancing skills and knowledge of macro-economics and finance, in particular on the prevention and mitigation of financial crises and the restoration of stability in member countries following crises, tax policy and administration, expenditure management and financial integration.

4 The IMF's Engagement in Achieving Sustainable Development Goals

Increased IMF involvement in the implementation of sustainable development priorities has been evident since the mid-1990s. The main areas of IMF activity related to the implementation of this strategy are concessional lending, technical assistance and debt relief for underdeveloped member countries. These activities are carried out using the global public goods managed by the Fund. These are financial resources and human capital along with the knowledge.

4.1 *Concessional Lending for Underdeveloped Member Countries*

For the poorest countries and those which are not well positioned on the financial markets, IMF loans are often the only way to obtain external financing. They are granted on concessional terms. The core area of IMF support for the poorest member countries – concessional lending – has evolved over the years to best meet the needs of the beneficiaries of this assistance and to contribute effectively to the implementation of the sustainable development strategy by eradicating poverty and economic and social inequalities, resulting in a sustained high level of economic growth (IMF, n.d.-d). Since the second half of the 1990s, the IMF's involvement in the creation of new assistance instruments for countries with the lowest level of GNI per capita has increased, as has the value of the financial resources transferred by the Fund for this purpose.

In 1999, the Poverty Reduction and Growth Facility (PRGF) was created. It was structured according to the needs of the lowest income countries. The funds made available under these facilities supported the implementation of poverty reduction programs in individual member states, but also stimulated economic growth in the poorest countries. The PRGF facility existed for 10 years. In 2009 the IMF made changes to the concessional facilities and financial design, transforming the PRGF-ESF into the Poverty Reduction Growth Trust (PRGT), which has been in place since January 7, 2010, to finance the costs of poverty reduction and economic growth in underdeveloped countries under three new facilities that have been made available to them since July 2009 on changes to lending to this group of countries. The PRGT is currently the IMF's largest trust account. Funds transferred to it by the donors and lenders are made available by the Fund – as administrator of the account – in the form of loans to the poorest countries. The scope of contemporary concessional credit assistance to the lowest income countries from the PRGT includes (IMF, n.d.-e):

- *The Extended Credit Facility* (ECF) was created to better tailor poverty alleviation programs to the individual strategies of countries facing the problem (IMF, 2022a). The ECF functions as one of three contemporary concessional lending facilities for low-income countries. Extended Credit Facility is provided when a member state is experiencing persistent balance of payments difficulties. Members may benefit from such assistance if the situation can only be improved in the medium to long term (IMF, n.d.-c). The objectives of the program concern the improvement of the balance of payments, sustainable economic growth, and the reduction of poverty. A new feature is that the flexibility of the assistance is improved, and it is better tailored to the needs of the beneficiary. The aid is granted for 3 to 4 years, in particular cases up to 5, with the possibility of renewal.

– *Funds under the Stand-by Credit Facility* (SCF) are available to members with a balanced macroeconomic situation that is sustainable in the long term, but there are risks associated with the possibility of short-term shocks that may cause an imbalance of payments. Therefore, the program is designed to, among other things, help maintain a stable economic situation and ensure economic growth. SCF financing is available to members qualified for preferential assistance. The duration of a loan agreement can range from 12 to 24 months. Countries benefiting from SCF are required to introduce reforms that will achieve a stable macroeconomic position in the short term (IMF, 2022c).
– *Another type of concessional financial assistance currently available to underdeveloped IMF member countries is the Rapid Credit Facility* (RCF). This facility is designed to optimize emergency assistance. The program is targeted at the poorest members that have been affected by sudden balance of payments problems and where a comprehensive recovery program offered by the IMF is either unnecessary or not feasible. Funds are made available in the form of a single disbursement of the total amount of the loan. It is worth noting that the repetition of such a disbursement, even several times (every 3 years), is possible if the imbalance of payments is caused by external shocks (IMF, 2022b). For example, in 2021 the IMF made 87.4 million SDRs (US$125.8 million) available under the SCF to Honduras due to the health crisis and recovery from tropical storms. The program aims to maintain macroeconomic stability while introducing economic and institutional reforms for inclusive growth. Priorities include reforms to improve the quality of fiscal policy, sustain efforts to mobilize revenues, protect social investment and spending, safeguard the financial stability of a public energy company and reforms to increase transparency and budget management (IMF, 2021).

4.2 *Technical Assistance to LICs*

At the same time, underdeveloped countries with stable macroeconomic situations and institutions that do not need or do not want PRGT assistance may request non-financial assistance from the IMF under the Policy Support Instrument (PSI) to cooperate in the design of effective economic and structural programs to maintain or reinforce macroeconomic stability, debt reduction, poverty, and sustainable development. They are designed to improve public sector governance, strengthen the financial sector, and build social safety nets in underdeveloped countries. The IMF assesses a country's economic and financial policies, which are monitored by donors, every 6 months. A PSI can be approved for 1 to 4 years, with a maximum of 5 years. If necessary, a country can avail of SCF and RCF in parallel with PSI, but no ECF facility is available (IMF, n.d.-i).

The IMF also provides technical assistance to LICs particularly in the areas of public revenue and expenditure management, taxation, banking activities, financial sector stability, exchange rate regimes, economic and financial statistics, and legal problems. This assistance is usually offered free of charge. Technical assistance for less developed countries is manifested in the systematic organization and delivery of training and thematic courses for the administrations of individual member states. Such trainings, conducted in Washington by the IMF Institute and its regional agencies (in Austria, Brazil, China, India, Singapore, Tunisia, and the United Arab Emirates), aim at strengthening the knowledge base of domestic institutions and thus improving the economic and public financial management process at the national level. Technical support also includes advisory and consultative assistance in the conduct of economic policy. The IMF promotes the implementation of appropriate standards, procedures, and the so-called good practices in the management of the economy and the related regulatory institutions. In particular, they refer to three main spheres: the need for transparency in the economic policy pursued and, in the preparation, and presentation of the necessary statistical data (sphere I), the effective supervision of the whole financial sector of a country (sphere II) and the implementation of clear rules of business activity at the microeconomic level (sphere III).

In recent years, the Fund has increased the financial and human resources allocated to the technical assistance. More than 80% of technical assistance funds are spent in countries with a low level of economic development. The IMF also cooperates with donors of development assistance, providing them with expert support on the macroeconomic situation in recipient countries and helping them to effectively channel financial resources to best meet IMF country-specific recommendations (IMF, n.d.-l). At the same time, the IMF attaches great importance to making technical assistance an instrument to increase the effectiveness of surveillance and the adjustment programs implemented.

4.3 *Debt Relief for Poor Countries*

To contribute to the achievement of sustainable development objectives, in 1996 the IMF started to cooperate with the International Bank for Reconstruction and Development and bilateral lenders. At that time, the G7 summit in Lyon, France, decided to balance the debt burden of the poorest countries under the Heavily Indebted Poor Countries (HIPC) Initiative. The aim was to reduce the external debt of the poorest countries to a level at which they could continue to service it, and to stimulate economic, social, and political reforms to increase growth as well as to reduce poverty. Debt reduction was to come down to eliminating the so-called debt overhang, which means too much debt discouraging investors from investing their money in a country. Overindebtedness means the anticipated increase in taxes for the state to repay the loans. The overhang is the amount that goes beyond the tolerable value, i.e., the state's ability to service its debt. The elimination of excessive debt is beneficial to the state and its creditors, as it provides a greater guarantee of debt repayment. On the other hand, poverty reduction under the initiative was to shift the funds hitherto needed for debt servicing towards the financing of social objectives such as combating natural disasters, feeding populations and increasing agricultural production, granting micro-credits for economic activities, and improving pension, health, and education systems.

After only 2 years of operation, the HIPC Initiative began to be criticized, mainly because of the low debt burden reduction, the long duration of the reduction process, and excessively demanding eligibility criteria for countries to join the program. Therefore, at the G7 summit in Cologne, Germany, in 1999, the HIPC Initiative was renamed the "Enhanced HIPC Initiative." It was originally intended to last for 2 years, but in fact has been extended. Its aim is to carry out the debt relief process more quickly, as well as to help more countries and to strengthen the interaction between debt relief and the eradication of poverty and changes in countries' social policies (IMF, n.d.-b). Therefore, the initiative encompasses multiple dimensions: debt relief, structural and social policy reform with a particular focus on health and basic education services. The program is open to all creditors: bilateral, multilateral, and trade creditors who financed it. The enhanced initiative implies, instead of rigid, floating debt reduction target points that depend on the progress achieved in reforms, a country could achieve debt relief earlier, i.e., before the targets are reached. Indeed, the level of debt relief depends on actual progress and not on projected achievements. The mechanism for granting assistance under the enhanced initiative consists of two stages. In the first stage, countries prepare over a period of 3 years to reach the decision point by developing a poverty reduction strategy. During the second phase, countries apply the policies set out in the decision point to reach the target smooth point. The IBRD and IMF provide transitional assistance, the Paris Club restructures debt in accordance with the Cologne[2] terms, and other creditors grant transitional debt relief on similar terms in support of a global poverty reduction strategy. The floating target point is linked to the pursuit for at least 1 year of a global poverty reduction strategy, in particular, stabilization and structural adjustment policies. All creditors provide the aid specified in the decision point. This assistance is not subject to any additional conditionality. Therefore:

- The Paris Club grants debt relief on Cologne terms.
- The other bilateral and commercial creditors grant at least the same debt relief.
- International organizations grant debt relief according to the option chosen.

The initiative is funded by the IMF and other international institutions such as the IBRD, the African Development Bank, the Inter-American Development Bank, and the Paris Club. The remainder comes from the participating countries' creditors.

In 2005, the G8 countries made a proposal to the International Monetary Fund, the International Development Association, and the African Development Fund to assist developing countries on a larger scale than the Enhanced HIPC Initiative. In fact, they proposed the creation of a new debt relief program, dubbed the Multilateral Debt Relief Initiative (MDRI). The aim of the program was complete cancellation of countries' debts and – thanks to that – freeing up financial resources to help them meet the Millennium Development Goals. Complete cancellation was to be carried out by 2015 by only three organizations without involving the others, especially bilateral creditors. As early as 2007, the Inter-American Development Bank joined the initiative, pledging debt relief to five countries in the western hemisphere (IMF, n.d.-h).

MDRI assistance was intended for countries that had already reached the so-called end point of the HIPC Initiative or had a GNI per capita of less than US$380 and at the same time outstanding obligations to the end of 2004. Liabilities after this date did not include the MDRI. The decision to allocate MDRI funds to a country was made separately by each organization, so the way in which debt relief was implemented varied. In deciding to implement the MDRI, the IMF modified the original G8 proposal to fit the IMF's modalities and to comply with the principle of equal treatment of members, in this case as regards the use of IMF resources. It was agreed that all countries with a GNI per capita of US$380 or less per year would receive debt relief from the IMF's own resources, i.e., from the MDRI-I Trust, and countries with a GNI per capita above this threshold from the MDRI-II Trust, i.e., additional contributions

2 A reduction of 90% or more of the NPV of debt.

from member countries administered by the IMF. To qualify for MDRI assistance, the IMF required evidence of a track record satisfactory to the Fund in
– Macroeconomic policy
– Implementation of poverty reduction strategies
– Public expenditure management

Due to the low eligibility of countries to benefit from MDRI funds on February 4, 2015, the IMF approved the decision to wind down the initiative and transfer the remaining funds of SDR 13.2 million from MDRI-I and SDR 38.9 million from MDRI-II to the Catastrophe Containment and Relief Trust (CCRT), which was established in February 2015 to assist developing countries affected by natural disasters or public health problems such as epidemics. The CCRT initiative puts money, which should go towards debt servicing, to solve the current urgent problems of underdeveloped countries, at its disposal.

In addition, a natural disaster must affect at least a third of the population, destroy a quarter of production capacity, or cause damage worth the equivalent of a country's GNI. Furthermore, the IMF does not enforce levies and debt repayments for 2 years after the natural disaster, and in exceptional cases of large and persistent external imbalances it can cancel the debt altogether. As far as epidemics are concerned, they must have a negative impact on a country's economy and spread to others, causing losses of at least 10% of the beneficiary country's GNI. The country then receives immediate aid equal to 20% of its IMF quota for debt relief. This can be increased if the IMF deems it necessary. At the same time, the beneficiary of the measures should apply the macroeconomic policy reforms indicated by the Fund to restore balance of payments sustainability.

As of December 2021, 31 member countries have approved a debt relief of US$976 million to fight the COVID-19 pandemic. In addition, the annual and cumulative RCF access limits are higher for major natural disasters (with estimated damage of 20% of GDP or more) than for other loans.

5 Conclusions

A stable financial system easily fulfills its assigned functions of a monetary, capital and redistributive, settlement, risk reduction, information, and control nature. The trouble-free performance of these functions ensures effective capital mobilization and its efficient allocation, efficient settlements and payments between market participants, effective risk diversification, and an adequate supply of money on the market. Therefore, international financial stability is extremely important for the functioning and sustainable development of states and the world economy. It is a global public good. Its guarantor is the activity of international organizations, especially the activity of the IMF.

The IMF's lending facilities are nowadays designed to address the diverse needs of the member countries, especially those with low gross national income (GNI) per capita. To meet the ever-increasing financing needs of its members, the IMF has significantly strengthened its lending capacity and flexibility (Shafik, 2012). Therefore, the Fund has begun to develop into an organization that not only provides financial resources and technical assistance to members facing balance of payments problems, but also to those facing social and developmental problems, especially poverty, natural disasters, or epidemics, actively contributing to the objectives of sustainable development.

IMF assistance under debt relief initiatives, financial and technical assistance, surveillance, and regulation contribute to the effectiveness of member countries' economic reforms and adjustment, as well as development programs (IMF, n.d.-f, p. 53). They also stimulate institutional capacity of member countries to conduct economic policy. With these activities, the IMF promotes sound economic and financial governance, which is an important contribution of the IMF to the sustainable development strategy and the management of global public goods.

Contemporary activities of the IMF are geared not only towards ensuring long-term economic and social stability, but also sustainable development through job creation, as well as reduction of economic and social inequalities together with enhancing social protection, as the most important economic pillars for achieving the Sustainable Development Goals.

References

Allen, W. A., & Wood, G. (2006). Defining and achieving financial stability. *Journal of Financial Stability, 2*(2), 152–172. https://doi.org/10.1016/j.jfs.2005.10.001

Bhasin, N., & Gupta, S. (2018). Reforms in International Monetary Fund (IMF): Challenges and the road ahead. *Management and Economics Research Journal, 4*(S1), 19–29. https://doi.org/10.18639/MERJ.2018.04.520665

Ciobanasu, I. C. (2012). Expanded mandate for the IMF: Global financial stability – Legal implications for the Articles of Agreement of the International Monetary Fund. *Minnesota Journal of International Law, 21*, 130–160. http://www.minnjil.org/?p=1320

Crockett, A. (1997). Why is financial stability a goal of public policy? *Economic Review (Federal Reserve Bank of Kansas City), 82*(QIV), 5–22. https://www.kansascityfed.org/documents/800/1997-Why%20Is%20Financial%20Stability%20a%20Goal%20of%20Public%20Policy%3F.pdf

Deutsche Bundesbank. (2003, December). *Report on the stability of the German Financial System.* Monthly Report. https://www.bundesbank.de/resource/blob/706378/d2cd736eb56e642772a94228124 63d3c/mL/2003-12-stability-data.pdf

Dicks-Mireaux, L., Mecagni, M., & Schadler, S. (2000). Evaluating the effect of IMF lending to low-income countries, *Journal of Development Economies, 61*(2), 495–526. http://dx.doi.org/10.1016/S0304-3878(00)00066-3

Drabczuk, M. (2021). Współpraca Ukrainy z MFW: w drodze do stabilności czy stabilnej zależności. *Komentarze IEŚ, 439*(136), 1–3. https://ies.lublin.pl/komentarze/wspolpraca-ukrainy-z-mfw-w-drodze-do-stabilnosci-czy-stabilnej-zaleznosci/

Edwards, K., & Hsieh, W. (2011). Recent changes in IMF lending. *Bulletin* [Reserve Bank of Australia], *December Quarter*, 77–82. https://www.rba.gov.au/publications/bulletin/2011/dec/8.html

Fidrmuc, J., & Schardax, F. (1999). Increasing integration of applicant countries into international financial markets: Implications for money and financial stability. *Focus on Transition, 2*, 92–109. https://www.bis.org/publ/confer08e.pdf

Gallego, S., Hotellerie-Fallois, P. L., & Lopez-Vincente, F. (2018, November 21). The International Monetary Fund and its role as a guarantor of global financial stability. *Economic Bulletin* [Banco de España], *4*, 1–14. https://repositorio.bde.es/bitstream/123456789/8992/1/beaa1804-art33e.pdf

Gao, H., & Gallagher, K. P. (2019). Strengthening the International Monetary Fund for stability and sustainable development. *G20 Insights*. https://t20japan.org/wp-content/uploads/2019/03/t20-japan-tf2-4-strengthening-international-monetary-fund.pdf

Hesse, H., & Čihák, M. (2007). Cooperative banks and financial stability. IMF Working Papers, WP/07/2. International Monetary Fund. https://www.imf.org/external/pubs/ft/wp/2007/wp0702.pdf

IMF. (2009, April 3). IMF overhauls nonconcessional lending facilities and conditionality. Public Information Notice no. 09/40. International Monetary Fund. http://www.imf.org/external/np/sec/pn/2009/pn0940.htm

IMF. (2014). 2014 Triennial surveillance review. Last updated July 28, 2017. International Monetary Fund. http://www.imf.org/external/np/spr/triennial/2014/index.htm

IMF. (2021, September 13). IMF executive board completes the fourth review under the IMF's Stand-by Arrangement and arrangement under the Stand-by Credit Facility for Honduras. Press Release, 21/262. International Monetary Fund. https://www.imf.org/en/News/Articles/2021/09/13/pr21262-honduras-imf-execboard-completes-4threv-under-imfs-sba-and-arrange-under-sbc-facility

IMF. (2022a, January 6). Extended Credit Facility. Retrieved February 24, 2022. https://www.imf.org/en/About/Factsheets/Sheets/2016/08/02/21/04/Extended-Credit-Facility

IMF. (2022b, March 7). Rapid Credit Facility. Retrieved March 8, 2022. https://www.imf.org/en/About/Factsheets/Sheets/2016/08/02/21/08/Rapid-Credit-Facility

IMF. (2022c, January 6). Stand-by Credit Facility (SCF). Retrieved February 24, 2022. https://www.imf.org/en/About/Factsheets/Sheets/2016/08/02/21/10/Standby-Credit-Facility

IMF. (N.d.-a). Articles of Agreement of the International Monetary Fund. Retrieved February 21, 2022. http://www.imf.org/external/pubs/ft/aa/index.htm#art27

IMF. (N.d.-b). Debt relief under the Heavily Indebted Poor Countries (HIPC) Initiative. Retrieved March 9, 2022. http://www.imf.org/external/np/exr/facts/hipc.htm

IMF. (N.d.-c). Financing the fund's concessional lending to low-income countries. Retrieved January 4, 2022. http://www.imf.org/external/np/exr/facts/concesslending.htm

IMF. (N.d.-d). The IMF and the Millennium Development Goals. Retrieved February 22, 2022. http://www.imf.org/external/np/exr/facts/mdg.htm

IMF. (N.d.-e). IMF lending. Retrieved February 22, 2022. http://www.imf.org/external/np/exr/facts/howlend.htm

IMF. (N.d.-f). IMF's response to the global economic crisis. Retrieved February 22, 2022. https://www.imf.org/external/np/exr/facts/changing.html

IMF. (N.d.-g). List of members. Retrieved February 21, 2022. https://www.imf.org/external/np/sec/memdir/memdate.htm

IMF. (N.d.-h). The Multilateral Debt Initiative. Retrieved March 9, 2022. http://www.imf.org/external/np/exr/facts/mdri.htm

IMF. (N.d.-i). The Policy Support Instrument. Retrieved March 8, 2022. http://www.imf.org/external/np/exr/facts/psi.htm

IMF. (N.d.-j). Research. Retrieved February 21, 2022. https://www.imf.org/en/Research

IMF. (N.d.-k). Standards & codes. Retrieved February 21, 2022. http://www.imf.org/external/standards/index.htm

IMF. (N.d.-l). Technical assistance. Retrieved March 8, 2022. http://www.imf.org/external/about/techasst.htm

IMF. (N.d.-m). Technical assistance and training. Retrieved February 22, 2022. http://www.imf.org/external/np/exr/facts/tech.htm

Large, A. (2003). Financial stability: Maintaining confidence in a complex world. Bank of England. https://www.bankofengland.co.uk/-/media/boe/files/speech/2003/financial-stability-maintaining-confidence-in-a-complex-world.pdf

Lastra, R. M. (2011). The role of the IMF as a global financial authority. In C. Herrmann & J. P. Terhechte (Eds.), *European Yearbook of International Economic Law* (pp. 121–136). Springer.

Mikita, M. (2021). Stabilność systemu finansowego Unii Europejskiej. *Studia Biura Analiz Sejmowych, 3*(67), 87–116. https://orka.sejm.gov.pl/WydBAS.nsf/0/90D913F763A9CDA5C1258766003FDB96/$file/5.Malgorzata_Mikita.pdf

Minsky, H. R. (1992). The financial instability hypothesis. Working Paper 74. Levy Economics Institute of Bard College. https://www.levyinstitute.org/pubs/wp74.pdf

Mishkin, F. (1991). Anatomy of financial crisis. NBER Working Paper Series, 3934. National Bureau of Economic Research. https://www.nber.org/system/files/working_papers/w3934/w3934.pdf

Mitrović Mijatović, M. (2013). Financial stability in open markets economy: Holistic approach in economic policy. *Journal of Central Banking Theory and Practice, 2*, 51–79. https://www.cbcg.me/slike_i_fajlovi/fajlovi/journal/vol2/no2/financial_stability.pdf

Morgan, P., & Pontiens V. (2014). Financial stability and financial inclusion. ADBI Working Paper Series, 488. Asian Development Bank Institute. https://www.shram.org/uploadFiles/20180116111859.pdf

Padoa-Schioppa, T. (2002). Central banks and financial stability: Exploring a land in between. Paper presented at the Second ECB Central Banking Conference, "The Transformation of the European Financial System," Frankfurt am Main, October 24–25, 2002. https://www.ecb.europa.eu/events/pdf/conferences/tps.pdf

Pandey, A. (2020, August 5). Promotion of currency stability vis-à-vis International Monetary Fund (IMF): An overview. SSRN. http://dx.doi.org/10.2139/ssrn.3667802

Schinasi, G. J. (2004). Defining financial stability. IMF Working Papers, WP/04/187. International Monetary Fund. https://doi.org/10.5089/9781451859546.001

Schinasi, G. J. (2006). *Safeguarding financial stability: Theory and practice*. International Monetary Fund.

Shafik, N. (2012, December). Rethinking sustainable development. *Finance & Development, 49*(4), 38–39. http://www.imf.org/external/pubs/ft/fandd/2012/12/straight.htm

Shirakawa, M. (2012, October 14). International financial stability as a public good. Keynote Address at a high level seminar co-hosted by the Bank of Japan and the International Monetary Fund (IMF) in Tokyo. https://www.boj.or.jp/en/announcements/press/koen_2012/data/ko121014a.pdf

Stiglitz, J. E. (2003). Democratizing the International Monetary Fund and the World Bank: Governance and accountability. *Governance, 16*(1), 111–139. https://doi.org/10.1111/1468-0491.00207

Taylor, J. B. (2015, June 15). IMF reforms and global economic stability. Testimony before the Subcommittee on Monetary Policy and Trade Committee on Financial Services, US House of Representatives. https://web.stanford.edu/~johntayl/2015_pdfs/House_MPTSC_testimony_June-2015.pdf

Trichet, J.-C. (2000). Introductory remarks. In: Indépendance et Responsabilité. Évolution du Métier de Banquier Central. Bicentennial Symposium Independence and Accountability Developments in Central Banking. Paris, Banque de France. https://www.banque-france.fr/sites/default/files/colbicengbdd.pdf

Vreeland, J. R. (2007). *The International Monetary Fund: Politics of conditional lending.* Routledge.

Zamorski, M. J., & Lim, V. C.-S. (2013). Financial stability insights from recent IMF/World Bank FSAP Assessments. *SEACEN Financial Stability Journal, 1*, 37–52. https://www.seacen.org/products/702002-100320-PDF.pdf

CHAPTER 11

International Financial Stability and Sustainable Development in EU Fiscal Policy

Agnieszka Kłos

1 Introduction

The scale and accelerating pace of changes in the world's economy and politics, which produce a number of risks to the economic and social order of the world, countries, and regions, make economic security, including financial security, grow in prominence and take on new meanings. Security and stability of public finances are two inextricable terms. One could say that financial stability determines financial security and vice versa: financial security determines financial stability.

Public financial stability, also referred to as fiscal stability, is the government's ability to maintain ongoing expenses, tax policy, and other related policies in the long term, without compromising its solvency, and being able to meet all the liabilities and the promised expenses. Public financial stability is not a matter of circumstances. It significantly influences the sense of intergenerational justice while simultaneously delineating enduring principles that are universally relevant to state governments, irrespective of their extant fiscal debt. The maintenance of a prudent level of public debt, coupled with the ability to issue it when necessary, constitutes an essential prerequisite for the optimal operation of the economy. The member states of the European Union must be capable of embracing unexpected circumstances beyond the government's control, such as high fluctuations of the economic cycle or economic crises. Failure to coordinate the decisions of respective EU member states could cause imbalance in the real economy and the financial system. Therefore, the rationale underlying the proposal for the construction of a sustainable Economic and Monetary Union (EMU) emphasizes the imperative of establishing frameworks for the harmonization of fiscal policies within the European Union.

This chapter is organized as follows. Section 1 deals with financial system as a public good as well as financial stability and security. Section 2 depicts the determinants behind the introduction of the Economic and Monetary Union in the European Union. Section 3 presents coordination of the fiscal policy at European Union level and Section 4 attempts to assess it.

DOI:10.1163/9789004687264_013

2 The Financial System as a Public Good

2.1 *Financial Stability and Security*

In specialist literature, the definition of "financial system" may vary depending on the trend one favors. The interpretative approaches to the issues pertaining to financial system perspectives are not mutually exclusive, but rather overlap and complement each other. From an institutional and structural perspective, a financial system is a complicated mechanism of interconnected elements complementing one another. Hence, if a financial system is to be stable, its various individual links must interconnect. The most prevalent idea is that such stability is achieved when economic activity is not disrupted due to asset price changes or problems experienced by financial institutions. Laker (1999) broadly defines a financial system as an avoidance of such disruptions to the financial system that are likely to result in significant increases in actual production costs. Such disruptions may be traced back either to difficulties affecting financial institutions or to financial market disruptions. Crockett (1997b) indicates that as much as monetary stability refers to an overall price level stability, financial stability refers to the stability of the major institutions and markets that make up the financial system. In his view, two conditions have to be met to achieve financial stability:

- The key institutions in the financial system must be stable, with a high degree of confidence that they can continue to meet their contractual obligations without interruption or outside assistance.
- The key markets must be stable, so that participants can confidently transact in them at prices that reflect fundamental forces and that do not vary substantially over short periods when there have been no changes in fundamentals. (Crockett, 1997a, 1997b)

In addition, Svensson notes that it is necessary to distinguish between monetary policy and financial stability policy. In devising a better financial stability policy, it is important to understand that the monetary policy is distinct and different from financial stability policy. These two policies differ in terms of goals and the choice of various instruments. The responsibility for monetary policy and control of the monetary policy instruments rests with the central bank, but the responsibility for financial stability policy and control of the financial stability instruments are in most countries shared between several authorities (Svensson, 2011).

This difficult task of defining financial stability has also been undertaken by Padoa-Schioppa (2002), Schinasi (2004), Davis (2001), Foot (2003), Williamson (2000), etc. Notably, Schinasi (2004, pp. 8–10) points to key principles for developing a definition of financial stability. However, given the broad character of financial stability, two interconnected definitions come in handy: "A financial system is entering a range of instability whenever it is threatening to impede the performance of an economy" and "A financial system is in a range of instability when it is impeding performance and threatening to continue to do so" (Schinasi, 2004, p. 6).

Financial security is yet another issue related to financial stability (Shkolnyk et al., 2021). The level of a country's financial security depends on the character of the financial architecture in place and the degree of its economic and financial advancement. For a high level of financial security and, consequently, stability of the financial system, the so-called economy "unshadowing" level becomes of importance. It means an effective financial monitoring, which primarily aims to employ appropriate resources to fight the shadow economy and money laundering (Bukhtiarova et al., 2020). There are internalities in every economy which can impact economic and financial security. They are: budget deficit, high unemployment or high inflation, as well as rising internal and external debt. It is natural for the factors to occur, but if a rising tendency is observed (of budget deficit, sovereign debt, unemployment, and inflation) over an extended time horizon, it could be indicative of a crisis. Therefore, public finance instability is named a potential threat to economic security. Given the state's role in providing economic sovereignty and independence in making economic decisions, a question arises on the degree of such sovereignty, as globalization and global integration processes are constantly deepening. It is also about what options the state has in decision-making and the influence on economic functioning amid rising international links.

In every country, a financial system works in a strictly defined environment, which has a strong impact on the functioning of the very system and its components. Thus, a structured financial system falls into:

– A market financial system which, due to the participation of financial institutions, is a mechanism of money co-creation and cash flow.
– A public financial system as a mechanism ensuring that public authorities provide social benefits and public services. The public financial system is made up of fiscal and budgetary institutions, fiscal instruments, and public financial instruments. The existence of a public financial system is attributable to the recognition of financial stability as a public good, as well as to market deficiencies and external factors. (Dobrzańska, Kosycarz & Pietrzak 2016, p.22A review of global literature on the public sector economy allows for the formulation of quite a clear and precise definition of a public good. It is a good to serve the general public, universal, social, and non-private. The public good category is of particular importance for the science of public

finance, and it is the need for such goods to exist and to be provided to society that underlies the accumulation and allocation of public funds.[1] Holcombe defines a public good as a good characterized by the following two features: it can be consumed by an additional consumer at no additional costs, and none of the consumers can be excluded from its consumption (Holcombe, 1997, p. 1). These two characteristics are referred to as non-rivalry and non-excludability (Samuelson & Nordhaus, 1989, p. 45). In a similar vein, Musgrave (1959) and Buchanan (1965, 1968) point to the principle of a public good in providing public goods. The stability of a financial system meets the criteria to be classified as a public good, as it is a non-competitive good and it is practically impossible for anybody to be excluded. One may say it is a global public good, as it is up to international/state bodies to prepare the relevant legal framework to govern the financial system so that institutions have relevant supervising instruments to perform their functions in providing the public good and ensuring the financial security of society.

3 The Determinants behind the Introduction of the Economic and Monetary Union in the European Union

The concept of creating a single-currency zone in Western Europe has a long history. Following World War II, a federalist movement emerged in Europe. It promoted the idea of political unification of the Western Europe and a formation of the United States of Europe or a European Federation. These ideas can be traced back to the unique political and economic circumstances that the European states were facing at the time. They were rooted in the experiences of armed conflict, with ensuring the preservation of stability and peace throughout Europe as the main goal of the federalist movement. Adopting a federal system would have involved certain sovereign powers being relinquished by individual states interested in participating in such a union in favor of a supranational entity which would serve as the federal governing body and would be subject to democratic oversight by a parliament chosen in direct and universal elections. The federalist movement was based on the idea of first unifying the countries in political terms, followed by economic unification (George & Bache, 2001, pp. 46–49). This concept, however, was not welcome by the countries. It was decided to shift the focus from political integration to

1 For more on the issue of public goods, see Chapter 1

economic integration. In 1951 in Paris, following these decisions, six countries (France, Germany, Italy, Holland, Belgium, and Luxembourg) signed a treaty establishing the European Coal and Steel Community, while on 25 March, in the capital of Italy, the Treaties of Rome were signed, setting up the European Atomic Energy Community (Euratom), and the European Economic Community (EEG), which aimed to establish a common market of the member states, introduce a customs union, and set common economic policy.

When the Western European countries signed the said treaties back in the 1950s, the Bretton Woods currency regime was in place globally. The issues of currency integration were not given much attention at that time. On 15 August 1971 Richard Nixon, the then US president, decided to suspend the international convertibility of the US dollar to gold, which caused a breakdown of the Bretton Woods system and a shift to a floating rate system in the majority of countries. The foreign exchange (FX) market turmoil along with the oil crisis forced European leaders to intensify their efforts for currency integration. At that time attempts were made to devise plans for a monetary union (Barre Plan of 1969) or an economic and currency union, the so-called Werner Plan (1970), which was to be complete by 1980, It envisaged:

- Full convertibility of the member states' currencies at irrevocably fixed rates
- Full freedom of the flow of goods, services, capital, and labor among the member states
- Centralized budgetary policy and uniform monetary policy pursued by a supranational central bank with an exclusive right to issue a common currency
- Strengthening and coordination of regional and structural policy
- Closer cooperation of social partners, i.e., trade unions, industry, and governments

As a result of the overambitious plans to centralize fiscal and structural policy, and difficulties in implementing the concept of the so-called European currency "snake," whereby FX rates of six participant countries were to fluctuate within a range of ±2.25%, the countries started withdrawing their currencies from this commitment and the Plan failed (European Commission, 1970; Danescu, 2017; Van Esch, 2009).

In the 1970s, numerous economists undertook an analysis of costs and benefits of a currency union based on an optimum currency area (OCA) theory (Grubel, 1970; Ishiyama, 1975; Tower & Willet, 1975). The optimum currency area theory was formed in the 1960s, and was to address the question in what situation and under what circumstances adopting one currency or fixing FX rates by two currency areas would be a convenient solution. An optimum solution is deemed to be one that guarantees that the fundamental goals of the economic policy (price stability, full employment, and external equilibrium) are met. The founder of the OCA theory is said to be Robert Mundell (1961), who attempted to fix an optimum FX rate system under various economic circumstances. In analyzing the results of demand shocks, he tried to assort an optimum FX rate system to match the economic circumstances in place (Mundell, 1961, p. 658). As part of his research, he endeavored to construct a comprehensive set of tools for shaping economic policy with the ultimate objective of optimizing the attainment and perpetuation of favorable inflationary stability and low rates of unemployment. McKinnon, Kenen, Minz,[2] Magnifico, and Fleming,[3] and Frankel and Rose[4] also contributed largely to the optimum currency area theory. McKinnon (1963) held that it is unprofitable for a small economy to create/maintain its own currency given its negligible importance globally and conversion difficulties in international trade. He also compared the effectiveness of two tools restoring external equilibrium: the liquid FX rate and internal fiscal and monetary policy, depending on how open an economy is. He maintained that the more open a country, the better a candidate to join the common currency area (with the notion of "economy openness" meaning trade integration with other economies measured by the share of goods and services exchanged versus the totality of goods produced and consumed domestically (McKinnon, 1963). Kenen (1966, 1969), in turn, was of the opinion that the current account balance is less likely to get upset as a result of terms of trade worsening when the export structure is more diversified. He emphasized that demand shocks affect the economies to a lesser degree when the latter's output is more diversified, because the shock will only impact a portion of output. Thus, Kenen's considerations lead to a conclusion that a currency union could be established by countries with a diversified economic structure as a more diversified economy will be less willing (than an economy with less diversified production) to use the FX rate as a tool to improve the terms of trade (Kenen, 1969, p. 46; Kenen, 1966, pp. 13–14). The most important stage in the history of the European currency union was the Delors Report of 1989, which features a plan to launch a common European currency. The genesis of the creation

2 Political integration is of primary importance to create an optimum currency area, as it is necessary to pursue common goals: economic growth, inflation, unemployment, etc.

3 Minz noted that the countries belonging to a single currency area should run an anti-inflationary policy and be similarly inclined to accept inflation.

4 Frankel and Rose developed the concept of the optimum currency area criteria being endogenic. They challenged the earlier exogenic OCA theory and came up with a new approach. They claimed that the countries joining the common currency are not required to meet the exogenic criteria ex ante as defined by OCA, because it is the adoption of a single currency that will bring their economies closer.

of the Economic and Monetary Union constitutes a multifaceted economic process encompassing distinct phases and stages that result in progressively more advanced causal relationships, known as stages of economic integration (Committee for the Study of Economic and Monetary Union, 1989).

The formation of the Economic and Monetary Union was to follow three stages:

- *Stage 1 (1990–1993)*. Physical, technical, and fiscal barriers are to be removed, coordination of economic policies strengthened, regional and structural funds reformed, budgetary coordination and the process of surveillance of the performance of the practices agreed.
- *Stage 2 (1994–1998)*. Community authorities undertake the first operational functions.
- *Stage 3 (1999–)*. FX rates are irrevocably fixed and the Community launches its monetary policy. The procedure starts with budget deficit constraints.

These stages were to be implemented provided a new treaty was adopted. On February 7, 1992, the Maastricht Treaty was signed, which became effective in the beginning of 1993. The Treaty established the European Union, largely amended the earlier treaties, and, most importantly, specified convergence criteria to be met by a country willing to join the economic and monetary union.

Convergence criteria fall into two main groups: nominal and legal. The legal criteria regard the compatibility of the legislation of a country candidate with the community law (i.e., with the Treaty on the Functioning of the European Union, Statute of the European System of Central Banks, and the Statute of the European Central Bank). The criteria are set out in Article 140 (1) of the Treaty on the Functioning of the European Union and Protocol 13 to the Treaty (Treaty on the Functioning of the European Union, 2012).

The nominal criteria, commonly referred to as the Maastricht Criteria, include:

- *FX rate criterion* – a country willing to adopt the euro must join European Exchange Rate Mechanism (ERM II) at least 2 years ahead. Participation in ERM II means that the FX rate of a given country must fluctuate within a normal range versus the central bank rate (currently ±15%). In addition, according to this criterion, a given currency rate must not be devalued over the period nor must it undergo severe tensions.
- *Price stability criterion* – an average yearly inflation rate (in the year prior to the test) must not exceed more than 1.5 percentage points of an average inflation rate of three countries with the lowest inflation. All EU countries are taken into account in this respect, even those from outside the eurozone.
- *Interest rate criterion* – in the year prior to the test, an average long-term interest rate must not be higher than by 2 percentage points than the

average rate determined for three countries with the lowest inflation. Again, all of EU countries are taken into account, not just the eurozone.

– *Fiscal criterion* – it comes down to the eurozone candidate's assessment with respect to excess deficit. Two economic indicators are taken into account to find whether a given country is subject to an excess deficit procedure:
  a The level of the country's budget deficit: it may not exceed 3% of the country's GDP.
  b The sovereign debt level: it may not exceed 60% of GDP. (European Council, n.d.-a)

What deserves attention is that every country willing to adopt the common currency had to meet the said criteria as at the adoption date. On the other hand though, if a currency union member exceeds the agreed criteria, no exclusion will ensue.

The countries that decided to adopt the common euro currency and met the necessary criteria had to accept the fact that they would not be able to conduct their own monetary policy, as henceforth it was to be conducted at the EU level. Since January 1, 1999, the European Central Bank has been in charge of the monetary policy. The Bank's primary goal is to keep stable prices, whereas the implementation of the main areas of the monetary policy, including money supply control and FX and interest rate policies, is aligned with the primary goal. In addition, the ECB, along with the central banks of all the EU 27 countries, form the European System of Central Banks. In turn, in the eurozone, there is the Eurosystem, which includes the ECB and the central banks of the member states of the Economic and Monetary Union.

As the common euro currency was launched, the monetary policy was delegated to a supranational level. It did not concern fiscal policy, which remained with the eurozone countries' domestic governments. The division was due to the nature of fiscal policy, which depends on a given country's administrative system, system of revenue collection and spending, economic and social situation, geographical location, and many other complex factors. The idea of a common fiscal policy emerged, but it faced strong opposition by some governments in response to the excessive constraints of the individual countries' authority over their own budgetary policies. In addition, there is the problem of possible financing of state-assigned tasks (such as social, health, or pension policies) with the state budget's funds. And then there is the potential coordination of tax systems. What would it look like if every country had a distinctive administrative system and varying needs? So far, only indirect taxes (such as VAT or excise tax) have been harmonized at EU level with regards to their maximum and minimum rates; direct taxes are the exclusive responsibility of the member states' central authorities.

Even if the fiscal policy is not centralized, it does not mean that every country is free to spend public funds by irresponsible fiscal policy, bearing no consequences. The principles, or rather, constraints, concerning the fiscal policy were included in the Maastricht Treaty, but still numerous countries find it problematic to observe the criteria in practice. In spite of the convergence criteria being formulated in so much detail, once countries met them and joined the eurozone they became less motivated to comply and pursue the correct fiscal policy, in particular, as regards eschewing excess budget deficit Therefore, 3 years after the adoption of the Maastricht Treaty, in order to make the criteria from the Treaty more specific, the Stability and Growth Pact (SGP) was drafted, which included a precise provision on the fiscal criterion, its implementation, observance, and enforcement. Adopting the Pact[5] was to prevent the eurozone countries from approaching the convergence criteria too leniently.

The principles on public financial stability as laid down in the treaties are an answer to the sustainable development concept. In line with the fundamental principles of sustainable development, financing of investment projects should be aligned with the development results, which integrate and synergize three dimensions of sustainable development, i.e., economic, social, and environmental, as expressed in the Rio+20 outcome document (United Nations, 2012) to ensure intra- and intergenerational equality.

A full implementation of the sustainable development concept is chiefly due to the observed climate change which calls for increasing financial outlays and the necessity to incur ever higher costs in both private and public sectors. The institutions of the EU (being an international organization) prepare the relevant legal framework to ensure the proper conditions for lasting and sustainable development, not only in the EU, in general, but also in the individual member states. Therefore, it is important for member state governments to remain prudent with respect to the potential macroeconomic challenges of financing sustainable development favoring social inclusion by maintaining fiscal balance and price stability. Within the development-oriented macroeconomic framework, the decision-makers are required to manage the domestic and external sovereign debt prudently so as to minimize its negative impact on inflation, the FX rate, the interest rates, and growth with respect to a potential risk. The requirement's important element is for the governments to accumulate funds necessary to invest in sustainable development. It is the governments' responsibility to unblock the fiscal space for investment-oriented expenditure for sustainable development. Countries may, for instance, increase their debt

5 The Stability and Growth Pact is an agreement of EU member states of June 17, 1997, made during a Council of Europe summit in Amsterdam.

at home or abroad. They may also create fiscal space by increasing the effectiveness of public spending in place and/or changing the priorities of public spending to make it more development-oriented. Countries may also mobilize their domestic funds by adapting the public income structure accordingly (e.g., tax and non-tax income) (United Nation, 2014, pp. 2–4, 14).

4 Coordination of the Fiscal Policy at the European Union Level

One of the pressing problems in the development of the global financial system is the excessive growth of sovereign debt, which has numerous negative consequences for the financial system of any country. Therefore, the spotlight should be turned to creating an effective state debt management system based on the debt's projected values (Zhuravka et al., 2021, p. 65).

The Stability and Growth Pact is among a few mechanisms ensuring the coordination of economic policies in the urozone. However, member states have always found the principles for economic policy coordination to be controversial. On the one hand, individual member states are keen to preserve the sovereignty of their fiscal policies, especially considering what has already been lost in terms of monetary policy. On the other hand, an economic and monetary union formed by 12 different countries implies that the actions of one member state necessarily affect the others. That is one reason why economic policies need to be coordinated. The belief is that only better coordination can provide for the policies growing more coherent, which would ultimately result in a better policy mix for the entire EMU (Zsolt de Sousa, 2004, p. 3).

The fiscal framework of the EU is an institutional safeguard against the externalities of the domestic fiscal policies in the economic and monetary union. Commonly agreed principles and institutions aim to ensure the long-lasting stability of public finances so as to protect the autonomy and effectiveness of the centralized monetary policy (Larch et al., 2020, p. 3).

There are many institutional participants in the fiscal policy coordination process and many procedures have been devised to achieve this goal (Treaty on the Functioning of the European Union, Articles 121, 126, 136). Among the institutions participating in the coordination process, the European Commission (EC) holds the central position, participates in the meetings of all the other bodies, and sets forth procedures on the financial stability of the member states. The Council (Council of the European Union) shall, on a recommendation from the Commission, formulate a draft for the broad guidelines of the economic policies of the member states and of the Union, and shall report its findings to the European Council. The European Council shall, acting on the basis of the report from the Council, discuss a conclusion on the broad guidelines of the economic policies of the member states and of the Union. On the basis of this conclusion, the Council shall adopt a recommendation setting out these broad guidelines. The Council shall inform the European Parliament of its recommendation (Treaty on the Functioning of the European Union, Article 121). The Economic and Financial Affairs Council (ECOFiN) is a section of the Council of the European Union dealing with government deficits, spending, and taxes, and is a center for coordinating economic policies of the member states. The European Central Bank (ECB) holds the right to participate in the meetings of the ECOFiN in order to foster dialogue on economic policy between these institutions. At the same time, the president of the ECOFiN sits on the EBC Governing Council. Although the president holds no voting rights, he or she may submit notions to this body (Panico & Vàzquez Suàrez, 2007, p. 6).

The Stability and Growth Pact consists of three elements:

1. A resolution of the European Council on the Stability and Growth Pact (Resolution of the European Council, 1997) (a resolution is an act that is not legally binding) – this is a political commitment of all the parties implementing the Stability and Growth Pact (the European Commission, the member states, and the European Council) to fully implement the process of budgetary surveillance while respecting the predefined dates.
2. Council Regulation (EC) no. 1466/97 of 7 July 1997 on the strengthening of the surveillance of budgetary positions and the surveillance and coordination of economic policies (Council Regulation, 1997a); the provisions included in the regulation are preventive in nature.
3. Council Regulation (EC) no. 1467/97 of 7 July 1997 on speeding up and clarifying the implementation of the excessive deficit procedure (Council Regulation, 1997b); the provisions included in the regulation are corrective in nature. This regulation allows for sanctions for countries with excessive deficits in order to prevent the occurrence of such deficits. Whenever the Council decides to impose sanctions to a participating member state, a non-interest-bearing deposit is, as a rule, required. If the excessive deficit results from non-compliance with the criterion relating to the government deficit ration, the amount of the first deposit comprises a fixed component equal to 0.2% of GDP, and a variable component equal to one-tenth of the difference between the deficit as a percentage of GDP in the preceding year and the reference value of 3% of GDP. Each following year, until the decision on the existence of an excessive deficit is abrogated, the Council shall assess whether the participating member state concerned has taken effective action in response to

the Council notice. If, following the assessment, an additional deposit is decided upon, it shall be equal to one-tenth of the difference between the deficit as a percentage of GDP in the preceding year and the reference value of 3% of GDP. Regulation (EC) no. 1467/97 specifies the upper limit of the deposits, which should not exceed 0.5% of GDP.

The provisions laid down in the Stability and Growth Pact cover all EU countries, while its correcting part only refers to urozone countries (Panico & Vàzquez Suàrez, 2007, p. 3). The purpose of the preventive function is to ensure that fiscal policy is sustainable throughout the business cycle, i.e., that the medium-term budgetary objective, individual for each member state, is achieved. On the other hand, if the domestic budgetary deficit exceeds 3% of GDP or the sovereign debt exceeds 60% of GDP (values as laid down in the Treaty), EU states shall undertake correcting measures. Under the Stability and Growth Pact, the financial policy rests on the medium-term budgetary objective. During the European Semester it is assessed whether the member states meet this objective or what correcting measures they undertake to meet it. Hence, a medium-term budgetary objective refers to a structural budgetary balance (between public income and spending), which is to protect against exceeding the treaty-based budget deficit threshold of 3% of GDP over the economic cycle and to ensure a long-lasting stability of public finances. The way each country should every year pursue this objective is called "adjustment paths to the medium-term budgetary objective." Each country figures out their own path individually. During the European Semester not only is the path's progress assessed, but the issue of whether the increase in public spending is fully covered by budget revenues is also analyzed (the benchmark for expenditure). In accordance with the Stability and Growth Pact, the member states are required to submit their stability (urozone countries) and convergence (countries awaiting urozone entrance) systems for assessment at EU level (European Council, n.d.-b).

However, as it turned out in the late 1990s and early 2000s, Europe's observance of the principles of the economic and budgetary policy was rather ailing. It was a time of stagnation in Europe, with almost non-existent economic growth. In the majority of countries, deficits would rise as a result of automatic stabilizers employed. Some of the countries exceeded the deficit ceiling set by the Stability and Growth Pact (Portugal, Holland). What is more, employment also failed to reach the rate set in Lisbon, and investments declined. Moreover, in the consecutive periods GDP growth lost its momentum, which meant that, in spite of recovery signs, the urozone officially plunged into recession. For most of the time inflation was above the 2% ceiling, and some claim that the ECB failed to reduce the interest rates as aggressively as it should have. During that time France and Germany surpassed their deficit limit[6] while being the urozone's largest economies. Nevertheless, the principles of the Stability and Growth Pact were still valid. Since that time and given the constrains on both monetary, as well as fiscal, policy, the key urozone countries insisted that the Pact principles be made more flexible, as the countries themselves were struggling to observe them (Zsolt de Sousa, 2004, pp. 7–8).

In 2005 the Stability and Growth Pact was reformed. The conditions for the assessment whether a given country has been affected by excessive deficits were eased and the timelines for the procedure were extended. As a result of the reforms, a safe margin for a possible surpassing of budgetary deficit threshold was introduced. The margin was so broad that it could accommodate the public sector's investment projects, pension reforms (both for the urozone, as well as ERM II) necessary for a given country.[7] The acceptable deficit was to fit into a range of –1% of GDP and the budgetary balance or surplus (Council Regulation, 2005a, 2005b). Pursuant to the Pact's amendments, the member states were obliged to present, inter alia, one-off factors which came to be listed among points to consider in the assessment of public finances. Such measures taken by the EU were dictated by the fact that some countries were using creative accounting or introducing one-off measures to improve public finances (e.g., levying one-off taxes) in order to avoid sanctions while ignoring adjustments (Beetsma & Debrun, 2004). In due course, following the onset of the crisis in the United States in 2007, a number of European Union member states experienced the repercussions of utilizing creative accounting methods in their public finances. As a result of high debt and deteriorated rating, in Spain, Greece, and Portugal there was a sharp slowdown in foreign capital inflow and debt rollover problems appeared. With a deficit (Eurostat, 2022a, 2022b) of more than 10% of GDP in Greece in 2009 and 2010 (as well as in Ireland, Portugal, and Spain), or approaching 10% in other EU countries, it was necessary to provide new solutions as regards fiscal policy coordination. In 2001 the so-called Sixpack legislative measures (five regulations and one directive) were

6 In 2003, following a recommendation from the Commission, the Council found that Germany and France were running an excessive deficit, and recommended that the deficit be reduced to an acceptable level by 2004. The Council failed to obtain a majority in the vote. Therefore, the European Commission brought action against the European Council before the European Court of Justice (ECJ). In its judgment of July 13, 2004, in Case C-27/04, the ECJ found that "the Council's conclusions adopted in respect of the French Republic and the Federal Republic of Germany respectively must consequently be annulled in so far as they contain a decision to hold the excessive deficit procedure in abeyance and a decision modifying the recommendations previously adopted by the Council under Article 104(7) EC."

7 It is a mechanism dedicated to countries awaiting eurozone admission.

adopted, including provisions for EU countries both inside and outside of the urozone. The Regulations (Regulation (EU), 2011a, 2011b, 2011c, 2011d), apply to EU countries, except for Regulations no. 1173/2011 and no. 1174/2011, which are meant for urozone countries. Two out of five regulations (Regulations no. 1175/2011 and no. 1177/2011) are concomitantly regulations that amend the Stability and Growth Pact, which they are a part of. Under the preventive arm (Regulation (EU), 2011b, 2011d) the focus was on the member states achieving and maintaining medium-term budgetary objectives. They are defined in the structural dimension, by adjusting the nominal balance by the effect of the economic cycle and following an adjustment by one-off and interim events. They are defined individually for each country given its economic and budgetary situation and with financial stability in mind. They may deviate from the general government balance requirement at the same time allowing for a safety margin before the 3% of GDP threshold for deficit is surpassed.

The scope of the information required to be disclosed in stability and convergence programs was broadened. The programs should additionally include the following: the planned growth path of government income and spending; information on implicit liabilities related to population ageing; and contingent liabilities, such as public guarantees. In addition, the stability and convergence programs should emphasize the assessment of the measures taken under the budgetary and economic policy. The assessment should cover cost–benefit analysis of significant structural reforms that give rise to improved public finances in the long term. Under the corrective arm (Regulation (EU), 2011e), the excessive deficit procedure was specified in more detail and made more restrictive. Where the general government debt exceeds the reference value, the debt-to-GDP ratio should be considered as sufficiently diminishing and approaching the reference value at a satisfactory pace, provided that over the previous three-year period its distance from the reference value has declined at an average rate of 1/20 per year, based on the trends over the preceding 3 years for which data are available.

Another important step to strengthen the public finance discipline of urozone countries and to step up the mechanisms of economic and budgetary surveillance was the Council adopting two regulations referred to as "two-pack" and signing the Treaty on Stability, Coordination and Governance in the Economic and Monetary Union, referred to as the Fiscal Compact. "Two-pack" regulations (Regulation (EU), 2013a, 2013b) introduce certain obligations and procedures concerning all urozone countries, as well as urozone countries subject to excessive deficit procedures. Among other things, a system of gradual monitoring by the Council and the Commission was introduced to ensure timely and sustainable correction of excessive deficits, and the possibility of early identification of risks associated with a member state's failure to comply with the Stability and Growth Pact. Another document to govern fiscal policy is the so-called Fiscal Compact (Treaty on Stability, Coordination and Governance, 2012), which is an international agreement of March 2, 2012, signed in Brussels, outside the EU legal framework, by the leaders of 25 EU countries. Out of the then EU member states it was the Czech Republic and the United Kingdom that failed to sign the Treaty. The Czech Republic adopted and ratified the Treaty in 2014, aiming to incorporate it into its domestic legislation later on. Croatia was not a signatory either. It failed to sign it on joining the EU, which took place on July 1, 2013. The Fiscal Compact became effective on January 1, 2012, after the ratification condition was satisfied by 12 EU member states, the urozone participants. The fiscal treaty introduces the so-called "budgetary pact," which incorporates guidelines having an immediate relationship with the procedures stipulated by Articles 119–144 of the Treaty on the Functioning of the European Union (TFEU), Protocol 12 to the TFEU, the provisions of the Stability and Growth Pact, and the Sixpack. The economic parameters referred to in the Treaty are also governed by the Compact, the Sixpack and the TFEU being a faithful reflection.

5 Coordination of Fiscal Policy at EU Level versus Ensuring Sustainable Development Conditions: an Assessment Attempt

As mentioned in the second section of this chapter, within the monetary union the monetary policy is centralized while fiscal policy is shaped by member states on an individual basis. Normally, each country's policy is based on discretionary measures, the strength of which may be determined by decision-makers shaping economic policy.

Undertaking discretionary measures in the area of fiscal policy should be preceded by an identification of an economic shock in place, analysis of its triggers, and a preparation of an action plan with the instruments intended to mitigate the shock. For the discretionary measures to succeed it is important whether, in the initial phase, its triggers are correctly analyzed and whether the tools for its reduction and the action plan are adequately selected. This is because, at the next stage, they will be the basis for developing relevant legislative solutions so that they could be used in practice.

It should be noted that between the stage of economic shock identification and the preparation of legislative solutions, months-long lags may occur. In addition, the adopted legislative solutions may prove to be incorrect or underdeveloped, which will translate into their ineffectiveness in practice. Moreover, attention should also be paid to the relationship between the state's debt and externalities. Demertzis and Viegi (2021) argue that a heavily indebted country, in running its fiscal policy, will adversely affect the EU. In turn, a low-debt country will have a positive external effect (Demertzis & Viegi, 2021).

In theory, striving for the long-term stability of public finances in line with the rules should be coherent with the finances' short-term stability. Still, there is ample evidence that a discretionary fiscal policy on the domestic level does not follow the intended or ideal path. On the contrary, numerous countries have high debts and their discretionary fiscal policy will amplify rather than stabilize the cyclical fluctuations of output (Larch et al., 2020, p. 2). Studies on the performance of the Stability and Growth Pact conducted in the 1990s by Buti et al. (2003) and Kopits and Symansky (1998) show that the sanctioning mechanisms did not meet the desired criteria (Buti et al., 2003; Inman, 1996; Kopits & Symansky, 1998). The economic situation of the EU and the respective EU member states is evolving as affected by changing global, regional, or national circumstances. Therefore, the studies on the coordination of fiscal policy at the EU level should be deepened, and enhanced with new observations, depending on the goals in place or the analyzed factors.

In the early 21st century Debrun (2007, pp. 5–6) devised a politico-economic model of fiscal policy aimed at identifying the relationship between policymakers' actions and the fiscal policy pursued. He claims that electoral uncertainty is endogenous and rooted in asymmetric information about policymakers' motivations and competence. Rational voters re-elect the incumbent administration only if the latter demonstrates sufficient ability to deliver a quantity of public goods deemed commensurate to tax revenues. In fact, policymakers themselves are uncertain as to whether their actions will be successful in delivering enough public goods, and there is no systematic difference in the level of competence between political parties. The less tolerant the voters vis-à-vis policy failures, the greater the electoral uncertainty and the larger the deficit bias. In this context, a simple balanced-budget rule can be enacted, with its enforcement strict enough to discourage the policymaker from deviating from the optimal policy. The problem is that a credible enforcement of the rule can only result from the decision of a non-partisan body, because a partisan decision-makers will always have an incentive to revert to the discretionary outcome (Balassone & Franco, 2001). Larch, Orseau, and Van der Wielan (2020) conducted a study analyzing the stabilizing effects, whether pro- or counter-cyclical, of the implemented fiscal policy, as well as the primary determinants thereof. They conclude that discretionary fiscal policies tend to be pro-cyclical both in the EU and beyond. They note that the alternative cyclical indicators that are observable in real time (less susceptible to revisions and politically more meaningful) also point to ill-timed discretionary fiscal stabilization. This suggests that pro-cyclicality is first and foremost a matter of political economy, not uncertainty. They also stress the crucial role of sustainability development constraints, because they may prove more important than the stabilization objective.

Moreover, the trade-off between stabilization and stability is not dealt with in the same manner for all levels of debt. Fiscal rules based on nominal aggregates, such as the nominal budgetary balance and the debt-to-GDP ratio, do not allow for the automatic effect of the economic cycle. In practice, the stability of public finances is an ill-defined and not a unique condition to apply to every country. It also depends on the economic governance framework – for instance, whether the central bank is independent, how credibly governments correct slippery fiscal trends, and what budgetary instruments are available to stabilize the economy in addition to national budgets. The researchers also emphasize that there is no central fiscal capacity, which implies that national budgets are directly exposed in case of major shocks. In comparison with a fully-fledged monetary union, such a solution may, on the other hand, impose stricter conditions for sustainable development, which renders the trade-off with fiscal stabilization difficult (Larch et al., 2020, pp. 29–30).

A special report is also worth mentioning here. It was prepared by the European Court of Auditors, which in 2018 audited whether the European Commission used the powers granted to it by a regulation to ensure adequate implementation of the preventive arm. The control of procedures under the preventive arm focused on six member states (five from the eurozone and one from outside of it). The Court also analyzed the interaction between the preventive and corrective arm of the Stability and Growth Pact, as far as it regards the preventive arm. It was concluded that the effectiveness of the preventive arm largely depends on how it is implemented by the Commission. The implementation rules decided by the Commission and its operational decisions do not ensure that the main objective of the regulation is met – i.e., that member states converge toward medium-term objectives in a reasonable period. Implementation rules on flexibility stem from 2005 reforms of the regulation but were not formally operationalized until 2015, when they reflected considerations prompted by the Great Recession. Moreover, the rules set by the Commission do not distinguish enough between those member states that do have a high level of debt and others. Instead of tightening the framework as the economic recovery was progressing, the Commission further weakened it in 2017, introducing a new "margin of discretion."

The structural reform allowance is no longer linked to the actual budget costs of the reform, but it is used as an "incentivizing instrument." All allowances (except for the pension reform) increase spending not only in the particular year for which they are granted, but also in the following years. The cumulative effect of all these allowances have resulted in multiyear delays in effective deadlines for reaching medium-term budgetary objectives. The credibility of the preventive arm was further eroded by the developments in the corrective arm. The Commission considers that the requirements of the corrective arm can be fully met just by cyclical recovery, which is also facilitated by the Commission's practice of proposing to Council granting multi-year extensions for exiting excessive deficit procedures. As a result, member states under excessive deficit procedures do not have to fulfill the requirements for improving their structural balances they would otherwise have to observe if they were under the preventive arm (European Court of Auditors, 2018, pp. 11–13, 73).

On March 13, 2020, in response to the outbreak of the COVID-19 pandemic, the European Commission announced a "coordinated economic response to the COVID-19 epidemic" (European Commission, 2020), in which, amid macroeconomic and financial effects of the COVID-19 epidemic, it called for a bold and coordinated response to mitigate the pandemic's negative impact on the overall economy. The EC ruled it was necessary to use all available EU tools and a flexible EU framework for member states action used to its full (European Commission, 2020, p. 4). Pursuant to the Communication, the budgetary effect of one-off social measures used to counteract the economic effects of COVID-19 was excluded. The Stability and Growth Pact can accommodate targeted exceptional expenditure. Support measures such as these urgently needed to:

- Contain and treat the pandemic
- Ensure liquidity support to firms and sectors
- Protect jobs and incomes of affected workers

This can be considered as one-off budgetary spending. The Commission considered that the flexibility to cater for "unusual events outside the control of the government" is applicable to the current situation. When an unusual event outside the control of a government has a major impact on a member state's fiscal position, the Stability and Growth Pact envisages that member states can be allowed to temporarily depart from required fiscal adjustments. As a result, this clause can also accommodate exceptional spending to contain the COVID-19 outbreak. In particular, the clause can apply to health care expenditure and targeted relief measures for firms and workers, provided they are temporary and linked to the outbreak. The Commission stood ready to propose to the Council that EU institutions activate the general escape clause to accommodate a more general fiscal policy support. This clause would suspend the fiscal adjustment recommended by the Council in case of a severe economic downturn for the euro area or the EU as a whole (European Commission, 2020, p. 13).

The member state governments responded to the EC's Communication swiftly and decisively to save the lives of their citizens and to keep their public finances on a sustainable path while reaching the stabilization goals. The states used a variety of ways to adjust their fiscal rules, including the activation of escape clauses, temporarily suspending fiscal rules, and modifying the limits of fiscal rules. A study by Davoodi et al. (2022) shows that, as of end 2021, about 105 economies adopted at least one fiscal rule, as opposed to fewer than 10 economies that had them in the early 1990s. At the end of 2021, more than 50 countries had established fiscal councils. Many countries incorporated flexibility provisions into their fiscal rules, most of the time in the form of escape clauses. The rules-based fiscal framework came under pressure during the COVID-19 pandemic, with countries using different ways to adapt their fiscal rules in response to the crisis. The widespread activation of escape clauses showed how fiscal rules can be highly flexible during large shocks. Experience suggests that fiscal rules allowed for a forceful response to the pandemic, disclaiming the concerns that rules are rigid in constraining the governments' response in bad times. However, fiscal rules did not prevent a large and persistent debt build-up over time. Studies show that deviations from deficit and debt rules were common across countries, but reached unprecedented levels with the pandemic. "On average, countries exceeded the deficit and debt limits by about 50 and 42 percent in the time during 2004–2021, respectively. The COVID-19 economic and health crisis, and the associated fiscal responses, led to a sharp rise in deficits and debt. Almost all countries with deficit rules exceeded the limits – by an average of 4% of GDP in 2020". (Davoodi et al., 2022, pp. 13, 25).

6 Conclusions

The process of building the Economic and Monetary Union is a long-term and complicated venture that requires a multilevel design. The EMU is formed by countries which fulfilled the Maastricht Treaty's criteria in various periods and at various levels of economic development. Across countries, the way in which a fiscal policy is conducted depends on a given country's administrative system, revenue collection system, the foci and objectives of public finance spending, the current economic and social situation, geographical location, and other factors. If implemented in the EU, a common fiscal policy would be confronted with the strong objection by individual governments in response to the excessive constraint on the individual countries affecting their budgetary policies. Worsened budgetary situations and increased sovereign debt across the EU make the stability of public finances a political challenge. Therefore, coordination of the EU's fiscal policy following the same principles as monetary policy in the eurozone is impossible. What remains to ensure financial system stability and the conditions for economic development of all the EU member states is only to devise a mechanism for coordinating fiscal policy. A mechanism that would be not only acceptable for all the member states, but also respected by them. Reckless fiscal policy may impact the level of interest rates, the rate of inflation, or money value, which, in turn, affects a society's welfare level. Failure to respect commonly agreed rules and principles for coordinating the EU's fiscal policy by respective member states is a dangerous precedent, and spawns a number of questions about whether it is advisable for some member states to incur efforts to reduce budget deficit and sovereign debt considering the entire eurozone and the whole international organization, while the remaining states are not held accountable nor bear any consequences for excessively expansionary fiscal policy.

Notes: Research presented in this chapter constitutes a part of the implementation of the "European Financial Security in the Global, Regional and National Dimension" (EUSEC) project funded by the European Education and Culture Executive Agency (EACEA) within the framework of the Erasmus+, Jean Monnet Activities: Jean Monnet Modules, no. 620453-EPP-1-2020-1-PL-EPPJMO-MODULE.

References

Balassone, F., & Franco, D. (2001). EMU fiscal rules: A new answer to an old question. In *Fiscal Rules*. Public Finance Workshop, Research Department, Banca d'Italia.

Beetsma, R., & Debrun, X. (2004). The interaction between monetary and fiscal policies in a monetary union: A review of recent literature. In. R. Beetsma et al. (Eds.), *Monetary policy, fiscal policies and labour markets: Macroeconomic policymaking in the EMU*. Cambridge University Press.

Buchanan, J. M. (1965). An economic theory of clubs. *Economica, 32*(125), 1–14.

Buchanan, J. M. (1968). *The demand and supply of public goods*. Rand McNally.

Bukhtiarova, A., Semenog, A., Razinkova, M., Nebaba N., & Haber J. A. (2020). Assessment of financial monitoring efficiency in the banking system of Ukraine. *Banks and Bank Systems, 15*(1), 98–106. doi:10.21511/bbs.15(1).20 20.10

Buti, M., Eijffinger, S., & Franco, D. (2003, January). Revisiting the Stability and Growth Pact: Grand design or internal adjustment. Economic Papers, no. 180. European Commission.

Committee for the Study of Economic and Monetary Union. (1989). *Report on economic and monetary union in The European Community*. European Commission. https://ec.europa.eu/economy_finance/publications/pages/publication6161_en.pdf

Council Regulation (EC). (1997a). No. 1466/97, Official Journal, L 209, 2.8.1997.
Council Regulation (EC). (1997b). No. 1467/97, Official Journal, L 209, 2.8.1997.
Council Regulation (EC). (2005a). No. 1056/2005, Official Journal, L 174/5, 7.7.2005.
Council Regulation (EC). (2005b). No. 1055/2005, L 174/1, 7.7.2005.
Crockett, A. (1997a, April). The theory and practice of financial stability. Essays in International Finance, no. 203, Department of Economics, Princeton University.
Crockett, A. (1997b). Why is financial stability a goal of public policy? *Economic Review (Federal Reserve Bank of Kansas City), 82*(QIV), 5–22. https://www.kansascityfed.org/documents/800/1997-Why%20Is%20Financial%20Stability%20a%20Goal%20of%20Public%20Policy%3F.pdf
Crockett, A. (2020). Why is financial stability a goal of public policy? In J. Rabin & G. L. Stevens (Eds.), *Handbook of monetary policy*. Routledge.
Danescu, E. (2017). University of Luxembourg, C2DH. The Werner Report of 1970 – a blueprint for EMU in the EU? Panel on *Architects of the euro*, EUSA, Miami, May 2017, Chair: Amy Verdun; Discussant: Erik Jones. the website https://webcache.googleusercontent.com/search?q=cache:Avtd42ZDKx4J:https://www.eustudies.org/conference/papers/download/467+&cd=14&hl=pl&ct=clnk&gl=pl&client=firefox-b-e
Davis, E. (2001). A typology of financial instability. In *Financial Stability Report 2001*, no. 2, pp. 92–110, Central Bank of Austria.
Davoodi, H. R., Elger, P., Fotiou, A., Garcia-Macia, D., Han, X., Lagerborg, A., Lam, W. R., & Medas, P. (2022). Fiscal rules and fiscal councils: Recent trends and performance during the COVID-19 pandemic. IMF Working Paper, Fiscal Affairs Department, WP/22/11, pp. 13 and 25. International Monetary Fund.
Debrun, X. (2007, January). Tying hands is not commitment: Can fiscal rules and institutions really enhance fiscal discipline? Bruegel Working Paper no. 2007/01. Bruegel.
Demertzis, M., & Viegi, N. (2021, December 20). *Policy coordination failures in the euro area: Not just an outcome, but by design*. Bruegel. https://www.bruegel.org/2021/12/policy-coordination-failures-in-the-euro-area-not-just-an-outcome-but-by-design/
Dobrzańska, A., Kosycarz, E., & Pietrzak, B. (2016). Stabilność systemu finansowego w gospodarce – rozważania teoretyczne i praktyczne aspekty. In A. Alińska & K. Wasiak (Eds.), *Mechanizmy stabilności systemu finansowego*. C. H. Beck.
European Commission. (1970). Report to the Council and the Commission on the realisation by stages of Economic and Monetary Union in the Community, "Werner Report," Council-Commission of the European Communities, Supplement to Bulletin 11–1970 of the European Communities. https://ec.europa.eu/economy_finance/publications/pages/publication6142_en.pdf
European Commission. (2020). Communication from the Commission to the European Parliament, the European Council, the Council, the European Central Bank, the European Investment Bank and the Eurogroup: Coordinated economic

response to the COVID-19 outbreak. COM/2020/112 final. https://eur-lex.europa.eu/legal-content/EN/TXT/?uri=CELEX%3A52020DC0112

European Council. (N.d.-a). Conditions for joining the euro area: Convergence criteria. https://www.consilium.europa.eu/pl/policies/joining-the-euro-area/convergence-criteria/

European Council. (N.d.-b). European Semester: A guide to the main rules and documents. https://www.consilium.europa.eu/en/policies/european-semester/european-semester-key-rules-and-documents/

European Court of Auditors. (2018). Special report: Is the main objective of the preventive arm of the Stability and Growth Pact delivered? No. 18.

Eurostat. (2022a). General government deficit/surplus. Eurostat. https://ec.europa.eu/eurostat/databrowser/view/tec00127/default/table?lang=en.

Eurostat. (2022b). General government gross debt. Retrieved March 17, 2022, from Eurostat website. https://ec.europa.eu/eurostat/databrowser/view/sdg_17_40/default/table?lang=en

Foot, M. (2003, April). What is "financial stability" and how do we get it? The Roy Bridge Memorial Lecture, Financial Services Authority.

George, S., & Bache, I. (2001). *Politics in the European Union*. Oxford University Press.

Grubel, H. (1970). The theory of optimum currency areas. *Canadian Journal of Economics, 3*(2), 318–324.

Holcombe, R. A. (1997). Theory of the theory of public goods. *Review of Austrian Economics, 10*(1), 1–22.

Inman, R. P. (1996). Do balanced budget rules work? US experience and possible lessons for the EMU. NBER Working Paper, no. 5838. National Bureau of Economic Research.

Ishiyama, Y. (1975). The theory of optimum currency areas: A survey. IMF Staff Papers, vol. 22. International Monetary Fund. https://www.elibrary.imf.org/view/journals/024/1975/002/article-A004-en.xml

Kenen, P. B. (1966). Toward a supranational monetary system. International Economics Workshop Columbia University.

Kenen, P. B. (1969). The theory of optimum currency areas: An eclectic view. In R. Mundell & A. Swoboda (Eds.), *Monetary problems of the international economy*. University of Chicago Press.

Kopits, G., & Symansky, S. (1998). Fiscal rules. Occasional Paper, no. 162. International Monetary Fund.

Larch, M., Orseau, E., & Van der Wielan, W. (2020). Do EU fiscal rules support or hinder counter-cyclical fiscal policy? CESifo Working Paper no. 8659. Center for Economic Studies and Ifo Institute for Economic Research.

McKinnon, R. (1963). Optimum currency areas. *American Economic Review, 53*(4), 717–725.

Mundell, R. A. (1961). A theory of optimum currency areas. *American Economic Review, 51*(4), pp. 657–665. https://www.aeaweb.org/aer/top20/51.4.657-665.pdf

Musgrave, R. A. (1959). *The theory of public finance.* McGraw-Hill.

Padoa-Schioppa, T. (2002). Central banks and financial stability: Exploring a land in between. Paper presented at the Second ECB Central Banking Conference, "The Transformation of the European Financial System," Frankfurt am Main, October 24–25, 2002. https://www.ecb.europa.eu/events/pdf/conferences/tps.pdf

Panico, C., & Vàzquez Suàrez, M. (2007). Scheme to coordinate monetary and fiscal policies in the euro area. Working Paper Series, no. 143. Political Economy Research Institute, University of Massachusetts Amherst.

Regulation (EU). (2011a). No. 1173/2011 of the European Parliament and of the Council, Official Journal L 306/1, 23.11.2011.

Regulation (EU). (2011b). No. 1174/2011 of the European Parliament and of the Council, Official Journal L 306/8, 23.11.2011.

Regulation (EU). (2011c). No. 1175/2011 of the European Parliament and of the Council, Official Journal L 306/12, 23.11.2011.

Regulation (EU). (2011d). No. 1176/2011 of the European Parliament and of the Council, Official Journal L 306/25, 23.11.2011.

Regulation (EU). (2011e). No. 1177/2011 of the European Parliament and of the Council, Official Journal L 306/33, 23.11.2011.

Regulation (EU). (2013a). No. 472/2013 of the European Parliament and of the Council, Official Journal L 140/1, 27.5.2013.

Regulation (EU). (2013b). No. 473/2013 of the European Parliament and of the Council, Official Journal L 140/11, 27.5.2013.

Resolution of the European Council. (1997). Resolution of the European Council on the Stability and Growth Pact Amsterdam, 17 June 1997, Official Journal, C 236, Volume 40, 2 August 1997.

Samuelson, P. A., & Nordhaus, W. D. (1989). *Macroeconomics.* McGraw-Hill.

Schinasi, G. (2004, October). Defining financial stability, IMF Working Paper, no. WP/04/187. https://doi.org/10.5089/9781451859546.001.

Shkolnyk, I., Kozmenko, S., Kozmenko, O., Orlov, V., & Shukairi, F. (2021). Modeling of the financial system's stability on the example of Ukraine equilibrium. *Quarterly Journal of Economics and Economic Policy, 16*(2), 377–411. doi:10.24136/eq.2021.014

Shkolnyk, I., Kozmenko, S., Polach, J., & Wolanin, E. (2020). State financial security: Comprehensive analysis of its impact factors. *Journal of International Studies, 13*(2), 291–309. doi:10.14254/2071-8330.2020/13-2/20

Svensson, L. E. O. (2011). Monetary policy after the crisis. Speech by Mr. Lars E O Svensson, deputy governor of the Sveriges Riksbank, at the conference "Asia's Role in the Post-crisis Global Economy," Federal Reserve Bank of San Francisco, November 29, 2011.

Tower, E., & Willet, T. (1976). The theory of optimum currency areas and exchange rate flexibility. International Finance Section, no. 11. Princeton University.

Treaty on Stability, Coordination and Governance. (2012, March 2). Treaty on Stability, Coordination and Governance in the Economic and Monetary Union (also known as the Fiscal Compact). https://eur-lex.europa.eu/legal-content/EN/TXT/HTML/?uri=LEGISSUM:1403_3&from=PL

Treaty on the Functioning of the European Union. (2012, October 26). *Official Journal of the European Union*, C 326/47.

United Nations. (2012). The future we want, Rio de Janeiro, Brazil, 19 June 2012, A/CONF.216/L.1

United Nations. (2014). Sustainable development financing: Perspectives from Asia and the Pacific. Background paper, Asia-Pacific Outreach Meeting on Sustainable Development Financing, Jakarta, June 10–11, 2014.

Williamson, O. E. (2000). The new institutional economics: Taking stock, looking ahead. *Journal of Economic Literature, 38*(3), 595–613.

Van Esch, F. A. W. J. (2009). The rising of the phoenix: Building the European monetary system on a meeting of minds. *L'Europe en Formation, 3–4*(353–354), 133–148. https://www.cairn.info/revue-l-europe-en-formation-2009-3-page-133.htm

Zhuravka, F., Filatova, H., Šuleř, P., & Wołowiec T. (2021). State debt assessment and forecasting: Time series analysis. *Investment Management and Financial Innovations, 18*(1), 65–75. doi:10.21511/imfi.18(1).2021.06

Zsolt de Sousa, H. (2004, April). The future of the Stability and Growth Pact as a tool for economic policy co-ordination. Policy Papes, no. 9. Notre Europe. https://institutdelors.eu/wp-content/uploads/2020/08/policypaper9_02-1.pdf

PART 5

Green Energy, Health Care, and Intellectual Property: International Global Public Goods?

CHAPTER 12

Green Energy as a Sustainable Development Model Leading to a Gradual Improvement of the Quality of Life

Anna Wójtowicz

1 Introduction

The progressive process of globalization has resulted in numerous threats taking on a much broader dimension in the modern economy than before. New global problems have become apparent, i.e., the degradation of natural resources, climate change, and the strong dependence of many developed economies on imports of energy resources. These issues pose a real danger in today's world, since a stable supply of energy is essential to any economy. Furthermore, the world is currently experiencing the severe effects of climate change, i.e., extreme weather events, floods, drought, melting glaciers, or rising sea and ocean levels. International organizations can play a significant role in overcoming these development barriers. Individual states are often unable to deal with the effects of global challenges on their own, which is why the role of international organizations as coordinators of activities aimed at managing global public goods is so important. Priority global public goods include energy conservation and environmental protection, covering the climate, and combating climate change. Managing the environment and energy efficiently is extremely important to improve the environment and human health, and stimulate economic growth through increased innovation, clean technologies, and the creation of new jobs.

Environmental and energy management can only be achieved through the wide distribution of green energy, which is perfectly compatible with the model of sustainable development. Equally, using green energy contributes to protecting the environment, increasing access to energy, and improving people's quality of life. Renewable energy sources (RES) increase the diversification of energy supply and thus improve energy security. Furthermore, renewable resources are climate-neutral, limit environmental degradation, and are inexhaustible. Nevertheless, the development of green energy requires coordinated global efforts and costly investments in clean and modern technologies based primarily on the generation of energy from renewable sources. Thus,

DOI:10.1163/9789004687264_014

international organizations are focusing increasingly on managing global environmental and energy public goods. Examples of organizations taking action in this area include the United Nations (UN), the World Bank (WB), and the European Union (EU). It is also worth mentioning the financial institutions that support this type of investment. This is the European Investment Bank (EIB) within the European Union, while internationally, the financial institution that supports the green transition is the European Bank for Reconstruction and Development (EBRD).

This chapter aims to show the importance of global public goods such as environmental protection and energy conservation, and to verify whether the actions taken by international organizations in favor of the green transition fit into the model of sustainable development. The analysis includes international organizations such as the UN, WB, and EBRD, but special attention is paid to the EU and EIB, as these organizations have taken on the extremely ambitious challenge of achieving EU climate neutrality by 2050.

This chapter is structured around the presented goal. The first section demonstrates the importance of global public goods (i.e., environmental protection and energy) in the UN concept of sustainable development. The second section of the chapter presents the key role of green energy in implementing environmental and energy sustainability objectives. The third and final section outlines how international organizations support the development of green energy to manage global public goods (i.e., environment and energy) effectively. In particular, it highlights activities undertaken by the WB and EBRD, but also pays attention to EU and EIB measures to achieve climate neutrality.

2 Environmental Protection and Energy: Relevance to the Concept of Sustainable Development

Sustainable development is a global concept of an interdisciplinary nature that is based on balanced economic, social, and environmental development. This concept is fluid in that it does not contain a well-defined range of activities, but rather evolves (changes) over time as new development challenges emerge. Sustainable development is most often defined as development that seeks to achieve intra- and intergenerational equity and ensure high ecological, economic, and sociocultural standards for all generations, within the Earth's natural limits (Rogall, 2005, p. 12).

Intergenerational equity, i.e., making sure present and future generations have equal access to resources, plays a significant role in sustainable development. Energy resources are a very important resource and necessary for the smooth functioning of any economy. In today's world, stable access to energy is critical to economic development. It has a significant impact on the world economy. Energy raw materials, which are a source of energy, are essential for the functioning and development of humanity, and when there is a shortage of energy raw materials, social, political, and economic problems arise, posing a significant threat to humanity. The supply of energy raw materials is, therefore, a global problem. That is why it is extremely important to manage the Earth's natural resources in a sustainable manner, i.e., to ensure that they will also benefit future generations. If not exploited properly, even the quality of natural resources considered inexhaustible, such as air, can decline significantly. As for renewable (vegetation, soil) and non-renewable (oil, coal) resources, their overexploitation and unchecked development of the world economy threaten to deplete some of them irretrievably.

In the 1980s, Richard Ullman analyzed the global threat of a shortage of energy resources. He identified two main dangers: "natural" – depletion of energy resources, and "artificial" – actions of governments of individual countries, e.g., boycotts, embargoes, restrictions on the supply of these resources (Ullman, 1983, pp. 140–145).

The growing danger of natural resource degradation and environmental pollution has also attracted the attention of global international organizations. In 1983, UN Secretary-General Javier Perez de Cuellar established the independent World Commission on Environment and Development, chaired by Norwegian prime minister Gro Harlem Brundtland. The Commission aimed to identify current world problems, and its work resulted in the *Our Common Future* report, published in 1987. The report defined the term "sustainable development" for the first time, recognizing that sustainable development "is the development that meets the needs of the present without compromising the ability of future generations to meet their own needs" (United Nations, 1987, p. 24).[1] The report warns against equating the term "development" with purely economic development and against an equally narrow understanding of the definition of "environment." Therefore, it was the first time that environment and development problems were treated as a single global issue. The report also demonstrates the strong relationship between the environment and poverty, stating that poverty is both a cause and an effect of global environmental problems. Furthermore, it has been emphasized that sustainable development requires decisive changes in the use of natural resources, investments, further technical development, and political structures (Eissel & Rokicka, 1996, p. 59).

1 The concept of sustainable development is thoroughly discussed in Chapter 1 of this book.

The *Our Common Future* report recognizes that there is no single blueprint for sustainable development, as it is necessary to consider that socioeconomic systems and ecological conditions vary considerably between countries. Although the *Our Common Future* report recognizes sustainable development as a global goal, each country has to develop its own policies for action (Baker et al., 1997, p. 4). The report brought about a real revolution in views, contributing to the reduction of ecological destruction and the formation of new concepts of development.

Daly draws attention to the need for sustainable use of natural resources and the environment, highlighting that if there is no change to the current methods in which they are exploited, there will be a collapse of the economy and even an ecological disaster is likely. Therefore, natural resources and the environment should be used consistently and sustainably. Daly thus proposed three key principles for sustainable use of resources and the environment (Daly, 2007, p. 14):

1. With regard to renewable resources: the sustainable withdrawal of resources cannot exceed the regeneration of resources.
2. With regard to non-renewable resources: the sustainable withdrawal of non-renewable resources cannot exceed the rate of production of their renewable substitutes – the total amount of natural capital should remain unchanged.
3. With regard to pollutants: the sustainable rate of pollutant emissions cannot exceed the rate at which the pollutants will be recovered, absorbed or disposed of by the environment. (Tester et al., 2005, p. 262)

The current problems faced in addressing the world's major global issues were identified on September 25–27, 2015, at the United Nations Summit in New York. At that time, the document entitled "Transforming Our World: The 2030 Agenda for Sustainable Development" was adopted, setting 17 Sustainable Development Goals for the period 2015–2030 (United Nations, 2015b). These goals are discussed in detail in Chapter 1 of this book. However, two of the goals indicated relate directly to energy and the fight against climate change, respectively Goal 7: "Ensure access to affordable, reliable, sustainable and modern energy for all," and Goal 13: "Take urgent action to combat climate change and its impacts." The United Nations' classification and listing of the 17 Sustainable Development Goals, which specifically mandate the guarantee of universal access to energy and the mitigation of climate change, represents a pivotal stride towards the enhanced management of these vital global public goods.

To sum up, one of the most important factors prompting the emergence of the concept of sustainable development was the increasing danger of degradation of natural resources and pollution of the environment. In the *Our*

Common Future report, the UN highlighted for the first time that the degradation of natural resources and the environment is a major global issue. It also shows that there is a strong correlation between the environment and poverty, emphasizing that poverty is both a cause and an effect of global environmental issues. Over the years, with the advance of globalization, these problems have become even more relevant. Ensuring stable and universal access to energy while protecting the environment is one of the most important Sustainable Development Goals.

3 Green Energy and Its Impact on Improving Quality of Life

It is worth highlighting that energy demand continues to increase. The US Energy Information Administration and the International Energy Agency predict in annual reports that energy consumption will increase by 71% between 2003 and 2030. Meanwhile, the increased demand for energy is accompanied by a continuous decline (depletion) of fossil resources. Moreover, carbon dioxide emissions continue to rise, with an increase of 50% in 2015 versus 1990 (United Nations, 2015b, p. 52). Thus, in order to meet the major challenges of sustainable development in the 21st century, i.e., increasing energy demand, resource scarcity, and climate change, it is necessary to approach environmental and energy protection as part of sustainable development.

The term "green energy" is commonly used to describe electricity generated from renewable sources. In principle, all natural resources are renewable, but at very different times. If the renewal time of the resource is short, it is considered renewable. However, if the renewal occurs over a somewhat longer period of time, but still within our lifetime, the resource is considered potentially renewable. Renewal of some natural resources is only possible as a result of geological processes of such duration that for practical purposes they are called non-renewable resources. Their reserves are exhaustible in terms of human life expectancy (Afgan et al., 2004, p. 5). For this reason, energy raw material resources are commonly divided into non-renewable raw materials (e.g., coal and lignite, oil, natural gas, uranium) and renewable raw materials (e.g., hydropower, biomass solar and geothermal energy, wind energy, etc.).

Non-renewable sources are limited in quantity, and intensive exploitation over the past century has significantly depleted them. Unfortunately, it is not possible to increase the reserves of non-renewable raw materials within a conceivable time frame through recovery or new discoveries. Conversely, renewable sources have the special property that they are not consumed in the process of exploitation, so that future generations will be able to use them as needed.

As it is based on non-renewable resources, conventional energy contributes significantly to environmental degradation – pollution of soil, water, and the atmosphere. Renewable energy is less burdensome for the environment, as much less pollution is involved in its production. Although renewable energy sources do not consume natural resources and are the most climate-friendly source of energy generation, it should be borne in mind that using them also involves some environmental interference. For example, the generation of wind energy causes a lot of noise from generators driven by this energy and a reduction in bird populations as a result of them colliding with wind turbines. Also, offshore turbines can disturb ecosystems through vibration and noise. In turn, dams contribute to the disruption of water relations in the ecosystem (changes in the flow of oxygen and nutrients) and become a physical barrier to migrating fish. These are just a few examples showing that renewable energy sources are not completely neutral to the environment, but it should be borne in mind that there is currently no source of energy generation that has no environmental impact at all. Nevertheless, green energy contributes only marginally to its degradation in contrast to the conventional energy sources described earlier. In addition, renewable energy sources allow for experiments and innovative actions to transform the environment, as yet unexplored due to widespread dependence on fossil fuels.

In sum, energy from renewable sources has many beneficial characteristics:

- Low environmental impact
- Resource renewability
- Saving fossil fuels (eliminates consumption of coal, oil, and natural gas)
- A nationally dispersed energy source that does not need to be transported and can be sourced anywhere, thus eliminating the losses incurred in distribution and the construction of costly transmission lines

A factor that determines the need for spreading and using green energy is the fight against climate change, the consequences of which are increasingly perceived by society. Another factor in favor of using green energy is the increasing demand for energy. As conventional resources become scarcer and steadily depleted, only renewable energy sources are able to ensure continued access to energy, both for current and future generations at an affordable price.

It is worth noting that the use of green energy directly contributes to the two Agenda 2030 Sustainable Development Goals – universal energy access (Goal 7) and combating climate change (Goal 13). However, indirectly, using green energy also contributes to almost all of the Sustainable Development Goals, including mainly the first goal, which focuses on poverty eradication. In fact, green energy does not emit pollutants into the atmosphere, and is therefore an effective tool for combating climate change, which is the main cause of environmental disasters. At the same time, disasters such as hurricanes or droughts significantly exacerbate poverty, causing major economic losses. Thus, green transformation plays a huge role in implementing the concept of sustainable development. It even lays the foundation for the sustainable development of the whole world, and thus for the effective management of global public goods.

To conclude, the development of green energy is an essential element for the implementation of the concept of sustainable development, as well as a necessary tool for efficiently managing global public goods in terms of energy and environmental protection. First of all, using renewable energy sources (RES) to generate energy is emission-free and does not exacerbate climate change, which is a fundamental global problem. Another important advantage of renewable resources is regeneration, thus saving fossil fuels. Surely the solution to the global issues of energy access, environmental protection, and climate change is to use a mechanism to implement sustainable development with green energy.

4 Green Transformation Efforts by International Organizations (WB, EBRD, WHO) and, in Particular the EU and the EIB

A major event that has driven international action to tackle climate change is the Paris Agreement, which entered into force on November 4, 2016 (Council Decision (EU), 2016). Its main thrust is to strive to keep the global temperature rise well below 2°C (and to make every effort to keep it at 1.5°C) relative to pre-industrial levels, and to bring about a rapid reduction in emissions. Signature of the agreement by two of the most carbon-emitting countries, China and USA,[2] was a great success. The Paris Agreement complements Agenda 2030 and the 13th Sustainable Development Goal on climate change (United Nations, 2015b).

– World Bank (WB)

Using green energy is one of the most important tools for combating climate change. Individual countries also support global international organizations to implement their commitments under the Paris Agreement. One such organization is certainly the World Bank, which launched in April 2021 a new Climate Change Action Plan (CCAP). In the CCAP, the Bank made a

2 The United States formally withdrew from the Paris Agreement on November 4, 2020, due to a decision of President Donald Trump, but rejoined on February 19, 2021, due to a decision made by the new president, Joe Biden.

commitment to increase climate finance to 35% of total commitments over the next 5 years (World Bank Group, 2021, p. 17).

– World Health Organization (WHO)

The WHO also draws attention to the fact that the Paris Agreement is a fundamental agreement on public health. At the 2018 UN Climate Change Conference in Bonn, WHO officials expressed concern that 9 out of 10 people breathe air with high levels of pollution, and around 7 million people die each year from exposure to fine particles in polluted air (United Nations, 2018).

– European Bank for Reconstruction and Development (EBRD)

EBRD also plays an important role in managing global environmental and energy public goods. The EBRD was established by the European Council in December 1989 and became operational in March 1991. Its main objective was to facilitate the transition of the Central and Eastern European countries to a market economy. Currently, the EBRD is owned by 71 countries, as well as the EU and EIB (EBRD, 2023). EBRD members work towards sustainable development, including environmental protection. The Bank promotes the slogan "Green economy transition," implying ecology as the priority of its activities and, in particular, combating climate change. In July 2020, the EBRD presented *The Green Economy Transition GET 2021–2025*, which aims to finance projects that accelerate the transition to a sustainable, low-carbon economy. As part of GET 2.1, the EBRD made a commitment to "aligning its activities with the principles of international climate agreements, including principally the Paris Agreement" (EBRD, 2020, p. 6). Therefore, the EBRD actively supports countries that seek to fulfill their commitments under the Paris Agreement. As a result of these measures, in 2021, climate change expenditure accounted for 51% (€5.4 billion) of the Bank's total investments (€10.4 billion) (Bennett, 2022). All financial flows by the EBRD are consistent with Article 2.1 of the Paris Treaty, which obliges signatories to make "finance flows consistent with a pathway towards low greenhouse gas emissions and climate-resilient development." In June 2021, the EBRD published a methodology for public consultation to define how the EBRD determines whether projects to be financed by the Bank are consistent with the Paris Agreement (EBRD, 2021).

– European Union (EU) and European Investment Bank (EIB)

The institution that has been particularly active in promoting the effective implementation of the Paris Agreement is the EU. In December 2019, the European Green Deal was established, a new strategy of action under which the EU aims to achieve climate neutrality by 2050. In order to implement the European Green Deal, the European Commission announced a new "Fit for 55" package on July 14, 2021 (European Commission, 2021). The package aims to decarbonize the European economy by at least 55% by 2030 compared to 1990 emission levels. The package contains 13 legislative proposals to achieve this goal, including a proposal to amend the renewable energy directive. It proposed to raise the current EU target of 32% RES in gross final energy consumption to at least 40% by 2030. The Commission also proposed to amend the Energy Efficiency Directive to raise the current EU target to improve energy efficiency from 32.5% to 36% of final energy consumption by 2030. The package also includes a proposal to revise the EU Emissions Trading System (EU ETS), which has been in place since 2005 and aims to reduce greenhouse gas emissions in the EU. Under this mechanism, the EU sets an overall cap on emissions allowances, and companies buy or receive these allowances. This cap is gradually being lowered so that emissions also decrease progressively. As per the amendment to the act within the package, each year, the permissible emission caps are to be reduced even more rapidly, so that the price of emission allowances will rise at the same time. Additionally, free emission allowances for aviation are to be gradually phased out and maritime transport emissions are to be included in the scheme. The new Carbon Border Adjustment Mechanism (CBAM) included in the package is particularly noteworthy. The CBAM is supposed to operate in parallel with the ETS and counteract "carbon leakage." Therefore, the project aims to avoid a situation where the EU's efforts to reduce emissions are undermined by increased emissions outside its borders, either through relocation of production to countries outside the EU (where climate change policies are less demanding than the EU's) or through increased imports of carbon-intensive products. The package also includes changes to the carbon dioxide emission standards for passenger cars and commercial vehicles. From 2035, no cars or commercial vehicles with combustion engines will be allowed on the EU market. Furthermore, an amendment to the legislation has been included in the package to accelerate the development of infrastructure for charging or refueling vehicles using alternative fuels. The package also involves air transport (ReFuelEU Aviation project) and maritime transport (FueEU Maritime) in meeting the EU's climate targets, intending to reduce greenhouse gas emissions through the use of renewable and low-carbon fuels in air and maritime transport (last updated March 25, 2022).

The EU attends the UN Climate Conferences every year, where participants reflect on how to accelerate global climate action. During the last COP 27 Conference in November 2022 in Sharm el Sheikh, the EU postulated to continue to increase the scale of international financing of actions related to climate change (European Council, 2022).

The financial institution actively involved in implementing climate neutrality in the EU is the European Investment Bank. In November 2019, the EIB Board of Directors decided to increase the EIB Group's commitment to the climate and environment. It was decided to transform the EIB from "the EU bank supporting the climate" into "the EU climate bank." Therefore, the Bank has adopted a new climate strategy, as well as a new energy lending policy. The EIB is committed to aligning all its financing activities with the goals of the Paris Agreement. To do this, the Bank has declared that by 2025 it will increase the share of investment to at least 50% of total funding under its "climate action and environmental sustainability" priority, a level of more than €30 billion per year. In addition, the EIB stopped financing conventional fossil fuel projects from the end of 2021 (European Parliament, 2021).

As the EU climate bank, the EIB focuses mainly on financing projects concerning (EIB, 2020, p. 15):

– Energy efficiency, including building and housing refurbishment, better road lighting and green transport
– Emission-free energy supply to contribute to the EU's goal of increasing energy from renewable sources
– Electricity networks connecting new, low-carbon energy sources
– Innovation in energy generation, storage and use

Reducing emissions, especially in the industrial sector, is a very difficult task. For this reason, the Bank is implementing projects to help businesses make the transition to a low-carbon model. Between 2016 and 2020, the EIB financed energy infrastructure to the tune of around €60 billion. The Bank financed energy-related projects worth €11.6 billion, including €5.8 billion for energy efficiency, €4 billion for renewable energy sources, €963 million for electricity, €455 million for gas, and €351 million for heat (EIB, 2021b, p. 3).

The establishment of the €100 million Breakthrough Energy Ventures Europe (BEV-E) investment fund, in collaboration with the European Investment Bank (EIB), the European Commission (EC), and Breakthrough Energy Ventures, represents a salient development deserving noteworthy attention. The fund is the first large-scale clean energy investment and focuses on significant emission reductions. The fund aims to support European companies that develop cutting-edge technologies that contribute to reducing greenhouse gas emissions (EIB, 2019).

Currently, companies are increasingly willing to invest in this type of project as they are increasingly aware that climate change seriously impacts their business. According to a qualitative survey conducted by the EIB in 2021, as many as 58% of companies with operations in the EU are aware that climate change is negatively affecting their businesses. Spain (78%), Romania (72%), Portugal

(72%), and Malta (44%) had the highest number of companies aware of the implications of climate change for their business (EIB, 2021a, p. 28).

To conclude, the EU and the EIB are making every effort to achieve climate neutrality in the EU economy by 2050 through the deployment of green energy. The increasingly stringent EU climate change standards and EIB financing for green energy projects are very concrete steps towards climate neutrality. However, it should be emphasized that in order to ensure universal access to energy as well, and effectively mitigate climate change, energy supplies must also be adequately diversified. A stable supply of energy is essential to the smooth operation of any economy. Unfortunately, the European Union is highly dependent on energy imports from external suppliers and is therefore vulnerable to sudden increases in energy prices and energy crises. Even at the end of 2021, there was an increase in energy prices in Europe, which was caused by a sharp increase in the price of natural gas on world exchanges. This increase was the result of increased demand for gas resulting, among other things, from the EU's climate policy and departure from fossil fuel – based power generation, as well as a reduction in the gas supply from major suppliers, mainly Russia. In December 2021, gas prices on world markets increased by 170% compared to December 2020 (last updated March 31, 2022). In contrast, the Russo – Ukrainian War (February 24, 2022) resulted in an even greater increase in the price of natural gas – by 38.6% at its peak in March 2022 compared to January of that year (Horton et al., 2022). Certainly the conflict with Russia has exposed the flaws in the EU's energy policy of overdependence on Russian energy imports, but it has also motivated the EU to accelerate its RES-based energy transition.

In March 2022, the EC communicated a plan to make Europe independent of Russian fossil fuels before 2030 (European Commission, 2022). The EC stressed that as a result of Russia's invasion of Ukraine, urgent action must be taken to bring about an even faster energy transition in the EU. The EC highlighted that the EU is heavily dependent on conventional fuel imports from Russia. As much as 45.3% of gas imports in 2021 came from Russia. The rest of the gas suppliers had a much smaller share of EU imports: Norway (23.6%), Algeria (12.6%), the USA (6.6%), Qatar (4.9%), and others (7.1%). Also, in 2021, more than 27% of oil and 46% of coal were imported from Russia. In order to become independent from Russian gas by 2030, the EC has proposed the REPowerEU plan, which includes diversification of gas supplies through increased imports of liquefied natural gas (LNG) and pipeline imports from non-Russian suppliers. In addition, the plan is to increase the production and import of biomethane and hydrogen and to reduce the use of fossil fuels more quickly. Attention was also drawn to the need to improve energy efficiency, increase the share of RES in final energy consumption, and address infrastructure constraints. The full implementation of the proposals under the "Fit for 55" package described earlier is intended to achieve these objectives. The EC estimates that these measures could reduce EU demand for Russian gas by two-thirds by the end of the year. The communication stresses that the significant increase in energy prices is hitting people in the poorest households (who spend a significant proportion of their income on energy bills) particularly hard, as well as those in fuel poverty. In turn, this contributes to exacerbating social disparities and inequalities, while constituting a huge barrier to achieving the UN's first Sustainable Development Goal – eradicating global poverty.

To summarize, today, international organizations such as the UN, WB, EU, EBRD, and EIB are taking many steps to manage the global public goods of environment and energy effectively. The EU is the undisputed leader in green transformation measures and the pursuit of climate neutrality. However, effective energy and climate management, in line with the sustainable development model, should incorporate environment protection, and also secure and stable energy supply at affordable prices. Unfortunately, there has not been adequate diversification of imported fuel supplies in the EU for many years, as most energy supplies depend on a single supplier – Russia. The Russo – Ukrainian War has highlighted the serious consequences for the EU of becoming heavily dependent on a single energy supplier. These consequences are a reduction in the supply of energy and a large increase in its price on the EU market, with a consequent rise in inflation and a significant fall in the population's real incomes. In the wake of these events, the EU is now taking a number of steps to reduce its dependence on energy imports from Russia. Under these circumstances, the green transition is an even more necessary and extremely important development, as the increase in energy generated from RES increases the diversification of supply and thus improves energy security. In addition, climate change and the degradation of natural resources are now a real global concern for society. Therefore, every effort should be made to achieve climate neutrality, while bearing in mind that stable and affordable access to energy is also an important element affecting people's quality of life.

5 Conclusions

Due to the world's growing population and economic development, the global demand for increasingly scarce energy resources continues to rise, and the global economy is under threat of increasing energy deficits and, consequently, significant environmental degradation and climate change. The solution to providing society with stable and affordable access to energy and combating climate change is green energy. Therefore, international organizations should implement green energy to manage global public goods such as the environment and energy effectively.

The present chapter has effectively accomplished its objective by highlighting the salience of global public goods, specifically those pertaining to environmental preservation and energy conservation. Moreover, the current discourse has substantiated that the measures undertaken by international organizations in support of the green transition align with the model of sustainable development.

The development of green energy contributes to the efficient management of global public goods, i.e., environmental protection and energy. Green energy is a direct opportunity to meet at least two of the current Sustainable Development Goals set out in the 2030 Agenda, i.e., ensuring access to affordable, reliable, sustainable, and modern energy for all, and taking urgent action to combat climate change and its effects. Moreover, using green energy indirectly contributes to almost all of the Sustainable Development Goals and is particularly strongly linked to the goal of poverty eradication. As a result of climate change, numerous disasters have occurred, including hurricanes and droughts, which have caused great damage and have consequently contributed to global poverty. To achieve sustainable development, it is imperative to implement and make extensive use of clean, modern technologies and renewable energy sources.

Since the adoption of the Paris Agreement, international organizations, i.e., the EU, WB, EBRD, and EIB, have made every effort to manage the global public goods – environment and energy – effectively. Concrete legislative measures and financial solutions supporting projects related to the development of green energy are a manifestation of these efforts. Undoubtedly, this provision of support is of utmost significance and necessity, as it constitutes a vital component of the sustainable development model, thereby enhancing the standard of living for all individuals.

In summary, global international organizations are exerting commendable efforts towards the effective management of global public goods pertaining to the environment and energy. Certainly, a necessary tool for the efficient management of these goods is the systematic implementation of green energy under the sustainable development mechanism. Using green energy reduces climate change, saves fossil fuels, and improves energy security by increasing energy generation sources. Thus, providing widespread access to green energy is seamlessly aligned with the model of sustainable development, while promoting environmental protection and improving people's quality of life.

References

Afgan, N. H., Bogdan, Z., & Duic, N. (Eds.). (2004). *Sustainable development of energy, water and environment system: Proceedings of the Conference*. A. A. Balkema Publishers.

Baker, S., Kousis, M., Richardson, D., & Young, S. (1997). *The politics of sustainable development, theory, policy and practise within the European Union*. Taylor & Francis Group.

Bennett, V. (2022, January 13). EBRD green finance in 2021 hits record 51 per cent of €10.4 billion total. European Bank for Reconstruction and Development. https://www.ebrd.com/news/2022/ebrd-green-finance-in-2021-hits-record-51-per-cent-of-104-billion-total.html

Council Decision (EU). (2016). Council Decision (EU) (2016/1841) of 5 October 2016 on the conclusion, on behalf of the European Union, of the Paris Agreement adopted under the United Nations Framework Convention on Climate Change (OJ L L282). https://eur-lex.europa.eu/legal-content/EN/TXT/PDF/?uri=CELEX:32016D1841&from=EN

Daly, H. E. (2007). *Ecological economics and sustainable development: Selected essays of Herman Daly*. Edward Elgar.

EBRD. (2020, July 10). Green economy transition approach 2021–2025. BDS20-082 (Final). European Bank for Reconstruction and Development.

EBRD. (2021). Guidance Note: Methodology to determine the Paris Agreement alignment of directly financed EBRD investments. European Bank for Reconstruction and Development.

EBRD. (2023, March 1). Shareholders and board of governors. European Bank for Reconstruction and Development. https://www.ebrd.com/shareholders-and-board-of-governors.html

EIB. (2019). The European Commission, EIB and Breakthrough Energy Ventures establish a new eur 100 million fund to support energy investments. European Investment Bank. https://www.eib.org/en/press/all/2019-141-the-european-commission-european-investment-bank-and-breakthrough-energy-ventures-establish-a-new-eur-100-million-fund-to-support-clean-energy-investments

EIB. (2020). The green thread. 2019 activity report. European Investment Bank. https://www.eib.org/attachments/general/reports/eib_activity_report_2019_en.pdf

EIB. (2021a). EIB investment survey 2021. European Union overview. European Investment Bank. https://www.eib.org/attachments/publications/eibis_2021_european_union_en.pdf

EIB. (2021b). Energy overview 2021. European Investment Bank. https://www.eib.org/attachments/thematic/energy_overview_2021_en.pdf

Eissel, D., & Rokicka, E. (1996). Sustainable development and democracy. In D. Eissel, J. Leaman, & E. Rokicka (Eds.), *Towards sustainablility: Challenges to the social sciences and local democracy* (pp. 53–67). University of Łódź.

European Commission. (2021, July 14). "Fit for 55": Delivering the EU's 2030 Climate Target on the way to climate neutrality. Communication from the Commission to the European Parliament, the Council, the European Economic and Social Committee and the Committee of the Regions, Brussels, COM(2021) 550 final. https://eur-lex.europa.eu/legal-content/EN/TXT/PDF/?uri=CELEX:52021DC0550&from=EN

European Commission. (2022, March 8). REPowerEU: Joint European action for more affordable, secure and sustainable energy. Communication from the Commission to the European Parliament. The European Council, the Council, the European Economic and Social Committee and the Committee of The Regions, Strasbourg, COM(2022) 108 final. https://eur-lex.europa.eu/resource.html?uri=cellar:71767319-9f0a-11ec-83e1-01aa75ed71a1.0001.02/DOC_1&format=PDF

European Council. (2021). Energy price rise in 2021 – infografika. Last updated March 31, 2022. Retrieved April 4, 2022. https://www.consilium.europa.eu/pl/infographics/energy-prices-2021/

European Council. (2022, October 24). Council sets out EU position for UN climate summit in Sharm El-Sheikh (COP27). https://www.consilium.europa.eu/en/press/press-releases/2022/10/24/council-sets-out-eu-position-for-un-climate-summit-in-sharm-el-sheikh-cop27/

European Council. (N.d.). Fit for 55. Retrieved April 2, 2022. https://www.consilium.europa.eu/en/policies/green-deal/fit-for-55-the-eu-plan-for-a-green-transition/

European Parliament. (2021). Control of the financial activities of the European Investment Bank – annual report 2019, 2020/2245(INI). https://oeil.secure.europarl.europa.eu/oeil/popups/printficheglobal.pdf?id-720374&l-en

Horton, J., Palumbo, D., & Bowler, T. (2022). Ukraine war: How reliant is the world on Russia for oil and gas? *BBC*. https://www.bbc.com/news/58888451

Rogall, H. (2005). Climate protection as a sphere of action towards a sustainable economy. Rio 5: World Climate & Energy Event, Rio de Janeiro, February 15–17, 2005.

Tester, J. W., Drake, E. M., Driscoll, M. J., Golay, M. W., & Peters, W. A. (2005). *Sustainable Energy: Choosing among options*. MIT Press.

Ullman, R. (1983). Redefining security. *International Security, 8*(1), 140–145.

United Nations. (1987). *Report of the World Commission on Environment and Development: Our common future*. Transmitted to the General Assembly as an Annex to document A/42/427 – Development and International. Co-operation: Environment.

United Nations. (2015a). *The Millennium Development Goals report 2015*.

United Nations. (2015b, October 21). Transforming our world: The 2030 Agenda for Sustainable Development, A/RES/70/1. https://www.refworld.org/docid/57b6e3e44.html

United Nations. (2018). *The Paris Agreement is a health agreement – WHO*. https://unfccc.int/news/the-paris-agreement-is-a-health-agreement-who

World Bank Group. (2021). *Climate Change Action Plan 2021–2025: Supporting green, resilient, and inclusive development*.

CHAPTER 13

Governing Global Health by International Organizations amid the Global Challenges of Today, and Its Impact on Sustainable Development

Ewa Kosycarz

> Without health, SDGs cannot be achieved, and all the SDGs must be achieved in order to improve living conditions and, ultimately, human health and well-being.
>
> WORLD HEALTH ORGANIZATION (2017a, 3)

1 Introduction

This chapter corresponds with the monograph's research field in that it analyzes a given area of GPGs: global health. This chapter aims to show the role of international institutions in the process of providing health-related global public goods (GPGs) that meet the Sustainable Development Goals 2030 (SDGs).

Why are global public goods so important in ensuring global health? Less than one-third of the world's population lives in relative prosperity, while more than two-thirds cannot satisfy their basic needs, including health needs. Thus, ensuring global health has become a significant challenge. The problem only seems to have been aggravating recently due to the most serious health crisis in more than a hundred years due to the SARS-CoV-2 virus.

The consequences of the crisis do not only affect health, but also the economy as a whole, which may translate into difficulties with financing GPGs. The war in Ukraine is yet another threat to global health, as it may result in food supply shortages affecting poor countries, implying a serious toll on the health of the regions' inhabitants. Ukraine produces and exports wheat, corn, and sunflower oil, all of which are imported by low-income countries in Africa and the Middle East. The following countries are fully dependent on wheat imports from Ukraine and Russia: Somalia, Benin, Laos, Egypt, Sudan, DR Congo, Senegal, and Tanzania. This means a catastrophic risk of famine,

 | DOI:10.1163/9789004687264_015

which will affect the health of people living far from where the armed conflict is taking place.

The chapter contributes to the understanding of the challenges of providing global health GPGs in the context of the new sustainable development paradigm, health crises, and famine caused by armed conflicts.

The content of the chapter is structured into six sections. The first section deals with the concept of global public goods related to global health, referring the various definition in the literature. The second section outlines the issues of governing global health. The third section provides a synthetic analysis of the direct and indirect presence of the global health concept in the Sustainable Development Goals 2030. The fourth section presents selected international institutions which, directly or indirectly, pursue the goal of global health. It also includes the activity of grassroots social initiatives aimed at improving the level of health from a global perspective. The fifth section focuses on the activities of institutions and EU-related initiatives concerning the provision of global health goods. The final section analyzes the anticipated and observed difficulties in meeting SDGs for global health. The chapter ends with the presentation of some conclusions.

2 Global Health and Related Global Public Goods

When discussing global health, we first think of it from the humanitarian perspective, that is equal access to medical care and knowledge. Being a growth driver, it is also of importance in the context of economic growth. In recent decades public health has also risen in significance in terms of safety. This has been due to: (1) the spread of communicable diseases, with poor countries being given the most prominence due to ailing or non-existent health-care systems, (2) biological weapons and bio-terrorism threats, and (3) political strategies used in conflicts and influence gaining.

The term "global health" is not unambiguously represented in the literature. Missoni et al. (2019, based on a literature review largely researched by Bozorgmeher) identify four meanings of global health. The first is "all around the world" or "everywhere." The second one relates to health problems that are not limited by state boundaries (e.g., pandemics and the spread of communicable diseases). In line with the third approach, the term "global health" is interpreted as a multidisciplinary concept. It implies that, the study of global health is the study of social, political, economic, biological, and technological relationships that affect health in various ways. The fourth approach applies a term introduced by Scholte: "supra-territoriality," that is, social links which transcend administrative territorial geography (Missoni et al., 2019). Frenk et al.

reconceptualize the term "global health" as "the health of the global population, with a focus on the dense relationships of interdependence across nations and sectors that have arisen with globalization" (Frenk et al., 2014, p. 94). For the analysis in this chapter, we define the term "global health" as public health for world's population with the inevitable impact of globalization processes.

The term "global public goods" (GPGs) is defined as goods that are non-excludable and non-rivalrous in consumption and their provision of benefits to every country (Barrett, 2007). But this is the definition of pure public goods. In addition to pure public goods, impure public goods and club goods are more common in the real world. The concept of global public goods is comprehensively presented in Chapter 1 In this chapter, the focus is on all types of global public goods related to global health. From the point of view of the considerations of this module, it is irrelevant to which category of global public goods the discussed examples belong. However, let us be aware that, like all global public goods, global health-related goods are characterized by differing intensities of consumption characteristics (non-excludable and non-rivalrous).

The literature provides varying definitions of global public goods for global health. They may be broadly interpreted as cross-border functions or interventions that contribute to a higher level of health and which are not produced by market forces (UN, 2020).

It is clear that global health as a concept cannot be just simply physically delivered. However, the provision of global public goods can contribute to global health by serving selected population needs.

In the context of a healthy society, examples of needs provided for by the supply of global public goods are: peace and security, fundamental rules of behavior, and regulations to protect health or knowledge of how to prevent and treat diseases (Moon et al., 2017). Health-related global public goods should, therefore, target these areas. Moon et al. (2017) divided GPGs into three categories: research/assessment, normative functions, and managing externalities.

In the first category, research/assessment, the following were classified as key for health: health technology R&D, marketing approval (e.g., the Food and Drug Administration [FDA], the European Medicines Agency [EMA]), health technology assessment (e.g., UK National Institute for Clinical Excellence [NICE]), product quality assessment (e.g., World Health Organization [WHO]), pre-qualification, good manufacturing practices (GMPs) certification, guidelines/forms (e.g., treatment guidelines, reimbursement decisions), delivery/health systems research/implementation research.

For the second category, normative functions, they named standard setting (e.g., International Classification of Diseases [ICD], Codex Alimentarius [GMP]), regulation (e.g., Framework Convention on Tobacco Control [FCTC], WHO pre-qualification), and policies to preserve the efficacy of antimicrobials.

The last category, managing externalities, embraced public goods such as: communicable disease surveillance, strategic stockpiles of drugs and vaccines for pandemics, and early-warning systems for natural disasters.

Barrett (2007) divided GPGs with respect to who provides and finances the GPG. He distinguished the following categories: *single best efforts* (only a single successful intervention would be required, all the other countries are beneficiaries), *weakest links* (can only be provided with the active participation of every country, requires universal cooperation), *aggregate efforts* (depends on the total efforts of all countries). All these GPG categories need financing. However, Barrett points out two other categories of GPGs which do not need financing: *mutual restraint* and *coordination.*

For the analysis in this chapter, it seems reasonable to address why it is worth delivering certain public goods in the health domain globally. Isn't the care of national systems sufficient? There are a number of arguments for the delivery of GPGs:

- They offer potential benefits to all countries, even if single countries bear the costs.
- Local measures may not ensure that the goal is met, even if huge outlays are made (preventing climate changes, containing the virus from spreading).
- Certain public goods, for instance, the *weakest links* category, would not be effectively delivered if not for international cooperation.
- International cooperation consists of information exchange and may prevent global health emergencies.
- Acting globally, it is possible to partly attend to health prevention and promotion, which largely determine healthy life expectancy.

As pointed out by Barrett (2007), global public goods must be supplied voluntarily. International cooperation could be a kind of organized volunteerism. Therefore, the chapter argues that international cooperation is possible thanks to the major role of international organizations.

3 Global Health Governance

Improving the health of the world's human population is among the main challenges of the 21st century. The various aspects of ensuring healthy societies require the interaction of countries within a region and even between continents. Hence the importance of global health governance (GHG). GHG may be understood as "formal and informal institutions, rules and processes by states, intergovernmental organizations, and non-state actors to deal with health challenges that require cross-border collective action to be addressed effectively" (Fidler, 2010, p. 3).

GHG forms a complex system that can be characterized as multi-sectoral, multi-actor, multi-institutional, multi-principle, and multi-instrumental system, as described in Chapter 2 In the context of Chapter 2, for each of these characteristics, some main developments can be discerned:

- *Subjects*: As in the general case of global governance, differentiated governance systems have emerged in GHG, depending on the fields of action. Interventions stem from differentiated measures to raise the level of global health. For example, prevention against communicable diseases (vaccination), health promotion for non-communicable diseases, clean air, access to nutritious food, systems for monitoring the spread of diseases, or building effective and efficient health systems. Over time, the thematic scope of the system has expanded considerably. Moreover, some IOs have increased their area of interest. The best example is the World Bank (WB), which has entered the remit of the WHO and, up to a certain point, competed with it.
- *Actors*: As Moon writes, "GHG can best be characterized as a network, in which independent purposive actors negotiate the rules that will regulate their relations, rather than a hierarchy or market" (Moon, 2021, p. 235).
- *Legal forms and competences*: Hundreds of actors have engaged in GHG influencing agendas, rulemaking, implementation, monitoring, and enforcement (Moon, 2021). These actors work in different forms of formal and informal governance arrangements. Some institutions are large, international treaty-based organizations with strong bureaucratic and financial support (WHO, WB). Others consist of transnational private (Bill and Melinda Gates Foundation [BMGF]) or hybrid arrangements (Gavi, the Vaccine Alliance). In addition to structures with a strong formal basis, the occurrence of civil society organizations (CSOs) is also observed.
- *Principles*: In the case of GHGs, the adoption of common principles seems unproblematic. However, the history of the WHO shows that adopted priorities for international action can be influenced by international politics (Moon, 2021).
- *Instruments*: In the case of GHG, soft instruments such as monitoring, persuasion, dissemination of standards, information exchange, etc. predominate among the instruments used.

In the case of the evolution of GHGs, an additional feature should be mentioned: the *sources of funding* and the associated pressure on expenditure allocation. Funds raised in the form of statutory contributions from countries affiliated to an international institution appear to be less subject to pressure from donor countries. In the case of funds from donors not bound by co-financing treaties, there is a risk of dedicating the donation to a specific purpose that the donor has, not necessarily the international organization.

There are at least two main risks in the way of proper GHG: the risk of inefficient and ineffective governance resulting from the structure of the IO network and the risk of insufficient financial resources.

The first one stems from underperformance in managing a network of fragmented actors. This is due to uncoordinated initiatives, often competing for funding. Such undertakings are typically focused on certain diseases, types of intervention, and population groups. Globally, it is the lack of a coordinating body and even of any adjustment mechanism that is to blame. This leads to an inefficient allocation of resources, carried out on the basis of ad hoc criteria decided by the attractiveness of aspects such as donor indications, public opinion assessment, foreign, economic or security policy priorities, etc., rather than the rationale of global health needs (Lee & Brumme, 2012).

The second risk stems from irrational priorities in the global community. It is worth noting the proportions in health spending by key institutions, such as the WHO, versus the incomes of top managers or the world's military spending. The Health Assembly – approved program budget for 2018–2019 totaled US$4.4 billion (WHO, 2020). During the 2008 financial crisis, when the world economy was deep in recession, the Wall Street bankers paid themselves bonuses amounting to US$18.4 billion (Węcławski, 2015), while in 2019 alone military spending was estimated at US$1.922 trillion (Glapiak, 2020).

According to Frenk (Frenk, 2010, p. 1): "Health has been increasingly recognized as a key element of sustainable economic development, global security, effective governance and human rights promotion." Hence, it seems obvious to link global health to the Sustainable Development Goals Agenda 2030.

4 Global Health in Sustainable Development Goals 2030

> The health-related targets are not limited to only SDG 3; many of the SDG s also have targets directly and/or indirectly related to health, reflecting the complex pattern of health determinants.
>
> WORLD HEALTH ORGANIZATION (2017A, 3)

Ever since the 1990s, the assessment of countries' economic development has come to include broadly understood human health. Amartya Sen, the Nobel prize winner, pioneered this approach. His theory inspired the *Human Development Report 1990: Concept and Measurement of Human Development* (UNDP, 1990). In later years there were numerous international discussions, which had laid the foundations for what gave rise to the Millennium Declaration of 2000. Another major step involve human beings in the assessment model of sustainable economic development was the United Nations Conference on Sustainable Development of June 2012 which decided on the development of the Sustainable Development Goals (SDGs).

The determinants of global health are multifaceted and encompass a range of factors, beyond those exclusively associated with the development and accessibility of health technologies. They include such areas as the development of communication technologies, consequences of climate changes, energy prices, environmental pollution, food quality and accessibility, the level of social inequality, and consequences of economic crises:

- *Communication technology* has massively affected the transmission and storage of information on hazards, e.g., epidemiological hazards.
- *Climate changes* have their adverse effect on food supply and water access, and in extreme cases some areas are exposed to the risk of flooding, which forces their inhabitants to migrate.
- *Energy prices* affect the prices of food and medicine transportation, as well as the accessibility of travel to medical facilities, which is of particular importance in poorer regions of the world. Energy prices will also affect living conditions in low temperatures, which may, in turn, influence the level of health.
- *Environmental pollution* impacts human health through the respiratory system (air pollution), as well as through contaminated food and water (e.g., microplastics).
- *Shortage of nutritious and diversified food* directly affects the health of the population.
- *Social inequality* leads to economic crises affecting real disposable income, which inhibits access to medical benefits and supplies.
- *Economic crises* national health systems to reduce health-care financing and so do international organizations, which find it increasingly difficult to raise funds.

With such a broad array of global health determinants, it is clear that pursuing the third SDG (Goal 3: To ensure healthy lives and promote well-being for everyone at all ages) is partly realized through other SDGs. It includes, in particular, the following goals: Goal 1 (End poverty in all its forms everywhere), Goal 2 (End hunger, achieve food security and improved nutrition and promote sustainable agriculture), Goal 4 (Ensure inclusive and equitable quality education and promote lifelong learning opportunities for everyone), Goal 5 (Achieve gender equality and empower all women and girls), Goal 6 (Ensure availability and sustainable management of water and sanitation for all), Goal 7 (Ensure access to affordable, reliable, sustainable and modern energy for all), Goal 10 (Reduce inequalities within and among countries), Goal 13 (Take urgent action to combat climate change and its impacts), Goal 14 (Conserve and sustainably use the oceans, seas and marine resources for sustainable development), Goal 15 (Protect, restore and promote sustainable use of terrestrial ecosystems, sustainably manage forests, combat desertification, halt and reverse land degradation and halt biodiversity loss). The aforementioned goals are strictly related to the health of the world's population. The pursuit of the remaining goals, which were not directly mentioned in this paragraph, will indirectly improve humans' living conditions, which, in turn, will positively affect their health.

In addition to the actions of "ordinary citizens," governments, and national NGOs, international organizations play a leading role in achieving the goals of Agenda 2030. International organizations serve as pivotal actors in this regard, gathering a diverse array of states and private entities. The following section provides a succinct overview of selected institutions and concise depictions of their respective missions.

5 Governing Global Health by International Organizations and its Impact on Sustainable Development

As mentioned earlier, GHG forms a complex system that can be characterized as multi-sectoral, multi-actor, multi-institutional, multi-principle, and multi-instrumental system. The institutions that manage, finance, and deliver global public goods related to global health form a network rather than a hierarchy. These institutions come in diverse legal forms and operate in different geographical areas and sectors related to global health. For the purposes of this subsection, we propose to present them in three subgroups: classical international institutions, civil society organizations, and initiatives based on information and monitoring systems.

5.1 *Classical International Organizations*

According to Moon et al. (2017), the global health system must perform four main functions: managing cross-border externalities; mobilizing global solidarity for disadvantaged populations; stewardship of the overall functioning of the system; and ensuring the adequate provision of GPGs. There are numerous international organizations that aim to perform the aforesaid functions. Their origins date back to the 19th century, when international health management came to be consolidated under the International Sanitary Conference of 1851 held in Paris. The subsequent steps to establish international organizations managing global health included the formation of the International Sanitary Bureau in 1902, the Office International d'Hygiène Publique (OIHP) in 1907, and the Health Organization of the League of Nations in 1920, as well as the World Health Organization (WHO) in 1948. In recent years, the role of private entities in global health management has grown. It takes on varied forms, including as coalitions, alliances, and more or less structured public and private partnerships.

Performing the said functions via a broad array of institutions aiming to ensure better global health often coincides with the pursuance of Agenda 2030. Not only is it directly through following SDG 3, but also indirectly through other SDGs, as shown in the preceding paragraphs. Table 13.1 shows examples of international organizations and their programs pursuing the health goals of Agenda 2030.

Examples of institutions managing cross-border externalities include the WHO, the Centers for Disease Control and Prevention (CDC), and the European Centre for Disease Prevention and Control (ECDC).

Functions mobilizing global solidarity for disadvantaged populations are demonstrated in the activities of most of the organizations in Table 13.1,

TABLE 13.1 International organizations and their health initiatives under agenda 2030

International organization	**International organization/ Policy framework/ Program/Action**	**Short description**
World Bank (WB)	International organization	"WB is like a cooperative, made up of 189 member countries. The World Bank Group is one of the world's largest sources of funding and knowledge for developing countries. Its five institutions share a commitment to reducing poverty, increasing shared prosperity, and promoting sustainable development" (World Bank, n.d.).
World Health Organization (WHO)	International organization	The WHO is an agency of the United Nations responsible for international public health It strictly implements the goals of the 2030 Agenda. Even the structure of the organization is being adapted to the more effective implementation of the 2030 Agenda.

TABLE 13.1 International organizations and their health initiatives under agenda 2030 (*cont.*)

International organization	International organization/ Policy framework/ Program/Action	Short description
United Nations Children's Fund (UNICEF)	International organization	UNICEF is an agency of the United Nations. Main activities: providing immunizations and disease prevention, enhancing childhood and maternal nutrition, improving sanitation, promoting education, and providing emergency relief in response to disasters.
Coalition for Epidemic Preparedness Innovations (CEPI)	Foundation	"CEPI is an innovative global partnership between public, private, philanthropic, and civil society organizations. We're working together to accelerate the development of vaccines against emerging infectious diseases and enable equitable access to these vaccines for people during outbreaks" (CEPI, n.d.).
Gavi, the Vaccine Alliance	Public – private partnership	Gavi helps vaccinate half the world's children against some of the world's deadliest diseases. It brings together developing country and donor governments, the World Health Organization, UNICEF, the World Bank, the vaccine industry, technical agencies, civil society, the Bill & Melinda Gates Foundation, and other private sector partners (www.gavi.org).
COVID-19 Vaccines Global Access (COVAX)	Worldwide initiative	COVAX is co-led by CEPI, Gavi, and WHO, alongside key delivery partner UNICEF.
WHO Regional Office for Europe	Overall activity	WHO/Europe's efforts to address the social determinants of health can be grouped into the following six areas of work:

TABLE 13.1 International organizations and their health initiatives under agenda 2030 (*cont.*)

International organization	International organization/ Policy framework/ Program/Action	Short description
		"1. Technical assistance services to countries, including capacity building and learning exchange 2. Evidence, data collection, and analysis 3. Gender and health 4. Promoting the health of vulnerable groups 5. Strengthening local-level governance – Healthy Cities 6. Strengthening governance at subnational level – Regions for Health Network" (WHO, 2011, p. 2)
Health 2020: WHO Regional Office for Europe	Policy framework	Health 2020 is the health policy framework for the European region (53 countries) supporting action across government and society for health and well-being. "It focuses on improving health for all and reducing health inequalities, through improved leadership and governance for health" (WHO, 2013, p. ii).
The International Federation of Red Cross and Red Crescent Societies (IFRC)	Overall activity	"With our 192 member National Red Cross and Red Crescent Societies worldwide, we are in virtually every community reaching 160.7 million people annually through long-term services and development programmes, as well as 110 million people through disaster response and early recovery programmes" (IFRC, 2021).

TABLE 13.1 International organizations and their health initiatives under agenda 2030 (*cont.*)

International organization	International organization/ Policy framework/ Program/Action	Short description
Global Alliance on Health and Pollution (GAPH)	GAHP is a collaborative body of more than 60 members and dozens of observers that advocate for resources and solutions to pollution problems	"GAHP is a network of international and national level agencies committed to a collaborative, multi-sectoral approach to address the global pollution crisis and the resulting health and economic impacts" (GAHP, n.d.).
More than a hundred mayors from leading cities and towns from around the world at the 9th Global Conference on Health Promotion	Shanghai Consensus on Healthy Cities 2016; policy framework	Participants of the conference "reaffirmed the vision of Healthy Cities and the Ottawa Charter for Health Promotion and committed politically to growing the global Healthy Cities movement" (WHO, 2017b).
Over 1,100 organizations and more than 58,000 networks involved in the preparations of the New Urban Agenda	New Urban Agenda; policy framework	"By readdressing the way cities and human settlements are planned, designed, financed, developed, governed and managed, the New Urban Agenda will help to […] improve human health and wellbeing" (New Urban Agenda, 2016).
European Health Information Initiative (EHII)	WHO network	Stakeholders include member states, WHO collaborating centers, health information networks and associations such as the European Association of Public Health (EUPHA), and charitable foundations such as the Wellcome Trust. The European Commission and the Organisation for Economic Co-operation and Development (OECD) are also active participants.

TABLE 13.1 International organizations and their health initiatives under agenda 2030 (*cont.*)

International organization	International organization/ Policy framework/ Program/Action	Short description
WHO, European Health Information Initiative, Central Asian Republics Information Network (CARINFONET)	Network	"CARINFONET is a collaborative network of five countries and a platform for improving health information systems. It promotes collaboration within and between countries in the region of central Asia to produce relevant, objective and accurate statistics" (WHO, n.d.).
Pure Earth	International non-profit organization	Pure Earth is dedicated to solving toxic pollution problems (lead and mercury) in low- and middle-income countries, where human health is at risk (Pure Earth, n.d.).
Institute for Health Metrics and Evaluation (IHME)	Research organization	"IHME works with collaborators around the world to develop timely, relevant, and scientifically valid evidence that illuminates the state of health everywhere" (IHME, 2014).
UNHCR, the UN High Commissioner for Refugees	International organization	"UNHCR works with governments and partners to provide emergency health services, improve local health services and include refugees in national health systems and plans" (UNHCR, n.d.).
EU + United Kingdom, Iceland, Norway, Montenegro, North Macedonia, Serbia, and Turkey	EU Civil Protection Mechanism	"The EU Civil Protection Mechanism is a system established in 2001 for coordinating rescue and humanitarian assistance in the event of natural and man-made disasters whose scale or nature exceeds the response capabilities of the affected country (legal basis – Decision 1313/13/EU)" (Government of Poland, n.d.).

TABLE 13.1 International organizations and their health initiatives under agenda 2030 (*cont.*)

International organization	International organization/ Policy framework/ Program/Action	Short description
Emergency Response Coordination Centre (ERCC)	Integrated operational center	"ERCC is the heart of the EU Civil Protection Mechanism. It coordinates the delivery of assistance to disaster-stricken countries, such as relief items, expertise, civil protection teams and pecialized equipment" (European Commission, n.d.-a).
European Centre for Disease Prevention and Control (ECDC)	International/European organization	"ECDC is an EU agency aimed at strengthening Europe's defenses against infectious diseases. The core functions cover a wide spectrum of activities: surveillance, epidemic intelligence, response, scientific advice, microbiology, preparedness, public health training, international relations, health communication" (ECDC, n.d.).
European Medicines Agency (EMA)	International/European organization	"The mission of the EMA is to foster scientific excellence in the evaluation and supervision of medicines, for the benefit of public and animal health in the EU" (EMA, 2018).
Centers for Disease Control and Prevention (CDC)	National organization in USA	"CDC is the nation's leading science-based, data-driven, service organization that protects the public's health" (CDC, 2022).
Food and Drug Administration (FDA)	National organizations in USA	"The Food and Drug Administration is responsible for protecting the public health by ensuring the safety, efficacy, and security of human and veterinary drugs, biological products, and medical devices; and by ensuring the safety of our nation's food supply, cosmetics, and products that emit radiation" (FDA, 2021).

SOURCE: OWN ELABORATION

especially the International Federation of Red Cross and Red Crescent Societies or the United Nations Children's Fund (UNICEF). The WHO and its regional branches are the best examples of performing the stewardship function for how the system works in general. The last function, ensuring the adequate provision of GPGs, is extremely important. Gavi, the Vaccine Alliance, is an international organization that performs this function. The institutions often cooperate by combining different functions in providing GPGs. In this way, new institutional arrangements emerge in the form of partnerships and networks. The eradication of smallpox in 1977 is an example of such successful cooperation, as it was achieved thanks to WHO coordination combined with financing from rich countries. Unfortunately, it was not possible to eliminate all diseases, such as malaria, although the number of cases and deaths has been considerably shrinking (Brown et al., 2006).

5.2 *Civil Society Organizations*

In tandem with the international organizations established by governments, it is also imperative to recognize the significance of informal international organizations, originating from the bottom up, and fostered by the passion and dedication of volunteers. They do not use public funds or public infrastructure, but they provide the international community with public goods. An example is Global Citizen (https://www.globalcitizen.org), which was set up in 2008 as a Global Poverty Project in Melbourne, Australia. Its founder, Hugh Evans, defined the overall goal of Global Citizen as the ending of extreme poverty by 2030. This precisely corresponds with the goals of Agenda 2030. Through mass volunteer activities, Global Citizen seeks to influence politicians deciding on issues such as health, security, and climate, and to raise funds for particular causes from individuals, companies, or governments. In the area of health they launched campaigns such as COVID-19 vaccinations, polio eradication, "Help Raise Awareness about the World's Most Neglected Diseases." "Stand up for Ukraine" (Global Citizen, 2022a) is an example of a recent fundraising campaign, in which US$10.1 billion was pledged in new grants and loans to support those who have had to flee their homes in Ukraine (Global Citizen, 2022b). It very well illustrates the strength when people come together to realize a common good across borders.

5.3 *Initiatives Based on Information and Monitoring Systems*

In the case of the current coronavirus pandemic, a quick response and identification of potential virus outbreaks are key to the global health concept. To achieve these, activities aimed at an early diagnosis and immediate response that are to prevent the spread of communicable diseases have been carried out. Numerous online surveillance systems have been developed, which process data in real time using a wide range of technology and data sources so as to prevent communicable diseases; the systems are still being expanded and monitored (Choi et al., 2016; Lombardo et al., 2003).

Many organizations worldwide, international, and national, seek to gather information on epidemic hazards. Next to traditional data collection, internet-based disease surveillance programs have been developing in recent years. They base on information from various sources, including social media. Among the first of such systems was ProMED-mail, which started in the US in 1994. Its task was to detect emerging communicable diseases and toxins dangerous to humans, animals, and crops, as well as the risks associated with their potential use for bioterrorism (Madoff & Woodall, 2005). At the outset, ProMED-mail included 40 scientists from seven countries. Its first report provide information from an American laboratory on infections with the Sabia virus, which caused Brazilian hemorrhagic fever. Information on identified disease emergencies was disseminated via electronic mail. The network of scientists, medical and veterinary doctors, and institutions affiliated with ProMED-mail grew very quickly, which proved the velocity whereby information circulated in the world. In 2020 the system had over 80,000 subscribers representing almost every country in the world (Bonilla-Aldana et al., 2020). In numerous cases, it was from ProMED-mail members that the WHO learned about epidemic hazards. SARS became first known to the Western world thanks to a report generated by the network on February 10, 2003 (Madoff & Woodall, 2005). Systems such as ProMED warn international communities of disease cases in the world, and they support communities in identifying new epidemic outbreaks. However, they require further formalization. Indeed, as suggested by the authors of "Coronavirus Infections Reported by ProMED," reports sent to the system should be standardized for better quality (Bonilla-Aldana et al., 2020).

Monitoring systems are not institutions, but a priceless tool in the hands of international and national institutions, enabling globalization of health management. They can even be treated as a public good. Next to ProMED-mail, other systems for collection and immediate dissemination of health hazard data also deserve attention. They include the Canadian GPHIN, GOARN (run by the WHO and the UN), the American EpiSimS, Health Map, EpiSPIDER and Google Flu Trends, the Japanese BioCaster, Swedish GET WELL, as well as the European MedISys and Influenzanet (Choi et al., 2016; Lombardo et al., 2003, Velasco et al., 2014).

6 Regional Public Goods in Health Care: the European Union Experience

In the European Union, health policy is the responsibility of member states, especially in terms of financing and managing health systems. However, it does not mean that the EU alone is totally passive in the area of health.

Analysis of Article 168 of the Treaty on the Functioning of the European Union (TFEU) shows that a substantial part of areas where EU institutions should be involved concerns ensuring health across borders, i.e., combating, warning against, and examining the causes of epidemics. Article 168 is about measures in the area of both veterinary and phytosanitary studies to directly protect public health. In other words, it concerns problems on which a part of the objectives of Agenda 2030 is focused.

In its activity so far, the European Union has demonstrated health efforts from two perspectives: long-term efforts aiming to provide good health to the community's inhabitants and crisis management in health emergencies.

6.1 *Long-Term Health Efforts*

In the first case, the European Union particularly emphasizes preventing non-communicable diseases by promoting health. Coupled with prophylactics, promotion is of vital importance today because, as shown by the outcome of research by McKeown (1973) and McKinlay and McKinlay (1977), medical progress affects the average life expectancy to a lesser degree than environmental factors, also including those that can be labeled lifestyle components (Ostrowska, 1999). Whether and how the aspects are attended to determines the spending on curative medicine. Depending on the research, the degree to which certain habits making up human behavior will affect health is between 30% and 50% (Espey et al., 2014; McGinnis et al., 2002). Meanwhile, in line with literature's estimates, the influence of medical care in this case is between 10% and 20% (McGovern, 2014), and according to McGinnis, Williams-Russo, and Knickman, the spending of medical service accounts for around 95% of total health-care spending (McGinnis et al., 2002).

Efforts in the area of promotion and prophylactics focus on the introduction of regulations (such as Directive 2014/40/EU of the European Parliament and of the Council of 3 April 2014, on the approximation of the laws, regulations, and administrative provisions of the member states on the manufacture, presentation, and sale of tobacco and related products and repealing Directive 2001/37/EC) and the launch of programs to finance the efforts of individual member states. They concern education and promotion of healthy lifestyles, building infrastructure to foster healthy lifestyles, taking care of the environment, including clean air, water and biodiversity. One of the European Commission's priorities for 2019–2024 also fits into this context, namely the European Green Deal strategy (European Commission, n.d.-b).

Other long-term health efforts at the EU level include the establishment of institutions at the community level: the European Food Safety Authority (EFSA), the European Centre for Disease Prevention and Control (ECDC),[1] the European Medicines Agency (EMA). These institutions, often jointly, pursue health efforts. An example is A European "One Health" Action Plan against Antimicrobial Resistanc. Statistical data shows how important these initiatives are. In the case of antimicrobial resistance alone, 25,000 deaths yearly are recorded in EU countries and the related costs are estimated at €1.5 billion (The EU Action Plan against Antimicrobial Resistance[2]).

6.2 *Crisis Management in Health Emergencies*

With regard to analysis of EU activities from the perspective of crisis management in health emergencies it is worth mentioning Strategic Plan 2016–2020 – Health & Food Safety, which allows for such objectives as "better preparedness, prevention and response to human, animal and plant health threats" (European Commission, 2016).

1 The ECDC is the major monitoring institution for COVID-19. As part of its activities, it provides risk assessments to assist member states and the EC in their response to individual pandemic developments. See "ECDC Novel coronavirus" (2020), https://www.ecdc.europa.eu/en/novel-coronavirus-china (retrieved on May 16, 2020). The ECDC has drafted numerous documents, including technical reports, statements, risk assessments, and algorithms which relate to, among other things, diagnosing, managing, and preventing the spread of COVID-10. See, e.g., "ECDC statement following reported confirmed case of 2019-nCoV in Germany," https://www.ecdc.europa.eu/en/news-events/ecdc-statement-following-reported-confirmed-case-2019-ncov-germany (retrieved on May 16, 2020); "ECDC algorithm for management of contacts of probable or confirmed 2019-nCoV cases," https://www.ecdc.europa.eu/en/publications-data/algorithm-management-contacts-probable-or-confirmed-2019-ncov-cases (retrieved on May 16, 2020); "ECDC Infection prevention and control for the care of patients with 2019-nCoV in health-care settings," https://www.ecdc.europa.eu/en/publications-data/infection-prevention-and-control-care-patients-2019-ncov-healthcare-settings (retrieved on June 25, 2020); "Public health management of persons having had contact with novel coronavirus cases in the European Union," https://www.ecdc.europa.eu/en/publications-data/public-health-management-persons-having-had-contact-novel-coronavirus-cases (retrieved on May 16, 2020); "ECDC Risk assessment: Outbreak of acute respiratory syndrome associated with a novel coronavirus. China: The first local transmission in the EU/EEA – third update," https://www.ecdc.europa.eu/en/publications-data/risk-assessment-outbreak-acute-respiratory-syndrome-associated-novel-1 (retrieved on May 16, 2020).

2 https://audiovisual.ec.europa.eu/en/video/I-139884?lg=PL (retrieved on May 26, 2020).

Decision no. 1082/2013/EU of the European Parliament and of the Council of 22 October 2013, which introduces a crisis management system in the case of threats to health in the European Union, was a very important step in implementing health safety coordination for EU citizens. This solution is based on cooperation and coordinating efforts among member states. The abovementioned decision concerns the cooperation of various institutions, the activities of which include: transmission of diseases between the human and animal worlds, bacterial drug resistance, plant-borne biotoxins, and environmental threats, including climate change. This decision also made it possible to place joint orders for medical supplies (e.g., vaccines or medications), encouraged knowledge and good practices sharing, and enabled epidemiological surveillance over a few dozen diseases in Europe. In addition, ad hoc monitoring is envisaged for health, environmental, or biotoxin contamination hazards. Pursuant to the decision, the EU Health Security Committee was set up.[3]

The said decision is not the first step to coordinate health hazards in the EU. Almost a decade earlier, the Parliament and the Council issued a Regulation (EC) no. 851/2004 of 21 April 2004 establishing the European Centre for Disease Prevention and Control (ECDC). The ECDC has competencies in surveillance and risk assessment of human health threats from communicable diseases and diseases of unknown origin. It is also responsible for the Early Warning and Response System (EWRS), which is an internet-based platform providing a link between the European Commission, ECDC and public health authorities in member states.

The coronavirus pandemic accelerated the formation of regional health management structures, and it strengthened the to-date institutions. During the pandemic, institutions such as ECDC and EMA had their scopes of competencies broadened. The first one expanded its powers and tasks to include: a network of reference laboratories, modern epidemiological surveillance, issuing recommendations on activities to control epidemic outbreaks, and specific response recommendations. In addition, the EWRS was enhanced. The EMA was conferred additional powers to monitor and minimize the effects of

3 The HSC's tasks are the following: (a) supporting the exchange of information between member states and the Commission on the experience acquired with regard to the implementation of this Decision; (b) coordination in liaison with the Commission of the preparedness and response planning of the member states in accordance with Article 4; (c) coordination in liaison with the Commission of the risk and crisis communication and responses of member states to serious cross-border threats to health, in accordance with Article 11 (quoted from Decision no. 1082).

shortages of drugs and medical devices due to serious circumstances, to advise on drugs that can be used to treat or diagnose the disease causing an epidemic outbreak or to prevent it, to coordinate studies monitoring the effectiveness and safety of vaccines, and also to coordinate and advise on clinical trials of drugs. In September 2021 the European Commission launched the Health Emergency Preparedness and Response Authority (HERA). HERA is to be a major pillar of the European Health Union and bridge the gap in the EU health emergency response and preparedness system.

The initiatives and institutions mentioned earlier on in this section bear more on regional management of the health of the European Union's population, with possible benefits for neighboring regions, such as, for instance, the European Green Deal. However, both the authorities and the member states of the European Union are aware that health management should be perceived more broadly and multidimensionally, hence the EU global health policy was defined in 2010. It announced working in partnership with all other relevant organizations and interest groups for global health, in the areas of trade, financing, development aid, migration, security, climate change and environment action, and research and innovation.

A breakthrough moment for global health came on May 19, 2022, at a G7 Development and Health Ministerial meeting, whereby work started on a new EU Global Health Strategy. Experts point to a number of reasons why it is necessary to introduce an EU Global Health Strategy:

- The primary reason is the need for an agreed set of principles and priorities to guide the European Union's activities and investments in global health.
- To create the conditions for the EU to be represented in external relations when deciding on global health.
- To prepare the conditions for the European Health Union to function.
- To enable a better understanding of the links between national, regional, and global health.
- The strategy, when adopted, will allow the promotion of European values in the global arena, such as universal values of human rights, equity, solidarity, and cooperation.
- It will help build partnerships in health with regions from other parts of the world.
- Global health is a geopolitical issue.

As health is interlinked with numerous policies, such as, climate, trade, security, and social policies, the Global Health Strategy is vital with regards to pursuing the goals of Agenda 2030.

7 Causes of Hampering the Supply of Global Public Goods for Global Health

In spite of the efforts of existing international institutions (and any other more or less formalized organizations) to supply global public goods in health care, the results are not spectacular. A lot of work is still required, as well as extensive funding to global public goods, in order to meet the global health goals of Agenda 2030.

It was the coronavirus pandemic that painfully brought to light the limited effectiveness of activities for the health of the international community. From the very onset of the pandemic we have observed inequality in access to medical supplies and medications, from personal protective equipment to vaccines.

In particular, market failures and the institutional deficits are to blame for failed management and supply of global public goods:

- Market failures appear when players' optimization decisions do not reach the social optimum. In the case of health decisions, market failures are connected with externalities, public goods, and information asymmetry. They also entail consequences for the present and the future generations. When a person decides whether or not to be vaccinated, they focus on the benefits and costs while ignoring the positive externalities imposed on strangers.
- Yet another market failure is related to insufficient efforts targeting epidemiological surveillance and intelligence.
- The world's wealthy countries are more willing to subsidize the fight against hazards they may be directly affected by themselves. Hence the worse results in providing GPGs with regards to measles, poliomyelitis, and dracunculiasis.
- High income elasticity and low price responsiveness of certain medications and treatment regimens motivate pharmaceutical companies to concentrate on diseases that are more important for high income countries.
- The activities of numerous international institutions (formal and informal) are not necessarily coordinated, which impedes their effectiveness and efficiency on a global scale.
- The activities of public and private (as well as charity) organizations often produce impressive results. However, according to Peacock (2022), there are many potential conflicts of interests in the case of public and private partnerships that are neither democratically elected nor publicly accountable.

8 Conclusions

The SARS-Cov-2 pandemic highlighted the importance of global public goods in the area of health, which contributes to the realization of the Sustainable Development Goals 2030. The global public goods in health that were provided by international institutions during the pandemic included: monitoring of virus spread; quarantine requirement and enforcement; development of the vaccine and medications; knowledge of how to treat it, what the symptoms are, and therapeutic procedures; acquisition and dissemination of knowledge on how to protect oneself on a daily basis to avoid infection; acquisition and dissemination of knowledge of how to organize hospitals or the health-care system; vaccination programs for indigent regions; social campaigns convincing member of the public to get vaccinated; joint purchase of medications, medical supplies, personal protective equipment, etc.

Fruitless efforts of certain institutions were also very conspicuous. In the initial phase, ineffective action allowed the virus to spread around the world. When the pandemic became established, huge deficiencies were disclosed, in particular in personal protective and medical equipment (ventilators). As a consequence, disparate access to medical technologies, including but not limited to vaccinations and therapeutic interventions, has been observed. The period of the pandemic has served as a litmus test for the efficacy of global and regional institutions, which regrettably, have not all emerged unscathed. The roots of this failure, resulting in excess deaths and lasting complications, are to be traced back to institution underfinancing, lack of adequate coordination, lack of proper preparation for a fast production of, for instance, personal protective equipment or vaccines, and nationalism, which was particularly noticeable in vaccine redistribution. Sharing intellectual property rights also became a problem.

The year 2022 is a time when the prospect of maintaining global health and pursuing the Sustainable Development Goals 2030 seems extremely difficult. Events of the past 2 years will have serious consequences, which will require international organizations to intensify their efforts to accumulate financial sources and step up activities to provide global public goods.

The war in Ukraine entails a real risk of reduced food supply worldwide. This will particularly affect poor countries that need the most support in building better living conditions, including the aspect of health. Moreover, the war is accompanied by economic sanctions imposed on Russia and Belarus, which is globally driving energy prices. As already mentioned, it also has an adverse effect on global health. Economic sanctions hit both sides of the conflict, hence economic problems are to be expected. Regrettably, they will be negatively reflected in the level of accessible funds devoted to global health.

Economic problems may be aggravated by subsequent COVID-19 lockdowns and the related disrupted supply chains (e.g., lockdown of Shanghai, a city of 24 million people in April 2022[4]). Problems related to the economy and access to gas may affect the pace of realization of Goal 7 (Ensure access to affordable, reliable, sustainable and modern energy for all) and Goal 13 (Take urgent action to combat climate change and its impacts).

Each armed conflict causes forced migration, which normally entails a deterioration of the refugees' living conditions, and thus their health. According to the UNHCR, the number of refugees has been steadily growing for 11 years due to persecution, armed conflicts or human rights violation. In mid-2022, the number of people fleeing reached 103 million people.[5] Given the current elevated figures and the exponential surge in refugee populations, it will be challenging for international and national organizations to realize Target 10.7 (Facilitate orderly, safe, and responsible migration and mobility of people, including through implementation of planned and well-managed migration policies).

It seems that in order to achieve the health-centered goals of Agenda 2030 it will be necessary to focus maximum efforts on coordinated international cooperation to boost effectiveness and efficiency of global public goods provision. The world cannot afford to waste any funds due to particular interests, fragmentation of efforts, lack of coordination, no success guaranteeing priorities in place, or failing to conscientiously pursuit them. The situation demands that the international community be open to global needs, dialogue, and acceptance of compromise, which is normally not satisfactory for all sides. The world is facing a difficult task indeed.

References

Barrett, S. (2007). *Why cooperate? The incentive to supply global public goods*. Oxford University Press.

Bonilla-Aldana, D. K., Holguin-Rivera, Y., Cortes-Bonilla, I., Cardona-Trujillo, M. C., García-Barco, A., Bedoya-Arias, H. A., Rabaan, A. A., Sah, R., & Rodriguez-Morales, A. J. (2020). Coronavirus infections reported by ProMED, February 2000–January

4 The port of Shanghai is the world's largest in terms of the size of container transshipment.

5 https://www.unhcr.org/spotlight/2023/01/2023-a-moment-of-truth-for-global-displacement/

2020. *Travel Medicine and Infectious Disease*, 101575. https://doi.org/10.1016/j.tmaid.2020.101575

Brown, T. M., Cueto, M., & Fee, E. (2006). The World Health Organization and the transition from "international" to "global" public health. *American Journal of Public Health*, *96*(1), 62–72. https://doi.org/10.2105/AJPH.2004.050831

CDC. (2022, June 15). About CDC. Centers for Disease Control and Prevention. https://www.cdc.gov/about/index.html

CEPI. (N.d.). A global coalition for a global problem. Retrieved April 10, 2022. https://cepi.net/about/whoweare/

Choi, J., Cho, Y., Shim, E., & Woo, H. (2016). Web-based infectious disease surveillance systems and public health perspectives: A systematic review. *BMC Public Health*, *16*(1), 1238. https://doi.org/10.1186/s12889-016-3893-0

ECDC. (N.d.). About ECDC. European Centre for Disease Prevention and Control. Retrieved July 18, 2022. https://www.ecdc.europa.eu/en/about-ecdc

EMA. (2018, September 17). About us. European Medicines Agency. https://www.ema.europa.eu/en/about-us/what-we-do

Espey, D. K., Jim, M. A., Cobb, N., Bartholomew, M., Becker, T., Haverkamp, D., & Plescia, M. (2014). Leading causes of death and all-cause mortality in American Indians and Alaska Natives. *American Journal of Public Health*, *104 Suppl 3*(Suppl 3), S303–S311. https://doi.org/10.2105/AJPH.2013.301798

European Commission. (2016, July 19). Strategic plan 2016–2020 – Health and Food Safety. https://commission.europa.eu/publications/strategic-plan-2016-2020-health-and-food-safety_en

European Commission. (N.d.-a). Emergency Response Coordination Centre (ERCC) factsheet. Retrieved April 10, 2022. https://ec.europa.eu/echo/what/civil-protection/emergency-response-coordination-centre-ercc_en

European Commission. (N.d.-b). A European Green Deal: Striving to be the first climate-neutral continent. https://commission.europa.eu/strategy-and-policy/priorities-2019-2024/european-green-deal_en

FDA. (2021, June 28). What we do. Food and Drug Administration. https://www.fda.gov/about-fda/what-we-do

Fidler, D. P. (2010, May). The challenges of global health governance. Working Paper. Council on Foreign Relations.

Frenk, J. (2010). The global health system: Strengthening national health systems as the next step for global progress. *PLoS Medicine*, *7*(1), e1000089. https://doi.org/10.1371/journal.pmed.1000089

Frenk, J., Gómez-Dantés, O., & Moon, S. (2014). From sovereignty to solidarity: A renewed concept of global health for an era of complex interdependence. *The Lancet*, *383*(9911), 94–97. https://doi.org/10.1016/S0140-6736(13)62561-1

GAHP. (N.d.). The Global Alliance on Health and Pollution. Retrieved April 10, 2022. https://gahp.net/

Glapiak, E. (2020, June 17). Świat się zbroi. Na cele militarne rocznie przeznacza blisko 2 biliony dolarów [The world will arm itself. It spends nearly $2 trillion annually on military purposes]. *Business Insider*. https://businessinsider.com.pl/finanse/w-ciagu-ostatnich-20-lat-na-swiecie-podwojono-wydatki-na-armie/spb2x6s

Global Citizen. (2022a). Tell us and the world why you're standing up for Ukraine. https://www.globalcitizen.org/en/action/take-the-pledge-stand-up-for-ukraine/

Global Citizen. (2022b, April 9). $10.1 billion (€9.1 billion) pledged in new grants and loans as part of the Stand up for Ukraine event to support those who have had to flee their homes in Ukraine. https://www.globalcitizen.org/en/content/stand-up-for-ukraine-impact-report/

Government of Poland. (N.d.). Union Civil Protection Mechanism. Ministry of the Interior and Administration. Retrieved April 10, 2022. https://www.gov.pl/web/mswia-en/union-civil-protection-mechanism

Handley, L. (2017, October 16). *Hugh Evans: Being a global citizen*. CNBC. https://www.cnbc.com/2017/10/10/global-citizen-founder-hugh-evans-on-how-to-end-extreme-poverty.html

IFRC. (2021). Strategy 2030. International Federation of Red Cross and Red Crescent Societies. https://www.ifrc.org/document/strategy-2030

IHME. (2014, February 26). About IHME. Institute for Health Metrics and Evaluation. https://www.healthdata.org/about

Lee, K., & Brumme, Z. L. (2012). Operationalizing the One Health approach: The global governance challenges. *Health Policy and Planning*, *28*(7), 778–785. https://doi.org/10.1093/heapol/czs127

Lombardo, J., Burkom, H., Elbert, E., Magruder, S., Lewis, S. H., Loschen, W., Sari, J., Sniegoski, C., Wojcik, R., & Pavlin, J. (2003). A systems overview of the Electronic Surveillance System for the Early Notification of Community-Based Epidemics (ESSENCE II). *Journal of Urban Health: Bulletin of the New York Academy of Medicine*, *80*(Suppl 1), i32–i42. https://doi.org/10.1007/PL00022313

Madoff, L. C., & Woodall, J. P. (2005). The internet and the global monitoring of emerging diseases: Lessons from the first 10 years of ProMED-mail. *Archives of Medical Research*, *36*(6), 724–730. https://doi.org/10.1016/j.arcmed.2005.06.005

McGinnis, J. M., Williams-Russo, P., & Knickman, J. R. (2002). The case for more active policy attention to health promotion. *Health Affairs*, *21*(2), 78–93. https://doi.org/10.1377/hlthaff.21.2.78

McGovern, L. (2014). The relative contribution of multiple determinants to health. *Health Affairs Health Policy Brief*. https://doi.org/10.1377/hpb20140821.404487

McKeown, T. (1973). *The role of medicine: Dream, mirage or nemesis*. Basil Blackwell.

McKinlay, J. B., & McKinlay, S. M. (1977). The questionable contribution of medical measures to the decline of mortality in the United States in the twentieth century.

The Milbank Memorial Fund Quarterly: Health and Society, *55*(3), 405–428. https://doi.org/10.2307/3349539

Missoni, E., Pacileo, G., & Tediosi, F. (2019). *Global health governance and policy: An introduction*. Routledge. https://doi.org/10.4324/9781351188999

Moon, S. (2021). Global health: A centralized network searching (in vain) for hierarchy. In J. C. W. Pevehouse, K. Raustiala, & M. N. Barnett (Eds.), *Global governance in a world of change* (pp. 234–264). Cambridge University Press. https://doi.org/10.1017/9781108915199.009

Moon, S., Røttingen, J.-A., & Frenk, J. (2017). Global public goods for health: Weaknesses and opportunities in the global health system. *Health Economics, Policy and Law*, *12*(2), 195–205. https://doi.org/10.1017/S1744133116000451

New Urban Agenda. (2016). The New Urban Agenda. https://habitat3.org/the-new-urban-agenda/

Ostrowska, A. (1999). *Styl życia a zdrowie. Z zagadnień promocji zdrowia*. Wydawnictwo Instytutu Filozofii i Socjologii PAN.

Peacock, S. J. (2022). Vaccine nationalism will persist: Global public goods need effective engagement of global citizens. *Globalization and Health*, *18*(1), 14. https://doi.org/10.1186/s12992-022-00802-y

Pure Earth. (N.d.). About Pure Earth. Retrieved July 18, 2022. https://www.pureearth.org/about-us/

UN. (2020, July 21). Recovering from COVID-19: The importance of investing in global public goods for health. UN Department of Economic and Social Affairs. Retrieved March 25, 2022. https://www.un.org/development/desa/dspd/2020/07/recovering-from-covid19/

UNDP. (1990). *Human development report 1990: Concept and measurement of human development*. United Nations Development Programme (UNDP). https://www.hdr.undp.org/en/reports/global/hdr1990

UNHCR. (N.d.). Public health. United Nations High Commissioner for Refugees. Retrieved July 18, 2022. https://www.unhcr.org/public-health.html

UNHCR. (N.d.). 2023: A Moment of Truth for Global Displacement, 7 November 2022. Retrieved July 18, 2022. https://www.unhcr.org/spotlight/2023/01/2023-a-moment-of-truth-for-global-displacement/

Velasco, E., Agheneza, T., Denecke, K., Kirchner, G., & Eckmanns, T. (2014). Social media and internet-based data in global systems for public health surveillance: A systematic review. *Milbank Quarterly*, *92*(1), 7–33. https://doi.org/10.1111/1468-0009.12038

Węcławski, J. (2015). Wielkie banki i ich rola w kryzysie finansowym. *Annales Universitatis Mariae Curie-Skłodowska, sectio H – Oeconomia*, *47*(1), 219. https://doi.org/10.17951/h.2013.47.1.219

WHO. (2011). Promoting health and reducing health inequities by addressing the social determinants of health. World Health Organization. https://apps.who.int/iris/handle/10665/349969

WHO. (2013). Health 2020: A European policy framework supporting action across government and society for health and well-being. World Health Organization. https://www.euro.who.int/en/about-us/regional-director/regional-directors-emeritus/dr-zsuzsanna-jakab,-2010-2019/health-2020-the-european-policy-for-health-and-well-being/publications/2013/health-2020-a-european-policy-framework-supporting-action-across-government-and-society-for-health-and-well-being

WHO. (2017a). Roadmap to implement the 2030 Agenda for Sustainable Development, building on Health 2020, the European policy for health and well-being (EUR/RC67/9). World Health Organization. https://www.euro.who.int/en/health-topics/health-policy/sustainable-development-goals/publications/2017/eurrc679-roadmap-to-implement-the-2030-agenda-for-sustainable-development,-building-on-health-2020,-the-european-policy-for-health-and-well-being

WHO. (2017b). Shanghai consensus on healthy cities 2016. *Health Promotion International*, *32*(4), 603–605. https://doi.org/10.1093/heapro/dax038

WHO (2020, May 18). *WHO Results report 2018–2019 – Driving impact in every country*. World Health Organization. Retrieved February 28, 2023. https://www.who.int/about/accountability/results/2018-2019

WHO. (N.d.). Central Asian Republics Information Network (CARINFONET). World Health Organization. Retrieved July 18, 2022. https://who-sandbox.squiz.cloud/en/data-and-evidence/european-health-information-initiative-ehii/central-asian-republics-information-network-carinfonet

World Bank. (N.d.). Who we are. Retrieved April 10, 2022. https://www.worldbank.org/en/who-we-are

CHAPTER 14

Intellectual Property in Light of the WTO, the WIPO, the EU, and the OECD

Ewa Osuch-Rak

1 Introduction

When it comes to growth, the economies of both developed and developing countries increasingly rely on innovations driven by knowledge, technology, and human creativity, all of which are supported by intellectual property. Unprecedented global challenges reveal certain problems related to the absence of adequate and flexible means that would be conducive to an effective use of innovation and intellectual property in the context of sustainable development. In some cases, the global system of intellectual property works in a manner that is inconsistent with the principle of sustainable development, for instance, hindering innovation in agriculture, increasing the cost of producing medicine, or promoting the development and sale of "dirty" technology.

Paradoxically, confronted with widespread disagreement as to the impact of intellectual property on sustainable development, the questioning of intellectual property as a global public good, the challenges of the Fourth Industrial Revolution, and an increasingly complex, multilateral intellectual property system, international organizations building this system may see their role in the process as increasingly important. There is a growing need for coordinating different policy areas and activities fragmented and dispersed at local or national level, for coordinated financing, providing reliable information and data, and strengthening the political will by inducing governments to design intellectual property solutions for the purpose of sustainable development.

The 2030 Agenda for Sustainable Development (Transforming Our World: The 2030 Agenda for Sustainable Development), adopted by the United Nations (UN) in 2015, provides little guidance on how the Sustainable Development Goals (SDGs) set out in the Agenda should be taken into account within the international intellectual property system. No direct reference to intellectual property is made in the SDGs. Moreover, the Global Indicator Framework for the SDGs, which sets specific indicators for each goal, involving various organizations and agendas in the implementation and measurement of the degree of implementation of individual SDGs, does not take into account SDG indicators

DOI:10.1163/9789004687264_016

related to intellectual property, which may be explained by an ambiguous relationship between intellectual property and several SDGs, in particular, those related to health, education, and food security.

In the context of new global processes and conditions, rethinking the context and principles governing the international intellectual property system has become urgent, as has the role played within it by international organizations. In this chapter we shall analyze the approach of selected international organizations that form part of the intellectual property system to the sustainable development agenda, and discuss when and how the SDGs became part of the policies, agendas, and programs of these organizations.

The first section presents the importance of intellectual property for innovative development and economic growth, highlighting the complex and ambiguous nature of these relationships, which makes managing the international intellectual property regime require special competencies. The second section focuses on analyzing the characteristics of knowledge and intellectual property as global public goods, and presenting the relationship between them. The third section is devoted to an analysis of selected international organizations – the World Trade Organization (WTO), the World Intellectual Property Organization (WIPO), the European Union (EU), and the Organisation for Economic Co-operation and Development (OECD), which form the basis of the architecture of the international intellectual property system. Based on the concept of global public goods, an attempt was made to assess the degree to which these organizations implement the concept of sustainable development, based on a study of their programs and activities. The chapter ends with some conclusions and inferences.

2 Intellectual Property and its Importance in the Modern World

According to the definition of the World Intellectual Property Organization (WIPO), intellectual property is a set of laws relating, inter alia, to literary, artistic, and scientific works, interpretations of artistic performances, scientific discoveries, trademarks, and service marks, as well as other rights resulting from intellectual activity (WIPO, 2004). Intellectual property, therefore, includes intangible creations of the human mind, usually expressed in the form of material objects. It relates to pieces of information or knowledge that are embodied in specific products – goods, but also services. Intellectual property rights, in turn, are the rights held by a person with respect to their intellectual creation. These rights are to best protect the interests of creators, i.e., innovators who have the exclusive right to manage their ideas, including how the ideas are used by other people, for example, through paid licensing.

Intellectual property – and knowledge that is inextricably linked to it – is the most important resource of the modern economy. This is reflected both in research on intellectual property rights (IPRs) (e.g., Hanel, 2006; Paasi et al., 2010; Unger, 2019) and in studies on innovation based on the latest economic data. For example, surveys conducted by the European Patent Office (EPO) and the European Union Intellectual Property Office (EUIPO) showed that, in 2014–2016, industries that make an intensive use of intellectual property (IP) contributed to the creation of 29.2% of jobs within the European Union (EUIPO, 2019). These industries stimulate economic growth, as over 42% of the EU's GDP is generated by IP-intensive industries. IP ownership is also an important element of commercial transactions. The relationship between IPRs, trade, and sustainable development is discussed in detail in Chapter 6 In 2016, trade in goods and services from IP-intensive industries represented as much as 80% of EU imports and 82% of EU exports (EUIPO, 2019).

The role of IP in developing economies is also growing, China being the most striking example of this phenomenon. According to Global Innovation Index data, China is consistently strengthening is position among the world's most innovative economies; in 2021 it ranked 4th globally (WIPO, 2021). Importantly, the share of income generated in China from intellectual property organizations has been rising: in this respect, China ranked 76th in 2015 and 36th in 2021 (Cornell University et al., 2015; WIPO 2021). China has also recorded a significant increase in the value of PCT patents, moving from 27th place (globally) in 2015 to 13th in 2021 (Cornell University et al., 2015; WIPO, 2021). The country has become an innovation leader among middle-income economies and one that actively uses and generates IP; at present, around 13% of the Chinese GDP is generated by patent-intensive industries.

However, relationships between the processes of knowledge generation, intellectual property protection, innovations, and economic and social development remain ambiguous. The role of intellectual property rights has been amply discussed in literature. Arrow, one of the precursors of the economy of innovation, saw intellectual property rights as a key factor driving research and development, innovation, and economic growth (Arrow, 1962). He agreed with Machlup, who claimed that a time-limited monopoly favors an increase in the number of registered intellectual property rights, allowing more inventions to become commercially applicable (Machlup, 1961). When analyzing the impact of patents on research and development, as well as on economic growth, Eaton and Kortum (1999) argued that lifting patent protection would both reduce investment in research and development, and hinder economic growth. In their empirical study, Arora, Ceccagnoli, and Cohen (2008) proved that patents are an important incentive for research and development, even though the majority of innovations are never patented and an average patent does not provide the owner with a financial bonus in any of the surveyed industries, with the exception of the medical devices sector. Bielig (2015), in turn, estimated the economic effect of the four main categories of intellectual property rights and, using the linear regression model, showed that intellectual property rights had had a positive impact on the German economy.

However, intellectual property rights can also prove an important obstacle to research and development, as well as innovation. For example, Grossman and Helpman (1991), who in their research referred directly to the concept of knowledge as a public good, claimed that a strong protection of intellectual property rights limits the possibility of observing and analyzing competing solutions (spillover effects), which, in turn, has a negative effect on innovation and economic growth. Hall and Harhoff (2012) explained that although patent rights create incentives for research and development, they also make it difficult to pool new ideas and inventions; what is more, they increase transaction costs. Similar trends have also been found in relation to other forms of intellectual property (Landes & Posner, 2003). In developing economies, the direct impact of intellectual property on economic growth depends on many factors, including per capita income, research and development potential, institutional efficiency, or human capital (Maskus, 2000; Forero-Pineda, 2006; Chu et al., 2014; Mehlig Sweet & Eterovic Maggio, 2015).

Thus, a higher level of intellectual property protection may have both positive and negative effects on the level of innovation and economic growth. Intellectual property rights have specific economic and social consequences, and may be more or less significant depending on the industry, state of the technology, or geographic region. For example, patents are of key importance for certain sectors of the manufacturing industry, including the pharmaceutical, chemical, and electronic industry; copyright is the primary protection instrument for audiovisual and literary works; trademarks are paramount for industries where brand value provides an important competitive advantage.

Intellectual property systems affect, inter alia, technological progress by affording certain mechanisms to deal with infringement, piracy, and the unauthorized use of intellectual property; in addition, they provide information to society, since all forms of intellectual property, except trade secrets, are made public. Nevertheless, it is emphasized that both the creation of innovation and economic and social development can take place without the protection of intellectual property rights (e.g., Cozzi, 2009; Stiglitz, 2008). In this respect, Stiglitz stresses the importance of basic research, of academia and public R&D-funding institutions, as well as the role of the open source movement, in particular with regard to software (Stiglitz, 2008).

3 Knowledge and Intellectual Property as a Global Public Good

Knowledge may be one of the most illustrative examples of a public good (Arrow, 1962; International Task Force on Global Public Goods, 2006; Stiglitz, 2008). Once produced, it can be shared and used by many people at the same time, and its creators are limited in their attempts to maintain exclusive ownership over it. For example, while knowledge about the production of rayon (a type of artificial fiber) was protected by a patent, other inventors used it to develop alternative synthetic fibers (Stiglitz, 1999). The production of knowledge, just as the production of other public goods, involves great costs, borne mainly by governments; however, knowledge can be disseminated at very low marginal costs, and in certain cases even at zero marginal cost (Stiglitz, 2008). In addition, knowledge, just as other public goods, generates a number of significant externalities; these are social and public benefits (Ndofirepi & Cross, 2017), including, inter alia, effects in the area of education or technological progress that contribute to the general development of civilization. Knowledge, therefore, inspires and stimulates the material, social, and cultural progress of humanity.

Knowledge is not only a national, but also a global public good. With accelerating globalization processes, the dynamic development of information and communication technology (ICT), the increasing mobility of people, as well as unprecedented changes to the work environment, e.g., triggered by the COVID-19 pandemic (e.g., remote and hybrid work, cooperation of global virtual teams), knowledge and information now flow between people, companies, countries, and continents with almost no impediments. Undoubtedly, certain types of knowledge are deeply rooted in a specific place or cultural context (e.g., traditional knowledge), but scientific and technological knowledge functions irrespectively of national boundaries or geographic conditions. It can also be easily disseminated on a global scale. This process is supported by the global scientific community, which, through the use of electronic communication channels, integrates dispersed groups, helps to establish bonds, and creates communities around various concepts and issues.

Knowledge as a global public good has yet another important feature: to effectively use knowledge, potential users must first invest their time and financial resources in assimilating and adapting it. Consequently, there is less freedom in the process of acquiring and using knowledge than in the case of other public goods (Przybylska, 2019). It also has important implications for policies implemented at the national or global level. Catching up on development requires the implementation of active learning policies, as well as building knowledge absorption and innovation capacities within society.

Knowledge is an example of a global public good of a mixed nature: it implies the absence of rivalry in consumption, but its excludability is an artificial construction reflected in intellectual property rights (Archibugi & Filippetti, 2015). The argument underlying public policy intervention aimed at limiting the use of knowledge is that without it the market economy could not protect private entities (Breitwieser & Foster, 2012). Consequently, these entities would not be sufficiently incentivized to undertake long-term, capital-intensive and risky investments in research, development, and innovation, which are nowadays commonly regarded as the main sources of sustainable socioeconomic development. Thus, intellectual property rights and their systems represent an institutional solution offered by both national governments and international organizations in the hope of solving the key problem of the insufficient production of public goods (Archibugi & Filippetti, 2015).

4 Knowledge and Intellectual Property Management by Selected International Organizations (WTO, WIPO, EU, and OECD) and Sustainable Development

The role of international organizations in the management of intellectual property and knowledge is multidimensional. The most important organizations in the global intellectual property system are the World Trade Organization (WTO) and the World Intellectual Property Organization (WIPO); the European Union (EU) and the Organisation for Economic Co-operation and Development (OECD) also play an important role in the process.

4.1 *World Trade Organization* (WTO)

The World Trade Organization (WTO) administers and implements trade agreements that incorporate intellectual property rights into the global trading system. The 1995 Agreement on Trade-Related Aspects of Intellectual Property Rights (TRIPS) is the most comprehensive multilateral agreement on intellectual property rights to date. TRIPS is the first WTO agreement that requires members of this organization to implement a set of legal norms and procedures into national law in order to enforce them more effectively and ensure that the minimum standards of intellectual property protection, guaranteed by the Agreement, are respected. As indicated in Chapter 6, the shape of the WTO regulations has a profound impact on sustainable development of the world.

TRIPS has introduced many changes to the global system of IPRs, including the principle of minimum protection, which means that any agreement negotiated subsequently may only introduce a higher standard of intellectual property protection (the so-called TRIPS-plus), or the dispute resolution mechanism in which each WTO member country has the right to bring a case before a specially appointed committee of independent experts.

The WTO perceives its role as key in the process of implementation of the SDGS:

> [T]he WTO is central to achieving the 2030 Agenda for Sustainable Development and its Sustainable Development Goals (SDGs), which set targets to be achieved by 2030 in areas such as poverty reduction, health, education and the environment. The SDGs put significant emphasis on the role of trade in promoting sustainable development, and recognize the contribution that the WTO can make to the 2030 Agenda. (WTO, 2018)

The implementation of the concept of sustainable development in the WTO system takes place on three levels: first, the principles and rules of the WTO; second, special programs and initiatives; third, multilateral negotiations for trade liberalization, known as negotiation rounds (Zajaczkowski, 2016).

4.1.1 Principles and Rules

The general objectives and principles of TRIPS are reflected in the preamble to the Agreement, which states that by establishing them, member states strive to minimize distortions and impediments to international trade, to promote effective and adequate protection of intellectual property rights, and to ensure that such measures and procedures to enforce intellectual property rights do not become barriers to legitimate trade (WTO, 2005, Preamble). The preamble completes the provisions of Article 7 of the Agreement, stating that its purpose is "the protection and enforcement of intellectual property rights," except in a manner that does not restrict trade, but contributes to the promotion of technical innovation and to "the transfer and dissemination of technology, to the mutual advantage of producers and users of technical knowledge, and in a manner conducive to social and economic welfare and to a balance of rights and obligations" (WTO, 2005, Article 7). No direct reference is made to the concept of sustainable development in the Agreement, while the absence of trade restrictions, the development and promotion of technology, and their transfer being conducive to social and economic welfare seem to tally primarily with the assumptions of two of the three dimensions of sustainability, namely economic and social order.

4.1.2 Special Programs

Within the WTO system, sustainable development appears most often in the context of developing and least developed countries (LDCs). The best way to attain the goal of sustainable development of these countries is to integrate them more fully into the international trading system, including the intellectual property system. Agreement initiators believed that the imposition of temporary monopolies under private intellectual property rights would bring broad benefits to society and encourage foreign direct investment, technology transfer, and licensing, and that it would foster the dissemination of knowledge to developing countries.

However, the TRIPS Agreement was received with widespread criticism due to its potentially negative impact on development (Chang, 2001; Kumar, 2003; McCalman, 2005). Among many reasons is the fact that the rules introduced by TRIPS hinder access to drugs necessary to curb the spread of AIDS and other epidemics in developing countries, and also increase their cost. Furthermore, the Agreement does not protect traditional knowledge, which is a fundamental resource of many developing countries and plays an important role in the global economy (Dutfield, 2001). The TRIPS Agreement was only amended in 2017; this change was significant, first of all, from the point of view of health protection. The protocol adopted then by two-thirds of the WTO members introduced additional possibilities of granting compulsory licenses to produce medicine intended for export; as a result, non-patent-holding companies could manufacture and sell equivalents of patent-protected medicine in the event of a public health emergency in the importing country.

Additional initiatives taken by the WTO in an attempt to improve intellectual property standards involve, for example, the protection of traditional knowledge, which is often applied in various sectors of the economy, such as the pharmaceutical industry, cosmetology, or agriculture, as well as forestry or biodiversity management.

In 2017, relationships between intellectual property and the public interest were first taken into account by the WTO TRIPS Council. This largely contributed to the general understanding of knowledge and intellectual property as a global public good. Members of the TRIPS Council discussed, inter alia, such new matters as micro, small, and medium-sized enterprises, technology partnerships between universities and industries, regional models of innovation, including those supporting the fight against certain communicable diseases, as well as the practical protection of public interest under competition policies. In 2022 the TRIPS Council adopted a stance to intellectual property in the context of the COVID-19 pandemic, outlining practical ways to clarify, streamline, and simplify procedures so that governments can, under certain conditions, waive patent rights to diversify the production of COVID-19 vaccines (WTO, 2022).

4.1.3 Multilateral Negotiations

The implementation of the concept of sustainable development by the WTO is also reflected in negotiation rounds conducted by the organization. In 2001 a round of multilateral trade negotiations was launched in Doha; this "development round" was aimed at further liberalizing world trade, with particular emphasis on the interests of developing countries. Its goal was to adopt rules that would advance the interests of developing countries and allow them to join the multilateral trading system under the auspices of the WTO to a greater extent than any existing agreements had ever done. The negotiating round has remained in a deadlock since 2008. To overcome the impasse, a new approach is being called for, taking into account both major changes in the level of development of individual countries, and the new complexity and divergence of interests within the three pillars of the WTO, with some developing countries becoming the main trade partners and competitors of developed countries.

4.1.4 Assessment

Intellectual property, as a key resource, should be instrumental in the attainment of the SDGs. Although indirectly and through numerous references to common values and fundamental human rights, this concept formed part of the TRIPS Agreement from the very beginning. However, facing dynamic changes and the need not only to redirect the trajectory of economic and social development onto a path of sustainability, but also create a systemic capacity for transformation that will allow for a dynamic response to unprecedented global and national phenomena, it is necessary to closely link the goals and tasks of the WTO regarding intellectual property rights with the SDGs and ensure that the system meets sustainable development priorities, while strengthening the position of developing countries within the system. Measures taken by the WTO over the past few years denote that the organization is becoming increasingly aware of the complex relationship between intellectual property law and sustainable development, but also that it is more capable than ever of working out specific solutions.

4.2 *World Intellectual Property Organization* (*WIPO*)

WIPO is a specialized agency of the United Nations (UN) established in 1974 and endowed with a mandate to act in accordance with the objectives of many other UN bodies and agencies dealing with innovation, intellectual property, and development. Under the Agreement concluded between the United Nations and WIPO, the latter has been empowered to act, inter alia, by concluding treaties and agreements aimed at the protection of intellectual property and at facilitating the transfer of industrial property technologies to developing countries with a view to accelerating economic, social, and cultural development.

4.2.1 Content and Development

The pillars of WIPO's activities include, in particular, actions aimed at consolidating rules and principles within a sustainable intellectual property system, as well as those designed to promote innovation and creativity, and to bolster infrastructure in order to provide highest quality services and facilitate access to patent information from databases throughout the world; equally important is capacity building through training targeted at all users of the intellectual property system (e.g., decision-makers, lecturers, creators, or inventors). The scope of WIPO's activity is, therefore, broad and comprehensive, and it includes the creation and administration of intellectual property treaties (at present, there are 26 international treaties), stimulating the development of intellectual property protection through creating partnerships and cooperating with developed and developing countries in the management of IP systems, or providing infrastructure for IP protection, as well as reliable knowledge and information to the users of the IP system.

In assessing its potential and real contribution to the achievement of the SDGs, WIPO focuses primarily on SDG 9: "Innovation, industry, infrastructure," declaring that innovation is at the heart of its mission, with SDG 9 being the most relevant (WIPO, 2019, p. 2):

> Of all the SDGs, Goal 9 is most closely aligned with WIPO's mission, which is to lead the development of a balanced and effective international intellectual property (IP) system that enables innovation and creativity for the benefit of all. Innovation is also essential in achieving SDG 2 (zero hunger), SDG 3 (good health and well-being), SDG 6 (clean water and sanitation), SDG 7 (affordable and clean energy), SDG 8 (decent work and economic growth), SDG 11 (sustainable cities and communities), and SDG 13 (climate change). In a wider policy setting, innovation can also assist in achieving SDG 1 (no poverty), SDG 8 (decent work and economic growth), SDG 14 (life below water), and SDG 15 (life on land). Other SDGs are also achievable within an innovation policy framework, notably SDG 5 (gender equality), SDG 8 (decent work and economic growth), SDG 10 (reduced inequalities), and SDG 12 (responsible consumption and production). (WIPO, 2019, p. 2)

The adoption of the Development Agenda in 2007, including 45 recommendations grouped into six thematic clusters, and the establishment of the Committee on Development and Intellectual Property (CDIP) was a breakthrough in WIPO's measures for sustainable development. Effective implementation of this Agenda is a priority and a major component of WIPO's assistance provided to member states with a view to attaining the SDGs. A wide range of reforms was initiated by the Agenda, aiming to transform WIPO, to redirect it towards growth and to change the way it is managed, creates policies, and provides technical assistance (Lerner, 2008). The Agenda was regarded as affording an unprecedented opportunity, in particular for developing countries and public interest organizations, to place the interaction between IP and different aspects of development at the very heart of the intellectual property debate. However, it has also been the subject of severe criticism, inter alia, for its failure to take into account public health issues, even though access to medicine in developing countries is a major driver of the development process (Lerner, 2008).

Copyright, which is within the area of WIPO's competence, is fundamentally related to education and R&D, as well as to incentives to create and disseminate educational materials and intellectual works (Chon, 2006). Copyright law may prevent access to educational material, especially in developing countries (Chon, 2006). As a solution to this problem, free and open access to copyrighted works has been proposed, as well as compulsory licensing (Chan et al., 2011; Willinsky, 2006). The WIPO Copyright Treaty (2002), concluded under the auspices of this organization, applies to copyright in the digital environment.

Two new WIPO treaties entered into force in 2020: the Beijing Treaty on Audiovisual Performances and the Geneva Act of the Lisbon Agreement on Appellations of Origin and Geographical Indications. The latter is of particular importance, as greater protection of geographical indications contributes to the advancement of developing countries (Chabrol et al., 2017). In addition, they also have numerous traits, typical of public goods, that affect local sustainable development in the economic, social, and environmental dimension (Belletti et al., 2017).

Since 2013 WIPO has been implementing the WIPO Green program in order to promote and disseminate green technology through connecting entities interested in new technology and suppliers thereof. As part of this initiative, an electronic platform was launched to integrate patent data and green technology offered by businesses, including small and medium-sized enterprises. WIPO sees its role as much broader. The overriding goal of the organization is to contribute to the implementation of the SDGs by supporting innovation, disseminating green technology and ensuring that intellectual property contributes to a greater extent to solving the most urgent global challenges, such as climate change, health, and food security.

In 2021 WIPO adopted a new strategy, i.e., the Medium-Term Strategic Plan for 2022–2026, based on four pillars closely related to the SDGs. Following the

Development Agenda, this is another milestone on WIPO's path towards transforming itself into a sustainable development – oriented organization.

4.2.2 Assessment

Despite close links between intellectual property and the SDGs within the WIPO system (Rimmer, 2018), the organization perceives its role in attaining them rather narrowly, i.e., primarily in terms of its contribution to the achievement of SDG 9: "Industry, innovation and infrastructure," and, in particular, with a focus on supporting innovation. WIPO sees itself as an organization that promotes innovation. On the other hand, WIPO documents do not refer to intellectual property as a potential source of inequality and a factor that slows down the process of attaining the SDGs.

4.3 *The European Union (EU)*

The concept of sustainable development is an overriding political priority of the European Commission led by Commissioner Von der Leyen. Its political guidelines for 2021–2024 set out its six overriding targets for Europe, closely related to the UN's SDGs (Von der Leyen, 2019). The key elements of the new, comprehensive approach of the European Commission to the implementation of the 2030 Agenda include the adoption of policies that have a great transformative potential, such as the "European Green Deal," aimed at transforming the EU into a modern, resource-efficient, and competitive economy, or the EU's digital transformation strategy adopted in 2020 in the document entitled *Shaping Europe's Digital Future*.

4.3.1 Content and Development

These programs set ambitious goals for the EU and its member states. They also define the directions and the pace of action in the years to come. However, their attainment depends on innovations – mainly industrial, but also digital. Their importance is emphasized in the "New Industrial Strategy for Europe" updated in 2021. In the latter document, which is a response to the challenges posed by the COVID-19 pandemic, the European Commission emphasizes the importance of a double transformation – ecological and digital – for sustainable competitiveness. In the new multiannual financial framework for 2021–2027, the EU is to allocate over €150 billion to research and innovation, digital transformation, strategic infrastructure, and the single market (Gabriel, 2021). The latest budget of the Horizon Europe program, the most important research and innovation funding program in the EU, was increased by as much as 30 percent compared to the previous budget, now standing at over €95 billion (Gabriel, 2021).

The EU's intellectual property policy is designed to support the attainment of overarching goals, but is also an important instrument in building technological sovereignty in Europe and is closely related to EU policy regarding small and medium-sized enterprises. Given the important economic role of intellectual property, in 2020 the European Commission published an action plan for the development of intellectual property protection in Europe entitled "Making the Most of the EU's Innovative Potential – An Intellectual Property Action Plan to Support the EU's Recovery and Resilience." The main objective is to help enterprises, in particular small and medium-sized enterprises (SMEs), to make the best use of their intellectual property, and to provide them with benefits that will also affect the entire European society and economy.

The intellectual property system in the EU is governed by international and national law, but also by European legal acts. Since 2009, i.e., since the entry into force of the Treaty on the Functioning of the European Union (TFEU), the EU has been endowed with certain powers in the field of intellectual property rights (Article 118). Article 118 of the TFEU states that in the context of the establishment and functioning of the internal market, the European Parliament and the Council shall establish measures for the creation of European intellectual property rights to provide uniform protection of intellectual property rights throughout the Union, as well as for the setting up of centralized Union-wide authorization, coordination, and supervision arrangements. Legislative measures taken by the European Union mainly consist of harmonizing certain aspects of intellectual property rights within its own system, for instance, in relation to the EU trademark or design, and in the future also in relation to patents. As early as in 1975 the EU Council stated: "[T]he creation of such a Community patent system is [...] inseparable from the attainment of the [internal market] objectives of the Treaty" (De Lange, 2021, p. 1079). Over the past 50 years, significant progress has been made in terms of EU trade harmonization within the internal market. However, one of the main constraints for further integration and attaining by the EU the position of the world's most competitive economy is precisely the lack of progress in the integration of the European patent system, compared to the overall harmonization of the internal market (De Lange, 2021).

4.3.2 Assessment

The European Union, which has placed both sustainable development and intellectual property (and, more broadly, innovation and technology) at the heart of its policy and activity, has been focusing mainly on strengthening its internal market and building technological sovereignty and an innovation-based competitive advantage. Despite, for instance, being the world's largest donor of development aid, intellectual property and its transfer have yet to be granted a place commensurate with their importance in the strategic documents of this organization.

4.4 *Organisation for Economic Co-operation and Development* (OECD)

The OECD is an intergovernmental organization and an association of the world's 30 most developed countries. Its primary goal is to promote policy focused on achieving highest levels of sustainable economic growth and employment, as well as rising standards of living in member countries, while maintaining financial stability, and thus to contribute to "sound economic expansion" in member as well as non-member countries in the process of economic development. Achieving these goals is based on working together for balanced economic development, as well as to contribute to the expansion of world trade on a multilateral and non-discriminatory basis in accordance with international obligations.

4.4.1 Content and Development

In 2021 the OECD set a policy stance based on a new narrative on economic growth that is to improve the well-being of societies, in line with the 2030 Agenda and its 17 Goals. The new policy is based on three overreaching priorities:

- Combining growth and economic efficiency with inclusiveness, resilience and sustainability goals in the OECD's advisory activity aimed at a strong and rapid recovery
- Helping governments build a strong social contract with current and future generations aimed at reducing inequalities in education, health care, infrastructure, and exposure to environmental threats
- Adopting a long-term approach to challenges related to climate change, biodiversity loss and environmental degradation, including, inter alia, transforming production and consumption patterns in order to avoid the worst consequences of impending environmental crises (OECD, 2021)

The OECD does not have many instruments of so-called hard power, such as economic sanctions, financial penalties, financial aid programs (such as those implemented by the EU), development aid programs (such as those of the World Bank), or structural adjustment programs (such as those of the IMF). The organization does, however, have soft power, creating the most important ideas and concepts used in numerous public policies, in particular in areas related to economic and social policy. In addition, the OECD shapes political discourse by shaping the views of the most important political leaders, economic decision-makers, and public opinion (Martens & Jakobi, 2010). The

OECD, therefore, supports governments and other organizations in delivering a wide variety of public goods, and is itself an active participant in the delivery of global public goods. This includes generating, legitimizing, and diffusing economic ideas and economic policies; creating an analytical framework, surveys and evaluations; and coordination and harmonization through the use of peer pressure methods and the principles of "naming and shaming" of individual practices and countries. The OECD is also a standard-setting organization.

The OECD is a pioneer in the field of innovation research. In 1992 it published the Oslo Manual, which is a standard international textbook of methodology for statistical research on innovative activities. Every 2 years it also publishes a report entitled *The OECD Science, Technology and Innovation Outlook*, which includes guidance for policymakers and analysts on the most important trends in science. Such sources of knowledge as databases, reports, and substantive support provided by the OECD can be perceived as important tools of international management (Erkkilä & Piironen, 2014).

Education is seen as a driver of growth and the OECD is committed to improving the quality, equality, efficiency, and effectiveness of education systems in its member states. The emphasis on generating human capital has become a cornerstone of the OECD's educational framework. Education is a key factor in creating human capital, which in turn has a positive effect on economic growth, employment prospects, health, and community involvement.

4.4.2 Assessment

Sustainable development and intellectual property are at the heart of the OECD's strategy and activities. This organization plays an important role in the coordination of international policy, which, in the face of global challenges, has significantly increased the demand for internationally oriented knowledge. The OECD has also assumed a key role in managing IP-based policies, in particular the innovation and education policy.

5 Conclusions

The international intellectual property system is complex and dichotomous in nature and creates tensions that can be eliminated through appropriate management. This involves, on the one hand, the need to constantly stimulate technological progress by maintaining an adequate level of IP protection and, on the other, the need to create appropriate conditions for the diffusion of innovation and technology transfer. Knowledge and technology transfer is of particular importance for developing economies. It requires the involvement of stakeholders at all levels: global, national, and local. In the case of global public goods, although the implementation of many decisions must take place at the national and regional level, strong international cooperation is necessary for setting priorities, defining and sharing responsibilities and competences of developed and developing countries, concluding binding agreements, and deciding on funding and law enforcement mechanisms.

Knowledge as a global public good plays an increasingly important role in the implementation of the concept of sustainable development. It generates externalities that extend beyond national borders, involving numerous social groups among both present and future generations. The use of new knowledge often requires taking additional action related to the strategy of active learning, or increasing the absorption capacity of enterprises, which in turn involves a greater number of beneficiary stakeholders and causes permanent changes in the global innovation system. Intellectual property may amplify these positive development effects, but on the condition that the negative effects of intellectual property agreements, for example, those that favor entities from highly developed countries or create privileged conditions for the development of selected sectors of the economy, are eliminated.

Here, we ought to mention the role of international organizations that create global programs and strategies of action, set new directions for governments and other international entities, establish common rules and principles of conduct, and disseminate innovative ideas and knowledge. Organizations such as the WTO, WIPO, EU, and OECD provide the architectural framework for the international intellectual property system. This analysis suggests a gradual shift of priorities towards the SDGs, which finds confirmation in the strategic documents of all of the above organizations. The intellectual property system is related to a wide range of sustainable development matters, including health, climate, and education. International organizations incorporate them in their activities to varying degrees. For example, the WTO (trade, health) and OECD (education) tend to specialize in selected areas, while the approach of WIPO is rather comprehensive. Furthermore, these organizations also exert diverse degrees of power through different instruments; for example, the WTO may impose sanctions for failure to comply with agreement terms, while the OECD only has soft power. There are also differences in the scope of impact. While the EU treats intellectual property rules as an instrument for deepening integration and building the EU's competitive advantage internationally, WIPO and the OECD focus on promoting the idea of intellectual property on a global scale.

As international organizations are established by states to solve their shared problems, they also strive to build knowledge that can be used for general purposes: they establish and maintain common norms and standards, provide reliable and up-to-date data, transfer knowledge and technical competences, and create and support research centers. For example, the European Union has established several international centers affiliated with the Joint Research Centre (JRC) in research areas where the costs and risks of research are particularly high, e.g., energy and transport, food and health, as well as data and digital transformation. Numerous research centers have been established by the United Nations University or under the auspices of specialized UN agencies. In this way, international organizations are directly involved in the process of creating knowledge, which is a global public good.

The general image of sustainable development and intellectual property conveyed in the discourse of the above international organizations is positive. It is important that international intellectual property system organizations analyze the SDGs as a whole, taking into account both the benefits and costs of intellectual property and its system for economies and societies. Only then will the strategies and activities of these organizations respond more dynamically to the actual needs of all entities within the system.

References

Archibugi, D., & Filippetti, D. A. (2015). Knowledge as global public good. In D. Archibugi & D. A. Filippetti (Eds.), *The handbook of global science, technology, and innovation* (pp. 425–446). John Wiley & Sons. doi:10.1002/9781118739044.CH23

Arora A., Ceccagnoli M., & Cohen, W. M. (2008). R&D and the patent premium. *International Journal of Industrial Organisation, 26*(5), 1153–1179.

Arrow, K. (1962). Economic welfare and the allocation of resources for invention. In K. J. Arrow (Ed.), *The rate and direction of inventive activity: Economic and social factors* (pp. 609–626). Princeton University Press.

Belletti, G., Marescotti, A., & Touzard, J.-M. (2017). Geographical indications, public goods, and sustainable development: The roles of actors' strategies and public policies. *World Development, 98*, 45–57. doi:10.1016/j.worlddev.2015.05.004

Bielig, A. (2015). Intellectual property and economic development in Germany: Empirical evidence for 1999–2009. *European Journal of Law and Economics, 39*(3), 607–622.

Breitwieser, A., & Foster, N. (2012, June). Intellectual property rights, innovation and technology transfer: A survey. Working Paper 88. The Vienna Institute for International Economic Studies.

Chan, L., Kirsop, B., & Arunachalam, S. (2011). towards open and equitable access to research and knowledge for development. *PLoS Medicine, 8*(3), e1001016. https://doi.org/10.1371/journal.pmed.1001016

Chang, H.-J. (2001). Intellectual property rights and economic development: Historical lessons and emerging issues. *Journal of Human Development and Capabilities, 2*(2), 287–309.

Chabrol D., Mariani, M., & Sautier, D. (2017). Establishing geographical indications without state involvement? Learning from case studies in Central and West Africa. *World Development, 98*, 68–81. http://dx.doi.org/10.1016/j.worlddev.2015.11.023

Chon, M. (2006). Intellectual property and the development divide. *Cardozo Law Review, 27*, 2821–2912. https://digitalcommons.law.seattleu.edu/faculty/558.

Chu, A. C., Cozzi, G., & Galli, S. (2014). Stage-dependent intellectual property rights. *Journal of Development Economics, 106*, 239–249.

Cornell University, INSEAD, & WIPO. (2015). *The Global Innovation Index 2015: Effective innovation policies for development.*

Cozzi G. (2009). Intellectual property, innovation, and growth: Introduction to the special issue. *Scottish Journal of Political Economy, 56*(4), 383–389. https://doi.org/10.1111/j.1467-9485.2009.00490.x

Cross, M., & Ndofirepi, A. (2017). Knowledge as a public good. In M. Cross & A. Ndofirepi (Eds.), *Knowledge and change in African universities, vol. 1: Current debates* (pp. 41–57). BrillSense.

De Lange, D. (2021). EU patent harmonization policy: Reconsidering the consequences of the UPCA, *Journal of Intellectual Property Law & Practice, 16*(10), 1078–1090. https://doi.org/10.1093/jiplp/jpab096

Dutfield, G. (2001). TRIPS-related aspects of traditional knowledge. *Case Western Reserve Journal of International Law, 33*(2). https://scholarlycommons.law.case.edu/jil/vol33/iss2/4

Eaton, J., & Kortum, S. (1999). International technology diffusion, theory and measurement. *International Economic Review, 40*, 537–570.

Erkkilä, T., & Piironen, O. (2014). (De)politicizing good governance: The World Bank Institute, the OECD and the politics of governance indicators. *Innovation: The European Journal of Social Science Research, 27*(4), 344–360. https://doi.org/10.1080/13511610.2013.850020

EUIPO. (2019). *IPR-intensive industries and economic performance in the European Union: Industry-level analysis report.* European Union Intellectual Property Office.

Forero-Pineda, C. (2006). The impact of stronger intellectual property rights on science and technology in developing countries. *Research Policy, 35*, 808–824.

Gabriel, M. (2021). *Budget: Horizon Europe – The most ambitious EU research & innovation programme ever.* European Union.

Grossman, G. M., & Helpman, E. (1991). Trade, knowledge spillovers, and growth. *European Economic Review, 35*, 517–526.

Hall, B. H., & Harhoff, D. (2012). Recent research on the economics of patents. *Annual Review of Economics, 4*(1), 541–565. https://doi.org/10.1146/annurev-economics-080511-111008.

Hanel, P. (2006). Intellectual property rights business management practices: A survey of the literature. *Technovation, 26*, 895–931.

International Task Force on Global Public Goods. (2006). *Meeting global challenges: International cooperation in the national interest. Final Report.*

Kumar, N. (2003, January 18). Intellectual property rights, technology and economic development: Experiences of Asian countries. *Economic and Political Weekly*, 209–225.

Landes, W. M., & Posner, R. A. (2003). *The economic structure of intellectual property law.* Harvard University Press.

Lerner, J. (2008). Intellectual property and development at WHO and WIPO. *American Journal of Law & Medicine, 34*(2008), 257–277.

Machlup, F. (1961). Patents and inventive efforts. *Science, 133*(3463), 1463–1466.

Martens, K., & Jakobi, A. P. (2010). Introduction: The OECD as an actor in international politics. In K. Martens, & A. P. Jakobi (Eds.), *Mechanisms of OECD governance: International incentives for national policy-making?* (pp. 1–25). Oxford University Press.

Maskus, K. E. (2000). Intellectual property rights and economic development. *Case Western Reserve Journal of International Law, 32*(3), 471–506.

McCalman, P. (2005). Who enjoys "TRIPS" abroad? An empirical analysis of intellectual property rights in the Uruguay Round. *Canadian Journal of Economics, 38*(2), 574–603.

Mehlig Sweet, C., & Eterovic Maggio, D. S. (2015). Do stronger intellectual property rights increase innovation? *World Development*, 66(C), 665–677. doi:10.1016/j.worlddev.2014.08.025

OECD. (2021). *Trust in global cooperation – the vision for the OECD for the next decade.* Organisation for Economic Co-operation and Development.

Paasi, J., Luoma, T., Valkokari, K., & Lee, N. (2010). Knowledge and intellectual property management in customer – supplier relationships. *International Journal of Innovation Management, 14*(04), 629–654. doi:10.1142/S1363919610002805

Przybylska, K. (2019). Globalne dobra publiczne. In K. Przybylska (Ed.), *Zawodność rynku w teorii i praktyce* (pp. 83–102). Warszawa: PWN.

Rimmer, M. (2018). A submission on intellectual property and the United Nations Sustainable Development Goals. Senate Standing Committee on Foreign Affairs, Defence, and Trade, Australia. https://eprints.qut.edu.au/215474/

Stiglitz, J. E. (1999). Knowledge as a global public good. In I. Kaul, I. Grunberg, & M. A. Stern (Eds.), *Global public goods: International cooperation in the 21st century* (pp. 308–325). Oxford University Press.

Stiglitz, J. E. (2008). Economic foundations of intellectual property rights. *Duke Law Journal, 57*(6), 1695–1724.

Unger, R. M. (2019). *The knowledge economy*. Verso.

Von der Leyen, U. (2019). *Political Guidelines for the Next European Commission 2019–2024.* https://ec.europa.eu/info/sites/default/files/political-guidelines-next-commission_en_0.pdf

Willinsky, J. (2006). *The access principle: The case for open access to research and scholarship*. MIT Press.

WIPO. (2004). The concept of intellectual property. In *WIPO Intellectual Property Handbook* (Chapter 1). World Intellectual Property Organization. WIPO Publication no. 483 (E).

WIPO. (2019). *Report on WIPO's contribution to the implementation of the Sustainable Development Goals and its associated targets*. CDIP/23/10. World Intellectual Property Organization.

WIPO. (2021). *Global Innovation Index 2021: Tracking Innovation through the COVID-19 Crisis*. World Intellectual Property Organization.

WTO. (2005). Agreement on Trade-Related Aspects of Intellectual Property Rights as Amended by the 2005 Protocol Amending the TRIPS Agreement. World Trade Organization. Retrieved June 20, 2022. https://www.wto.org/english/docs_e/legal_e/trips_e.htm

WTO. (2018). *Mainstreaming trade to attain the Sustainable Development Goals*. World Trade Organization.

WTO. (2022). TRIPS – Trade-Related Aspects of Intellectual Property Rights. World Trade Organization. Retrieved June 13, 2022. https://www.wto.org/english/tratop_e/trips_e/trips_e.htm

Zajaczkowski, M. (2016). Concept of sustainable development and global public goods in the World Trade Organization. In E. Latoszek, M. Proczek, & M. Krukowska (Eds.), *Sustainable development and global public goods in the theory and practice of international organizations* (pp. 131–145). ELIPSA.

PART 6

Digital Transformation and Smart Settlements as a New Paradigm of Strategic Sustainable Development

CHAPTER 15

Digital Transformation Processes in Society and the Economy: The Role of the International Labour Organization and the European Union

Małgorzata Dziembała and Mirela Mărcuț

1 Introduction

Technological development is a key process fueling changes in society and the economy. The Fourth Industrial Revolution is not only a continuation of the previous transformation processes brought about by technological development. For instance, production was automated in the Third Industrial Revolution with the power of computers and electronics, but the world maintained the same social relations and policies as before. In comparison, according to Klaus Schwab, the Fourth Industrial Revolution is different from three points of view, namely its speed, its breadth, and its overall impact (World Economic Forum, 2015). The overreaching impact of these transformations goes beyond the production process; they extend into the management, the work structure itself, and into the basic fabric of society. The sharing economy, the platform economy, as well as business models derived from the collection of data and automation, reshape industrial relations and challenge jobs. In this sense, these changes may be extensive, but they are not entirely positive.

Additionally, they require a concerted approach, which is difficult to attain. States have different interests and may enact different public policies to help mitigate the difficulties and to foster technological development. Therefore international organizations, due to their scope and activity, could address the challenges related to digitalization via the provision of global public goods (GPGs). Sustainable Development Goal (SDG) 9, entitled "Build resilient infrastructure, promote inclusive and sustainable industrialization and foster innovation," also focuses on the provision of GPGs. Within this goal eight targets were specified (United Nations, n.d.). The international organizations by providing GPGs respond to this development goal and enable their member countries to cope with the challenges related to digitalization which are of multidimensional nature.

The purpose of this chapter is to investigate the role of international organizations in influencing and channeling the processes of transformation in

DOI:10.1163/9789004687264_017

society and the economy brought about by digitalization. Focus is both on the International Labour Organization (ILO), as a global organization that can help set standards, and on the European Union (EU), as a regional integration project that helps negotiate legislation between member states and one that scan influence other jurisdictions as well in the so-called "Brussels Effect" (Bradford, 2020). The chapter is structured along three main sections. The first section deals with a theoretical analysis of digitalization and its effects in society and the economy. The second section is conceptual and focuses on challenges to labor, education, and skills. Finally, the third section is an empirical analysis into the roles of the two international organizations, namely the ILO and the EU.

2 Theoretical Framework

This section provides a theoretical framework for the empirical analysis on the role of international organizations in the digitalization processes in society and the economy. It starts from a simple question to establish a clear conceptual framework: Do we discuss digitization, digitalization, or digital transformation? Then, it ties digital transformation with automation, so that it can specify the challenges with which society and the economy are confronted.

The discussion regarding digital transformation is founded on the concept of the Fourth Industrial Revolution or Industry 4.0. It refers to a change in the production system, not only in the sense that technology is upgraded, but that "real and virtual" systems work together without too much human supervision (World Economic Forum, 2015). These are called cyber-physical systems, as they blend data and technology with machines. The Fourth Industrial Revolution is not a revolution of the machines; it is the result of decisions made by the people developing the technology guided by the purposes they aim to achieve (DeNardis, 2020). Productivity increase is one such purpose. There is an intertwining between the designers of these technologies and governments, which aim to deploy resources to help boost these gains. At the same time, these governments must also take into consideration another side of this effort, namely, the unavoidable changes in labor and education. Considering this, we should not only talk about digitalization, but also about digital transformation, because the digital systems blend with the physical objects. Hence, actions do not take place only in the digital sphere.

Digitization, digitalization, and digital transformation are catch-all terms that have gained attention in public discourse in recent years. In the EU, the current digital transition discourse, and the post-pandemic recovery with the help of the Resilience and Recovery Framework, have contributed to this development (European Commission, 2022). Decision-makers use them interchangeably, but the literature makes a distinction between them (Venkatraman, 2017; Verhoef et al., 2021). Verhoef et al. consider that the three concepts are phases in digital transformation, beginning with digitization and working towards digital transformation. First, "digitization" is a shift from analogue to digital tasks, or, more simply put, the integration of IT technologies into the existing processes. Other researchers share this technical point of view as well (Van der Zande et al., 2019). Next, "digitalization" intervenes in business processes by helping create new ways of communicating and managing resources. Digitalization pushes for optimization of processes both at an internal level and with the exterior (Pagani & Pardo, 2017). This second phase focuses on improvement, optimization, and change within an entity, so that it can create new sources of value (Van der Zande et al., 2019). Finally, Verhoef et al. describe "digital transformation" as the most pervasive phase, since it aims to transform the entity from the foundation, be it a company or a public institution (Verhoef et al., 2021).

Larsson also notices the misuse of the terms in public discourse, and emphasizes the broader outlook of digital transformation, which requires several transformative processes within the entity. He also states that digitalization and digital transformation can be used interchangeably to analyze the core changes happening in society (Larsson & Teigland, 2019, p. 3). Other studies also agree that digital transformation represents an evolution in terms of ICT-enabled transformation, focused both on the significant changes brought about by ICT, but also on the expected means of action that are necessary to channel these changes for the better (Majchrzak et al., 2016). At the same time, Van der Zande et al. (2019) clarify the differences between the three concepts and use "digital transformation" to describe the wider effects of digitalization on society.

Regardless of the terminological overlap, the various definitions of digital transformation can offer significant insights into its effects in society and the economy (Majchrzak et al., 2016). While most definitions focus on the internet underpinning this process, they also delve into the challenges that digital transformation creates. For instance, Bowersox et al. (2005) focus on the idea that digital transformation is a process by which businesses reinvent themselves, as well as re-energize themselves by using technology in their supply chain management. In a similar manner, other authors focus on the idea of the evolution of an entity, in line with the technological revolution (Mazzone, 2014). Mazzone deliberately emphasizes the idea that it is an ongoing process, hence it requires constant and conscious adaptation to the wave of technology.

These approaches point to a deterministic and instrumentalist view of technology, namely the idea that this technological wave sweeps society and the economy entirely with only positive benefits. However, a deeper look into the definitions of digital transformation in the literature implies that this process requires a conscious effort from both the private and the public sector. As a matter of fact, research also focuses on the actors' efforts to channel digital transformation (Schallmo et al., 2017).

The barriers between digitalization and digital transformation are clear in business, but in policy these terms are used interchangeably. This interchangeable use is adopted in the chapter, but with the following definition that subscribes to the business perspective presented above:

> The conscious and ongoing effort of an entity to integrate information and communication technologies (ICTs) in growing facets of its activity by taking advantage of the process of data collection and analysis enabled by technology, as well as of emerging technologies, to facilitate its activity and balanced functioning.

This definition balances between the improvements in terms of efficiency and optimization that ICT can bring about and the need for conscious actions to mitigate the challenges that it creates. In short, it strives for a societal approach to digital transformation.

While most of the literature on digital transformation stems from a business perspective, a social science perspective is also required to understand the effects of technology in society and the economy. In this sense, Salento (2018) criticizes the mainstream interpretation that digital transformation is deterministic and will bring about only positive change. He points to the popular idea from public discourse that the negative effects of digital transformation will be offset by new opportunities, especially on the labor market. In this sense, the key concept from the definition provided above is "balanced functioning", since digital transformation should be conceptualized as a process by which actors and entities strive not only for efficiency and optimization, but also for better quality of life. In this sense, according to Salento (2018), digital transformation can also be a threat to citizens.

A complementary process adds to the challenges of digital transformation, namely automation, the process by which technology replaces humans from performing routine and non-routine tasks. To round up the theoretical discussion surrounding the effects of technology in society and the economy, automation needs to be conceptualized, as well.

Automation works towards the goal of efficiency and optimization of organizations, considering that it creates productivity gains by eliminating human errors or friction. As with the three concepts discussed above, there is also a great deal of confusion regarding "automation", as it also appears interchangeably in discourses with "robotization" or, in fact, "digitalization" (Van der Zande et al., 2019). The main difference between automation and digitalization is that the former focuses on improving existing processes within an entity, while the latter is a wider effort to develop new ways to add value within that particular entity (Van der Zande et al., 2019). The main goal of automation is the inherent improvement of the functioning of an entity, but it has a fixed goal in that it does not transform the underlying logic of processes. A particular technology simply replaces what was originally performed by humans (Van der Zande et al., 2019). Considering that automation is a more concrete application of digital transformation in society and the economy, it will be analyzed further in the next section dedicated to changes in the labor market.

This brief theoretical framework has explored the potential of automation, digitalization, and digital transformation to challenge existing socioeconomic relations. The next section delves deeper into their effects into society and the economy, by mapping the transformations triggered, as well as the predictions for the future.

3 Contextual Framework: Challenges to Society and the Economy

Based on the theoretical framework presented above, this section deals with the challenges brought about by digital transformation, digitalization, and automation. It approaches this discussion in two manners. Based on the literature review, it maps the transformations that are already underway. The section provides conceptual clarity and serves as a bridge towards the discussion on the role of international organizations in channeling processes of digitalization in society and the economy.

3.1 *Transformations in the Labor Market*

This subsection analyzes the current labor market trends influenced by digitalization. It focuses on the job perspectives affected by automation, but also by platformization. Platformization refers to the process by which digital platforms penetrate significant infrastructures, social relations, and institutions, causing substantial changes in a variety of sector (Poell et al., 2019). It also penetrates the world of work and has contributed to the development of the gig economy or the platform economy, with significant impact on the future of work.

Along with digitalization and digital transformation, automation is also included in the wide domain of research entitled "future of work," since it significantly impacts the labor market and, with it, education, and social relations. Several studies have analyzed these effects, with varying degrees of optimism regarding the effects of automation and digital transformation in society and the economy. One of the landmark studies regarding the potential of automation to displace jobs is Acemoglu and Restrepo (2018), who adopt a task-based approach meant to quantify more clearly the potential for job disruption in the American economy. They conclude that the replacement of humans with machines reduces the demand for labor, as well as wages and overall unemployment. At the same time, production costs will decrease, leading to more automation. Nevertheless, they maintain an optimistic perspective by emphasizing the potential of automation to create new tasks and, hence, new skills.

Van der Zande et al. (2019) use a similar task-based approach to map the changes brought by automation in tandem with the categorization of human capabilities in the workplace. They stress the idea that the more complex and non-routine a task is, the more difficult it is for an automated system to perform it. Van der Zande et al. (2019) illustrate this idea with the example of natural language processing, which is developed, but has not reached human-like potential. Other examples include the capacity to recognize human emotions or fine motor skills. While certain tasks have been replaced by machines, there is no clear consensus regarding the complete elimination of jobs that require complex human thinking, according to Van der Zande et al. (2019). The task-based approach in relation to the impact of digital transformation on the labor market opens the door not necessarily to the elimination of jobs, but to their transformation. Indeed, there is a trend towards more human – machine interaction in manufacturing or other industries rather than the complete elimination of jobs (Acemoglu & Restrepo, 2019).

In this sense, the policy trend is to invest in reskilling and upskilling, considering integration of technology into the world of work. Schmidpeter and Winter-Ebmer (2021) have analyzed the relation between risk of automation and probability that the displaced workers find new job opportunities. Often, job seekers must shift sectors to find employment. They conclude that the higher the risk for automation, the more difficult is for workers to find new opportunities. They also assess the potential of training policies for the mitigation of these adverse effects and find that labor market training is significant in boosting chances for re-employment for those who have been displaced by automation.

Another effect of automation and digitalization relates to the polarization of the labor market, with a reported decrease of the share of mid-sector jobs and a rise in low-skilled and high-skilled jobs (Frey & Osborne, 2013). The reason behind this trend is that most middle-skilled jobs contain tasks that have been automated, while many new jobs require more complex skills, such as programming.

The decline of the middle-class sector can be seen in tandem with another trend observed by researchers, namely reshoring. Reshoring is the opposite process to offshoring and it refers to the return of production back to the more developed countries, but the processes are not symmetrical. Reshoring can take place when automated manufacturing returns to the original production sites, but requiring fewer employees with a higher skill set. Research argues that reshoring is still a limited occurrence and may just be anecdotal (De Backer et al., 2016). Nevertheless, growing discussions around "taking back control" over global supply chains are poised to reignite the debate on bringing jobs back.

The second trend related to digitalization is the so-called "platformization". This trend has resulted in significant changes in the labor market as well. With the advent of platforms and the gig economy, the traditional model of the employer – employee relationship has shifted. Employees become collaborators or self-employed persons who find work using digital platforms.

Although the narrative of these platforms focused on the flexible worker experience, the reality is different. Protests by taxi drivers in Barcelona against Uber, accusations of surveillance by other platform workers, or the lack of willingness to ensure basic social rights to gig workers have reignited the debate over the gig economy and the role that such platforms should assume. They face regulation both at a national and at a European level to mitigate the side effects of a technological change that is meant to make workers more flexible, but which can also be destructive to social rights. The European Union is stepping up its efforts; its intervention will be analyzed in the section dedicated to international organizations.

3.2 *Transformations in Education*

Education is also affected by digitalization, not only with the way technology can improve teaching and students' experiences, but also with transformations to the curriculum and to adult training with consequences on the labor market and in the economy. We focus on three aspects: digital inclusion, skills, and training.

Firstly, the literature on digital inclusion provides interesting insights into the changes brought about by digitalization for the education system. Digital inclusion research stresses the significance of a layered approach to integration in the new digital society, starting from building motivation, continuing with providing access, building skills, and culminating with usage of technologies (Van Dijk, 2005).

In this sense, if education policy does not prioritize the deployment of digital technologies and the subsequent adaptation to digital society, then it risks contributing to digital exclusion and, eventually, damaging the labor market. The educational system is the appropriate environment to build motivation and provide internet access, especially in disadvantaged or rural areas prone to more social exclusion. In this sense, we refer to the effect that digital transformation has on the curricula, content, and teaching. Digital technologies should underpin teaching to contribute to the development of well-trained digital citizens and an inclusive digital society.

Secondly, digitalization influences what students should learn because it creates the need for new skills. Additionally, the educational sector should support the development of a proper workforce. The discussion above related to reskilling and upskilling is significant here as well. Symeonidis et al. (2021) analyze the EU discourse with regards to education policy and find a strong connection between digital transformation and a developing discourse on reskilling and upskilling the European workforce. The lifelong learning approach is at the forefront of these efforts, since these two terms relate especially to adult training rather than to the traditional education sector. Indeed, research shows that labor market training plays a role in mitigating some of the effects of automation (Schmidpeter & Winter-Ebmer, 2021). Companies, as well as the education system, should adapt to the new requirements in the economy and to the innovative technologies and create agile teaching programs aimed at teaching hard IT skills necessary for working with machines, artificial intelligence, or with big data, as well soft skills.

Thirdly, the *Future of Jobs* report released by the World Economic Forum illustrates the urgency for rethinking education and training, considering the "double disruption" trend that describes the displacement of jobs by the pandemic and by digital transformation (World Economic Forum, 2020). The report argues that job destruction has surpassed job creation, considering the accelerated pace of digitalization in the wake of the pandemic. This has a double effect on the education sector, considering that it will render some specializations obsolete, but it will also pressure the institutions to adapt, to reskill trainers, and to deliver updated content.

4 The Role of International Organizations: the ILO and the EU

The challenges brought about by the processes described in the previous section require multiple interventions by a variety of actors in light of their widespread effects. Considering that technology knows no borders, efforts should be concentrated at various decision-making levels, not only at the state level. International organizations are well-equipped to offer guidance and a governance umbrella for states and other actors involved in the digitalization process. The core premise of this chapter is that multilateralism is the solution, given that states share similar socioeconomic challenges and interests. Multilateralism is also a significant venue for sharing of best practices and for creating common regulations and standards. This section first deals with the International Labour Organization as a venue for cooperation between employers, workers, and member states. The role of the European Union in promoting standards and regulations in relation to the digital economy, digital education, industry, and so on is then discussed.

4.1 *The Role of the ILO in Promoting Mechanisms to Respond to Digital Challenges*

The processes of digitalization and digital transformation affect workers and different social groups, causing some to be excluded from the labor market, which may contribute to increasing socioeconomic inequalities. The challenges of digitalization have been reconsidered and addressed by recently adopted policies, programs, and activities of international organizations.

Two organizations and their activities are noteworthy: the International Labour Organization and the European Union. They have adopted diverse policy agendas and actions in order, on the one hand, to meet the challenges and seize the opportunities presented by digitalization processes and, on the other, to counter the risks that can inevitably be observed. This is also due to the specificity of the mentioned organizations that provide public goods. Global public goods are "thought and action on common concerns that affect a substantial proportion of humanity" (Sagasti & Bezanson, 2001, p. i). However, as was stressed in Chapter 1, there are public goods with benefits that are not limited to national borders but extend the border of one country. A distinction can be made between core and complementary activities, where core activities refer to all activities that produce international public goods, while complementary activities are prepared by countries "for consumption" of international public goods (World Bank, 2001, p. 110, after Sagasti & Bezanson, 2001, p. 22).

4.2 *Role of the ILO*

The International Labour Organization (ILO) provides global public good by easing the transition of people to the future of work and facilitating the acquisition of skills, competencies, and qualifications to cope with the challenges of digitization. Today an agency of the United Nations based in Geneva, the ILO was originally created in 1919 as an organization of representatives of three parties: government, employers, and workers (International Labour Office, 1920, Article 393). It was based on the 1919 Treaty of Versailles and its first members were representatives of nine countries. Gradually, the number of members grew. Today, the organization has 185 member states (ILO, n.d.-c) and, as stated in the Preamble of the ILO Constitution, "whereas universal and lasting peace can be established only if it is based upon social justice" (ILO, n.d.-g, Preamble), underlies the need to promote social justice, including, among other things, attention to vocational and technical education (ILO, n.d.-g, Preamble). Since its inception, education has been of paramount importance to the ILO, but today it faces certain challenges due to digitalization.

The ILO operates through the following bodies, which include the three parties mentioned above: the International Labour Conference or the General Conference, meeting annually in Geneva, which is also a forum for discussion, held at least once a year; the Governing Body, which is the executive council of the ILO, responsible for ILO policy, program, and budget; and the International Labour Office, which is the permanent secretariat of this organization and with a director general appointed by the Governing Body. The work of the ILO is supported by tripartite commissions and committees of experts (ILO, n.d.-d; ILO, n.d.-g, Article 2–8). This organization has some instruments at its disposal.

In its daily activities, the International Labour Conference adopts the following instruments: conventions, recommendations, and others, such as declarations (of wide application). The following declarations (which were also updated) were adopted: the Philadelphia Declaration on the Aims and Objectives of the ILO (1944), the Declaration on the "Apartheid" Policy of South Africa (1964), the Declaration on Gender Equality, the ILO Declaration on Fundamental Principles and Rights at Work (1998), the Declaration on Social Justice for a Just Globalization (2008), and the relatively recent Centenary Declaration for the Future of Work (ILO, n.d.-f) adopted in 2019, which is of great importance for further considerations in this chapter.

The Declaration for the Future of Work (hereafter referred to as the Declaration) was adopted at the International Labour Conference held in Geneva during the 108th session of the ILO. It affirmed that there has been a transformational change regarding the "world of work", which is driven by, among other things, technological innovation, and persistent inequalities, which will affect the future of work. The primary areas of action envisaged by the Declaration relate to investments in people's capabilities, in work institutions, and in decent and sustainable work (ILO, n.d.-f).

The Declaration indicated that ILO efforts must ensure the transition to the future of work, harness the potential of technological progress, and stimulate and support the acquisition of skills, competencies, and qualifications over the course of workers' professional lives. It also stressed the need to enhance the capacity of workers to take advantage of opportunities relevant to decent work. The need to promote effective policies that facilitate the transition to work after education and training was also emphasized (ILO, n.d.-e, pp. 3–6). Members were urged to promote a "human-centered approach to the future of work" (ILO, n.d.-e, pp. 6–7) and to improve people's ability to seize the opportunities a changing world offers by, inter alia, promoting lifelong learning, and ensuring the quality of education. Another course of action is to strengthen labor institutions to protect all workers, and to promote sustainable employment and decent work (ILO, n.d.-e, pp. 6–7).

However, the pandemic has created new circumstances for the world of work. The pandemic, as highlighted by the ILO, has caused significant changes related to the world of work, namely technological change, alongside environmental sustainability, or demographic change. During the COVID-19 pandemic, the digitalization of work accelerated, and remote working was introduced, but it was not a trend. Some people have been unable to take full advantage of this phenomenon. The reasons for this situation are due to the nature of work or connectivity problems. The dramatic situation caused by the COVID-19 pandemic was reflected in the labor market figures, as the global number of working hours in 2020 fell by about 9 percent compared to 2019 (through the last quarter), representing a loss of 255 million full-time jobs (ILO, 2021c, pp. 10, 7). Thus, the pandemic has accelerated the process of digitalization, which inevitably affects people at work and work organization.

The transformational changes observed inevitably affect the world of work and required the development of skills adapted to the needs of the labor market, with a particular focus on digital skills. Therefore, the role of the ILO in this area is to (a) support the development of skills policies and systems to meet the demands of the labor market, (b) create relevant competencies that are required for future jobs, and (c) promote the social inclusion of disadvantaged groups through skills development (ILO, n.d.-k).

The aforementioned activities are implemented in collaboration with member countries, where the ILO has a supportive role in policy planning, governance, as well as regulation. Referring to one of the key activities focusing on strengthening skills policies and systems in member countries, the ILO is collaborating in skills systems on improving planning and governance policies. This cooperation is also aimed at greater involvement of workers' and employers' organizations in skills development and improving the quality of skills to promote socioeconomic development. To achieve this, research is conducted, and technical assistance is offered. ILO activities in this area include digitizing skills systems by working on the impact of technology on TVET (technical and vocational education and training) and the skills system (ILO, n.d.-a). It is emphasized that digital transformation in TVET includes digital innovation, digital adaptation, and digital acceleration (ILO, 2020a).

The importance of digitalization has been recognized by the ILO and its Skills Branch, whose work examines the impact on TVET and skills systems that leverage technologies, and supports greater commitment to digital transformation, digital inclusion, and bridging the digital divide (ILO, n.d.-a). There are some research initiatives dedicated to digitalization. One example is the project "Digitalization, the Future of Work and the Teaching Profession," which commenced in November 2019 (through December 2021). Carried out by the ILO and the Deutsche Gesellschaft für Internationale Zusammenarbeit (GIZ), the project examines the impact of digital technologies on the primary and secondary educational systems of a range of countries and includes a coronavirus and digitalization perspective on teaching and education. The countries analyzed were Ethiopia, Kenya, Malawi, Rwanda, and the United Republic of Tanzania. It was highlighted that these countries are making efforts to use technology to improve the quality of teaching and learning, although these efforts are rather diverse. Some measures aimed to ensure access to quality digital education services while others designed policies to guide digitalization in education, increase investment in digital technologies, develop digital skills of teachers, ensure decent working conditions for teachers, and improve social dialogue (ILO, n.d.-b; ILO, 2021b).

To create the right skills required by the labor market, a strategy for skills anticipation must be developed. Therefore, the ILO is working on "Skills Strategies for Future Labour Markets,", both in terms of research on the adaptation of skills to future labor markets and by providing technical assistance relating to knowledge and tools for skills anticipation (ILO, n.d.-k). This work focuses, among other things, on skills related to technological change, meaning that technological change makes it necessary to change skills, retrain them or upgrade them because they are sometimes outdated. Two aspects of their activity were identified: (a) technological change skills, which refers to a focus on the demand for digital skills, as well as other skills and digitalization, and (b) technological skills foresight (STF),which focuses on collaborative skills anticipation, primarily at the sector level and working with sector stakeholders (ILO, n.d.-j). Society should adapt to these changes because "digital transformation not only means that some jobs disappear, but also that the vast majority of the existing work tasks with traditional jobs will be modified" (ILO, 2021a, p. 9). For instance, the Training for Rural Economic Empowerment (TREE) program, which addresses the challenges in rural areas by providing essential skills, is implemented in more than 20 countries (ILO, 2020b).

Another area of ILO work includes activities aimed at improving the labor market and the quality of work for disadvantaged groups, including women, youth, migrants, refugees, and rural workers, as well as activities aimed at establishing TVET systems and active labor market programs, which are the focus of the ILO activity (ILO, n.d.-i). By promoting the development of right skills required by the market in the face of digitalization, the activities undertaken by ILO contribute also to SDG 9, where promotion of inclusive and sustainable industrialization is underlined.

4.3 *The Role of the EU in Promoting Mechanisms Related to Digital Challenges*

4.3.1 A Common Online Market Tackling Digital Challenges

As underlined, digitalization brings about some opportunities for EU countries and their regions, for citizens and businesses. However, there are certain groups of European citizens and entities/actors who may be excluded from the digital market. The creation of a Digital Single Market, which aims to remove barriers to online transactions in the EU, enables the potential of digitalization, and, by promoting digital skills and learning related to digitalization, all European citizens should be able to benefit from this process. It can be argued that the creation of the Digital Single Market by the EU provides global public goods, including a legal framework and mechanisms for adoption. Financial support from the EU will support the efficient implementation of the Digital Single Market. Thus, the multidimensional benefits provided by this market cover the EU, but extend even beyond it, thus fulfilling the Sustainable Development Goal 9.

The Digital Single Market is a market where the free movement of factors of production is ensured "where individuals and businesses can seamlessly access and exercise online activities under conditions of fair competition, and a high level of consumer and personal data protection, irrespective of their nationality or place of residence". (European Commission, 2015, p. 3). The Digital Single Market Strategy consists of the following three pillars:

- "Better access for consumers and businesses to online goods and services across Europe."
- "Creating the right conditions for digital networks and services to flourish."
- "Maximizing the growth potential of our European Digital Economy."

The first pillar of the strategy focuses on removing barriers to cross-border online activity. The main proposals regard the creation of an appropriate framework for e-commerce by introducing certain cross-border e-commerce rules common to cross-border online and digital purchases or ensuring quality cross-border parcel delivery at affordable prices. Additionally, the strategy focuses on removing unjustified geo-blocking practices, and improving access to digital content by implementing a harmonized copyright regime and reducing barriers to cross-border e-commerce resulting from different VAT regimes.

The second pillar refers to promoting high-speed networks and services that protect consumers and ensure privacy and data protection. The proposed actions in this pillar include aligning telecommunications laws and providing a regulatory framework for telecommunications, as well as a regulatory framework for media, platforms, and intermediaries, and ensuring the security of digital services, personal data, and privacy.

The third pillar promotes big data, cloud services, and the Internet of Things, which are key issues for EU competitiveness, promoting interoperability and standardization. The Digital Single Market should be inclusive by promoting digital skills; it can benefit not only from e-services, but also e-government, e-justice, e-health, e-energy, or e-transport (European Commission, 2015). The growing pace of regulations and directives proposed and discussed within the European Union is a testament to the idea that there is consensus at the member state level regarding the idea that a European governance umbrella is required for mitigating the risks of digitalization and channeling its potential.

On June 20, 2019, the European Council agreed on "A new strategic agenda 2019–2024" for a five-year period identifying four priorities, also important as a direction for the institution (European Council, n.d.). "The development of a strong and vibrant economic base" was identified as a priority. The document emphasizes that digital transformation will develop and address infrastructure, connectivity, services, data, regulation, and investment. All aspects of the digital revolution and artificial intelligence should be taken into consideration (European Council, 2019).

These have been translated into policy priorities for the European Commission for 2019–2024 and the following six priorities have been defined: "A European Green Deal, an economy that works for people, a Europe fit for the digital age, protecting our European way of life, a stronger Europe in the world, a new push for European democracy" (European Commission, 2019, p. 4).

4.3.2 Tackling Societal Challenges Brought by Digital Transformation

The focus of European policymaking has shifted from economic to societal challenges related to digital transformation. The priority of "a Europe fit for the digital age" underlines that Europe should seize the opportunities of the digital age, highlighting the role of digital technologies, including artificial intelligence (AI). Proposed actions include legislation on the human and ethical implications of AI; investment in AI; and a new Digital Services Act that will help strengthen the Digital Single Market. Moreover, the need to provide people with the opportunities for education and skills acquisition is emphasized. Therefore, the objective under the priority is to create by 2025 the European Education Area by reducing barriers to education and increasing access to quality education, facilitating transition between education systems, and promoting lifelong learning. A particular priority is the improvement of digital skills among young people and adults using the potential of the internet (European Commission, 2019, pp. 13–14).

The objectives are specified in detail, namely they refer to "technology that works for people, a fair and competitive economy and open, democratic and sustainable society" (European Commission, 2020). The March 2021 Digital Compass provides a vision for 2030 in terms of key milestones and measures that are being used to achieve clearly defined goals. As underlined in the document, digital ambitions are translated into targets and an improved monitoring system that will include milestones and cardinal points. These points refer to a digitally skilled population and digital professionals, secure and sustainable digital infrastructure, digital transformation of businesses, and, finally, digitalization of public services (European Commission, 2020).

The Digital Decade is the mission policy defined by the EU to shape the digital society for the Europeans. The policy discourse, as well as public appearances of EU leaders, focuses on a European digital society, where digital rights and principles are enshrined into legislation and policies that favor a more humane approach to digital transformation. For instance, *Shaping Europe's Digital Future* presents the overall vision regarding digital transformation in the EU and it starts off with a bold desire:

> [T]he Commission wants a European society powered by digital solutions that are strongly rooted in our common values, and that enrich the lives of all of us: people must have the opportunity to develop personally, to choose freely and safely, to engage in society, regardless of their age, gender or professional background. (European Commission, 2020)

This vision clearly mirrors the theoretical discussions in the previous section on the societal impact that digital transformation has. In this vision, digital solutions are shaped around European values and European society and not the other way around, pointing away from the deterministic, mainstream vision that Salento (2018) criticizes. This is also evident in the priorities that the strategy discusses. Technology serves socioeconomic relations and not the reverse.

The strategy presents the policy program regarding digital policy and the following initiatives will shape digitalization processes in society and the economy in the mandate of the Von der Leyen Commission:

- Developing gigabit connectivity by means of action plans for 5G and 6G, revisions of the Broadband Cost Reduction Directive and other initiatives to boost connectivity
- The Digital Education Action Plan, "to boost literacy and competences at all levels of education"
- An updated Skills Agenda, as well as a "reinforced Youth Guarantee to put a strong focus on digital skills in early career transitions"
- Regulatory initiatives for platform workers
- The Digital Services Act and Digital Markets Act (European Commission, 2020)

At the same time, the societal orientation of digital transformation in the EU is evident also in the Digital Compass Communication. The document crystallizes the European vision for a digital society as follows: "The European way to a digitalised economy and society is about solidarity, prosperity, and sustainability, anchored in empowerment of its citizens and businesses, ensuring the security and resilience of its digital ecosystem and supply chains" (European Commission, 2021e). Additionally, this vision is distilled into four cardinal points that map out the next decade:

- A digitally skilled population and highly skilled digital professionals
- Secure and sustainable digital infrastructures
- Digital transformation of businesses
- Digitisation of public services (European Commission, 2021e)

Moreover, the document also contains a list of digital principles that are the cornerstone of the European digital society, namely:

- Universal Access to internet services
- A secure and trusted online environment
- Universal digital education and skills for people to take an active part in society and in democratic processes
- Access to digital systems and devices that respect the environment
- Accessible and human-centric digital public services and administration
- Ethical principles for human centric algorithms
- Protecting and empowering children in the online space
- Access to digital health services (European Commission, 2021e)

The strategy of the European Union does not stop at promoting best practices or encouraging common standards, but it focuses on shaping the socioeconomic relations in the digital society of the future. It does so in two ways: by providing regulatory frameworks for the digital challenges and by providing a model for the digital society, based on the model for the social market economy. These two facets reinforce each other. To exemplify this idea, we focus on specific examples in the labor market and education, namely the initiatives for the gig economy and the new agenda for skills in the digital age.

The platform economy, also known as the gig economy or the sharing economy, has been one of the major disruptors of social relations in the digital sphere. From food delivery to freelancing, major platforms have become marketplaces for work in the European Union. The EU estimates that approximately 28 million Europeans work in the platform economy with a steady growth potential. According to the accompanying Communication on better working conditions in the platform economy, platforms are indeed effective in matching supply and demand for labor, thus offering numerous opportunities for work, while challenging the traditional labor model. However, the Communication also emphasizes that this new model has the potential to undermine the European social model (European Commission, 2021b). The challenges stem from the fact that platform work "does not automatically translate into quality jobs" (European Commission, 2021b). Additionally, the Commission states some of the challenges that platform workers face in this disrupted labor market:

- Difficult working conditions
- Ambiguity regarding the status of workers
- Limited access to rights and protections associated with the worker status
- Challenges related to surveillance, mismanagement of data, equality, and potential algorithmic discrimination
- Lack of transparency and predictability of contractual arrangements to health and safety challenges
- Limited social dialogue

Taking these difficulties into consideration, the solution proposed by the Commission in the form of a directive aims to clarify the employment status of platform workers and to build a solid framework for their protection against the potential challenges mentioned above. In terms of employment, the directive creates a set of criteria that will determine whether one such platform classifies as an employer. If this happens, then the people involved in contractual relations with that platform will automatically be classified as workers. Once the workers attain this status, they are entitled to a set of rights, such as the "right to a minimum wage, collective bargaining, working time and health protection, the right to paid leave or improved access to protection against work accidents, unemployment and sickness benefits, as well as contributory old-age pensions" (European Commission, 2021c). Platforms will also have a right to dispute this classification, but they must prove that "there is no employment relationship" between them and the worker. Other significant provisions from the directive focus on algorithmic management, namely the idea that workers understand how algorithmic decisions are taken on the platform and how this influences their rights and activities on that platform.

The situation of this proposed legal framework is rather peculiar, considering the limited social policy competences that the EU has. At the same time, it is also a perfect example of the idea that international organizations, such as the EU, can offer a governance umbrella for their member states because it does not aim to change the existing social policy mechanisms from the national level. It rather focuses on a wide set of rules that are applicable in every member state and are neutral from a legislative point of view, given that it creates a legal framework where many member states do not have one yet. It intervenes in an area that has not been completely covered by national legislation, while respecting the existing social rules at the national level.

For instance, the set of rights that workers may enjoy once their status is recognized is the right to minimum wage, a notoriously contentious issue in the EU nowadays. However, the right is only valid where it is applicable under the national law. Indeed, the proposed directive cites the support competence of the EU to provide a framework for worker protection, by setting a set of minimum standards and, at the same time, by abstaining from "imposing administrative, financial and legal constraints" (European Commission, 2021d).

The second example that aims to illustrate the role of the EU in channeling the processes of digital transformation in society and the economy refers to its constant push towards the improvement of citizens' digital skills. While the previous example focused on a proposal for legislation that would become hard law, the EU Skills Agenda is classified as soft law, a set of policy initiatives spearheaded by the Commission in tandem with the member states and other stakeholders.

If we refer to the principles set within the Digital Decade and the Digital Compass, we observe that the first cardinal point relates to the digital skills of Europeans. At the same time, the Resilience and Recovery Framework (RRF) incentivizes member states to upskill and reskill their citizens to adapt to digital transformation. In fact, one of the seven major priorities of the RRF refers to reskilling and upskilling, both in terms of adult education, as well as in the education system that needs upgrading to the new requirements of the labor market (European Commission, 2021a). Yet again, the Commission has no direct competences with relation to the national education systems, but it does create yet another framework by which it incentivizes member states to act. In terms of reskilling and upskilling, the financial assistance by means of the RRF pushes member states to create their own programs, which are adapted to the national specificities.

5 Conclusions

The main objective of this chapter has been to highlight the role that international organizations play in developing policies for the challenges brought about by digitalization in society and the economy. The chapter starts with short overview of the theoretical framework of digitialization. It further assesses the contextual impact of digitalization on the world of work and education, being the basis for the analysis of the activities of international organizations. Labour market polarization, changes in the educational system due to the requirement of new skills on the labor market, or platformization are the main effects that digital technologies have on society and the economy. These challenges are inherently transnational, and they require transnational policies.

Within this context, the chapter analyzed the activity of the ILO and of the EU. On the one hand, the ILO has a global outreach due to its statute as a UN agency. On the other, the EU is a regional integration project, but its legislation and policies echo across its borders and it can influence other jurisdictions as well.

Both organizations stress the need for a human-centered digitalization, but they have different angles to tackle this problem. The ILO cooperates with member states and organizes programs and projects, but its policies are not mandatory. The European Union, by virtue of its organization and logic, can issue legislation that is binding for the member states and its policies have the possibility to shape global trends as well. Data protection legislation is one example of a legal framework that the EU leveraged globally. Moreover, with its current strategy, the EU focuses on values at the foundation of digital transformation and aims to lead by example globally.

Both organizations' steering activities are essential for developing strong policies as answers to significant changes in society and the economy that digital transformation causes, especially because this process is ongoing.

References

Acemoglu, D., & Restrepo, P. (2018). *Artificial intelligence, Automation and work.* National Bureau of Economic Research, Working Paper no. 24196. https://doi.org/10.3386/w24196

Acemoglu, D., & Restrepo, P. (2019). Automation and new tasks: How technology displaces and reinstates labor. *Journal of Economic Perspectives, 33*(2), 3–30. https://doi.org/10.1257/jep.33.2.3

Bradford, A. (2020). *The Brussels effect: How the European Union rules the world.* Oxford University Press.

De Backer, K., Menon, C., Desnoyers-James, I., & Moussiegt, L. (2016). *Reshoring: Myth or reality?* OECD Science, Technology and Industry Policy Papers no. 27. https://doi.org/10.1787/5jm56frbm38s-en

DeNardis, L. (2020). *The internet in everything: Freedom and security in a world with no off switch.* Yale University Press.

European Commission. (2015). *A digital single market strategy for Europe.* Communication to the European Parliament, the Council, the European Economic and Social Committee and the Community of the Regions, Brussels, 6.5.2015, COM (2015) 192.

European Commission. (2019). *A Union that strives for more: My agenda for Europe, by candidate for president of the European Commission, Ursula von der Leyen, Political Guidelines for the next European Commission 2019–2024.* Retrieved March 28, 2022. https://ec.europa.eu/info/sites/default/files/political-guidelines-next-commission_en_0.pdf

European Commission. (2020). *Shaping Europe's digital future.* Publications Office of the European Union, Luxembourg. Retrieved March 28, 2022. https://commission.europa.eu/publications/communication-shaping-europes-digital-future_en

European Commission. (2021a). *Commission staff working document. Guidance to member states. Recovery and resilience plans.* Retrieved February 15, 2022. https://ec.europa.eu/info/sites/default/files/document_travail_service_part1_v2_en.pdf

European Commission. (2021b). *Communication from the Commission to the European Council, the European Economic and Social Committee and the Committee of the Regions. Better working conditions for a stronger social Europe: Harnessing the full benefits of digitalisation for the future of work.* Retrieved February 15, 2022. https://ec.europa.eu/social/BlobServlet?docId=24994&langId=en

European Commission. (2021c). *Improving working conditions in platform work.* Retrieved February 15, 2022. https://ec.europa.eu/commission/presscorner/detail/en/ip_21_6605

European Commission. (2021d). *Proposal for a directive of the European Parliament and of the Council on improving working conditions in platform work.* https://ec.europa.eu/social/BlobServlet?docId=24992&langId=en

European Commission. (2021e). *2030 digital compass. The European way for the digital decade.* Retrieved December 5, 2021. https://ec.europa.eu/newsroom/dae/document.cfm?doc_id=75375

European Commission. (2022). *Recovery and resilience facility.* Retrieved: 8 February 2023. https://commission.europa.eu/business-economy-euro/economic-recovery/recovery-and-resilience-facility_en

European Council. (2019). *A new strategic agenda 2019–2024* (2019). Retrieved March 27, 2022. https://www.consilium.europa.eu/media/39914/a-new-strategic-agenda-2019-2024.pdf

European Council. (N.d.). A *new strategic agenda for the EU 2019–2024.* Retrieved March 27, 2022. https://www.consilium.europa.eu/en/eu-strategic-agenda-2019-2024/

Frey, C. B., & Osborne, M. A. (2013). The future of employment: How susceptible are jobs to computerisation? *Technological Forecasting and Social Change, 114*, 254–280. https://doi.org/10.1016/j.techfore.2016.08.019

ILO. (N.d.-a). *Digitalisation of skills systems.* International Labour Organization. RetrievedMarch20,2022.https://www.ilo.org/skills/areas/skills-policies-and-systems/WCMS_822790/lang--en/index.htm

ILO. (N.d.-b). *Digitalization, the future of work and the teaching profession.* International Labour Organization. Retrieved February 21, 2022. https://www.ilo.org/sector/activities/projects/WCMS_776653/lang--en/index.htm

ILO. (N.d.-c). *History of the ILO*. International Labour Organization. Retrieved March 15, 2022. https://www.ilo.org/global/about-the-ilo/history/lang--en/index.htm

ILO. (N.d.-d). *How the ILO works*. International Labour Organization. Retrieved March 15, 2022. https://www.ilo.org/global/about-the-ilo/how-the-ilo-works/lang--en/index.htm

ILO. (N.d.-e). *ILO centenary declaration for the future of work.* International Labour Organization. Retrieved February 16, 2022. https://www.ilo.org/wcmsp5/groups/public/@ed_norm/@relconf/documents/meetingdocument/wcms_711674.pdf

ILO. (N.d.-f). *ILO centenary declaration for the future of work, 2019* International Labour Organization. Retrieved February 16, 2022. https://www.ilo.org/global/about-the-ilo/mission-and-objectives/centenary-declaration/lang--en/index.htm

ILO. (N.d.-g). *ILO constitution*. International Labour Organization. Retrieved March 15, 2022. http://www.ilo.ch/dyn/normlex/en/f?p=1000:62:0::NO:62:P62_LIST_ENTRIE_ID:2453907:NO

ILO. (N.d.-h). *ILO declarations.* International Labour Organization. Retrieved February 17, 2022. https://www.ilo.org/global/about-the-ilo/how-the-ilo-works/departments-and-offices/jur/legal-instruments/WCMS_428589/lang--en/index.htm

ILO. (N.d.-i). *Skills for social inclusion.* International Labour Organization. Retrieved February 16, 2022. https://www.ilo.org/skills/areas/skills-for-youth-employment/lang--en/index.htm

ILO. (N.d.-j). *Skills for technological change.* International Labour Organization. Retrieved March 21, 2022. https://www.ilo.org/skills/areas/skills-training-for-poverty-reduction/stech/lang--en/index.htm

ILO. (N.d.-k). *Skills, knowledge and employability.* International Labour Organization. Retrieved February 16, 2022. https://www.ilo.org/global/topics/skills-knowledge-and-employability/lang--en/index.htm

ILO. (N.d.-l). *Skills strategies for future labour markets*. International Labour Organization. Retrieved March 17, 2022. https://www.ilo.org/skills/areas/skills-training-for-poverty-reduction/lang--en/index.htm

ILO. (2020a). *The digitization of TVET and skills systems.* International Labour Organization.

ILO. (2020b). *Training for Rural Economic Empowerment (TREE)*. International Labour Organization. Retrieved March 21, 2022. https://www.ilo.org/skills/projects/WCMS_731670/lang--en/index.htm

ILO. (2021a). *Changing demand for skills in digital economies and societies: Literature review and case studies from low- and middle-income countries.* International Labour Organization.

ILO. (2021b). Digitalization in teaching and education in Ethiopia, Kenya, Malawi, Rwanda and the United Republic of Tanzania: Digitalization, the future of work and the teaching profession project. Synthesis report (2021). International Labour Organization. Retrieved February 21, 2022. https://www.ilo.org/wcmsp5/groups/public/---ed_dialogue/---sector/documents/publication/wcms_791865.pdf

ILO. (2021c). Work in the time of COVID. Report of the Director-General International Labour Conference 109th Session, 2021, ILC.109/Report I (B), International Labour Office. Retrieved February 17, 2022. https://www.ilo.org/wcmsp5/groups/public/---ed_norm/---relconf/documents/meetingdocument/wcms_793265.pdf

International Labour Office. (1920). *The labour provisions of the peace treaties.* Retrieved March 15, 2022. https://www.ilo.org/public/libdoc/ilo/1920/20B09_18_engl.pdf

Larsson, A., & Teigland, R. (Eds.). (2019). *The digital transformation of labor: Automation, the gig economy and welfare.* Routledge. https://doi.org/10.4324/9780429317866

Majchrzak, A., Markus, M. L., & Wareham, J. (2016). Designing for digital transformation. *MIS Quarterly, 40*(2), 267–278.

Mazzone, D. M. (2014). *Digital or death: Digital transformation: The only choice for business to survive smash and conquer.* Smashbox Consulting Inc.

Pagani, M., & Pardo, C. (2017). The impact of digital technology on relationships in a business network. *Industrial Marketing Management, 67,* 185–192.

Poell, T., Nieborg, D., & Van Dijck, J. (2019). Platformisation. *Internet Policy Review, 8*(4). https://policyreview.info/concepts/platformisation

Sagasti, F., & Bezanson, K. (2001, November). *Financing and providing global public goods: Expectations and prospects.* Institute of Development Studies Sussex, Stockholm.

Schallmo, D., Williams, C. A., & Boardman, L. (2017). Digital transformation of business models – Best practice, enablers, and roadmap. *International Journal of Innovation Management, 21*(08), 1740014. https://doi.org/10.1142/S136391961740014X

Schmidpeter, B., & Winter-Ebmer, R. (2021). Automation, unemployment, and the role of labor market training. *European Economic Review, 137.* https://doi.org/10.1016/j.euroecorev.2021.103808

Symeonidis, V., Francesconi, D., & Agostini, E. (2021). The EU's education policy response to the Covid-19 pandemic: A discourse and content analysis. *Center for Educational Policy Studies Journal, 11*(special issue). https://doi.org/10.26529/cepsj.1137

United Nations. (N.d.). The 17 goals. UN Department of Economic and Social Affairs. Retrieved April 23, 2022. https://sdgs.un.org/goals

Van der Zande, J., Teigland, K., Siri, S., & Teigland, R. (2019). The substitution of labor: From technological feasibility to other factors influencing the potential of job automation. In A. Larsson & R. Teigland (Eds.), *The digital transformation of labor: Automation, the gig economy and welfare*. Routledge.

Van Dijk, J. A. G. M. (2005). *The deepening divide: Inequality in the information society*. Sage.

Venkatraman, V. (2017). *The digital matrix: New rules for business transformation through technology*. LifeTree Media.

Verhoef, P. C., Broekhuizen, T., Bart, Y., Bhattacharya, A., Qi Dong, J., Fabian, N., & Haenlein, M. (2021). Digital transformation: A multidisciplinary reflection and research agenda. *Journal of Business Research*, *122*, 889–901. https://doi.org/10.1016/j.jbusres.2019.09.022

World Bank. (2001). *Global development finance 2001*, Washington, DC: World Bank (after Sagasti & Bezanson 2001).

World Economic Forum. (2015). *The Fourth Industrial Revolution: What it means and how to respond*. Retrieved February 22, 2022. https://www.weforum.org/agenda/2016/01/the-fourth-industrial-revolution-what-it-means-and-how-to-respond/

World Economic Forum. (2020, October). *Future of jobs 2020*. https://www3.weforum.org/docs/WEF_Future_of_Jobs_2020.pdf

CHAPTER 16

The Smart City as a Keystone between Sustainability and Public Good: Case Research on How the European Union is Supporting Smart Settlements in Poland

Agnieszka Domańska and Giuseppe T. Cirella

1 Introduction

The idea of transferring urban areas into more sustainable, accessible, and eco-friendly spaces can be to better our standard of living with the visionary idea of developing the "city of the future." Smart or "intelligent" cities, which in fact embody the success of past development, are characterized by how human settlements have evolved the fields and dimensions of public management, urban planning, mobility, and transportation in terms of environmental and social cohesion.

With the mass exodus of people moving from rural to urban towns and cities over the last century, this globally observed phenomenon has made these areas extremely congested, polluted, and resource scarce. These severe problems are a challenge that cannot be ignored and necessitate action from all levels of society. Moreover, such problems cannot be resolved by onetime operations but rather by wide-ranging international strategies that embrace long-term and forward-looking processes.

In this context, the underlined role of the United Nations (UN) is evident, as stated in the UN Charter Preamble. Dating back to the 1970s, the UN identified the growing global difficulties and problems connected to ever-increasing crowded urban areas as the harbinger of the broader debate on the magnitude and consequences of urbanization (UN, 1976). The manifestation of the issue was, among others, included in the city-related challenges of the UN Millennium Development Goals (MDGs) and its successor, the UN Sustainable Development Goals (SDGs).

The SDGs were established in 2015 with the target of achieving them in accordance with Agenda 2030. Needless to say, according to internationally reconciled and accepted assumptions, the Agenda constitutes the most future-looking and comprehensive approach of the 21st century to tackle the key

DOI:10.1163/9789004687264_018

issues and challenges that inhibit sustainable growth and development (UN, 2015b).

SDG 11 specifically is focused on fostering sustainability together with inclusion, safety, and resilience by making cities and urban space more livable as "incubators for innovation and growth" (UN, 2015a) by 2030. This leads to a better understanding of how to develop "intelligent" cities as well as to provide a high-quality standard of living as described by various international bodies and relating international indices.

Among international agreements underlining the importance of supporting smart city initiatives, the European Union (EU) continues to play a vital role in developing its "urban well-being" mission by allocating funds for various smart city projects and initiatives by its member states. The funds, which are aimed in particular at financing such projects, include the Smart Cities Marketplace, which merges two former platforms, the Marketplace of the European Innovation Partnership on Smart Cities and Communities and the Smart Cities Information System.

Progress in implementing the smart city concept has also been achieved in Poland – both within large agglomerations and small and medium-sized cities. Mainly thanks to EU funding (e.g., the Technical Assistance Operational Program [OP], the European Structural and Investment Fund [ESIF], and the European Regional Development Fund [ERDF]), numerous projects have been effective in implementing and modernizing Polish urban settlements. This includes an upgrading in the quality of the life which is irrefutable and visible in numerous aspects of Polish cities' everyday functioning. Positive changes are centered on urban planning and management, technological advancement of urban grids and public transport, digitalization of local administration, and social behavioral progress.

In this context, the chapter is structured in three main sections. Section 1 assesses the state of the art of both concepts, i.e., sustainability and city smartness. Section 2 explores how these two concepts are interrelated by definition and through the goals they serve. Section 3 gives special attention to the contribution and implementation of the smart city concept in Poland.

In reference to the title of this book and its key issues, it should be noted that measuring and reporting progress in achieving such targets is a manifestation of the actual practical engagement of the given international organization in the real world. As such, indicators from the following key indices, i.e., IMD – SUTD Smart City Index (SCI), IESE Cities in Motion Index (CIMI), EasyPark Cities of the Future Index (CFI), and the CITYkeys project, will be used to evaluate city smartness.

When presenting general conclusions on the commonalities between both concepts, as seen through the perspective of concrete indicators and data, one can reflect and measure them. Exploratory research into the role of international and supranational bodies that support city smartness can offer insight into how this might be achieved. The EU is this case is a suitable candidate since it has already implemented several smart city measures and policy reforms with its member states.

Case research in Polish cities can elucidate various projects financed from EU funds and focus on projects linking sustainability and city smartness to show how they can be commonly and concurrently realized in practice. Utilizing Polish cities pinpoints the progress made in respect to upgrading the level of sustainability of urban development and showcases the improvements and efficiency of local management in a relatively short period of time in comparison to wealthier Western cities.

In short, a breakdown of the chapter identifies the state-of-the-art literature, the relationship between sustainability and city smartness concepts and indicators, case research on Poland in terms of financial opportunities and progress in creating smart settlements, and concluding recommendations on how they can be commonly and concurrently put into practice.

2 The State of the Art of Sustainability and City Smartness

The relationship between sustainability and city smartness is fairly new in the literature. Their intertwining rapidly developed about a decade ago when a few authors argued how the smart city agenda contributes to sustainability (Al-Hader, 2009; Al Nuaimi et al., 2015; Bifulco et al., 2016; Vilajosana et al., 2013). De Jong et al. (2015) showed that the linkages between the "smart city" and the "sustainable city" had been relatively weak up to this time. In most cases, the methodology used to study the issue was based on qualitative surveys and interviews (Alawadhi et al., 2012).

A discursive connection between the two is highlighted and has been more intensively researched during the last 5 years (Cowley & Caprotti, 2019; Trindade et al., 2017). As such, some studies analyzing real-world projects and investments found little empirical evidence that smartness contributes to the sustainability of the cities (Yigitcanlar & Kamruzzaman, 2018). For example, Kramers et al. (2014) explored the opportunities of using information and communication technology (ICT) solutions targeting climate goals to reduce urban energy use. It was concluded that reaching climate targets for cities by way of ICT was primarily focused on the operation of transport and heating of buildings. Moreover, Haarstad and Wathne (2019) investigated smart cities and urban energy sustainability (i.e., energy efficiency, transport, and public services) in the cities of Nottingham, Stavanger, and Stockholm in order to check how urban energy sustainability initiatives were being implemented. It was shown that smart city initiatives did play a positive role and that sustainability did contribute to the local implementation of smart city projects – highlighting a positive correlation between the two. Among other authors investigating these concepts, Barresi and Pultrone (2013), Kitchin (2014), Gabrys (2014), and Martin et al. (2018) concentrated on how environmental consequences interlink with urban energy sustainability as a way of making cities more "intelligent."

One of the first to propose a specific combination of both concepts in relation to cities is Ahvenniemi et al. (2017), who recommended the use of a more accurate term "smart sustainable cities" instead of "smart cities." This approach is consistent with the concept proposed by Girardi and Temporelli (2017) and also developed by Kramers et al. (2014), who examine how smart cities pursue sustainability-oriented goals based on the so-called "smartainability" methodology.

However, the idea to redefine smart cities into smart sustainable cities originates from earlier works, in particular Giffinger et al. (2007), who conceptualized six characteristics which are often referenced and used today. They theorized indicators to measure city smartness and found specific metrics where sustainability is embedded, distinguishing in particular sustainable resource management in a sort of smart environment and sustainable transport system via the concept of smart mobility.

These methods are derived from the *Guidelines for Conducting a Cost-Benefit Analysis of Smart Grid Projects* (Giordano et al., 2012) and *Smart Cities – Ranking of European Medium-Sized Cities* (Giffinger et al., 2007), a publication from a project based on the assets – functionalities – benefits approach. An extent of the research examines how the "enabling technologies" are transferred into practical functionalities (i.e., services) which in turn find practical realization in benefits evaluated via qualitative and quantitative performance indicators.

Ahvenniemi et al. (2017) referred to this as the "smartability" concept in their broad analysis on how basic sustainability domains (i.e., environment, social, economic, and energetic) interlace. They looked at 16 sets of city assessment frameworks (i.e., eight smart city and eight urban sustainability assessment frameworks) covering 958 indicators and found a large number of indicators measuring environmental sustainability while smart city frameworks lacked environmental indicators. A strong focus was put on modern technologies and "smartness" in smart city frameworks compared to urban sustainability frameworks.

Similarly, the use of indicators, measures, and tools for sustainability rather than empirical studies of implementation was done by Lazaroiu and Roscia (2012), Lee et al. (2014), and Huovila et al. (2019). Huovila et al. (2019) compared seven recently published indicator standards for smart sustainable cities by using a taxonomy of 413 studied indicators against five conceptual urban focuses (i.e., types of urban sustainability and smartness),10 sectoral application domains (i.e., energy, transport, ICT, economy, etc.), and five indicator types (i.e., input, process, output, outcome, and impact). Their conclusions enabled, among others, discrimination between indicator standards suited for evaluating the implementation of predominantly smart city approaches versus standards more focused on sustainability assessment. It was suggested that the implementation of smart urban ICT solutions with impact indicators exhibit possible aftereffects to those solutions.

The state of the art of the concepts of sustainability and city smartness also include wider studies completed by Bibri and Krogstie (2017) and Lim et al. (2020, 2021). The former conducted a wide analysis examining the terms "smart sustainable cities" versus "sustainable smart cities" and found that the first category scored higher results, i.e., 403 to 321. Lim et al.'s (2020) first approach examined a "human driven method" and aimed to address the environmental and social aspects of the smart city. The second, i.e., a technology-driven study, targeted ICT and data challenges in building sustainable agglomerations (Lim et al., 2021).

In reference to these developments, it was found that ISO 37120:2014 is an index for measuring urban sustainability, i.e., utilizing indicators at the local level, that lacks standardization, consistency, or comparability over time or across different cities. To better focalize the index, indicators for city services and quality of life have been inserted as a contribution to the sustainability of a city – constituting part of the series of international standards – to uphold a holistic and integrated approach for the development of smart and resilient cities (ISO, 2022). The index itself is heavily discussed in the literature with both supporters and critics alike. Berman and Orttung (2020), for example, examined the index's content using Arctic cities and proposed some potential modifications of the standard that might improve its performance. They showed only half of ISO 37120:2014's 128 indicators actually measure future-oriented concerns – noting the importance of characteristic features of Arctic cities that produce unique sustainability challenges otherwise not appraised.

The terminology of smartability has been adopted by some European (i.e., CEN-CENELEC, 2015) and ETSI, 2015) and international (i.e., ITU, 2016) standardization bodies and plays an important role in piecing together the most recent developments of the two title concepts in the real world. Today, sustainability and smartness of cities have much in common and form the partial bedrock of future city development in response to the rapid growth of urbanization worldwide.

3 General Concepts and Indicators Used in Interlinking Sustainability and Smart Cities

3.1 *Premises*

Smartness of cities can be identified by the broad understanding of the quality of life of everyday citizens – i.e., how they feel psychologically, mentally, and physically as inhabitants of a given urban area – constituting a geographical, structurally defined, and administratively controlled residential environment. Sustainability, in turn, literally means the ability of something to maintain or "sustain" itself over time. This, however, is contemporarily defined as the need for economic and civilizational development in terms of the natural resources people have been "equipped" with as well as their ability to secure those resources for future generations. It can, ultimately, be conceived as a synonym of the widely understood term of well-being or "good" existence lived in concordance with nature, society, and to the satisfaction of broadly seen human needs in environmental, social, and economic perspectives (Elkington, 2018).

However, as both concepts are related to socioeconomic categories, defined quantitatively and qualitatively, and presented in various sources to understand how actually "sustainability" and "smart cities" are intertwined, the details of measuring them is explored. It is indispensable to investigate their relationship in both conceptual and practical terms, i.e., how they are denoted and reflected by indicators and data. Progress in measuring reflects, among many benefits, the real practical engagement of international and global bodies in realizing their functionality and best practices.

To examine a stricter conceptual axis of the interrelation between sustainability and smart cities, it is necessary to assess the current state of global goods. Moreover, to identify this, a direct reference to Agenda 2030, as an indisputable pillar of the global sustainability strategy, should be acknowledged. Established by the UN General Assembly in 2015, the SDGs and specifically SDG 11 ("Sustainable cities and communities") interconnect with Agenda 2030. It is divided into five areas of critical importance for humanity and the planet (i.e., the so-called 5Ps) via 17 SDGs and their related 169 targets.

To date, UN member states commit themselves to working towards the main targets such as the eradication of poverty and hunger, fulfillment of human individual potential in terms of dignity and equality, and living in a healthy environment. In the very essence, the Agenda, which is an unprecedented event in the history of mankind, puts people at the very center of its interest.

Hence, looking for the commonalities between two concepts is an obligatory start to see how city smartness can play an important role for urban inhabitants and their well-being. SDG 11's official mission is to "make cities inclusive, safe, resilient, and sustainable" (UN, 2015a). The idea of building intelligent cities is to provide primarily high-quality conditions for living by linking the two concepts and, ultimately, satisfying urban space by providing a "good life" for its inhabitants. This, in turn, comes down to the factors that can assure mental and physical health in which organizational, infrastructural, and technical (i.e., in conjunction with modern technologies) favor city development (Russo & Cirella, 2020). In sum, this fully responds to sustainability's ultimate goal – the well-being of human beings.

Such an approach also complies with the primary vision of the smart city model as represented by Lazaroiu and Roscia (2012, p. 327), i.e., a community "of average technology size, interconnected and sustainable, comfortable, attractive, and secure." As Girardi and Temporelli (2017, p. 810) stressed, the smart city paradigm "aims to improve citizens' quality of life in a scenario where the percentage of people living in urban areas is getting higher and higher."

The issue of creating good space for living is underlined by Addanki and Venkataraman (2017) who addressed the issue of developing new sustainable, accessible, and well-connected cities of future. The approach stressing the role of smart cities in creating widely understood, sound urban space complies with the definition presented by Anand et al. (2017, p. 211). They recognized the "efficient city center providing high quality of life by optimally using its resources." Calvillo et al. (2016, p. 273) described the smart city as "a sustainable and efficient urban center that provides a high quality of life to its inhabitants through optimal management of its resources."

Ahvenniemi et al. (2017) underlined that the general goal of smart cities is to improve sustainability with help of technologies. Moreover, it corresponds to the way a smart sustainable city is understood by many international bodies. For example, the International Telecommunication Union defines it as "an innovative city that uses ICTs and other means to improve quality of life, efficiency of urban operation and services, and competitiveness, while ensuring that it meets the needs of present and future generations with respect to economic, social, environmental as well as cultural aspects" (ITU, 2016).

It should be mentioned that smart cities are conditioned by the development of digitalization, ICTs, and eco-friendly transport; the concept – as a whole – is still relatively new. Considering this, the conditions or factors responsible for satisfying community mental and physical health are directly a result of the organizational, spatial, and structural aspects of city smartness. Table 16.1

TABLE 16.1 Mental and physical health factors that affect organizational, spatial, and structural aspects of sustainability and city smartness

City inhabitants	Factor	Definition
Mental health	– overcrowding and internal accessibility	– well developed, punctual, fast, and modern public transport network – regulations targeted at discouraging the use of private cars within the city center together with solutions such as park-and-ride for those commuting from the suburbs – policies restraining the overbuilding of the city territory, i.e., the construction of new residential sites restrictions and destroying the city space (e.g., damaging green areas, walking space, and general accessibility) – solutions to counteract traffic jams
	– noise level	– develop regulations to lower the noise level in cities – implement regulations to counteract acoustic smog from worsening using green spaces
	– living space	– provide enough living space as a fundamental condition for quality living
	– social well-being	– friendly, social environment to assure daily living – implementation of projects and regulations against any form of discrimination
	– medical care and health services	– adequate access to mental and psychiatric care, health services, and rehabilitation for all inhabitants
Physical health	– clean environment	– having clean, unpolluted air, water, and food – using clean and low emission technologies (i.e., CO_2, NO_x, $PM_{2.5}$, PM_{10}, etc.) – regulating energy resources for central heating and urban transport – adequate legal regulations concerning energy resources and infrastructure – high quality sanitation equipment – solutions caring for healthy food supply – modern waste management
	– medical supplies	– adequate supply of medical supplies
	– security	– adequate security for the protection against physical assault, violence, war, etc.

SOURCE: OWN ELABORATION

presents a current practical overview of how city smartness has developed, given the reviewed conceptual assessments and based on the available literature, datasets, and indices.

A practical examination of the commonalities between the two concepts, viewed through concrete indicators and data collected by various international organizations, pinpoints unique combinations inhabitants of a city may find essential to live adequately. The detailed analysis of the indicators reflecting the two concepts is based on the following sources: (1) the Department of Economic and Social Affairs of the United Nations (DESA) indicators of sustainable development (i.e., the precursor indicators of the SDGs) and Eurostat sustainable development indicators to represent sustainability and (2) SCI, CIMI, CFI, and CITYkeys to evaluate city smartness. From an overarching standpoint, steps to improve mental and physical health should also be taken into account by way of city planning and the modernization of management, infrastructure, and digital solution processes. Based on the collated data a "general typology" is formulated to summarize the indicators used by categorizing them within defined common areas.

3.2 *Sustainability Indicators*

Sustainability is recognized and implicit to represent the three pillars of sustainability – i.e., environmental, social, economic principles. To observe and record the effects of implementing these principles a wide variety of metrics, indicators, and indices as well as different benchmarks, audits, sustainability standards, reporting, and certification systems have been tried and tested, and continue to the developed and improved. Some of the more comprehensive and complicated aspects of these measures is that they are applied over a wide range of spatial and temporal scales (Alawadhi et al., 2012; Anand et al., 2017) and are usually treated in various combinations since environmental, social, and economic facets interrelate.

Furthermore, they are also addressed in different disciplines and fields of work, e.g., environmental, social, and governance reporting and triple bottom line (TBL) accounting focus on enterprises and the corporate business sector, while the World Sustainability Society environmental sustainability index and environmental performance index refer to the governance of individual countries. As an alternative approach, the UN Global Compact Cities Programme explicitly utilizes the Circles of Sustainability method to assess sustainability and manage projects connected with socially sustainable outcomes.

In terms of global metrics and how they fit into the bigger picture of sustainability, example metrics of the three pillars exhibit the multidimensional nature of what is functional (or dysfunctional) in society and how a system is maintained. For example, global environmental sustainability examines global warming potential, ozone depletion potential, energy resources use, aerosol optical depth photochemical ozone potential, waste treatment, freshwater use, and acidification potential. Key global social indicators look at employment and unemployment, health and safety, education, housing and living conditions, regional cohesion, and social security. International gridded economic datasets consider gross domestic product (GDP) per capita, purchasing power parity, income distribution, trade balance, and foreign direct investment.

Hence, in order to organize the disorder in selecting the metrics, specific organizations have grouped them into different categories and defined methodologies to implement specific measures. Several modeling techniques and indices compare and convert the scientific measures into easy-to-understand terms. In this case, the SDGs will be interrelated with the System of Integrated Environmental and Economic Accounting to formulate the primary source data in measuring the Agenda 2030 plan. Secondary sources will collate the Eurostat sustainable development indicators, i.e., a database structured along the SDGs, in which each particular goal is given a set of indicators, making the database both exhaustive, overall, and detailed. Over the past two decades, sustainability indicators have substantially evolved and show promise in better establishing sustainable development processes. The growing number of sustainability indicators is an evolving process that correlates with human – nature relations (i.e., at the ethos level), scientific discovery, and technological advancement to measure them.

3.3 *City Smartness Indicators*

In terms of urban environments, the idea of creating smart cities corresponds with the growing changes to sustainability indicators and shows promise for developing indicators in line with people's values as well as exposure level to understanding what is being measured. In this case, an overview of the four indices used to examine city smartness takes into account a wide perspective structured on mental and physical health of city inhabitants in Poland. First, SCI is presented as an index that collects data and information based on five indicators, i.e., from a list of 15, perceived as the most urgent. To perform this, information on the indexed cities is categorized according to UN Human Development Index and its three components: education. life expectancy, and per capita income. The methodology is formulated into two questionnaire pillars for which perceptions from residents are solicited: the "Structures" pillar, referring to the existing infrastructure of the city, and the "Technology" pillar, which describes the technological provisions and services available to the inhabitants. Then, priority areas (i.e., health and safety, mobility, activities, opportunities, and governance) are evaluated from the point of view of being more or less important for the city (IMD, 2021).

Second, CIMI examines 101 indicators for 174 cities, across 80 countries, of which 79 are capital cities. The index aggregates nine key dimensions: human capital, social cohesion, economy, governance, environment, mobility and transportation, urban planning, international projection, and technology. Each field is represented by a set of indicators which is cross-referenced with another source (e.g., UNESCO, World Happiness Index, Euromonitor, OpenStreetMap, Numbeo, Walk Free Foundation, Nomad List, etc.) and linked strategically to create a novel economic and social perspective of each city's entrepreneurial spirit, innovation, and social cohesion (IESE, 2020).

Third, EasyPark CFI integrates ICT to evaluate the level of technological advancement of cities using four categories: digital life, mobility innovation, business tech infrastructure, and environmental footprint. This index aims to find the most intelligent and future-proof cities in the world to unveil which cities are "best adopting new technological solutions to improve their sustainability and livability" (EasyPark, 2022). The index ranks the top 50 smart and future-proof cities worldwide in each category and cross-references its data from leading sources, such as the World Bank and International Monetary Fund.

Fourth, the CITYkeys project ranks European cities using six characteristics: smart economy (i.e., economic competitiveness as innovation, entrepreneurship, trademarks, productivity, and flexibility of the labor market), smart people (i.e., education, social interactions, and openness towards the "outer" world), smart governance (i.e., political participation, services, and local and international accessibility), smart mobility (i.e., availability of ICT and transport), smart environment (i.e., natural conditions, pollution, resource management, and environmental protection), and smart living (i.e., quality of life, culture, health, safety, housing, and tourism).

It is worth mentioning that the four indices utilize different measuring techniques to formulate their overall score. Nonetheless, in doing so, they all hold strong to the premise that city smartness can be improved and through accurate and controlled measure make things better for urban development and city life.

3.4 *Building a General Typology of the Two Title Concepts*

As a result of the investigated databases and indices used to assess commonality between sustainability and smart cities, Table 16.2 interlaces mental and physical health conditions as a requisite to defining a general typology of the two concepts. A typological breakdown is illustrated by intertwining "through the lens" of human mental and physical health (i.e., understood as the ultimate

TABLE 16.2 General typology of sustainability and city smartness

Dimension	Concept	Index	Indicator
Ecological safeguard	Sustainability	DESA	– percentage of population using solid fuels for cooking – emissions of greenhouse gases – CO_2 emissions – consumption of O_3 depleting substances – ambient concentration of air pollutants in urban areas – wastewater treatment – GDP per capita – material intensity of the economy – domestic material consumption – share of renewable energy sources in total energy use – generation of waste – generation of hazardous waste – waste treatment and disposal – management of radioactive waste
		Eurostat	– area under organic farming – harmonized risk indicator for pesticides, by groups of active substances (source: DG SANTE) – NH_3 emissions from agriculture (source: EEA) – NO_3 in groundwater (source: EEA) – estimated soil erosion by water, area affected by severe erosion rate (source: JRC) – biochemical O_2 demand in rivers (source: EEA) – phosphate in rivers (source: EEA) – water exploitation index plus (source: EEA) – share of renewable energy in gross final energy consumption by sector – greenhouse gas emissions intensity of energy consumption as well as by source sector (source: EEA, Eurostat) – air emission intensity from industry – tertiary educational attainment by sex – average CO_2 emissions per km from new passenger cars (source: EEA, DG CLIMA)

TABLE 16.2 General typology of sustainability and city smartness (*cont.*)

Dimension	Concept	Index	Indicator
			– circular material use rate – generation of waste excluding major mineral wastes by hazardousness – gross value added in environmental goods and services sector – mean near-surface temperature deviation (source: EEA) – climate-related economic losses by type of event, using the EU aggregate (source: EEA) – contribution to the international US$100 bn commitment on climate related expending (source: DG CLIMA, EIONET) – population covered by the Covenant of Mayors for Climate and Energy signatories (source: Covenant of Mayors) – share of renewable energy in gross final energy consumption by sector – global mean ocean surface acidity (source: CMEMS) – surface of marine sites designated under Natura 2000 (source: DG ENV, EEA) – estimated trends in fish stock biomass in the northeast Atlantic (source: JRC, STECF) – assessed fish stocks exceeding fishing mortality at maximum sustainable yield in northeast Atlantic (source: JRC, STECF) – bathing sites with excellent water quality by locality (source: EEA) – marine waters affected by eutrophication (source: CMEMS) – share of forest area – soil sealing index (source: EEA) – common bird index by type of species using the EU aggregate (source: EBCC) – grassland butterfly index using the EU aggregate (source: EEA, BCE) – share of environmental taxes in total tax revenues

TABLE 16.2 General typology of sustainability and city smartness (*cont.*)

Dimension	Concept	Index	Indicator
	Smart cities	SCI	– recycling services are satisfactory – public safety is not a problem – air pollution is not a problem – green spaces are satisfactory – website or app that allows residents to effectively monitor air pollution
		CIMI	– solid waste – future climate – methane emissions – environmental performance index – CO_2 emission index – pollution index – PM_{10} and $PM_{2.5}$ – percentage of the population with access to the water supply – renewable water resources – bicycles for rent
		CFI	– congestion levels – time spent in traffic during a commute – dissatisfaction due to long commute times – score that measures the share of each city's energy consumption that comes from renewable sources – the high score that indicates the high usage of renewable energy consist of (1) share of nation-wide energy consumed from renewable sources, (2) share of electricity consumption from renewable sources, and (3) number of certified green buildings – percentage of total buildings certified as green (note: cities are represented by country level data) – the high score that indicates low levels of waste generated and a high recycling rate consist of the recycling rate in each country and the city representation at the country level

TABLE 16.2 General typology of sustainability and city smartness (*cont.*)

Dimension	Concept	Index	Indicator
			– estimated percentage increase in greenhouse gas emissions – total CO_2 emissions from fuel combustion – expenditure on environment protection – change in CO_2 emissions per capita over time – number of climate laws, policies, and targets in place
		CITYkeys	– sewage discharge management and water pollution control with ICT measures
Quality of housing and living	Sustainability	Eurostat	– population living in a dwelling with a leaking roof, damp walls, floors, or foundation or rot in window frames, by poverty status – population having neither a bath, or a shower, or indoor flushing toilet in their household, by poverty status – population unable to keep home adequately warm, by poverty status – overcrowding rate, by poverty status – population connected to at least secondary wastewater treatment – bathing sites with excellent water quality by locality (source: EEA) – population living in households considering that they suffer from noise, by poverty status – settlement area per capita – general government total expenditure on law courts – perceived independence of the justice system (source: DG COMM) – Corruption Perceptions Index (source: Transparency International) – population with confidence in EU institutions by institution (source: DG COMM)

TABLE 16.2 General typology of sustainability and city smartness (*cont.*)

Dimension	Concept	Index	Indicator
	Smart cities	SCI	– basic sanitation meets the needs of the poorest areas – finding housing with rent equal to 30% or less of a monthly salary is not a problem – online platform where residents can propose ideas has improved city life – processing identification documents online to reduce waiting times
		CIMI	– number of people per household – percentage of the urban population with adequate sanitation services
Transport and accessibility	Sustainability	DESA	– percentage of population having paid bribes – adult secondary (tertiary) schooling attainment level – lifelong learning – bathing water quality – share of women in wage employment in the non-agricultural sector – modal split of passenger transportation – modal split of freight transport
		Eurostat	– patent applications to the European Patent Office – overcrowding rate by poverty status – Vshare of buses and trains in total passenger transport
	Smart cities	SCI	– traffic congestion is not a problem – public transport is satisfactory – most children have access to a good school – lifelong learning opportunities are provided by local institutions – minorities feel welcome – information on local government decisions is easily accessible – corruption of city officials is not an issue of concern

TABLE 16.2 General typology of sustainability and city smartness (*cont.*)

Dimension	Concept	Index	Indicator
			– residents contribute to decision-making of local government – residents provide feedback on local government projects
		CIMI	– secondary or higher education – schools – business schools – expenditure on education – female-friendly – female employment ratio – bicycle, moped, and scooter rental – bicycles per household – bike sharing – traffic inefficiency index – exponential traffic index – traffic index – length of the metro system – metro stations – high-speed train – commercial vehicles in the city
		CFI	– highly ranked universities for computer science degrees – highly ranked universities for engineering degrees – overall number of parking spaces per capita
Safety	Sustainability	Eurostat	– physical safety – economic safety – economically vulnerable groups – violence and crime rates
	Smart cities	CIMI	– crime rate – Peace Index – homicide rate
Technological advancement	Sustainability	DESA	– number of internet users per 100 inhabitants – mobile cellular telephone subscribers per 100 inhabitants

TABLE 16.2 General typology of sustainability and city smartness (*cont.*)

Dimension	Concept	Index	Indicator
		Eurostat	– gross domestic expenditure on R&D by sector – R&D personnel by sector – high-speed internet coverage, by type of area (source: DG CNECT, Eurostat) – exposure to air pollution by PM (source: EEA) – recycling rate of municipal waste – population connected to at least secondary wastewater treatment
	Smart cities	SCI	– online reporting of city maintenance problems provides a speedy solution – website or app that allows residents to easily give away unwanted items – free public Wi-Fi to improve access to city services – arranging medical appointments online – car-sharing apps and bicycle hiring to reduce congestion – apps that direct you to an available parking space to reduce journey time – online scheduling and ticket sales to make public transport easier to use – providing information on traffic congestion through mobile phones – online services provided by the city to make it easier to start a new business – current internet speed and reliability to meet the connectivity needs of the city's inhabitants
		CIMI	– e-government Development Index – research centers – open data platform – 3G coverage – Innovation Index – internet – online banking – online video calls – LTE/WiMAX

TABLE 16.2 General typology of sustainability and city smartness (*cont.*)

Dimension	Concept	Index	Indicator
			– mobile phone penetration ratio – personal computers – telephony – mobile telephony – internet speed – Web Index – Wi-Fi hotspots
		CFI	– number of app downloads and ranking in food, navigation, travel, education, and financial service categories – National Digital Infrastructure Index – Digital Economy Score – development of e-government services – Health Care Quality and Access Index – number of startups in the health-care sector in each city, both in absolute terms and on a per population basis – number of app downloads and ranking in the health-care and medical categories, excluding reference and utility apps – number of parking spaces capable of accepting digital payments – number of parking technology providers operating in the city – civilian adoption of parking technology – level of parking technology implementation – electric cars per capita and new electric car sales – electric car charging stations per capita – CO_2 emissions – Health care, lifestyle services, and media – financial services – percentage of the population that is in favor of a cashless society – percentage of the population that has been cashless since the beginning of the pandemic

TABLE 16.2 General typology of sustainability and city smartness (*cont.*)

Dimension	Concept	Index	Indicator
			– number of cashless retail transactions per 1,000 adults – credit card and debit card ownership – percentage of the population that paid bills or bought something online in the past year – internet services and median download and upload speeds – 5G deployment and government efforts to promote 5G – 5G availability in major cities and number of 5G providers per city
		CITYkeys	– number of ways in which citizens can communicate with the municipality (e.g., phone, mail, social media, etc.) – increased computer literacy of elderly people – proportion of homes using smart home monitoring systems – number of infrastructure components with installed sensors (i.e., traffic, public transit, parking, waste, water, and public lighting) – number of services integrated in a singular operations center delivering real-time data (i.e., ambulance, emergency and disaster response, fire, police, weather, transit, and air quality) – number of smart apps developed using open data platforms – internet penetration rate – share of intelligent buildings – use of smart mobility apps and share of electric car owners in the district – access to high-speed internet – access to public Wi-Fi internet connection
Social environment	Sustainability	Eurostat	– early leavers from education and training by sex – early leavers from education and training, by citizenship – tertiary educational attainment by sex

TABLE 16.2 General typology of sustainability and city smartness (*cont.*)

Dimension	Concept	Index	Indicator
			– participation in early childhood education by sex (children aged 3 and over) – underachievement in reading, math, and science (source: OECD) – adult participation in learning by sex – energy import dependency by products
Economic development	Sustainability	DESA	– ratio of share in national income of highest to lowest quintile – population growth rate – total fertility rate – dependency ratio – ratio of local residents to tourists in major tourist regions and destinations – percentage of population living in hazard prone areas – investment share in GDP – savings rate – adjusted net savings as percentage of gross national income (GNI) – inflation rate – debt-to-GNI ratio – employment – population ratio – vulnerable employment – labor productivity and unit labor costs – gross domestic expenditure on R&D as a percent of GDP – current account deficit as percentage of GDP – share of imports from developing countries and from lesser developing countries – average tariff barriers imposed on exports from developing countries and from lesser developing countries – net official development rate – assistance given or received as a percentage of GNIforeign direct investment net inflows and net outflows as percentage of GDP

TABLE 16.2 General typology of sustainability and city smartness (*cont.*)

Dimension	Concept	Index	Indicator
			– remittances as percentage of GNI – annual energy consumption, total and by main user category – intensity of energy use, total and by economic activity – energy intensity of transport
		Eurostat	– people living in households with very low work intensity – share of individuals having at least basic digital skills, by sex – gender pay gap in unadjusted form – gender employment gap – inactive population due to caring responsibilities by sex – seats held by women in national parliaments and governments (source: EIGE) – positions held by women in senior management positions (source: EIGE) – early leavers from education and training by sex – tertiary educational attainment by sex – primary energy consumption – final energy consumption – final energy consumption in households per capita – energy productivity – real GDP per capita – investment share of GDP by institutional sectors – young people neither in employment nor in education and training by sex – young people neither in employment nor in education and training by citizenship – employment rate by sex – employment rate, by citizenship – long-term unemployment rate by sex – in work at-risk-of-poverty rate

TABLE 16.2 General typology of sustainability and city smartness (*cont.*)

Dimension	Concept	Index	Indicator
			– inactive population due to caring responsibilities by sex – resource productivity and domestic material consumption – purchasing power adjusted GDP per capita – adjusted gross disposable income of households per capita – relative median at-risk-of-poverty gap – income distribution – income share of the bottom 40% of the population – asylum applications by state of procedure – people at risk of poverty or social exclusion by degree of urbanization – road traffic deaths, by type of roads (source: DG MOVE) – population reporting occurrence of crime, violence, or vandalism in their area by poverty status – resource productivity and domestic material consumption – energy productivity – official development assistance as share of GNI (source: OECD) – EU financing to developing countries by financing source (source: OECD) – EU imports from developing countries by country income groups – general government gross debt
	Smart cities	SCI	– employment finding services are readily available – businesses are creating new jobs – CCTV cameras has made residents feel safer – online access to job listings has made it easier to find work – ITC skills are sufficiently taught in schools

TABLE 16.2 General typology of sustainability and city smartness (*cont.*)

Dimension	Concept	Index	Indicator
		CIMI	– Gini Index – unemployment rate
		CFI	– number of startups in the health care, lifestyle, and internet service sectors in each city, both in absolute terms and on a per population basis

Abbreviations for sources: BCE = Butterfly Conservation Europe; CMEMS = Copernicus Marine Environment Monitoring Service; DG CLIMA = Directorate-General for Climate Action; DG CNECT = Directorate-General for Communications Networks, Content and Technology; DG COMM = Directorate-General for Communication; DG ENV = Directorate-General for the Environment; DG MOVE = Directorate-General for Mobility and Transport; DG SANTE = Directorate-General for Health and Food Safety; EBCC = European Bird Census Council; EEA = European Environment Agency; EIGE = European Institute for Gender Equality; EIONET = European Environment Information and Observation Network; JRC = Joint Research Centre; OECD = Organisation for Economic Co-operation and Development; STECF = Scientific, Technical and Economic Committee for Fisheries

SOURCE: OWN ELABORATION

goal of sustainability) how the given dimensions – using currently available datasets – is defined.

The broader categories of the topology are defined in seven dimensions: ecological safeguard, quality of housing and living, transport and accessibility, safety, technological advancement, social environment, and economic development. Specifically, within each dimension, the two concepts have divided the indices accordingly, i.e., sustainability (DESA and Eurostat) and smart cities (SCI, CIMI, CFI, and CITYkeys). The exact metrics of each indicator is not presented in full due to the length and explanation each individual indicator uses to calculate its measure.

The analysis can lead to further studies that may identify what the most commonly used smart city indices lack in view of sustainability, e.g., which indicators are least or not considered, so as to make the measures better focused and sustainability oriented. This, however, is outside the scope of this chapter and should be considered in the future. As such, this framing can be applied in other research aimed at analyzing the activities or projects implemented in settlements in other countries. For sake of space ands focus, Section 3 deals with a case research in Poland identifying projects and best match examples of interlinking sustainability and city smartness in Polish cities.

4 Case Research on Smart Projects, Settlements, and Cities in Poland

4.1 *Progress, Financial Opportunities, and European Union Support*

As an interlinking example of sustainability and city smartness, the EU has been at the forefront of this effort to develop responsibly in a forward-thinking manner. The implementation of the sustainability and smart city agenda specifically in Poland has been picking up nationally as well as from a top-down EU perspective.

Recently, Polish cities have made enormous progress in their use of ICT in several dimensions, including urban social, public, and economic life. It is fair to say that almost everything in the country has become digitalized. To achieve these high standards and performance Polish settlements and cities have strived to be "smart" by implementing a variety of solutions in line with the indicators presented in Table 16.2.

Moreover, since Poland has only been a market-oriented economy for about 25 years (i.e., dating back to the collapse of communism in 1989 and then being transformed from a centrally planned to market-oriented economy in the early 1990s), most changes took place only after it joined the EU in 2004 and started receiving enlargement support. EU funds kick-started the country by offering trade concessions, economic and financial assistance, and assistance for reconstruction, development, and stabilization. Polish municipalities significantly made a giant leap forward in terms of their development. It meant that settlements and cities inadvertently transitioned into "the smart city era" with novel public systems, administration, governance, etc. In short, key steps to Polish settlement and city smartness truly started with the introduction of EU-funded projects.

Projects related to city smartness have become popular throughout Poland. They are financed from a variety of public resources with substantial support from EU funds. In the period 2014–2020, mention can be made to the Technical Assistance OP, OP Infrastructure and Environment, and OP Intelligent Development.

Poland as the largest beneficiary of EU funds in terms of all its member states was allocated €67.3 billion in 2007–2013 and €105.8 billion in 2014–2020. According to the Ministry of Funds and Regional Policy, from 2004 Poland has effectively used €154.44 billion of the allocated funds to realize more than 273,000 projects (i.e., with public subsides totaling approximately €265.2 billion). Out of these projects, Polish cities realized 17,427 of them in which 722 initiatives were categorized as a part of the smart city agenda.

It is important to underline that the projects associated with smart cities "belong" in fact to different scopes and priorities and are "categorized" under various goals for funding – i.e., financed from different sources with different baseline goals. For example, the projects related to ICT in urban areas have received funding from almost all national and regional programs for the period 2014–2020 except from the European Maritime and Fisheries Fund. Other development projects that focused on transport (i.e., intelligent transport systems and local traffic control centers), power engineering (i.e., intelligent energy networks), and environmental protection (i.e., automation and robotics systems in sewage treatment and incineration plants) have come from OP Infrastructure and Environment and ERDF. Moreover, projects involving the automation of processes for the construction of data exchange systems in cities are co-financed mostly by OP Intelligent Development and ERDF. The European Social Fund finances, in turn, raises digital competences in areas related to the labor market, education, and social inclusion (e.g., digital schooling aimed at developing digital skills of teachers and students and providing schools with the necessary ICT equipment).

In addition, the Ministry of Investment and Development in 2017 announced the program-based competition called "Human Smart Cities" in which smart cities co-created by residents account for €18 billion that are aimed at making cities friendly via intelligence-based solutions. In this case, residents are co-responsible for their city's urban space and take an active participation in its management and co-decide on how it should be developed.

Human Smart Cities are financed from the Technical Assistance OP 2014–2020 and have benefited 25 projects Poland-wide (i.e., they are divided into three categories of cities: two large cities, 15 medium cities, and eight small cities). At present, the process of their implementation has been prolonged due to the COVID-19 pandemic.

The idea of most Polish settlements and cities progressing (i.e., transforming) sustainably in a smart city manner is shared by many researchers and scholars. According to Sikora-Fernandez (2018, p. 57), "the development of advanced technologies, as well as increasing expenditures on research and development in Poland are an important contributor to the pursuit of making cities smarter." Janecki and Karoń (2014, p. 100) stressed that in Poland "the intelligent city is characterized by investments in social capital, transport, communication infrastructure, fuel and sustainable economic development, and quality of life. A key determinant of these characteristics is cost-effective use of natural limited resources."

Furthermore, it cannot be understated that in Poland the rudimentary definition for city smartness, the sustainability of a city's economy, and its areas of operation are based on social participation and focused on high-quality two-way communication between city authorities and its inhabitants

(Stawasz & Sikora-Fernandez, 2016). This, by in large, is the model supported (and funded) by the EU as asserted by Stawasz and Sikora-Fernandez's (2016) examination of contemporary problems of the functioning and development of cities in Poland. It explicitly looked at the main barriers to urban development as well as the main problems and their consequences for the development of Polish cities.

4.2 *Positive Sustainability and Smart City Development in Poland*

In terms of sustainability-based initiatives and projects in Poland, extensive use of digital solutions both in larger cities and smaller settlements have been advancing all over the country. These projects are developed mostly in the areas of transport combined with ecology and energy efficiency (e.g., environmentally friendly public transportation), intelligent municipal grids, tourism, public administration, and urbanization initiatives. In terms of transport design, several fundamental improvements, funded by the EU, have paralleled Poland's extremely fast development, which has increasingly demanded better transport accessibility. For instance, in 2018 Poland had 1.6 million new passenger cars – an increase of 6.7% from the year precedent. In comparison, a decade earlier, in 2008 the increase was 50% less, i.e., 3.3%. This type of change has complemented its expanded highway network and urban reconstruction of settlements and cities towards a fast-tracked smart way of thinking.

In the era of sustainable development in Europe (i.e., versus pre-implemented sustainability-based principles), Poland's timely entry into the EU and its cohesion as a nation to develop and follow EU guidelines allowed it to modernize and advance smartly and efficiently as one of the fastest growing pre-COVID pandemic member states (European Commission, 2019; Eurostat, 2020). Several other positive changes Polish cities have experienced include the replacement of diesel-fueled motor vehicles with electric ones. This has helped in bettering urban air quality devices that operate via the Internet of Things and advanced public communication directives.

Additional change has sparked the modernization of tram lines and additional bus and trolleybus lines, i.e., in some cities, by integrating them into one supratransportation network. Moreover, the network can include bicycling (e.g., bike lanes) and pedestrian systems (e.g., pedestrian paths) to help facilitate smarter and more sustainable city designs. In effect, EU funds have supplemented domestic governmental resources to reduce (and eliminate) obsolete, old-fashion, and unecological rolling stock to be replaced with comfortable, clean, and eco-friendly transportation vehicles using advanced technological steering systems.

To the wider environment-friendly transport systems, many Polish cities have also upgraded their eco-vehicles to include city bikes, electric scooter rentals, and hybrid and electric car sharing systems. Generally, this has fostered a strong, positive societal reaction for the use of intermodal transport in urban commuting using several different transport modes (e.g., park and ride, kiss and ride, and park and bike).

An important aspect of the "smartness" of Polish settlements is their "eco-friendliness," i.e., environmental protection and energy efficiency to reduce energy consumption and emission levels. Among the energy-smart systems, in conjunction with eco-transport, there has been several changes to the street light systems in Poland by adopting energy-efficient technologies such as the 1 watt system (e.g., Sitraffic One introduced by Siemens) used for traffic lights, controllers, pedestrian buttons, and acoustic devices. Many cities, e.g., Wroclaw, replaced their municipal light bulbs with LEDs. Such tools bring not only less air pollution but also financial savings for the municipalities.

Moreover, Polish metropoles started to implement and run "smart grid" solutions. Smart electric grids are elements that are intelligently connected to enhance the overall functionality of the power delivery system, ensure reliability, optimize energy usage, and minimize environmental impact (Gontar, 2018). Other programs involve installing renewable energy facilities on public buildings, implementing intelligent building solutions, and supporting local energy utilities in new energy demand programs (e.g., the deployment of advanced metering solutions) (Gontar, 2018). Correspondingly, in Wroclaw, a modern water supply network system, called SmartFlow, was implemented in 2014, to save water. In its first year of operation, the city conserved about 500 million liters of water and reduced losses in the water supply network by 9% (SmartFlow, 2021).

In the field of municipal waste management numerous Polish cities have introduced eco-friendly ICT solutions, e.g., Warsaw, Cracow, Wroclaw, and Tychy. Throughout the country, a disposal system that utilizes a free app on a smartphone can inform the date of removal of waste from individual districts as well as rebound bulky waste and waste segregation. Such apps also contain links to environmental organizations and information about ecological events (Kola-Bezka et al., 2016). Wroclaw participates in the Smart Waste Management project, which aims, among other things, to optimize waste collection and reduce the related exhaust emissions.

On another front, tourism throughout Polish cities has integrated several smart-oriented projects in which most link ICT solutions (i.e., mobile solutions) such as QR codes, mobile timetables, city guides, virtual museums, and public hotspots with a growing e-tourism market. Similarly, most Polish municipalities have installed surveillance sensor networks with cameras and control modules to regulate urban video monitoring for congestion related and security measures.

Progress in ICT advancement has specialized the digitalization and computerization of public administration to the point where most communities today use easily available systems that operate via two-way communication with public offices. Computerization of social activities enables public institutions to operate dedicated systems and municipal apps for different devices. Most Polish cities offer apps for online payments for public transport and parking fees. Examples of projects in this area include e-bike rentals and public transport apps that allow for the payment of e-tickets by using one's smartphone.

Considering the institutional procedures and services of various public administration offices throughout Poland, user services made by schools and universities, municipal sport facilities, the health-care system, social pensions and benefits, the court system, libraries, and transport and communication the trend for digitalization and use of modern ICT solutions has substantially accelerated. In all, the use of mobile apps, in conjunction with relatively cheap access to the internet in Poland, has allowed its citizenry to positively integrate and modernize an EU-centric transition.

The majority of Polish settlements and cities have successfully implemented "participation budgeting" (i.e., the practical realization of the Smart City 3.0 concept), in which any inhabitant can create his/her own proposal for investments and projects in his/her city and apply for its financing from public sources. The inhabitants themselves vote online for the chosen projects and decide on the most desired ones. In this way, local communities have a tangible opportunity to be included in the decision-making process, in managing their life space, and in actively participating in city governance and strategic planning.

In terms of smart projects, settlements, and cities in Poland, the last decade has bolstered a strong focus on sound sustainability and forward-moving smart city design to enrich the standard of living – inclusive of mental and physical health – and to facilitate public good provision with the support of international and supranational bodies. The long list of urban projects implemented, and ongoing, link the two researched concepts of sustainability and city smartness and show positive signs for current and future generations in Poland.

5 Conclusions

Referencing the case research from Polish cities, smart city projects that are co-financed with EU funds is an example of how the proposed typological framework can draw general conclusions about public goods via an international organization. In Poland, most of the projects applied to the "ecological safeguard" and "transport and accessibility" dimensions. The provided cities in Poland had developed high-quality, comfortable, safe, and – most of all – eco-friendly transport (i.e., via electric, hybrid engines, etc.) which represents one of fundamental public goods for any city of the world. Low-emission, ecological, quiet, and safer buses, trams, and trolleybuses (and metro) has highly improved the quality of air in the cities and contributed to better public mental and physical health.

It should be mentioned that in this case priority for investments in transport, especially rolling stock, was indispensable and observable with Poland's accession in joining the EU in 2004. Other investments of high importance include accessibility and diminishing traffic congestion – both necessary for the ecological safeguarding of cities. Key development in this field revolves around intelligent transport systems implementation, which can also include eco-vehicles like city bikes and bike paths, electric scooter rentals, and hybrid and electric car-sharing systems. To date, several infrastructure projects combining city smartness with sustainability (such as intelligent municipal grids, new sewage treatment plants, installing renewable energy facilities on public buildings, and intelligent building solutions) elucidate the importance of combining the "ecological safeguard" and "quality of housing and living" dimensions to facilitate and improve inhabitant health and well-being.

In sum, the conclusions have identified the most important EU co-financed projects in Polish cities. However, a long, exhaustive list of smaller and less significant projects and programs have all contributed to developing a link between sustainability and city smartness since Poland became an EU member state in 2004.

As a result, the typological framework elaborated in this chapter, together with the discussed case research, create a base for further detailed studies concerning all actions and initiatives to make cities more smart, intelligent, and sustainable. It is recommended that future research continues to evaluate organization oversight by collecting data on projects that can detail and systematically categorize interconnectedness between the two analyzed concepts. This should include project information, e.g., cost of the project, organization contribution, and impact on well-being.

Although the analysis presented in this chapter only touches on the field, it does bring into light important additional deductions to how one might perceive future research implementation. Namely, international organizations have to play a vital role – and in some cases they are absolutely key actors – in helping countries become more resilient, sustainable, and responsible when trying to create their public policies under this strategic direction. This very special role acts as a keystone when approaching, designing, managing, and investing in public goods in countries and applies, due to financial constraints, mainly to countries which are not accounted to the most highly developed, those under transition, or emerging. The Polish case illustrates how the EU significantly contributed to making its cities more eco- and social-friendly. It serves as an optimal example of combining international support with national strengths to the success of integrating sustainability and city smartness into practice.

Notes: Research presented in this chapter constitutes a part of the implementation of the project "Smart Cities: Modelling, Indexing and Querying Smart City Competitiveness," funded by the National Science Centre (NCN) in Poland, OPUS 20, Grant no. DEC-2020/39/B/HS4/00579.

References

Addanki, S. C., & Venkataraman, H. (2017). Greening the economy: A review of urban sustainability measures for developing new cities. *Sustainable Cities and Society, 32*, 1–8. http://doi.org/10.1016/J.SCS.2017.03.009

Ahvenniemi, H., Huovila, A., Pinto-Seppä, I., & Airaksinen, M. (2017). What are the differences between sustainable and smart cities? *Cities, 60*, 234–245.

Alawadhi, S., et al. (2012). Building Understanding of Smart City Initiatives. In: H. J. Scholl et al. (Eds.), Electronic Government. *EGOV 2012. Lecture Notes in Computer Science*, vol. 7443. Springer. https://doi.org/10.1007/978-3-642-33489-4_4

Al-Hader, M. A. (2009). The smart city infrastructure development & monitoring. *Theoretical and Empirical Researches in Urban Management, 4*(2), 87–94.

Al Nuaimi, E., Al Neyadi, H., Mohamed, N., & Al-Jaroodi, J. (2015). Applications of big data to smart cities. *Journal of Internet Services and Applications, 6*(1), 1–15. http://doi.org/10.1186/S13174-015-0041-5/FIGURES/3

Anand, A., Dsilva Winfred Rufuss, D., Rajkumar, V., & Suganthi, L. (2017). Evaluation of sustainability indicators in smart cities for India using MCDM approach. *Energy Procedia, 141*, 211–215. http://doi.org/10.1016/J.EGYPRO.2017.11.094

Barresi, A., & Pultrone, G. (2013). European strategies for smarter cities. *TeMA – Journal of Land Use, Mobility and Environment, 6*(1), 61–72. http://doi.org/10.6092/1970-9870/1455

Berman, M., & Orttung, R. W. (2020). Measuring progress toward urban sustainability: Do global measures work for arctic cities? *Sustainability, 12*(9). http://doi.org/10.3390/SU12093708

Bibri, S. E., & Krogstie, J. (2017). Smart sustainable cities of the future: An extensive interdisciplinary literature review. *Sustainable Cities and Society, 31*, 183–212. http://doi.org/10.1016/J.SCS.2017.02.016

Bifulco, F., Tregua, M., Amitrano, C. C., & D'Auria, A. (2016). ICT and sustainability in smart cities management. *International Journal of Public Sector Management, 29*(2), 132–147. http://doi.org/10.1108/IJPSM-07-2015-0132/FULL/PDF

Calvillo, C. F., Sánchez-Miralles, A., & Villar, J. (2016). Energy management and planning in smart cities. *Renewable and Sustainable Energy Reviews, 55*, 273–287. http://doi.org/10.1016/J.RSER.2015.10.133

CEN-CENELEC. (2015). CEN-CENELEC. Retrieved June 15, 2022. https://www.cencenelec.eu/

Cowley, R., & Caprotti, F. (2019). Smart city as anti-planning in the UK. *Environment and Planning D: Society and Space, 37*(3), 428–448. http://doi.org/10.1177/0263775818787506

De Jong, M., Joss, S., Schraven, D., Zhan, C., & Weijnen, M. (2015). Sustainable-smart-resilient-low carbon-eco-knowledge cities: Making sense of a multitude of concepts promoting sustainable urbanization. *Journal of Cleaner Production, 109*, 25–38. http://doi.org/10.1016/j.jclepro.2015.02.004

EasyPark. (2022). EasyPark Cities of the Future Index. Retrieved June 16, 2022. https://easyparkgroup.com/studies/cities-of-the-future/en/

Elkington, J. (2018, June 25). 25 years ago I coined the phrase "triple bottom line." Here's why it's time to rethink it. *Harvard Business Review*. https://hbr.org/2018/06/25-years-ago-i-coined-the-phrase-triple-bottom-line-heres-why-im-giving-up-on-it

ETSI. (2015). ETSI – World of Standards. Retrieved June 15, 2022. https://www.etsi.org/

European Commission. (2019). *European economic forecast: Summer 2019*. European Commission, Directorate-General for Economic and Financial Affairs.

Eurostat. (2020). Which EU countries had the highest GDP in 2019? Retrieved June 17, 2022. https://ec.europa.eu/eurostat/web/products-eurostat-news/-/ddn-20200508-1

Gabrys, J. (2014). Programming environments: Environmentality and citizen sensing in the smart city. *Environment and Planning D: Society and Space, 32*(1), 30–48. http://doi.org/10.1068/D16812

Giffinger, R., Fertner, C., Kramar, H., Kalasek, R., Pichler-Milanović, N., & Meijers, E. (2007). *Smart cities – Ranking of European medium-sized cities*. Centre of Regional Science, Vienna UT.

Giordano, V., Onyeji, I., Fulli, G., Jimenez, M. S., & Filiou, C. (2012). *Guidelines for conducting a cost-benefit analysis of smart grid projects*. Publications Office of the EU. https://op.europa.eu/en/publication-detail/-/publication/5aba88eb-88b8-4716-99a6-0fea164f9308/language-en

Girardi, P., & Temporelli, A. (2017). Smartainability: A methodology for assessing the sustainability of the smart city. *Energy Procedia, 111*, 810–816. http://doi.org/10.1016/J.EGYPRO.2017.03.243

Gontar, Z. H. (2018). *Smart grid analytics for sustainability and urbanization*. SGH Warsaw School of Economics.

Haarstad, H., & Wathne, M. W. (2019). Are smart city projects catalyzing urban energy sustainability? *Energy Policy, 129*(February), 918–925.

Huovila, A., Bosch, P., & Airaksinen, M. (2019). Comparative analysis of standardized indicators for smart sustainable cities: What indicators and standards to use and when? *Cities, 89*, 141–153. http://doi.org/10.1016/J.CITIES.2019.01.029

IESE. (2020). IESE Cities in Motion Index 2020. Retrieved June 16, 2022. https://blog.iese.edu/cities-challenges-and-management/2020/10/27/iese-cities-in-motion-index-2020/

IMD. (2021). Smart City Observatory: Smart City Index 2021. Retrieved June 16, 2022. https://www.imd.org/smart-city-observatory/home/

ISO. (2022). ISO 37120:2014 – Sustainable development of communities – Indicators for city services and quality of life. Retrieved June 15, 2022. https://www.iso.org/standard/62436.html

ITU. (2016). ITU-T recommendation database ITU-T Y.4900/L.1600 (06/2016). Retrieved June 15, 2022. https://www.itu.int/itu-t/recommendations/rec.aspx?rec=12627

Janecki, R., & Karoń, G. (2014). Concept of smart cities and economic model of electric buses implementation. In *TST 2014: Telematics – Support for Transport, 471*, 100–109. http://doi.org/10.1007/978-3-662-45317-9_11/COVER/

Kitchin, R. (2014). The real-time city? Big data and smart urbanism. *GeoJournal, 79*(1), 1–14. http://doi.org/10.1007/S10708-013-9516-8

Kola-Bezka, M., Czupich, M., & Ignasiak-Szulc, A. (2016). Smart cities in central and Eastern Europe: Viable future or unfulfilled dream? *Journal of International Studies, 9*(1), 76–87. http://doi.org/10.14254/2071-8330.2016/9-1/6

Kramers, A., Höjer, M., Lövehagen, N., & Wangel, J. (2014). Smart sustainable cities – Exploring ICT solutions for reduced energy use in cities. *Environmental Modelling & Software, 56*, 52–62. http://doi.org/10.1016/J.ENVSOFT.2013.12.019

Lazaroiu, G. C., & Roscia, M. (2012). Definition methodology for the smart cities model. *Energy, 47*(1), 326–332. http://doi.org/10.1016/J.ENERGY.2012.09.028

Lee, J. H., Hancock, M. G., & Hu, M. C. (2014). Towards an effective framework for building smart cities: Lessons from Seoul and San Francisco. *Technological Forecasting and Social Change, 89*, 80–99. http://doi.org/10.1016/J.TECHFORE.2013.08.033

Lim, S. B., Abdul Malek, J., Hussain, M. Y., & Tahir, Z. (2020). Understanding the trends and characteristics of smart urbanism across continents. *Smart Cities and Regional Development Journal, 4*(1), 23–35. https://ideas.repec.org/a/pop/journl/v4y2020i1p23-35.html

Lim, S. B., Abdul Malek, J., Hussain, M. Y., & Tahir, Z. (2021). Malaysia Smart City Framework: A trusted framework for shaping smart Malaysian citizenship? In J. C. Augusto (Ed.), *Handbook of smart cities* (pp. 515–538). Springer. http://doi.org/10.1007/978-3-030-69698-6_34

Martin, C. J., Evans, J., & Karvonen, A. (2018). Smart and sustainable? Five tensions in the visions and practices of the smart-sustainable city in Europe and North

America. *Technological Forecasting and Social Change, 133*, 269–278. http://doi.org/10.1016/J.TECHFORE.2018.01.005

Russo, A., & Cirella, G. T. (2020). Urban sustainability: Integrating ecology in city design and planning. In G. T. Cirella (Ed.), *Sustainable human – nature relations: Environmental scholarship, economic evaluation, urban strategies* (pp. 187–204). Springer Singapore. http://doi.org/10.1007/978-981-15-3049-4_10

Sikora-Fernandez, D. (2018). Smarter cities in post-socialist country: Example of Poland. *Cities, 78*, 52–59. http://doi.org/10.1016/J.CITIES.2018.03.011

SmartFlow. (2021). SmartFlow: Water losses monitor. Retrieved June 17, 2022. https://www.smart-flow.eu/en

Stawasz, D., & Sikora-Fernandez, D. (2016). *Koncepcja smart city na tle procesów i uwarunkowań rozwoju współczesnych miast*. Wydawnictwo Uniwersytetu Łódzkiego.

Trindade, E. P., Hinnig, M. P. F., Da Costa, E. M., Marques, J. S., Bastos, R. C., & Yigitcanlar, T. (2017). Sustainable development of smart cities: A systematic review of the literature. *Journal of Open Innovation: Technology, Market, and Complexity, 3*(3), 1–14. http://doi.org/10.1186/S40852-017-0063-2/FIGURES/2

UN. (1976). United Nations Conference on Human Settlements: Habitat I. Retrieved June 14, 2022. https://www.un.org/en/conferences/habitat/vancouver1976

UN. (2015a). SDG 11: Department of Economic and Social Affairs. Retrieved July 14, 2021. https://sdgs.un.org/goals/goal11

UN. (2015b). United Nations Sustainable Development Goals. Retrieved May 3, 2019. http://www.un.org/ga/search/view_doc.asp?symbol=A/RES/70/1&Lang=E

Vilajosana, I., Llosa, J., Martinez, B., Domingo-Prieto, M., Angles, A., & Vilajosana, X. (2013). Bootstrapping smart cities through a self-sustainable model based on big data flows. *IEEE Communications Magazine, 51*(6), 128–134. http://doi.org/10.1109/mcom.2013.6525605

Yigitcanlar, T., & Kamruzzaman, M. (2018). Does smart city policy lead to sustainability of cities? *Land Use Policy, 73*, 49–58. http://doi.org/10.1016/J.LANDUSEPOL.2018.01.034

Evaluation and Conclusions

Ewa Latoszek and Agnieszka Kłos

1 Introduction

The role of international organizations (IOs) in responding to global and regional challenges related to economic, financial, and social changes has increased significantly over the past decade. Given the need for a specific "platform" of discussion that would result in the development of solutions to problems related to economic, financial, and social changes, the importance of IOs has been growing. The need to work out solutions through a compromise stimulates interactions between states and the development of mechanisms facilitating an effective delivery of global public goods (GPGs) in accordance with international principles and norms (Hooghe et al., 2019, pp. 2–5). In the globalized world, access to public goods provides benefits that go far beyond formal (political and geographical) borders of states, regions, and continents. Their indirect impact is, therefore, visible on a much larger scale than intended by their suppliers (Kaul et al., 1999; Stiglitz, 2003; Altvater, 2007; Kaul, 2001; Felício, 2005; Engerer, 2011). In today's world of increasing global uncertainty created by political, geo-economic, and social tensions, a new policy of providing and regulating GPGs by IOs is at the core of global sustainable development (Hughes, 1991; Sandler, 1999). Despite systemic changes introduced over the past decades to the functioning of economies and to the process of solving problems related to various types of crises, conflicts, etc., societies and decision-makers, including international organizations, are still looking for answers to important questions: How can peace and democracy be maintained? How can global warming be curbed? How can we prevent future pandemics and keep them in check? How can we avoid global economic and financial crises?

2 Conclusions

This publication fills the existing gap in research on the activities of IOs to find the multilateral consensus on providing and managing GPGs for fostering sustainable development to meet the needs of the increasingly interconnected worlds in the 21st century. The monograph is a synthetic analysis showing how the evolution of IO policy and activities under new global challenges in the world affects and thus increases the sustainability of member states through

 | DOI:10.1163/9789004687264_019

making GPGs more manageable. The nature and comprehensiveness of these processes require an interdisciplinary perspective, a multi-aspect analysis of the most important dimensions of contemporary GPGs and the ways of regulating as well as improving their provision by the IO to foster their impact on the sustainable development of member states.

The book provides answers to a number of important questions identified in the introduction and in subsequent chapters. As the world, economy, and politics are constantly changing, the reader is encouraged to reflect on the multilevel and multi-factor functioning of the world, including globalization processes, the role, place, and functioning of IOs, their impact on individual states, their economy, and society. This book can encourage reflection on future directions of research, without providing a closed catalogue of issues related to the distribution of public goods by IOs in their attempt at creating appropriate conditions for a more sustainable economy.

The book's conclusions indicate that GPGs cannot be adequately and sufficiently provided by national governments acting unilaterally, and therefore cooperation among multiple countries is necessary. It is important to improve effectiveness in the provision of GPGs through accountability measures aimed at increasing compliance with sustainable development and deliver better results by influencing member states' policies not only for more effective implementation, but also for adequately securing (private and public) support for GPGs. The global governance system has grown in number and types of partners, size, issue coverage, intrusiveness of instruments, and complexity of operational forms. All intellectual property organizations taken together show a significant increase in the authority of the IOs and a shift away from national states and private organizations, but the authority of the IOs is increasingly questioned. One way to improve the functioning of IOs is to change the institutional structure, and another is to increase management methods.

One important conclusion is that the existing system of international relations is subject to fierce competition; it is also becoming increasingly anarchic. Many IOs have been endowed with appropriate instruments or mechanisms to ensure the peaceful existence and functioning of their member states. Unfortunately, with the exception of internal relations within NATO and the EU, none of them has managed to pursue its principles, attain its goals, or carry out the tasks for which they have been established in the first place. This indicates the existence of certain weaknesses within the global community architecture. These need to be addressed. There is an urgent need to reform IOs, starting with the United Nations, the OSCE and a number of regional organizations, such as the Council of Europe.

In terms of migration, global governance is highly fragmented and consists of overlapping regimes that address different aspects of human mobility or different "types" of migration. The UNHCR, as the "custodian" of the international refugee regime, has played a key role in linking the Global Compact on Refugees with Sustainable Development Goals; it remains a crucial actor in the process of implementing it, actively combining sustainable livelihoods with the global asylum agenda.

Another important conclusion is that IOs need to ensure the rule of law. All public authorities should operate within the limits set by law, in conformity with the values of democracy and fundamental rights, including the right to non-discrimination, and under the supervision of an independent and impartial judiciary. If any of these elements is threatened, the principle inevitably becomes eroded.

The impact of IOs (such as the WTO, the OECD, and the EU) on international trade is analyzed on the macro level, i.e., from the point of view of trade liberalization, cooperation between the WTO and the EU, and on the micro level, which involves the analysis of export credits – an export support instrument used by the WTO. It has not been confirmed that trade liberalization, carried out within the multilateral framework of the WTO and supported by the OECD, contributes to sustainable development worldwide. Nevertheless, the WTO strives to create appropriate conditions for granting export credits in order to eliminate practices that favor one of the parties to the transaction; this forms the basis for the development of international trade as a GPG. There are a number of contentious issues that the WTO and the EU have yet to agree on regarding trade liberalization in the context of tariffs in the agricultural sector. The EU maintains much higher tariffs than those proposed by the WTO. The second issue is state aid. The EU proposes a more comprehensive approach to state intervention into trade, while the WTO argues that the EU supports a wide range of actors and sectors through a common budget. Importantly, it can be concluded that regardless of the profits generated through trade, it is crucial to ensure their fair distribution and future profits (Mendoza & Bahadur, 2002).

In terms of financial management and stability, the World Bank provides loans to the governments of developing countries to help them finance development projects, economic reforms, and technical assistance. However, the specific procedures employed by the World Bank Group to the processing of loan applications and to capital management means that aid is granted only to a specific group of countries. This leads to the conclusion that the Bank's overall commitment to GPG production should be more strategic. The World Bank should also focus on policies and projects that complement its core activity, for instance, domestic loans. Programs and strategies developed by the Bank should also involve external partners. The IMF's assistance through debt relief initiatives, financial and technical assistance, supervision, and regulation all contribute to the effectiveness of economic reforms and economic adjustments of the member states, as well as development programs (IMF, 2022, p. 53). As for the EU and its financial stability, the coexistence of two distinct approaches to fiscal and monetary policy restrains the impact of the EU, as an IO, on the financial stability of its member states.

The conclusions regarding green energy are, unfortunately, quite unsatisfactory. Despite all the efforts and actions undertaken by IOs (the World Bank and the EU), the financing of investments into energy security remains unsatisfactory. More effort is necessity, including greater financial commitments.

Not only has the COVID-19 pandemic brought the importance of GPGs in the area of health to the fore, but it also exposed the vain efforts undertaken by certain institutions. Excessive death tolls and persistent health problems are the consequence of the underfunding of institutions, inefficient coordination, inadequate preparation for emergency situations (e.g., the production of personal protective equipment or vaccines), as well as nationalistic attitudes, particularly evident in the redistribution of vaccines. Another problem is the sharing of intellectual property rights. With respect to these GPGs, certain decisions need to be taken at the national and regional level. Organizations such as the WTO, the WIPO, the EU, and the OECD provide the architectural framework for the international intellectual property system. In their actions they integrate the goals of sustainable development, including health, climate, and education to varying degrees. While the WTO specializes in trade and health, and the OECD in education, the scope of WIPO's actions is quite comprehensive. What is more, these organizations use different instruments to exercise coercion to varying degrees. They also differ in terms of their impact. While the EU uses intellectual property law as an instrument that deepens integration and enhances its competitive advantage on the international stage, the WIPO and the OECD focus rather on promoting the idea of intellectual property on a global scale.

Positive conclusions have been drawn with respect to digitization. Just as with intellectual property, the ILO – as a UN agency – acts on a global scale, while the EU is a regional integration project whose legislation and policies may also affect other jurisdictions.

When it comes to smart city projects, also in the context of sustainable development, the involvement of the EU in the implementation of smart city projects in Poland proves that IOs must play an important – if not crucial – role in helping countries become more resilient, sustainable, and responsible in the process of creating their public policies in this area. The skillful design of cities is very important for devising, managing, and investing in public goods; given financial constraints, this applies more to emerging countries and those in transition than to the most developed.

References

Altvater, E. (2007). Public goods for human security. *Papeles del Este, 14*, 1–19.

Engerer, H. (2011). Security as a public, private or club good: Some fundamental considerations *Defence and Peace Economics, 22*(2), 135–145.

Felício, T. (2005). Managing security as a regional public good: A regional – global mechanism for security. UNU-CRIS Occasional Papers, no. 19. Paper prepared for the Conference "Regionalisation and the Taming of Globalisation? Economic, Political, Social and Governance Issues," University of Warwick, UK, October 26–28, 2005.

Hooghe, L., Lenz, T., & Marks, G. (2019). *A theory of international organization*. Oxford University Press.

Hughes, B. B. (1991). *Continuity and change in world politics: The clash of perspectives*, Prentice Hall.

IMF. (2022). IMF's response to the global economic crisis. https://www.imf.org/external/np/exr/facts/changing.html.

Kaul, I. (2001). Global public goods: What role for civil society? *Nonprofit and Voluntary Sector Quarterly, 30*(3), 588–602.

Kaul, I., Grunberg, I., & Stern, M. A. (1999). Defining global public goods. In I. Kaul, I. Grunberg, & M. A. Stern (Eds.), *Global public goods: International cooperation in the 21st century* (pp. 2–19). Oxford University Press.

Mendoza, R., & Bahadur, C. (2002). Toward free and fair trade: A global public good perspective. *Challenge, 45*(5), 21–62. doi:10.1080/05775132.2002.11034175

Sandler, T. (1999). Intergenerational public goods: Strategies, efficiency and institutions. In I. Kaul, I. Grunberg, & M. A. Stern (Eds.), *Global public goods: International cooperation in the 21st century* (pp. 20–50). Oxford University Press.

Stiglitz, J. E. (2003). Democratizing the International Monetary Fund and the World Bank: Governance and accountability. *Governance, 16*(1), 111–139.

Index

Printed in the United States
by Baker & Taylor Publisher Services